WALLY'S BOYS

By Loran Smith

Based in part on the recollections of John Rauch
with an assist from Dan Magill, John Stegeman,
Edwin Pope, Jim Minter and Jesse Outlar.

DEDICATION

Faye, Jean and Nancy.
The triumvirate of Wally's girls who gave their time and heartfelt assistance.

John Rauch for getting this project started.
Nobody was ever more loyal to his coach than this modest and selfless Bulldog.

All Wally's Boys themselves who, with the passing of time,
continue to express enduring loyalty and love for their coach.

LONGSTREET
PRESS

PUBLISHED BY

LONGSTREET PRESS, INC.
325 Milledge Avenue
Athens, Georgia 30601

1st printing, 2005
ISBN: 1-563-52-738-3
Library of Congress Control Number: 0000000000

Printed in the United States of America

Jacket and book design by Thomas R. Bledsoe

Wally's Boys Show Thier Appreciation

This book has been made possible in part by a grant from the Georgia Student Educational Fund, Bill Hartman, chairman, and one from the University of Georgia Athletic Association, Vincent J. Dooley, Director of Athletics. Additionally financial support was generously provided by the Wally's Boys themselves, those who played for James Wallace Butts. A number of friends contributed also. A listing of those most valuable contributors follows:

Platinum

Sam Bailey (43-45); Edwin Pope, Sports Columnist, Miami Herald

All-American

Bill MacKenna (43, 46); Jimmy Harper (52-55); Fran Tarkenton (58-60)

Silver

Fred Brown (58-60); Jack Bush (46-48); John Donaldson (45-48); Pat Dye (58-60); Freddy Farah (60); Bobby Green (59-61); Green Keltner (39-41) by Elaine Keltner; Ken McCall (44, 47-49); Pud Mosteller (54-56); Carl Sanders (45); Frank Sinkwich (40-42) by Frank Sinkwich, Jr.; James Skipworth (39-40) by George Skipworth; Don Soberdash (57-59); Charley Trippi (42, 45-46)

Red and Black

Heyward Allen (39-41) by Buddy Allen; John Bell (53-55); Fred Bilyeu (50-52); Aaron Box (57-59); Bill Bradshaw (47-50); Zeke Bratkowski (51-53); Charley Britt (57-59); Bill Burt (53); Marion Campbell (49-51); John Carson (50-53); Cleve Clark (53-55); Bob Clemens (52-54); Joe Comfort (55-57); Ken Cooper (55-57); Leo Costa (40-42); Lee Cummings (59); Tony Cushenberry (54-56); J. B. Davis (55-57); Hinton Davis (55-57); Lamar (Racehorse) Davis (40-42); Art Decarlo (50-52); Nat Dye (56-58); Charlie Earnest (51-53); Willie Fowler (54-55); Bobby Garrard (52-55); Bill Godfrey (59-61); Ed Greenway (49-51); Bob Greer (48-50); Earl Gunn (51-52); George Hansen (57-58); Lauren Hargrove (50-52); Billy Hearn (56-57); Claude Hipps (44, 49-51); Paul Holmes (60-62); Cliff Kimsey (39-41); Derwent Langley (50-53); Don Leebern (57-59); Tommy Lewis, Jr. (57-59); Cicero Lucas (56-58); John Luck (54-56); Charlie Madison (52-54); Frank Malinowski (51-53); Hugh McCarley (48-49); Bill McKenny (59-61); Mike Merola (49-50); George Mitchell (54); Angelo Monti (55-56); Zippy Morocco (49-51); Butch Mulherin (53-55); Joe O'Malley (52-54); Jimmy Orr (55-57); Tommy Paris (58-60); Durward Pennington (59-61); Morris Phelps (41); Barry Phillips (46-48); Wyatt Posey (39-41); Ray Prosperi (48-50); Carter Ramsey (58-59); John Rauch (45-48); Bob Reed (53); Bernie Reid (44, 47-48); Jackie Roberts (50-52); Billy Roland (57-59); Theron Sapp (56-58); Bill Saye (53-55); Jimmy Sealey (58); Don Shea (53-55); Billy Slaughter (59); Pat Smith (59-61); Charles (Rabbit) Smith (43-46); Len Spadafino (54-55); Joe Tereshinski (42-46); Tommy Thompson (60); Albert Thompson (49-50); Don Tomberlin (60); Bobby Towns (57-59); Bobby Walden (58-60); Bob West (50-52); Walter White (53-55); George Whitton (56-58); Dale Williams (59-61); Jimmy Williams (52-55); Gene (Buck) Wilson (56-57); Bruce Wimberly (52-53); Bill Young (52-53)

Friends of Wally's Boys

Ken Bishop; Vernon Brinson; Louis Trousdale; John Withers

Acknowledgements

John Rauch. When he put down on paper, in long hand, his memories of his days on campus, he preserved details, fact, opinion, lore and remembrances which led to the publishing of this book. He spent a lot of time without compensation—truly a labor of love—interviewing and logging the memories and thoughts of his former teammates. After the project got underway, the computer made it easier, but it wouldn't have mattered. His love for Coach Butts meant that he would have done it with pad and pen, which is the way he began.

Faye Butts Jones, Nancy Butts Thompson, Jean Butts Jones, the Butts' daughters for providing information, photographs and valuable proof reading assistance.

Bill Hartman, for his advice and encouragement; his vivid recall of details of his long time association with Coach Butts and Georgia were invaluable.

Dan Magill. What would we have done without him? He helped soothe feelings during down times and never at a loss for (printed) words. Dan's recollections and memories appear throughout this book. He is Georgia's great football historian. He loves history like he loved The Little Round Man, his fellow Georgian.

Vince Dooley, who along with Coach Hartman, agreed to underwrite a major portion of the cost of producing Wally's Boys.

Damon Evans, Georgia Athletic Director for his support of Wally's Boys.

Sam Bailey for getting the Wally's Boys reunion underway and who is, along with Edwin Pope, the biggest individual contributor to this publication.

Edwin Pope, an Athens boy, still writing snappy and informative columns for the Miami Herald. Thanks for his financial assistance too.

Jim Minter, Jesse Outlar and the late John Stegeman. Terrific writers, all, who had passion for their work, their alma mater and their friend Wally. They, like Dan Magill, can claim membership in the Wally's Boys fraternity too.

Claude Felton, Georgia sports information director and his staff, including Karen Huff, Jordan Posey and Jenny Menkes for research, locating photos and general assistance.

George Harwood, excellent at editing and proofing, one of the best.

Bill Simpson, long time university public relations officer, an editor with the right stuff.

Lamar Lewis for accounting and financial management.

Tom Bledsoe, the book's designer, who delighted in the nostalgia that he discovered while bringing the manuscript to its final form.

Chris Martin, my son-in-law, who efficiently managed the manuscript process to the printer.

Dolores Hughes and Virna Mendoza for manuscript management and production.

My wife, Myrna, whose patience and assistance were a comfort in times of early morning and late afternoon stress of trying to meet deadlines.

Rob Zullo for general assistance and the collecting of all the photographs.

And to all those Wally's Boys who spent time and also generously contributed their money to bring this book about. I'm grateful.

Author's Note

Obviously, we could not include stories of every letterman who played for Coach Wallace Butts. We tried to include features and vignettes, not only about the celebrated stars, but those who never gained all-star status. We tried to make a sensitive effort to bring to print the stories of a cross section of Wally's boys.

Many lettermen recommended stories of other lettermen that the author and John Rauch included. It was not our intent to overlook any player, which is why we sought recommendations of all living captains. We apologize for any omission.

Foreword
By Vince Dooley

As I look back on it now after forty years, it was a daunting challenge when I accepted the head coaching position at the University of Georgia in December of '63. However, as a young 31 year old assistant coach, I never considered the challenge as intimidating, but rather as an extraordinary opportunity to reach a long range goal of becoming a head coach earlier than planned. It was a tremendous opportunity to coach at a major institution like the University of Georgia.

As I further reflect on the situation today, I never realized how daunting the challenge really was. I knew Georgia had gone through some difficult times, but I never realized until I took the job the great disharmony among the Georgia people.

After hiring an excellent staff, we focused all our efforts on the future. We allowed no time for dwelling on the problems of the past or to choosing sides – we simply rolled up our sleeves and went to work to gain credibility. You do that in the coaching profession by winning games and fielding a team that will battle hard for 60 minutes.

On the other hand, you would have had to be blind not to be aware of the problems. Facilities needed improving and upgrading; financially, there was a lot of red ink. Georgia had not done well in football in recent years, having fielded eight losing seasons in the previous eleven years. Additionally, there were three consecutive losses to Georgia Tech. The frustration brought about by the disassociation of Coach Wallace Butts as Athletic Director and the negative headlines of the Saturday Evening Post trial had left the Georgia people disconsolate, divided, and downcast, to say the least.

They were anxious for a change, and they were ready to see what the new staff could do, but I don't think they were ready for an unknown, freshman coach from a rival school to take over. Fortunately, we won seven games that first year including a bowl victory. We defeated Florida and Georgia Tech – a stimulating tonic, indeed, for alumni spirits. I always felt that one of the reasons we were accepted easily in the community was that we not only earned a bowl invitation, the Sun Bowl in El Paso, and defeated both Florida and Tech, but most Bulldog fans felt that our team played with a lot of fight and heart. Bulldog fans had always appreciated the hard-hitting teams that characterized Coach Butts' style. His teams fought hard and so did our first team at Georgia. As I think about it, I was very fortunate to inherit a lot of traditions at Georgia. Foremost among those traditions was the pride the Bulldogs took in fielding tough, hard-hitting football teams under Coach Butts.

Coach Butts established a reputation as a very demanding, tough task-master on the football field. I will have to admit that I was a little intimidated when, soon after arriving in Athens, I went by his office to visit with him. A few days later when I got home, Barbara told me an interesting story. She said, "The sweetest man came by to see me today and brought me a dozen red roses!" I said, "Who are you talking about?" When she said Coach Butts, my immediate reaction, recalling his hard nosed practice field reputation was, 'Barbara, I believe you have the wrong man!' "No, it really was Coach Butts," she said. That kind gesture really did give me insight into the generous and sensitive nature of the man.

What was inspiring from those early days when I took over was that Coach Butts not only attended all of our home games that year, he often followed us on the road. Every Monday, a letter from Coach Butts showed up on my desk after our Saturday game. He offered congratulations if we had won, and expressed encouragement if we had lost. He did that every season until he passed away. Those memories of his great support will always be special to me.

When he spoke to the Athens Touchdown Club and Quarterback Clubs around the state - just visiting with people as he pursued his insurance business - he was always complimenting us. You can imagine how uplifting that was for our young staff.

Many times I have said that I was a product of the Wally Butts system. When I played at Auburn under Coach Shug Jordan, I was aware that he brought a lot of the Butts' philosophy with him when he left Athens as the line coach to take over at Auburn. Of course, he also brought many of Coach Butts' former players who became assistant coaches at Auburn. The first thing I learned was we were going to hit and hit hard when we lined up. I was introduced to hard-nosed football under Coach Jordan, and it formed the basis for my approach to the game as a head coach. I always felt that Coach Jordan's philosophy was greatly influenced by Coach Butts. In that sense, I, too, am a "Wally's Boy" and am very proud of that.

I am very happy that the idea of this book began with John Rauch, one of Coach Butts' greatest players. It warms a coach's heart when you become aware of the intense loyalty that John has for Coach Butts. That admiration and respect has lasted a lifetime for Coach Butts' most successful quarterback at Georgia. In the section devoted to John's memories, you will not only appreciate his enduring affection for Coach Butts, you gain an insight into what life was like in Athens for a Bulldog player in the glory years of the forties. That section is not only stimulating and informative, it is heart warming.

When Loran Smith, the principal author, advanced the idea that the Georgia Student Educational Fund and the Athletic Association underwrite the cost of a portion of the book, Coach Hartman and I, representing these two organizations, were quick to advance approval. When we agreed to put up approximately forty percent of the cost, I remember Loran saying, "I'll raise the rest from his former players."

When I reviewed this with him as the book was going to press, Loran said, "It was the easiest money I ever raised for any project." Nobody turned him down, and many, I understand, gave more than the request letter called for.

There is a poignant reminder here. There is often a special and lasting bond between players and their coach. When you finish school and move on with your life, you look back at your career with great appreciation for your teammates and your coach.

Being in the profession now for over fifty years, I've heard a lot of testimonials from players across the country about their respective coaches. However, I have never known a more loyal group of players to their coach than those that stayed and played for Coach Butts and proudly became known as "Wally's Boys".

Presentation of Coach Butts' Hall Of Fame plaque. From left: Bernie Kish, Allison Yeomans, Nancy Butts Thompson, Page Allen, and Coach Vince Dooley.

PART I

JAMES WALLACE BUTTS

The Little Round Man

An Original

Colorful, Lovable, Unforgettable Wally

Wallace Butts was a lovable, colorful, and unforgettable character, a humorous and sensitive man who experienced the high of coaching his team to the national championship and the low of being accused by a sensational, muckraking magazine of attempting to fix a Georgia game when he was no longer the Bulldog coach.

Emotions, when it came to Butts, were never without passion. He is remembered for his taskmaster's style, which perhaps stemmed from being a little man, who distinguished himself on the football field as a player who could, as a result of unyielding tenacity, gain the better of those who possessed superior physical dimensions. He was a fierce competitor and combatant.

He was 5-feet, 6-inches tall, an almost meek and timid man off the field, but a driven, dominating and unrelenting force when his practice sessions began.

Butts stood behind his offense in wrinkled khaki pants, his over sized forearms (developed by his labor at a brickyard in his youth) folded neatly across his chest. He had those rare eagle eyes that few coaches have. He never missed anything. When the ball was snapped and the line fired out, he could see every individual player carry out his assignment. He had an overview of the team, functioning as a single unit. He immediately knew what was wrong when there was a breakdown. He knew instantly when an assignment was missed. His reaction was instantaneous, his critique was pointed and sharp, clever and, more often than not, sarcastic.

He was such a perfectionist that defeat plunged him into the depths of despair. Even in victory, he would moan over missed blocks and arm tackles.

One of his early players, John Stegeman, who later became a doctor and the UGA's foremost historian of the early days of Georgia football, had this to say about Butts when his coach suffered criticism in the fifties.

"...he had a hilarious assortment of expressions, and on the practice field he spiced them with timely oaths that brought great (but silent) glee to every player except the one being singled out. In later years, detractors of the coach and of the university were to seize on this profanity theme and distort it beyond recognition. I still have to fight my own blood pressure when I hear people, who don't know Wally, speak of his profanity, or reflect on his character. Such people have haunted him during most of his coaching career.

"Even now, years later, after a bad day, I still occasionally dream of Wally, imagining that he is watching my sloppy performance, and that I'll have to answer to him the following day. I'm still a little scared of him, perhaps, but I've never stopped loving him."

Stegeman spoke the sentiments of countless Butts' players.

Indeed, sloppiness Butts would never tolerate. No shirttails out. Run on and off the field. Perfection, he felt, was achievable through hard work and total discipline. If a player knew his assignment and practiced it over and over, then you should be able to execute effectively. You should be successful. You should win.

A man far ahead of his time with the passing game, he believed that discipline and precision were mandatory for victory. He never expected a player to perform at a level that exceeded his ability, yet he demanded every player from the gifted on right down to the clumsiest B-teamer give his very best.

Under game conditions, when the challenge weighs heavy, when the body is fatigued, when the odds are stacked against the team, only the disciplined... only those with the will to win, can survive victoriously. He agreed with Vince Lombardi that "fatigue makes cowards of us all."

Butts referred to this commitment to his favorite

sport as "paying the price." It was the most repeated football phrase in his vocabulary. To win and to win often, you simply had to pay the price. Any player who did, gained his eternal affection.

This approach to football was to bring him a bittersweet career, the bitter and the sweet almost in equal measure. Talented players who paid the price gained for them his highest tribute. Rebuke for those who didn't was predictably forthcoming. In the days when Butts did not or could not recruit successfully, the game was not good to him.

Frustration so overwhelmed him when he could not recruit well enough for desired results that he, himself, that little giant of discipline, finally broke. He lost his grip on his own discipline and suffered dreadfully before recovering. He was the toast of the state in the Forties, developing seven bowl teams in 10 years. The Fifties were lean and harsh until he came back to win his last SEC championship in 1959 with a hometown boy, Francis Tarkenton. His practices were, in the long standing football vernacular, hard nosed.

Butts believed that if you practiced harder, if you stayed on the practice field longer, that in all likelihood when the fourth quarter came around, you would have more in reserve, you would be able to perform more competitively than the other team because fatigue would not weigh as heavily on you as on your opponent. He expected his teams to be mentally tougher with the game on the line. Those rigorous practices, he felt, would be the difference.

That philosophy of "paying the price," he believed, would bring victory more often than not. In fact, that slogan could well have been the title for this book.

Those who paid the price developed an everlasting affection for Wallace Butts and the University of Georgia. His former lettermen would fight you about him. There were alumni and fans who felt the same way. Even today.

It has always been my belief that the warm feelings and enduring love that so many had for him, especially his players, were because they felt that he truly cared for them and for the University of Georgia. He gave of himself, an attribute not lost on his ardent supporters.

His generosity and his open house style endeared him and his family to countless alumni and friends, but unfortunately many who bellied up to his bar in good times later joined the corps of critics.

His story began and ended on a high note. Early success during which he was the toast of college football, was followed by mediocrity and in some years, losing records, but he rallied to exit on top. His last SEC championship, his fourth, came in the serendipitous season of 1959.

In 1960 he was one victory shy of another bowl invitation but resigned as head coach after defeating Georgia Tech in Athens, 7-6, for his fourth victory in a row over the Yellow Jackets.

He settled in as athletic director amid rancor and

Coach Butts as a baby; with his family (Jean, Faye, Nancy and wife, Winnie); in his early years as a coach

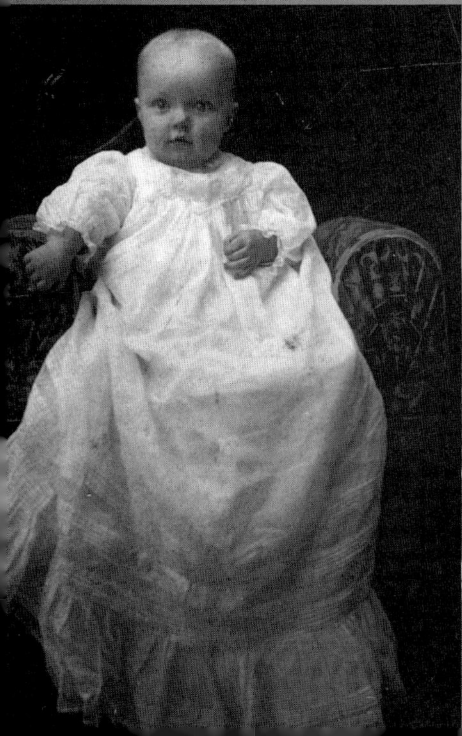

dissention, and it was obvious to those closest to him that he preferred to be on the field, teaching his vaunted passing offense to young athletes as he had done throughout his life.

It was the best of times, and the worst of times, in many respects – those final years of his career. Coach Butts knew what it was like to experience the thrill of victory, but he also was afflicted with the depression of down times.

Nothing was worse than the charge by the Saturday Evening Post in March 1963 that he and Paul "Bear" Bryant colluded to fix the Georgia-Alabama game in 1962.

How could two coaches fix a game? That was the reaction that most of his loyal followers and many detached observers expressed. Even those who were not passionate supporters of the University of Georgia asked that question.

A federal jury in Atlanta in August 1963 vindicated Coach Butts with a verdict that granted him a $3,060,000 judgment. (Later reduced by the judge to $460,000.) His worst nightmare had ended.

In typical fashion, he entered business with the same commitment and tenacity that characterized his playing and coaching career. He established an insurance company, which, with aggressive sales efforts, brought him financial comfort. He had a near perfect personality for a salesman, plus many people wanted to do business with a man they admired and loved. The demand for speaking appearances throughout the South grew rapidly. He was on top again.

Wherever he went, people greeted him with overwhelming affection. Airports, hotel lobbies, corporate offices – it didn't matter. They wanted to meet The Little Round Man of Georgia football. They sought his opinion on the state of the game.

They wanted his view on the big game coming up and his critique on the one just played. His knowledge always had credibility, and on top of that, no inactive coach ever enjoyed sitting down and talking with a fan of college football more than Coach Butts.

He made people comfortable. He provided clever and poignant insights about college football. If he had had the opportunity he would have been an informative television analyst, bringing both insight and levity to his commentary.

The golden years of his life were all too brief when a heart attack ended his life after a winter's jog, Dec. 17, 1973.

This book is about Wallace Butts the master of the forward pass of college football, the man who delighted audiences, including his players, with his witticisms. It is about a beloved coach who experienced the thrill of victory and the agony of defeat. It is not about the times when he stumped his toe, but a celebration of his successes. It is about his "boys," the many who paid the price and considered it an honor to have played for him.

This story began in the mid-nineties when John Rauch mentioned that he had, in long hand, penned his memories of Coach Butts and the teams on which he had played.

When I learned this, I thought there might be the possibility of publishing a book that would be important for Georgia and the players who played for Butts and the fans who remember and appreciate his legacy.

Rauch's hand written notes were transcribed, but sat in a corner of my office for months, gathering dust. I was not exactly sure how the book could be organized effectively for consideration by a publisher. In addition, I was simply too busy to get to it, but the idea remained alive – though dormant – in my thought process. When I would see John, I would remind him not to give up. "I'll get to it some day," I promised.

When he and Sam Bailey organized an annual reunion of former Butts' players, under the heading of "Wally's Boys," I had another conversation with Rauch about the book. "I've been thinking," Rauch said, "that if a book is done, it should be done about all his teams and as many players as possible."

About this time, long time Butts assistant, Bill Hartman, and I had a discussion about what could be done to advance John's candidacy for the Hall of Fame. Rauch's omission was a glaring oversight, but, typical of Rauch when I mentioned our interest in his candidacy, the accomplished quarterback and coach said, "Don't worry about me. Let's get Coach Butts in the Hall of Fame."

At the time, Butts had not been selected, another glaring oversight. Everybody went to work on that objective, giving it the highest priority.

After Coach Butts was finally elected in 1997, Coach Hartman and I met again to scheme a plan that might bring positive results in regard to Rauch being elected.

The National Football Foundation and Hall of Fame has a rule that stipulates when your class has been graduated fifty years, that you become ineligible. The list of nominations simply grows every year, and there is

Comic books and Wheaties honor the Top Dog

a backlist that is longer than the Empire State Building is tall. As a result, Rauch's name went off the list in 1998.

However, good news came about when the Hall of Fame created an "ole timers" committee with the purpose of addressing the nominations of those whose class had been graduated for fifty years.

Rauch was again nominated and recommendations were sent to the members of the ole timers committee. A number of those affiliated with the University of Georgia – Hartman, Coach Vince Dooley, who was a member of the Hall of Fame Honors Court; Edwin Pope, Georgia graduate and long time sports columnist for the Miami Herald; Dick Bestwick, former Assistant Athletic Director for Compliance at Georgia all lobbied on behalf of Rauch.

Bill Walsh, who won all those Super Bowls with the San Francisco Forty Niners, was eager to lend his support which was significant. In a conversation I had with Walsh, he commented that the genesis of the popular West Coast offense began when he was the backfield coach for the Oakland Raiders. Who was the head coach? John Rauch.

You could make the assessment that the West Coast offense had its origins with John Rauch when he played for Wallace Butts at Georgia in the Forties. All of this was enthusiastically noted to the Ole Timer's committee.

With Rauch being elected to the Hall in 2003, I felt that it was time to finalize a plan for this book. I asked Coach Dooley and Coach Hartman if they would help underwrite the cost of production of the book.

Hartman, representing the Georgia Student Educational Fund, and Dooley, representing the Georgia Athletic Association, agreed to provide approximately half the cost of producing the book, and I committed to a plan to raise the remainder. Wally's Boys, like always, pitched in out of deep reverence and affection for their old coach. They were eager to contribute and encourage their teammates to participate. That is how this publication came to be.

It is a book about Coach Butts, his players, and his teams. It principally covers the highlights. We've stated the football facts of Wallace Butts' life and career, including those losing teams and his down times at Georgia. The intention of this book is to underscore the high moments, not the negative.

Wallace Butts was a successful coach, one who was inducted into the College Football Hall of Fame. He was a popular and colorful character. He endeared himself to his friends and players, especially those who paid the price.

This is not a definitive biography. It is a tribute to Coach Butts and "Wally's Boys."

WALLY'S GIRLS

Wallace Butts was always an adorable and loving father to his three daughters—Faye, Jean and Nancy.

They were there for the glory years of the forties, and nobody stood by him in down times like this threesome. When he was elected to the College Football Hall of Fame, they, and their families, traipsed merrily to the Waldorf in Manhattan enmasse.

There were shopping excursions. They took in the latest hits on Broadway. But when the glorious hour of tribute became reality, it was difficult for them to contain themselves, they were so proud.

Nancy, his youngest, represented the family on the dais. In the audience were officials from the University of Georgia, former players and coaches, including his most loyal assistant through the years, Bill Hartman.

It was a warm, uplifting and exhilarating moment for the family. The daughters, in particular, were so appreciative, not just because of deserved and overdue recognition, but because they steadfastly loved their father.

Feelings run deep in the Butts family. Grandchildren who never knew him and some who barely remember him were on hand. Not on hand, but gloriously happy was his sister, Ruth Butts Coley back home in Cochran.

A losing season, like he experienced in the fifties, might have raised the ire of some Bulldog followers, but nobody stood by The Little Round Man, nobody loved him, nobody forgave him like his unflinchingly loyal daughters.

Their delightful recollections follow.

WALLY BUTTS
BY FAYE BUTTS JONES

"Life With a Football Coach" was originally written as a feature for a University of Georgia Journalism School class by Faye Butts, Coach Butts' oldest daughter, in the early fifties. Though not originally written for publication, it carried such an interesting tale that The Atlanta Constitution obtained the story in the belief that its readers would find it interesting and enjoyable reading.

One o'clock in the morning. The ringing of the telephone interrupts the silence, and I stumble out of bed to answer it. "Is Wally Butts there?" a drunken voice drawls on the other end of the line. "I want to give him hell for sending me some tickets behind the goal post!"

At all hours of the day and night, calls such as this come to our house. Someone is liable to call 10 minutes before time for a game asking, "who's gonna win the Tech-Georgia game today?" or "how much are tickets for the game today?" If you can't answer their questions, it's very likely that they will hang up without so much as a word of thanks, implying, of course, that you are terribly stupid for not knowing which team will win. Sometimes I feel like telling them to consult the stars, if they really want a prophecy.

In case it's not obvious, my father, Wallace Butts, is head football coach and athletic director at the University of Georgia. As a consequence, my life has been filled with a jumble of excitement – football games, crowded stadiums, cheering fans, and waving pennants.

Along with this excitement, however, there has sometimes been heartache and worry. A football game means much more to me, as the coach's daughter, than it does to the average fan. It was because of this that I decided to write about what it is like to be the daughter of a coach.

During football season, and, to a large extent between seasons, my mother, two sisters and I hardly ever see Daddy unless it's in a crowd of people or from the stands at a football game. Every morning, after a hastily eaten breakfast of fruit and coffee, he goes to the office, where he reads and answers mail. I often answer our telephone at home and direct calls to the office.

If Daddy receives a call after lunch between 1:00 and 2:00, I say, "you may be able to get him at the Huddle, or if he's not there try the Palace Theater." The Huddle is the place where Daddy usually eats a sandwich for lunch. The Palace Theater is where he often goes to relax at a movie. He likes the shoot 'em-up style.

I always look forward to dinner because that is about the only time that the family is all together. The conversation at dinner varies according to the day of the week. Sunday or Monday, after a Georgia victory the previous weekend, the atmosphere is rather gay.

Daddy calls Nancy, age 11, "Short One," and like the rest of us, is amused by the things she says. Once, after listening to Daddy's pessimistic comments about a Georgia game, Nancy said, very seriously, "Mother, I wish Daddy liked the games."

Once, back in the days when Daddy was coaching at Male High School in Louisville, Kentucky, he made the remark at the dinner table that if we lost to Manual High the next week, our family would probably have to move out of our house and away from Louisville.

He had forgotten all about this remark, but apparently my sister, Jean, who was five at the time, hadn't. Immediately after we lost the game she asked, "Daddy, when are we going to move?"

Every night during the week, Daddy goes to a meeting of the coaching staff and football team, in which they go over plays and discuss the next game on the schedule. After the meeting, Daddy comes home, answers the phone every few minutes, drinks a glass of buttermilk, and goes to bed.

Until about 2 o'clock in the morning, Mother and Daddy take turns answering the telephone. People not only want to discuss football, but they give him all sorts of advice, which ranges from the reasonable to the insane. There is an astrologer who is very thoughtful about helping Georgia. I once listened to a conversation between him and Daddy.

"Coach Butts," the astrologer said, "Saturn moved a few degrees to the left last week, and the new moon rose in a cloudy sky."

"Oh," mumbled Daddy, "that's fine."

"But this means" continued the astrologer, "that next week in the Auburn game, if Geri goes around right end on the first down of the second quarter, Georgia will make a touchdown."

You see, everyone tries to be helpful. Georgia has lots of friends.

Being a football coach's daughter has its assets. The most enjoyable of these is the chance to travel. The excitement and fun of going on football trips is special. However, since I've been at the University, I have been on fewer trips. Daddy doesn't approve of cutting classes. His philosophy is that one should work hard, putting business way ahead of pleasure, but at the same time do anything one can for everyone else, be thoughtful, honest and sincere. I have never known him to do anything contrary to this philosophy.

In fact it sometimes gets on my nerves. When I am riding to class with Daddy, in a hurry to get there on time, he stops at every corner and fills the car with students while I anxiously watch the minutes fly by. He also stops whenever he sees anyone with a flat tire or out of gas.

During the summer, sometimes Daddy finds time to go with us to the beach for a few days. He likes to keep in shape by trotting a mile up the beach every morning and he insists on Jean and me accompanying him. I pant and stagger and am feeling about like the marathon runner must feel by the time we get back to our starting point.

Then Daddy decides to do pushups. I leave before he gets any more ideas. What a way to spend a vacation! We do have wonderful times. Daddy doesn't hesitate to take us fishing, even though he is quite bothered by seasickness and is easily sunburned.

Naturally, since our lives have been built around it, we love football. During football season, I live for the weekends. When the football crowds come to Athens, there are many dances and parties. Of course, the game is the most important thing. I always chew gum so that I don't bite my fingernails when I get nervous. Daddy chews blades of grass. I hate to see him down on the field when Georgia is losing, because his dejection seems contagious.

Even when we are winning, I feel happier if I don't look at him, because he sees everything that goes wrong on a play. His reputation for pessimism is well founded, but I think it is often exaggerated.

I enjoy immensely the comments I hear around me at a game. After a touchdown by the opponents, someone invariably says, "Look at Ole Wally now," or "I'd hate to hear what Butts is saying."

Sometimes I hear someone asking the person next to them, "which one is Wally Butts?" The answer is always, "that little round man in the blue suit," or "the short one kneeling down, picking grass."

After a game there are dozens of people who drop by our house: friends, relatives, sports writers, and people who are just plain curious as to Daddy's opinion about the game. Daddy always says something like "pretty lousy," or "it was all right." Sometimes people ask my opinion – if they want a more optimistic answer. I'm quite the opposite from Daddy in this respect. I remember the good points in a game and try to forget the bad ones.

Everyone at my house reads the sports page. Nancy wants me to say that even Rip, our dog, reads it. But I won't go that far. Actually, the sports page takes a terrific beating while making the rounds at our house. I like the editors' columns best, and I read the game write-ups from start to finish.

Reading the sports page was what first interested me in journalism. I think writing has a close correlation to sports. This, among other reasons, is why I am now majoring in journalism at Georgia. Jean hasn't decided definitely, but I think that she will also major in journalism. When she was a senior in high school, she wrote up all the girls' basketball games for the Athens Banner-Herald.

At Athens High School, I was inspired to try out for the basketball team. During my sophomore year, I always sat on the bench and I knew that unless a miracle happened or we were leading by about 50 points, I would never get into a game. Nevertheless, before each game, Daddy wouldn't let me eat anything for supper except maybe a poached egg or milk toast.

"Daddy," I'd say, "please let me have a steak like everyone else. I'm not gonna play tonight anyway."

"Nope," Daddy would answer conclusively, "you can't be on the team unless you follow all the rules and keep in shape."

This incident proves that Daddy carries over his football principles into his home. He has decided now that Jean and I, who are both attending the university and living at home, shall live by the dormitory rules for freshmen and junior girls. He really is a stickler for discipline. Any of his football players will vouch for this. Mother will also tell you what a disciplinarian he is.

Which reminds me that I haven't introduced you to Mother. I think that she is the perfect football coach's wife. She never gets upset in the least when people crowd into our home before and after games. She simply accepts the fact that a football coach is always going to be surrounded by people, and does her best to be hospitable although many who show up are strangers. A coach's wife must, of necessity, have an even temper. Also, she must like football. And Mother does. She watched Daddy play at GMC and later at Mercer when they were sweethearts.

When Georgia loses a game, it always leaves me with a dull ache which I can't explain. I know the effect a loss has on Daddy, on the football players, and on the real Georgia fans.

The most heartbreaking loss of all was the Auburn game in 1942. Georgia had a perfect record and hopes of a bowl invitation. Auburn and Tech were the last two games on the schedule, and Auburn was supposed to be a pushover. They were all set emotionally, and we were over confident.

Naturally, everyone thought that Georgia's bowl chances were ruined after Auburn upset us. At my cousin's house in Columbus, the atmosphere was like that of a morgue. That is the only game that I can remember having such a morbid effect on Bulldog fans.

To brighten the story, though, Georgia was victorious in the Tech game the next week and the newspaper headlines screamed GEORGIA IN ROSE BOWL!

I didn't go to California for the Rose Bowl. But I went to Miami in 1941 for the Orange Bowl. In later years I went with the team to the Oil Bowl in Houston, the Sugar Bowl in New Orleans and the Gator Bowl in Jacksonville. These were all wonderful trips.

I have met lots of celebrities on football trips, mostly sports celebrities. Coach Frank Leahy, of Notre Dame, a close friend of Daddy's, is one of my favorite people. There are dozens of other well-known personalities who are Georgia rooters.

Out of season, Daddy goes on trips all over Georgia and the United States making speeches, visiting prospects, lecturing at coaching clinics, etc. Sometimes I go along.

One summer Daddy, along with others in the sports world, was invited (by Louis Wolfson) to attend the premiere of the "Babe Ruth Story" in New York. He couldn't make it because of a clinic, but Mother, Jean and I went.

Babe Ruth and his wife (who actually was from nearby Jefferson) sat directly behind me at the premiere. This gave added interest to the movie, which we thoroughly enjoyed.

After the premiere I met quite a few movie stars, including Joe E. Brown, Guy Madison, Gale Storm, Paul Kelly and Eddie Albert. I often wonder what kind of an impression I made on them, because I was so fascinated in their company that I hardly knew what I was saying.

Sometimes I think about the calm, quiet life I probably would have led as the daughter of a teacher, a businessman, or a merchant, and I realize all the fun I would have missed. The love of football as a sport, as well as a most important part of my life, has developed through the years. It has become as much a part of me as acting is a part of Ingrid Bergman. And I would not trade my life for hers or for anybody's for that matter.

It's quite exciting to be the daughter of Georgia Coach Wallace Butts.

MY DAD
BY JEAN BUTTS JONES

Growing up around "Bulldogs" was truly a child's dream. We three girls went to bowl games as children and often met famous coaches and movie stars.

We rode a bus to the Oil Bowl, wrote and sang Georgia fight songs all the way. We spent New Year's Eve in New Orleans at the Sugar Bowl. We went deep-sea fishing with the Orange Bowl team. We always celebrated my birthday in Jacksonville at the Georgia-Florida game.

We had crushes on several of "Wally's Boys" and we kept scrapbooks on many of them.

Dad kept a drawer full of yellow tablets at home. He spent endless hours analyzing plays and creating new ones. He was often so absorbed with football he would draw plays on tablecloths at restaurants. It was not surprising to us that nationally recognized coaches constantly called or visited him to talk football. Coach Frank Leahy of Notre Dame, among others, was frequently at our home.

I never heard my Dad say a "cuss" word though I'm aware that his football field language was not a "lack of vocabulary" but a language all its own. He never brought it home with him. As a matter of fact off the field he was a gentle man who rarely raised his voice.

Once when I was about five years old my mother insisted that Dad give me a spanking. He took me in the back room and closed the door. He swung me gently over his arm and barely tapped my bottom instructing me to "yell". I obliged and mother never knew that we were giggling between licks.

Though not much of a disciplinarian to us, he somehow instilled in us to always do our best in school. He taught us as he did others to "pay the price" and we were all three conscientious students. He was very proud when I graduated from Georgia with honors.

Dad loved animals and, though we had several pure bred dogs, his favorite was "Rip" the mixed breed that Faye bought for $2.00. Rip could go alone from our house near Five Points to the practice field and get back home each day. He knew just when practice would be starting.

Dad also loved birds. He fed them daily at a window feeder.

Those who knew him socially found him delightful. He could tell wonderful stories and jokes and had an infectious laugh. He loved to play telephone jokes on friends using various accents. He never could fool me

Another trophy for Wally and Winnie

but once he had Dan Magill call and play a joke on me. He was so much fun to be with because of his great sense of humor.

As a reporter for the Atlanta Journal after graduation, one of my feature columns was a story with color photographs for a game with Georgia Tech. The column was called "Dear Daddy." Supposedly I was scouting Georgia Tech for Dad. When the Journal wanted a picture of me drawing a Tech play in the stands, Dad's team was playing on the road, so I called coach Bobby Dodd and he actually drew the play for me.

It was quite natural for me to try out for cheerleader

at Georgia. One of my fondest memories of college is cheering for the Bulldogs and being on the sideline by my Dad. As girls we couldn't play football but we did what we could to help the team.

I am the genealogist of my family. Those who knew him would not be surprised to know that his ancestors, one and all, contributed in major ways to building our nation. His lineage is filled with burgesses, justices, sheriffs, and soldiers in every war. They were Indian fighters and legislators.

His great grandfather Arthur Irwin Butts, served in the Georgia legislature twice. He hid the Georgia state papers at his Hancock County farm so that Sherman couldn't find them. His great-great uncle Samuel Butts fought so bravely at the Battle of Challibee in Alabama against the Indians that Butts County, Ga. was named for him.

Three of dad's direct ancestors were burgesses in Virginia...Capt. Francis Clements, Col. John Simmons, and his son, Benjamin Simmons. Dad's immigrant ancestor Thomas Butts Jr. was a justice representing New Kent County, Va. for many years and was a vestryman of his church for 41 years.

Dad's grandfather, James Wallace Butts I, a surgeon, was a captain of the Baldwin Blues and Doles-Cook brigade in the Civil War. He lost a leg and the fingers on one hand and was described by a comrade as "brave to recklessness." Wally's Scottish ancestress was the granddaughter of clan chief, Patrick McGregor, and his wife, a daughter of a McDonald clan chief.

Wally's father James Wallace Butts II lived during Civil War reconstruction days. He was a "jack of all trades". He built houses for himself and his brother, ran a farm, a dairy, a brickyard, a moving and hauling business and grew most of his own food. His garden brings memories of delicious strawberries to mind. He taught his son to work harder than most people.

Dad attended Georgia Military College. He was so small when he went out for football they didn't issue him a uniform or cleats. They gave him oversized tennis shoes with paper stuffed in the toes. His bulldog tenacity soon overcame his small stature, and he became a star. He became captain of the football, basketball and baseball teams.

At Mercer University he earned sports recognition as an All-Southern end but also was a member of the Mercer Round Table, an organization that recognized academic excellence.

When Dad died we got many, many letters from people whose lives he had touched in positive ways. Years after his death we would hear stories of his generosity and kindnesses to people. I don't believe he ever heard of someone having a problem that he didn't try to help out. Yet he never once mentioned his own good deeds.

Wally Butts was a unique and wonderful human being, a little man with an outsized heart. How proud I am that I could call him "Dad."

Wally Butts
by Nancy Butts Thompson

When Georgia dedicated the Butts-Mehre Building, which houses the athletic offices, in the spring of 1987, Nancy Butts was asked to represent the Butts' family. Her touching remarks follow.

Wally and Nancy when she was a Georgia coed

We all have memorable, unforgettable days. There's that first day of school, and mine was right across the street (Barrow School); the time of first love; marriage; children; important milestones in life.

Those of us who are the ordinary members of the Butts family have enjoyed an extraordinary coattail ride to fame through our association with Wallace Butts. He truly lighted up our lives. Because of the "Little Round Man" our memories are overflowing.

There were Orange, Sugar, and Gator Bowls, even the Rose Bowl, and if you've never ridden through a city with police sirens blaring ahead announcing that the Georgia Bulldogs have arrived, then you haven't really lived.

All of the family are certified Bulldog fans. In 1980 many of us had the sheer unmitigated joy of returning from New Orleans across the entire states of Alabama and Mississippi waving our pennants and our shredded crepe paper and screaming, "We're No. 1!"

Dressed in our wrinkled red and black outfits, too proud to make a change, we shared that unique event along with thousands of our fellow Bulldog fans. What a memory! We owe that one to you, Vince.

Please allow a vintage cheerleader, Class of '59, to echo the words of the present-day cheerleading squad, "It's great to be a Georgia Bulldog!"... [Wallace Butts] never bore grudges nor nursed resentment. He was generous to a fault, especially with the University of Georgia.

Having observed his courage, his tenacity, and his fighting spirit firsthand, I feel that all the attributes, awards and honors he received during his lifetime, all the respect he commanded from his players and coaches, yes, even the naming of this great Heritage Hall in his honor, he richly deserved.

He was only five-feet-six inches tall, but in my estimation never was there a man so short in stature to stand so tall. He had players well over six-feet tall who honestly thought they were looking up when they talked with the coach.

Faye, Jean, and I have always been proud to be the daughters of Wallace and Winnie Butts. Proud on the days when he rode off the field on the shoulders of his players with those Georgia yells and chapel bell ringing out the victory. Proud even on the days when his battling Bulldogs suffered those few defeats. Proud when he made witty after-dinner speeches. Proud when he fought back in life and restored his good name, and never prouder than at this moment.

Nancy, who was a cheerleader for Georgia, has special memories of the times she spent with her dad in his late years including a memorable foreign trip.

It was September of 1973. Daddy had won a trip to Spain through a competition in the credit life insurance company with which he was affiliated.

Faye, Jean, my late husband George Murray and I accompanied Mother and Daddy on this wonderful, action-packed trip.

Some of my favorite memories stem from this family time together. I can picture Daddy now, dressed in coat and tie, astride a camel in Tangiers. That same day in a restaurant, the women sat in one section and the men in another as strains of Moroccan music filled the air. Daddy proceeded to stand up and "do the twist." We laughed so hard we were unable to eat.

In spite of the tour guides countless warnings not to tip, Daddy couldn't contain himself. He slipped money to a little boy who was begging. Pandemonium ensued! For the rest of the day, hordes of urchins hounded him; surrounding him at every stop, so much so that he could scarcely move, much less sightsee.

In Madrid Daddy added an "o" to the end of almost every word, his comical variation of speaking Spanish. He also came up with his own rendition of the flamenco, much to our delight. Part of this scene includes a picture of Jean with a rose in her teeth. Eat your heart out, Carmen!

Faye, Jean and I will always picture Daddy, smiling, teasing and making us laugh, as he was always wont to do.

Several months later in December, George and I were returning from a visit with Jean and her husband, Frank, in Richmond, Va. With us were our two youngest children, Taylor, who was five years old, and Jack who was four. Also, we had with us our five-year-old foster daughter, Susie, who was living with us at the time.

On the way back home to Griffin, we decided to detour and pay a visit to Mother and Daddy in Athens. I'm so grateful that we made that decision because that brief stop now holds a special place in my treasure trove of memories.

Upon arrival at my parents' home on Hill Street, we dressed the children in their pajamas, so that they'd be ready for bed when we got home.

They soon joined Daddy in a follow-the-leader hysterical parade all over Mother's antique filled house. Phew! We had some narrow misses as the boisterous foursome shrieked uncontrollably, hopped, leapt and rolled, accompanied by uproarious laughter.

Mother must have been relieved when we finally began our last lap home, and George and I laughed all the way back to Griffin while three exhausted children slept in the backseat. It was the last time I saw my dad.

He died the next day.

A Passing Fancy

Wally - The Recruiter When Times Were Hard

Those of us who were not around in the mid thirties after this great nation came out of the Depression can gain a greater appreciation for the game of football if we consider the environment that existed for most members of the American working class.

First of all, people were expected to work. Seeking gainful employment was the order of the day. People knew how to make do, especially in the rural South where there was plenty of farm land to offer the bulk of the population an opportunity to feed itself.

A lot of farm boys had to quit school to work in the fields, but education always remained at the forefront of every family's mind. You couldn't expect much more in life than manual labor if you didn't at least finish high school. College was out of the question for many Americans, but a great number, who otherwise would not have gotten a degree, became graduates as a result of playing football. There were country boys in so many cases making good.

Everybody—including many who lived in town—had a garden. Canning and putting up for the winter was a necessary survival practice for every family. Not many had disposable cash for "store bought" products.

There were countless people who moved about via horse and buggy or mule and wagon. In the country, paved roads and electricity were as scarce as a native of the Peach State voting Republican.

In 1928 Wallace Butts completed requirements for his degree at Mercer, and by fall he was the head football coach at Madison A&M.

With the hard times in the thirties, every man looked out for himself. The Great Depression, brought about by the Wall Street crash of 1929, gripped the nation. Self survival had never been more challenging. Not since pioneer days had the work ethic been more underscored.

Soup kitchens, especially in Northern cities multiplied. Unfortunately, so did crime. In 1932 Al Capone went to prison, not for murder, but for income tax evasion and in the same year Wallace Butts became head coach at G.M.C.

The hopes and expectations for the country lifted when Franklin D. Roosevelt was elected in 1932 and took office the following year. In 1933, FDR was it. He brought about the New Deal and a number of programs that stimulated employment. G-Men in 1934 got tough, eliminating the menace of gangsters Pretty Boy Floyd, Baby Face Nelson, John Dillinger and Bonnie and Clyde.

Meanwhile Wallace Butts was winning every Friday in the fall.

By 1936, things were looking up, hopes were renewed across the country. Bill Hartman was in his senior year at Georgia, ready for a year in the National Football League while Coach Butts joined Joel Hunt's staff, a year later, as end coach.

Serendipity was forthcoming for Wallace Butts. He had distinguished himself in the prep and high school ranks. He had prepared himself to be a college coach. His record proved that.

Bill Hartman remembers Butts arrival in Madison, population about 1,800. In his mind's eye seventy five years later, he can see Coach Butts and his wife, Winnie, sitting on the first row at the Madison Methodist Church. "He was very popular, he had the town eating out of his hand," Hartman said.

An indefatigable worker, Butts ran the single wing and immediately identified with passing concepts. His teams often threw the ball 20 to 25 times a game, unheard of in those days.

Much has been chronicled over the years about his

coaching ability, but Wallace Butts was just as diligent and effective as a recruiter as he was at designing a pass pattern that would go all the way.

Players from Florida and Ohio showed up to play for him at Madison A&M and subsequently Georgia Military College. He developed a vast network of friends and contacts. They sent him names of prospects, and he followed up by phone and/or letter. He was a prolific letter writer, and he was good with correspondence. Like a good salesman he asked for the order, and he followed through.

The A&M schools created an effective system for athletics. There was an A&M school (agricultural and mechanical) located in every congressional district. It was part of the educational setup in the state of Georgia. The schools had plenty of land and grew enough crops to feed matriculants. Growing boys were hungry boys, and living off the land covered the biggest cost in funding scholarships.

There was opportunity at these schools that did not exist in states like Ohio where Butts annually scouted for talent. He also brought in exceptional talent from central Florida and later expanded into Pennsylvania.

If a player from the North with credible reputation came to the South for prep school, he might parlay that experience into a football scholarship at a major university campus.

Many of Butts players at Madison A&M and G.M.C. enrolled and played football at Auburn, Georgia Tech, Clemson and, of course, the University of Georgia where Butts would eventually wind up.

Hartman watched with keen interest how Butts coached his Madison team. Hartman played for Madison High School, but the town was taken by what Butts developed with the local prep school.

The leading football team in the state was Boy's High, and Hartman remembers that Madison A&M played the state's best reputed team at Ponce de Leon Park in 1930, winning 7-0.

"You can't imagine what that did for our community," Hartman said. "They couldn't do enough for Coach Butts." That was a big deal in the state of Georgia. You beat the best school the biggest city in the state could offer and your reputation as a coach was elevated to major status.

"You have to remember that Coach Butts was only 23 years of age," Hartman points out. "He established a great reputation overnight as a coach, but he was more than that. He was an excellent English teacher, and he was one of the town's most respected citizens."

When Butts left in 1931 for Georgia Military College in Milledgeville, there was considerable disappointment in Madison, but the local gentry concluded that it would be difficult to keep him when G.M.C., one of the highest regarded military schools in the entire country offered him an opportunity in his own hometown.

In short order, Butts was to do for G.M.C. what he had done for Madison A&M. He won the Southern Prep Championship and never lost more than one game in any season.

Identifying talent beyond the Georgia borders, Butts picked up the recruiting pace at G.M.C. His teams played entertaining football and the consensus was that surely some college would snap up this coaching genius who was ahead of his time.

College coaching was in his future, but before that opportunity came about, he took an attractive job at Male High School in Louisville, Ky.

The pay was much better than what he had been used to, and he realized that he would be closer to the talent he had discovered over the years in Ohio and more recently in Pennsylvania. He wasn't there long, however.

When Harry Mehre moved on following the 1937 season, Butts was a candidate for the Georgia job, and Bill Hartman, headed for the Washington Redskins, lobbied for his G.M.C. coach to be hired in Athens.

"I went to see Mr. (Harold) Hirsch, who was very influential in Georgia and recommended that he hire Coach Butts. I had played for him, and I knew that nobody knew more football than he did.

"He was a good leader, an outstanding teacher, and his commitment and passion to succeed were as strong as you could find in a coach. On top of that he was just as tenacious as a recruiter."

It only took a year for the decision makers in Athens to agree with Hartman's assessment.

Pioneer Of The Forward Pass

Any seasoned football fan who has been on the scene more than a few years knows that the current offensive philosophy of football is a notable departure from the fifties, sixties and seventies – even the early eighties.

It wasn't all that long ago that Texas' Darrell Royal, who played split T-formation quarterback for the eminently successful Bud Wilkinson at Oklahoma in the late forties, noted that when you deploy the forward pass, three things can happen and two of them are bad.

When he was quarterbacking the New York Giants in the seventies, former Georgia quarterback, Fran Tarkenton, working with Y. A. Tittle, one time Giant quarterback from L.S.U., and Joe Walton, who became head coach of the Jets, described their approach to offensive football: "We honed the offensive passing game to where we felt that we could make first downs throwing ball as well as we could by running," said Tarkenton, who learned his basic offense under Butts.

"That," says Butts' longtime backfield coach, Bill Hartman, "is exactly how we felt starting out with Coach Butts."

The offensive minded coaches of today are predominately the head coaches in college and the pros. They believe to succeed you must put an efficient passing game on the field. Today's coaches like to air it out. Wallace Butts was doing just that over six decades ago.

If you research the early Butts years, you conclude that the coaching preference for offense today is exactly his approach, dating back to his days as an innovative prep coach. "We had the west coast offense at Georgia in 1939," Hartman suggests.

In Butts' time slugging it out with the power game was the order of the day. The leading coach in the Southeastern Conference when Butts began was Tennessee's Bob Neyland. The General played it close to the vest – no mistakes on offense, keep it conservative, and win with kicking and defense.

With Coach Butts, his objective was to move the ball. After World War II he quickly identified with the T-formation because it allowed even greater offensive flexibility.

"He just liked passing and exciting offense," Hartman says. "He had a fertile football mind. He would wake up at 4:00 a.m. and design a couple of dozen pass plays. When he walked in with those yellow legal pads, we knew he had been busy diagramming more plays for us to put into our offense."

Butts had an imaginative football mind, and he could fill up a yellow notepad with pass plays in a matter of minutes. There was nothing he enjoyed more than to talk football and diagram plays.

"It was not uncommon to go into a game with 75 or more individual pass patterns," Hartman says. "The staff used to beg him not to put in more plays. We were the first team to throw 35 passes in a game. That became routine."

If he were coaching today, the leading offensive minds – the avant garde of the college game – would be flocking to his side to talk offensive football.

Interestingly, while he was always eager to sign up for coaching clinics and huddle with coaches in restaurants and hotel lobbies, diagramming plays until the wee hours, his understanding of the passing game was essentially his own creation.

He didn't study under any expert. He was, in fact, the expert, and when he had the players, his teams moved the football better than anybody. The only time his teams could not move the ball was when he had lesser talent.

No one seems to know exactly what attracted Wallace

A Wally Clinic by Tanyard Creek

Butts to the forward pass, except, as Hartman says, he simply was fascinated by the excitement of the passing game. In his day, throwing the ball was not what most colleges emphasized. Most coaches didn't have the patience to work at developing passing precision from their players. He knew how to do it and he got results.

His early teams could be overpowering. Like all championship teams, there was competent talent, and most importantly there was balance. His best offensive teams always played winning defense and never lacked for a sound kicking game. Much of the latter emanated from the influence of Hartman, a classic punter when he played at Georgia.

Every successful coach is remembered for some feature or specialty. Some invent, some adapt, some perfect. Missouri's Don Faurot is credited with inventing the split T, Bud Wilkinson perfected it at Oklahoma. A high school coach designed the wishbone, Darrell Royal won national championships with it at Texas. Bill Yeoman developed the veer, a variation of the wishbone, and it became the offense of the seventies.

With Butts, it was the function and utilization of the forward pass.

He was throwing the ball in an era when defense dominated, and you earned your keep on offense with a power running attack. Most teams ran the single wing, as Butts did starting out, but the old Notre Dame box was still around at the outset of his career.

As the war years began, the professionals, most notably the Chicago Bears under the influence of Clark Shaunessey, the creator, moved to the "T," which became the formation of the future. Butts was seriously studying the "T," all along, and would make the switch during the war years. The "T" offered greater offensive flexibility, and he would produce outstanding individual passing stars, but few of his teams would ever match the offensive firepower of his 1941 and 1942 squads.

When Butts threw 35 times in a game, that was nearly half of a season's total for some college coaches.

As time went by, he would design eight and often ten different passing series with ten or more patterns off each series, which meant he could enter a game with at least 100 different pass plays.

It was difficult for his quarterbacks, who called the plays, to comprehend that much. He mastered the system, however, and expected his players to learn it. For example, he demanded that the fourth available receiver not slough off. If the other three were covered he wanted the fourth one to be ready and to run his route correctly and precisely. "You can't be a true decoy unless you think you might get the ball," he often told his receivers. No trotting through, no round angles. They had to be sharp. A safety picks up on a sloppily run route and will ignore you.

From one season to the next he would tinker with a dozen new pass series, and he might design four or five new pass routes during a single week of practice. He was always thinking, cogitating, and scheming.

In offensive drills, he threw the ball for 45 minutes in live situations. He would tell the defense what was happening to make his offense work hard to perfect its execution.

"When I got to the pros," Charley Trippi, perhaps, his greatest player, once said: "I could tell immediately that they didn't know half as much about the passing game as Coach Butts. He was way ahead of them.

"Fran Tarkenton became a scrambler at Georgia which influenced his success in the pros for one big reason. Coach Butts in the late fifties was the only college coach I knew of who sent out five receivers. He was doing it long before anybody else did, and when the defense broke through, Fran developed the scramble. He learned to scramble very effectively, but sending out all those receivers is what gave him the opportunity to improvise."

One September afternoon more than four decades ago, Zipp Newman, sports editor of the Birmingham News asked Coach Butts to tell him what he looked for in a passer and described his approach to developing a passing attack.

"At Georgia," Butts said, "we first try to find a passer with proper passing form." In addition to good form, Butts outlined for Newman these requirements for his passer:

- Throw from behind the ear with an overhand motion.
- Must follow through. We ask the passer to imagine that he is actually giving the ball to his intended receiver.
- Must throw ahead of the receiver.
- Should throw a pass easy for the receiver to catch.
- Must have the will to win, since the defense will rush him in the hope of interfering with his concentration on the pass pattern.
- In addition to mechanical ability to throw, the passer must have an innate ability to select the open receiver.

Over the years a great many coaches gained considerable passing knowledge from Butts. All they had to do to get him to impart his wisdom was to ask.

Rauch Remembers

This is the first of several detailed recollections of James Wallace Butts by his Hall of Fame Quarterback, John Rauch. His first person recollections appear throughout this book.

Spartan Coach And Humble Servant

Our coach at the University of Georgia, James Wallace Butts, Jr. was a legend, truly an unforgettable character. He was born near Milledgeville, in the central part of the state which once was the capital of the Empire State of the South. The family homestead was known in Baldwin County as Butts Crossing. The date of his birth was February 7, 1905. The home has long since burned to the ground.

However, for those many of us who loved and appreciated the intensely competitive man, that ground is sacred. From that middle Georgia turf sprang one of the greatest coaches in history of college football. However, the family cemetery and plot of land where he grew up is now accessible only by boat since the waters of Lake Sinclair have cut off the overland routes. Coach Butts passed away in the winter of 1973, a sad, sad day for those of us who played for him and loved him. His contributions to the University of Georgia and the Bulldogs are legendary. His coaching statistics, records, and awards can be found in the Butts-Mehre Building on the campus in Athens, but those raw statistics don't tell you the entire story of Coach Butts who for so many of us became our second father. I know that is the way I felt about him. I would like to tell you more about our coach and the Bulldogs who played for him, getting into his personality, which, perhaps, is more significant than the records his teams set.

His wife, Winifred (Coach Butts called her Winnie), called him Wallace. When she called him Wallace it had a ring of respect and dignity. Most of his close friends referred to him as Wallace. The legendary Coach at Notre Dame, Frank Leahy, called him Wallace.

He and Leahy were very close friends, dating back to the early forties. The two socialized together, but most of the time they were discussing football. At dinner they would diagram plays on napkins.

They had a deep and abiding love for the game. The two of them envisioned the "T" formation as the college offense of the future when they began their personal clinics in the forties. Most college teams of that era ran from some variation of single wing formation. The single wing was a power formation, requiring a tailback who could run and throw. Like Frank Sinkwich whose quickness enabled him to devastate defenses.

Sinkwich didn't have great top speed, but had such remarkable quickness that he often made long runs, bursting past the defense before they knew where he was. While I came after Sinkwich, I knew of his reputation as a runner and can imagine what explosive running ability meant to Coach Butts. But Coach Butts knew that to incorporate his passing objectives that the "T" formation gave him more options. The "T" was perfect for Charley Trippi.

The Chicago Bears and Clark Shaughnessy introduced the "T" in the early 40s to professional football with great success. Butts and Leahy installed the Pro "T" formation at their respective schools in 1944. They spent time together in South Bend and Athens during their spring practices.

Never will I forget the first time I met Coach Leahy. It was the spring of my sophomore year in 1946. The two coaches sat up in a tower overlooking the field while we scrimmaged for over two hours. Coach Butts would holler down from the tower, "run that play over again" or run this play or that play.

I'm sure we practiced every play in our playbook.

When they came down from the tower Coach Butts called everyone over. He introduced Coach Leahy, and the Notre Dame coach said a few nice remarks about our practice. Maybe I was young and easy to impress, but I thought Coach Leahy was the most gracious, articulate person I had ever met.

The Bowlmaster of the Forties

He commenced to shake hands with each player and called many by their first names. When he came to me he said with that Irish brogue I've often tried to imitate, 'Jawn, you are doing a nice job for Wallace. Keep up the good work.' Needless to say, I felt ten feet tall.

Over his lifetime Coach Butts had been called a lot of things. Some negative because of his Spartan regimen in preparing his teams but most with great respect. Football coaches and sportswriters (we had no television and not much radio coverage in those days) referred to him as Wally. Some coaches and writers, who were taken in by his pessimistic evaluation of his team's chances to win the next Saturday outing applied the moniker "Weepin' Wally." Even after years of his wringing out the crying towel, most of them still fell for Coach Butts sad stories over and over again.

True Bulldogs referred to him as the "Bowlmaster" for he was the master at taking his team to post season bowl games in the forties.

Except for the war years of '43 and '44, Georgia went to a bowl every year. There were outstanding teams, but you can't overlook the fact that the Bulldogs played exciting football. That meant a lot to bowl promoters in the era when filling seats in post-season matchups did not come easy.

You had to know and be around Coach Butts for a long period of time to understand all sides of him. My layman's analysis of him is that he was a great actor. He was gifted with that ability to change with the situation.

As a football coach he was naturally stern, disciplined, and a no nonsense teacher. Even today his former players like to recall his talks at the beginning of fall practice. He would first set the training rules: hours, meals, practice schedule, etc., then he would say something like, "I expect each and every one of you to obey these rules if you want to play football at the University of Georgia.

"If you cannot obey these rules you will not be paying the price it takes to win. I dislike losers. If there are any here step up now and well have it out." Needless to say there were never any takers.

We all knew it was Coach Butts' way or the highway. Several very fine players were sent packing for breaking training rules or for insubordination. I'm sure he hated this part of his duty but the team always came first.

He was known for long physical practices. He worried about his team's condition and preparation. He won a lot of games by having his team better prepared. With equal talent his Spartan style would insure his Bulldogs had the edge in the fourth quarter.

Away from competition he was humble, sincere, honest, and a softhearted man. He was a family man who loved his wife and children very much. I had a chance, early on, to see that side of Coach Butts.

After the 1946 season I got married, and when I brought my wife, Jane, to Athens there weren't many nice places we could financially afford to rent. This was after the war and the veterans overran the town and campus, taking advantage of the G.I. bill. A lot of them were married and there probably was never a more competitive circumstance in Athens in trying to find a residence in those years.

So we lived in a boarding house, a trailer, basement and garage apartments. Anything we could find. We were always upgrading on a very small budget.

Coach Butts approached me one day and said he wanted my wife and me to stay in his house while he and Winnie were out of town. How could I refuse my coach? Besides, it sounded like an order.

Wally with an early Bulldog; the first mascots were brindle

We packed a few things and went over at noon, the day the Butts left town. When we arrived the maid had a full meal prepared for the three daughters and us. We were amazed. What a meal. Ham, grits, cornbread, collard greens, black eyed peas, and strawberry shortcake for dessert. We lived like a king and queen for three days.

The greatest thrill was to be around the Butts' girls. Faye was the oldest. She was about 15 at the time. Jean was the middle daughter, and Nancy the youngest, about 10. They were adorable southern ladies who made my wife and me feel right at home. We could feel the family love in that house.

We enjoyed spending time with them when the girls returned home from school. The maid was terrific. She had worked for the family for several years and had everything under control. At night we would play games with the girls. As I remember, Nancy came down sick the second day. Although she was feeling poorly, she was a smiling and happy child. We enjoyed giving her special attention. We thought so much of Nancy we decided to name our first child Nancy.

The day Coach and Mrs. Butts came home it was close to noon, and the big meal had been prepared by the girls and the maid. Jane and I said we would be going but Mrs. Butts insisted we stay for lunch.

Mrs. Butts and the girls kept the conversation going about the trip, school, and Nancy's illness. Coach Butts and I were pretty much silent. In the middle of the meal Mrs. Butts said, "Wallace, did you bring in the jellies and jams from the car?" "No," he replied, "I'll get them later."

"Get them right now Wallace, I want John and Jane to take some with them," Mrs. Butts ordered. With that Coach Butts got up very slowly and fetched the jellies and jams. I could have crawled under the table. He might be king on the football field, but he was Wallace or Dad at home, and he always played second fiddle to four women.

James Wallace Butts was, as I have said, an actor. He could play the role of tough guy, saint, politician, orator, comedian – anything the situation called for. I liked him best as a football coach, but after that, I most admired his ability as a public speaker.

Several times I accompanied him to banquets where he had been invited to speak. He always received a standing ovation. He had perfect timing when he spoke. He always started off slow, like he was somewhat embarrassed to be addressing his audience. Then he would get into his stories and the words flowed smoothly. He was great at setting up the punch lines and his animations were always delightfully comical. He got better with each story and the more he talked the more the people loved it.

He spoke on a vast number of subjects but football with its many heroic or frustrating moments captivated his audience more than anything. He wasn't beyond poking a little humor at himself.

Coach Butts had a language of his own on the football field. He was so graphic, and his caustic remarks went right to the point. He made you understand what he wanted done and he was the best ever at getting his point across. "That's a terrible stance you have," he might say, "you look like a dog passing a peach seed."

When a player failed to get down field to make a block he would shout, "you'll never get down field if you don't get out of that damned Chinese trot." Sometimes players would get up tight, or try too hard, when he was riding them.

Picture this poor player messing up time after time until Coach Butts walked up to him and exclaimed, "Son, you'll never get it right being so tense. Your butt is so tight I couldn't drive a needle up it with a sledgehammer." That broke the tension because everyone laughed. The player soon improved significantly.

Coach Butts was a friend to us all. If we count all the kind things he did for others, you would understand why some of us referred to him as a saint. He never revealed any of his charitable contributions. He gave of himself, and his money, to friends everywhere, never asking anything in return. He pulled for the little guy. Not because he was short himself, but because he was a caring and generous person. He might have been short, but he was very muscular and tough. He was very conscious of his excellent physical condition.

Coach Butts was a fierce competitor. In his playing days he was a very good football player and a boxer who feared no one. He loved a challenge and the word quit was not in his vocabulary. Yet he had this soft side and you knew he cared about you.

He would amaze me when he talked to the quarterbacks before practice. He spoke with a soft southern voice, very fatherly and teacher like. When he finished, he would head to the practice field. First thing he'd do was pull his ball cap down tight on his head. Then his pace would quicken. Look out, he's a different person now. A real Jekyll and Hyde changeover if you know what I mean. If you had played for him, you'd know for sure.

It would be hard for him, with his generous personality and concern for kids, to coach today under the rules and regulations of the NCAA. He could not turn down anyone in need, especially one of his players. I cannot pinpoint every occasion, but I'm sure many players, coaches, and friends benefited from his generosity. Maybe this would be an infraction today. In his day, it was a matter of helping kids get an education.

When we traveled to away games, he insisted everybody wear a coat and tie. In 1946, I had a very worn sport coat and a tie I had received the past Christmas as a gift. It wasn't much, but it was all I had. So I qualified to travel under his rules.

The only problem was that the tie would glow in the dark. In our first game we beat the Chattanooga Moccasins on their home field and boarded the bus for the long ride home. It was getting dark, and as I climbed aboard one of the players noticed the glow from my tie. Well that tie and my coat were the brunt of many jokes and wisecracks all the way back to Athens.

On Monday after my first class I walked past the arch and into downtown Athens. As I passed a popular downtown men's store, a salesperson came running out, grabbed me by the arm and said, "I have something for you." He took me inside and said, "Pick out any sport coat you want in this store." I was flabbergasted.

When I asked why, I was told, "Don't ask any questions." I walked out with the best coat I ever owned in my life and the man gave me a nice tie to go with it. I wasn't very good at saying thank you, but a couple of days later when Coach Butts and I were alone, I mentioned the coat and tie. Before I could say "thanks" he said, "I don't know what you're talking about." End of conversation.

Then he walked out of the field house, pulled the ball cap down tight on his head and, you guessed it, his personality changed. He took care of me on the one hand, but on the other, when practice started, it was all business – the business of paying the price to win football games for the University of Georgia.

Humble servant, to me, is a proper description of Coach Butts. It was appropriate because he was so courteous and thoughtful to those who were in need or who provided services to others.

I recall a time when we rode to Atlanta together for a sports banquet at the old Henry Grady Hotel. We were staying overnight at the hotel and our luggage consisted of small overnight cases.

After checking the car with the parking lot valet he tipped him a bill that looked like a five. We carried our cases to the door and were met by at least five porters who insisted on carrying our bags. It was something to see those porters scramble to reach those two little bags.

Coach Butts commanded them to stop and then

handed a five-dollar bill to each of them. They all stuffed the bills into their pockets, and with chorus like voices said, "Mr. Butts, if there's anything else ya needs – call (whatever their respective names were)."

This was the first time I had witnessed a show like that but later I heard it was a regular performance whenever Coach Butts arrived at the hotel. He distributed plenty more five-dollar bills that night and the next morning as we left to return to Athens.

Wherever he went, he took a stack of five-dollar bills. Word gets around, you know. A five-dollar tip is big to me even today but imagine its magnitude back then.

Let me go back again and talk about Coach Butts' coaching ability and philosophies of football. I already mentioned how demanding he was on the field. He was an excellent teacher. Very meticulous with detail and artistic in diagramming plays on the blackboard.

I believe he liked the excitement of doing new or different things. At that time not many coaches devoted much time to the passing game. Most would schedule five or ten minutes to the passing game, and it generally showed after kickoff.

They would stress defense and running as well as kicking. Very important for success in football, but Coach Butts would devote at least fifteen minutes to passing before practice even started. I would say the passing game took up about one third of our practice routine.

If he felt the quarterbacks needed more throwing, he might eliminate wind sprints and have everybody run a straight path down the field as a receiver.

He would often add the challenge of, "catch a hundred straight passes and you can go in." Can you imagine the pressure that would build up when the count got to 70-80-90 straight catches? A few times we struggled to complete 20 in a row.

This would aggravate him and he would shout, "get your butts around the field until I tell you to stop." As this mass of dirty, tired players trudged around an area the size of four football fields you would hear some real grumbling. "You drop another one and I'm going to kick your tail." Or, "Phew I can't take this much longer." Usually one of the leaders would put it into perspective: "Let's get it back together men. If we make the man happy he'll send us in." After three or four laps Coach Butts would yell, "If you're ready to do it right, get back out here." We always got it right after that.

He and his assistant coaches devised many drills to enhance the performance of quarterbacks and receivers. However, I got the feeling he knew the passing game wouldn't work if there wasn't good pass protection in the line.

He and his staff worked hard at recruiting big, strong, and agile linemen. The linemen worked harder than any players on the team. Some of their drills were like war games. One of Coach Butt's most able assistants, J.B. Whitworth, worked the linemen both offensively and defensively. Their drills were packed with grunts, groans, sweat and blood.

All spectators at our practices got to their places early for a good view of the linemen war games. I never had much chance to observe those drills, but the ones I heard people talk about most were the one-on-one battles.

Coach Whit would designate an offensive and defensive player to oppose each other at the line of scrimmage. At the snap the two would charge into each other until one was declared the winner by penetration (defensive player) or by protecting the line of scrimmage (offensive player).

This was only the warm-up because Whit would then conjure up two on one, three on one, and for those he had his own reasons to punish, he might go four on one.

He would be heard shouting during these drills, "Don't be a quitter, go for his face, show me some blood." Life in the trenches was tough under Whit. If you had heart and fight, he would make you a successful lineman.

Another drill the spectators seemed to enjoy was the chicken coop. There was a cage like structure about three feet high with chicken wire over the top. It was about ten feet square with two four by four posts in the middle about three feet apart. Just enough room for a body or bodies to crawl under the wire but only one could make it between those posts in the middle.

The drill was to improve agility but in the end it enhanced hostility, something a lineman needs. Drill one had linemen crawl on all fours through the cage doing a figure eight between the inside posts. They went as fast as they could and as soon as one came out another player started. If you collapsed, Coach Whit was all over you.

To excite the spectators Coach Whit would start one player at one end of the coop and another at the other end. It was a test of agility, strength, and moxie as to which player would make it through the two center posts first.

It must have looked like a chicken fight in a chicken coop. Nobody got maimed as far as I know, but there was a lot of bloodshed under that chicken wire. The fans, who came to practice, loved it and it must have been a letdown when the linemen joined the rest of us for teamwork.

Coach Butts may well have picked his starting lineman by the skinned marks on their faces. Those were badges of courage. Broken noses, black eyes, missing teeth and skin marks – all Georgia linemen were marked.

All but one. The best looking guy on the team was Robert Blaze Sanders of Augusta, brother of quarterback Carl Sanders. Blaze was the perfect southern gentleman, a member of the elite Chi Phi fraternity with a face as flawless as any movie star.

Blaze spent more time in lineman drills than any other lineman. Yet he never had a blemish, never an ugly skinned mark on his face. It infuriated the other linemen and most went out of their way to try to do the job on him. Coaches Butts and Whitworth both loved the guy because he hung in there and got the job done.

We had outstanding coaches. Along with Coach Whit there were Quinton Lumpkin and Shug Jordan. All were hardworking men and effective teachers. The development of Georgia linemen was in good hands. It is a tribute to Coach Butts' organizational ability to hire these outstanding coaches. He believed you had to have more than a few good men in the trenches to win the big football games.

Everyone knows it takes motivation to become successful in football. Coach Butts was a master at motivation and psychology. He used a lot of it on me. In my case, I was not a great football player but did possess some athletic ability.

I loved to play all sports but other things were also important to me. Mainly it was my high school sweetheart who meant the most.

When I got to Athens, I was a long way from home for the first time in my life. I was being called on to make decisions and to do things on my own for the first time. Coach Butts must have realized this for he gave me special attention. He spent a little more time with me on and off the field than the other quarterbacks. He built me up when he thought I was getting depressed or homesick. But I might have become a little cocky from this early attention. That did not set well with Coach Butts.

In my first game against Murray State in 1945, I did fairly well. The second game against Miami, in Miami, I threw two touchdown passes. The second one was for the winning touchdown. I must have displayed some cockiness after that game.

Coach Butts didn't like that with his players. He wanted them confident but not cocky. The morning after the Miami game we were preparing to leave the hotel and return to Athens. Someone came up to me with a Miami newspaper and said, "You had better read this." I sat down anxious to read about myself and my great play.

After reading the accounts of the game there were stinging quotes from Coach Butts. He said in so many words that he was worried about his team. "There seems to be a lack of leadership," he noted. As a team the Bulldogs did not play very well. The quarterbacking was mediocre and he would possibly have to make a change at that position. I couldn't have been more hurt if he had stabbed me in the back. I felt lousy the whole train ride home.

It made me very humble. It might have been one of his psychological moves since he stuck with me the rest of my four years. But I was not a cocky kid on that train ride home. You can be sure of that.

Other times he motivated by challenge. He would challenge your guts, your manhood, or whatever it took to get your competitive spirit going. There was only one player I recall who fought back at him. That was Tom Greene, a lineman from Macon. It was before my time, but the story was passed along over the years. This is the story the way I heard it. Coach Butts was "motivating" Tom pretty hard on the practice field one day. A fight ensued. They players were aghast. (Dan Magill, who was at practice that day says Coach Butts kicked Tom in the seat of his pants after a sloppy performance. "Tom didn't know who had kicked him. He swung as he turned around which led to Coach Butts punching Tom, but Tom was so big, most of his punches landed on Tom's shoulder pads. Wyatt Posey was the one who broke it up.")

After the assistant coaches restored order, practice continued without further incident. There never was a formal apology from Tom or Coach Butts. I suspect behind closed doors the two settled their differences. Tom Greene was one of Georgia's outstanding linemen. I think he knew Coach Butts never held Tom's reaction in the heat of battle against him.

The two remained close friends for the rest of their lives. Just one of those practice field episodes which reflect the intensity that is part of the great game of football.

Other Voices

Edwin Pope
On Wally's Personal Payroll

Edwin Pope, long time columnist for the Miami Herald, is a native of Athens. He wore short pants when he first wrote sports for the old Banner Herald.

He grew up in the shadow of Sanford Stadium, and became a friend of Wallace Butts. He is vicariously one of Wally's Boys although he never played for the famous Bulldog coach.

A distinguished and award winning columnist, Edwin worked tirelessly to see that both Coach Butts and John Rauch were elected to the College Football Hall of Fame.

Joining the Miami Herald in 1959, John Edwin was the youngest winner of the Red Smith Memorial Award (1989), the most cherished accolade in the sports print media. In 1993 he was elected to the National Sportscasters and Sportswriters Hall of Fame. He has won a record three National Headliners Club awards as the nation's best columnist, two of them 26 years apart, and another record three Eclipse Awards for thoroughbred racing columns.

He has authored six books, including Football's Greatest Coaches; Baseball's Greatest Managers; Ted Williams' Golden Year and The Edwin Pope Collection. He is one of only a handful of writers to have covered every Super Bowl.

A major underwriter in the production of this book, Edwin's recall of a trip to Yeadon, Pennsylvania with John Rauch is a classic:

I flashback to Wally Butts a lot, but never by that exact name. It was impossible for me to address him any way except "Coach Butts." Long after he left us, I still can't.

Coach Butts was sort of my second father, stern whereas my real father was forgiving, but generous in a way that my real father, God bless him, simply could not afford.

Allow me to offer just one example. I worked two years for coach Butts in another age, as "Acting director of sports publicity" from 1944 through '46. It wasn't a lot of work then, even for only one person. It wasn't even considered a conflict of interest to do that job and another as sports editor of the Athens Banner-Herald at the same time.

Did anyone ever seriously think I was going to write nasty things about Coach Butts or the Bulldogs? Hey, that's why they called me "Bulldog."

Anyway, they only gave me the job because there was no one else. All the qualified people were in the armed forces. Then those people came back home, and Coach Butts beckoned me one night at a basketball game, and said, "The athletic board has abolished your temporary job, and someone else will take over permanently." Then, in a voice I didn't know he had until that minute, he said, "but if you'll just show up at the office now and then, I'll see that you get paid anyway."

I was a fairly simpleminded kid, but not so simpleminded I didn't know where the money was coming from. Out of Coach Butts' pocket. He wasn't making that much, around $15,000 a year (Georgia drew 17,000 customers for its '45 opener against Murray State, and you could still sit in the "bullpen," somewhere around the goal line at Sanford Stadium, for 40 cents, so football wasn't anything like the big-ticket item it is today). But he would have given me a piece of that if I'd let him.

That was so typical. Coach Butts was as openhearted as he was hugely demanding. He would give you everything he had. In return he expected everything you had. Your best was the least you could give. He awarded no points for trying. Only winning counted, but when you were up against it, there he was. There was nothing accidental about the deep reverence which all his ex-players have for him.

So when he recruited Johnny Rauch in '45, it was a meeting of souls, the coach no player (well, none except Charley Trippi and Frank Sinkwich) could ever satisfy, and the player who was never satisfied with himself.

Rauch must have been amused the last few decades hearing college coaches proclaiming confidence all over the place. That's a dramatic turn from days when the only time coaches admitted they had any real talent was when those players were hurt and couldn't play. Coach Butts was the master of that, as a celebrated sports writer of the time learned.

Carter "Scoop" Latimer, sports editor of the Greenville (SC) News, was looking for something different before the Georgia-Furman game there in 1946. So he ran down Coach Butts and started firing questions.

"Three-touchdown favorites!" Coach Butts snorted. He mourned that Trippi had a bad leg, and Rauch's timing was off, and there was no one to catch the ball even when his timing was on. "We may wind up having to use our fifth string," Coach Butts concluded bleakly.

Latimer had his scoop. Off he hustled to his typewriter. The next morning's headlines read: FURMAN WILL THRASH GEORGIA.

Coach Butts used his fifth string, all right. There was no other way to hold down the score when Georgia led, 70-7. "And you know," Latimer said later that night, "I talked to Wally after the game and I still don't see how Georgia won."

It would be extremely difficult for Coach Butts to convince his old players at Georgia Military College of his good heartedness. He actually worked some of those teams during halftimes of games. They wouldn't understand that he would go on to substitute for ministers on certain Sundays, that he never could pass up a hitchhiker, that he wouldn't let his daughters use the family car on occasions because the family pooch, Rip, was napping in it "and I don't want to wake him up."

One Sunday, after an especially painful loss, Coach Butts was found sitting in his office, patting Rip and saying, "You're the only friend I've got left in this world."

So, naturally, Rauch seldom saw this tender side of his coach until he was long into coaching himself, including taking the Oakland Raiders to Super Bowl II. Coach Butts simply saw what a diamond he had in Rauch, on the field and off it. He wasn't about to say so. He just kept polishing that diamond.

"Keep your feet together," he drummed into Rauch. "Twelve or fifteen inches will do it. Throw off the back foot and step into the target. Elbow close to body and keep it there! Now when you step off that left foot, no more than six to eight inches. That's it! Ball up from your chest about a foot – just to the right of your head. Turn your wrist in, line it up with your receiver."

Rauch was a gifted athlete, with magnificent reflexes if not especially fast on any straightaway. He was tough as hickory. He didn't go to the trainer about hangnails. Maybe Georgia's finest all-around player ever except for the remarkable Trippi and Sinkwich, he never missed a game on offense or defense or special teams. From 1945 through '48, be started every game and finished most, throwing, handing off, even running and receiving, then, defensively, coming up for tackles and making interceptions. He covered kickoffs, too. That's what Coach Butts asked Rauch to do, and it wouldn't have occurred to Rauch to question why.

I don't know if you could say Rauch was actually afraid of Coach Butts because he seemed to fear no one. But there was a day...

One summer, he and I hit the road together. We rode a train from Athens to Philadelphia so he could attend the high school graduation of his future wife. We had only a few bucks at the beginning and nothing when it came time to return to Athens. So we went to the thumb. The last night on the road, we were so broke we stayed in a flophouse in Greenville for 50 cents, total.

We had been lucky our first day out from Philly. Drivers picked us up and took us as far as they could. Then we ran into some less hospitable. We were pretty much down on life in general when we happened onto College Park, Maryland, and the then pristine campus of the University of Maryland.

Inevitably, I suppose, under the circumstances, Rauch looked up at a stretch of grass leading to a college building and said, "I wonder if Maryland would take me."

"What do you mean?" I said.

"It's just so far from my home to Athens," he said. "Maybe I'd be better off going to school up here closer, if they'd take me."

I panicked. "Oh, no," I said, ready to beg. "If I go back to Athens without you, Coach Butts would never forgive me."

It didn't seem important at the time that Coach Butts probably would never forgive Rauch, either. But Rauch would be a star anywhere, whereas I had no choice but to go back to my hometown. And I wasn't going to be the one to tell him that Johnny Rauch had decided to transfer to Maryland.

Just about then, a car picked us up and carried us on toward the flophouse in Greenville and closer to Athens. But I knew enough of how Rauch felt about Coach Butts to believe he never would have left him, no matter how tempting the idea of playing nearer to home.

Coach Butts thought as much of Rauch as Rauch did of him. That's another reason it is great for us that John Rauch put his memories of Coach Butts and his days at Georgia down on paper for Wally's Boys even if so many of us could never bring ourselves to call Coach Butts by his first name.

JESSE OUTLAR REMEMBERS WALLY

It was hard on Jesse Outlar, sports editor of the Atlanta Constitution, when it came to professional objectivity and his beloved University of Georgia.

It was a good job, and he enjoyed the big events—Kentucky Derby, Indy 500, World Series, Masters and in later years, the Super Bowl. But what he loved most was Georgia football. On top of that, he truly loved Wallace Butts.

Though he needed to be objective it was not easy with his emotions. He also had to cover Georgia Tech, and he did that fairly and professionally, but when the Yellow Jackets played his beloved Bulldogs, he was in knots, just like the man on the sideline he admired so much, Wally Butts.

What was hardest on Jesse, in addition to the long losing streak to Tech in the fifties, was the constant criticism of Coach Butts that reached a crescendo as the decade played out. There was only so much he could say in his column, but privately he blasted Butts' critics, often at public gatherings – even at dinner at a restaurant—when the subject of his friend came up.

Outlar never allowed anybody, Bulldog or stranger, to take a shot at his friend without a serious rejoinder. He would put up his dukes if necessary. He remained fiercely loyal to Butts, and at the ripe ole age of 81 put down on paper his remembrances of Coach Butts, whom he first got to know when he was an eavesdropping waiter at Memorial Hall where the coaches lounged for refreshments during the day.

A native of Omega, Jesse is a graduate of the University of Georgia Journalism School.

On a bright July day in 1973 Winnie and Wallace Butts were treating my Icelandic bride, Johanna, and me to lunch at the Athens Country Club. Johanna had heard many former Georgia players discuss Coach Butts. They admired him greatly but they all remembered those long days of "paying the price" in practice.

Charley Trippi served as consensus spokesman when he vowed that Coach Butts was the only person he'd ever been afraid of. You'd have to attend practice to discover why Charley and so many of his cohorts feared their coach.

"Coach Butts," my wife said " I can't understand why so many of those boys were afraid of you. You seem like such a nice little man."

Coach Butts smiled and Winnie laughed and laughed. Wallace Butts was indeed an extremely nice man – away from the practice field. The drillmaster's record of 140-86-9 reflect that he had the correct attitude on the field.

I was privileged to know Coach Butts and his family for thirty-three of his sixty-eight years. Regardless of how fearful he could sound at work, he was always very calm and overmatched when debating his wife and three daughters at home.

Someone inquired how I first met Coach Butts. Actually, I never was introduced to him. We just got to know each other over the years, dating back to my days as a journalism student.

I first saw him, along with members of his coaching staff, in 1941 when their offices were in Memorial Hall. That was also where the Memorial Hall grill was located. As a student waiter I frequently served the coaches coffee, donuts, and sandwiches.

Listening to Coach Butts and his aides gossiping about football and their players provided me the best field position I ever had as a sportswriter.

The coaches, of course, were unaware and didn't care that I was a rookie sportswriter for the *Red and Black*, the student newspaper.

Promoted to Sports Editor the next year I paid my first official call on Coach Butts for an interview. He promptly recognized me as the waiter and discovered my name for the first time. He then realized why I had been such an attentive listener during those conversations at "The Grill."

I never informed Coach Butts that I also knew many of his players. While visiting "The Grill" the players discovered that my dorm room was next door to the football domicile. They promptly invited themselves to smoke cigarettes in my room day and night. That's a great way to experience a football education – listening to the players talk and commiserate while enjoying a smoke in privacy.

Frank Sinkwich didn't smoke, but he shook up Coach Butts and the entire Bulldog nation when he declared that he intended to skip spring practice so he would have more time to drink beer and date the girls. You may easily reflect how that declaration brought a prompt analogue of Sinkwich's character from the coach.

Everyone, including Sinkwich, was surprised when Butts never invited his future Heisman Trophy winner to rejoin the team. However, fellow players quickly took care of matters and voted to welcome Sinkwich back to the squad. Frank frequently told me through the years how Wally promptly proved to him that football is a game designed for the team and not for an individual, even the star of the team.

It was unbelievable how Butts electrified Georgia students and alumni by producing the Bulldogs first bowl invitation, the first of eight post season trips in his career. Georgia whaled TCU 40 – 26, in the 1942 Orange Bowl game. The Bulldogs had led 33-7, at halftime prompting Butts, not noted for compliments, to later remark those thirty minutes were the finest of any of his teams. Sinkwich was the ringleader in an unbelievable exhibition of passing and running.

Though Georgia would visit the Rose Bowl the next season Butts always rated the '41 crowd as his most talented.

I was among those invited to visit Coach Butts and his family after games. It was always fun to be there when everyone was smiling about a victory. The lone exception was the coach.

It was also a pleasure to frequently enjoy lunch with Coach Butts all those years. He always amused me by ordering his favorite dish – turnip greens and cornbread at the Georgian Hotel.

Over the years, I watched and heard of the multiple things that Coach Butts did for former players. I doubt any coach ever assisted players obtain jobs more so than Wallace Butts.

Jimmy Orr, a pass receiver, poignantly summed up Coach Butts personality, "As a player I always thought Coach Butts liked me, but he never showed it until I graduated. Once you played for him you had a friend for life."

Butts was indeed an offensive football genius, but he had an uncanny knack of losing in his business endeavors until the end of his career. His football glory days at Georgia ended a season after the Orange Bowl in 1960 when Fran Tarkenton and Pat Dye led the Dogs to a victory over Missouri.

Pressured by a small influential alumni group, Butts was forced to resign as head coach. Two years later he bitterly stepped down as athletic director. Fortunately, as he'd always preached to his players, he never quit.

Jesse Outlar, devout Wally loyalist and Bill Hartman

I spent considerable time with Winnie, Wallace, and their three daughters during and after the Saturday Evening Post trial. Butts' ladies had accurately predicted that Wally would win his biggest game in the courtroom.

Of all his many accomplishments I admired most what Butts did in his final decade. He started as a rookie insurance salesman and wound up as the owner of a very prosperous insurance firm. He earned more money from insurance than he'd ever made in football.

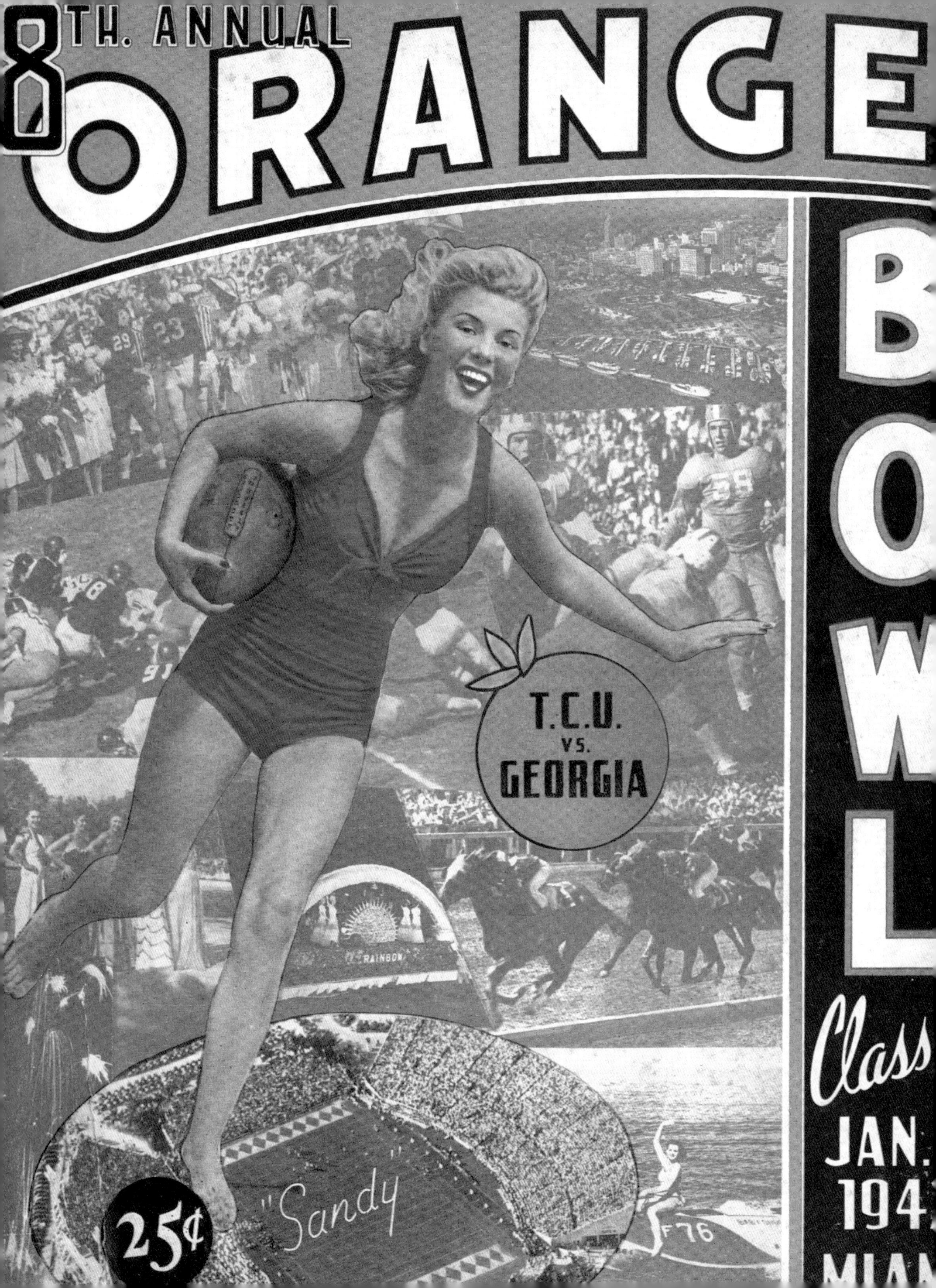
8TH. ANNUAL
ORANGE
BOWL
Class
JAN.
194
MIAM
T.C.U.
vs.
GEORGIA
"Sandy"
25¢
RAINBOW
F76

PART II

THE EARLY YEARS

Bowls, Championships and WWII

About John Stegeman

When I arrived in Athens, following high school graduation, I sure of what I wanted to do. Because of a farm background, I naturally enrolled in the College of Agriculture, with plans to major in entomology.

Today, I often comment that my choice of majors, "bugged me." While I remained unsure of what I wanted in the way of a degree, one thing was certain – I was not happy. My grades reflected my unhappiness. I knew I had to choose something different.

Following a senior class trip to Washington and New York, I, as class reporter, had written a two part series for my hometown weekly paper. It brought a positive reaction from my friends, but I never really considered journalism until the end of my immature freshman year. But enrolling in the Henry W. Grady College of Journalism was the right move.

Soon, I got to know Dan Magill. I had decided to give track a try, and, I recall it was my coach, Spec Towns, who introduced us.

Before long, I was happily studying for a journalism degree, living in Payne Hall where the athletes resided, and working for the school newspaper, The Red and Black. I also took up dry cleaning for Finley's Dry Cleaners.

Dan later hired me part time in the sports information office and also assigned me to assist the stat crew for home games in Sanford Stadium. Ten dollars cash in an envelope. That was a big deal in the late fifties.

Towns arranged for me to serve meals in Payne Hall where I also put up the mail for free room rent. He later put me on scholarship.

As time went by, Dan arranged for me to become campus correspondent for the Atlanta Journal and recommended me for the job of sports editor for the Athens Banner Herald. Life was good.

Many evenings were spent with Dan, who entertained the sports writers at Harry's Tavern at Five Points and Poss' Restaurant on the Atlanta Highway. He often invited me.

I was listening and learning. I was meeting people, including the Georgia coaches, former players and sports personalities who came to town – to see Georgia play, speak to the Athens Touchdown Club or to visit Coach Butts.

There was plenty of time to interact with Coach Butts. I had never been around a real celebrity before although in high school I did meet Eddie Robinson, who was a slugging first baseman at the time for the Chicago White Sox. A neighbor's brother from Baltimore brought him our way to quail hunt.

Everybody seemed in awe when in Coach Butts' company. Even after meeting him a few times with Dan, I was usually dumbfounded in his presence. I was afraid to say anything, but he usually displayed a warm smile and was generous in conversation which eventually made me feel comfortable around him.

On Bulldog Club trips with him and Dan, he occasionally asked questions about growing up in rural middle Georgia. My hometown of Wrightsville was not too far from Milledgeville, the place of his birth.

I have always been emotionally attracted to good humor and learned to appreciate story telling and the spinning of a yarn from several members of my family.

When people sat around on front porches and visited with the neighbors who dropped by, I was always eavesdropping. I was eager to learn and to hear the seasoned humorists in our community deliver their best. I suspect front porch yarn spinning was something that Coach Butts experienced growing up.

Coach Butts was eminently gifted at telling a story. Since my campus days, I have met many of the name coaches in the country over a period of time. There have been some with smooth style and delivery like Bud Wilkinson of Oklahoma and Paul Dietzel at LSU. Others like Frank Howard of Clemson and Peahead

Walker of Wake Forest, were more often than not, salty and acerbic. Colorful and accomplished at the art of applying the needle; ribald and raw humor often accompanied their presentations.

Shug Jordan of Auburn was most often referred to as a gentleman. Bear Bryant of Alabama roguishly colorful and Bobby Dodd of Georgia Tech, because of his overt penchant for saying something nice about everything and everybody, was known in many circles, as "old syrup mouth."

Author and Wally's Boy, John Stegeman

None had the one-liner gift or off-the-cuff rejoinders that Coach Butts had. Except, perhaps, for Duffy Daugherty of Michigan State. An Irishman, Duffy had a cherub face and a sly grin, and he could, perhaps, match Coach Butts with clever insights, creative and instantaneous banter before the mike.

When I first realized Coach Butts knew my name, I considered it a thrill that would rank up there with winning the Heisman Trophy if that had been my good fortune.

There was something about him that made you feel he had genuine warmth inside for people.

When he died, along with his players, I cried at his funeral. At that time in their lives they were literally weeping for Wally, their beloved coach.

One day, Dr. John Stegeman showed up at Dan's Stegeman Hall office. The building, which housed the expansive indoor swimming pool, was built by the Navy for training purposes during World War II and later named for John's father, Herman, a former Bulldog coach and athletic director. Coach Steg, as he was called, played for Amos Alonzo Stagg at the University of Chicago. I felt I was linked to the origins of the fundamentals of football.

Getting to know John Stegeman was one of the richest experiences I have had in my time in Athens. John was an accomplished writer who specialized in addition to Georgia's early football chronology and lore, the history of the War Between the States, principally relating to those from Athens who distinguished themselves in the conflict. Out of this latter interest came his book, These Men She Gave. It had to do with Athens' native sons who lost their lives in the Civil War.

John was the leading historian, the unparalleled expert, on the formative years of Georgia football. His book, Ghosts of Herty Field, disclosed some wonderful stories, and hidden gems, of the ole timers – all the way back to Dr. Charles Herty, who originated football at Georgia.

A man of enormous patience, John could spend hours at the University library researching microfilm and other preserved documents about an era which only a few remembered.

He wrote a second book, Touchdown, A Pictorial History of Georgia Football, which covered the beginning of the game on the campus through much of Vince Dooley's era.

John, who grew up with the most famous names in athletics, like Stagg for example, hanging around his house and staying overnight with his family, made an invaluable contribution to the history of football at Georgia with his exhaustive and dedicated research.

A lanky end on Coach Butts' first team, John remained loyal to his coach to the very end. His knowledge and research on Coach Butts' early career, through his books, newspaper articles and football program features are valuable archive material. His work is referred often in this book, and fortunately for all Bulldogs, what he researched and discovered made its way into print via his manual typewriter. It is preserved forever. Here's a mighty toast to John Stegeman.

1939

Even when Wallace Butts began his career at Georgia, nobody, based on his reputation of offensive innovation and his predilection for the passing game would have forecast that his team would have trouble scoring in the Southeastern Conference.

But that first season, his team was shut out four times. His defense was more efficient. The only team to score more than 14 points on his Bulldogs was Furman, which clipped the visitors from Athens 20-0 in Greenville.

The season ended with a 5-6 record, but there was not so much gloom about, for the Point-a-Minute Bullpups had the whole town of Athens eagerly awaiting 1940 when those sensational freshmen would be ready for varsity action.

Making His Way
End Coach To Head Coach

After a successful coaching run at Madison A&M and Georgia Military College, Butts moved to Male High in Louisville, Ky., in 1935 where he remained until 1938.

Following the 1937 season, Harry Mehre was forced to resign and became the head coach at Ole Miss. Joel Hunt, who enjoyed noteworthy success as a player at Texas A&M, was named to succeed Mehre.

Bill Hartman recalls that Hunt, Butts and Elmer Lampe were all brought to Athens to be interviewed. "Each thought that he might be named head coach," Hartman says. "That is the way I remember it."

Hartman surmises that when Hunt got the job, that he was advised that he should then hire the other two as assistants. If that is not exactly the way it was, that is what happened. Butts then became Hunt's end coach. Lampe coached the B-team and scouted the opposing teams.

When he took the assistant coaching position, it not only was obvious that Butts wanted to return to his Georgia roots, but also he had enough passion to coach for the University of Georgia that he took a sizeable pay cut to leave Male High and accept the opportunity in Athens. But his move was to prove a wise one in that following the 1938 season, Hunt was fired and Butts was named head coach.

"Hunt was never very popular in Athens," Hartman says. "He rubbed a lot of people the wrong way including Harold Hirsh of the Coca Cola Co., a long time benefactor of the University of Georgia."

Hartman believes Hunt's ego and arrogance were a potion too potent to overcome. "He spoke to the Rotary Club and infuriated a lot of folks, and I think it got back to Mr. Hirsch," Hartman says.

When Butts took over, he knew exactly what was on Georgia's mind. Winning a championship and playing in bowls was the hue and cry statewide. Mehre's teams enjoyed favorable success and only lost to Georgia Tech twice in ten years. But his teams never won the Southern Conference championship, nor the SEC, which was formed in 1933.

After Mehre's departure which was followed by Hunt's one year term, Butts began his college career which was to last 22 years.

He gave this account of his hiring, for a book, to his good friend, Jesse Outlar, longtime sports editor and columnist for The Atlanta Constitution.

"Dr. (W.O.) Payne (faculty chairman) told me they wanted me to coach the team. He offered me $5,500, but I told him that was too much. I offered to accept it for less. Then they made me an unusual offer. Somebody recommended that I receive five percent of any income generated by bowl teams.

"Georgia, of course, had never been to a bowl, so this did not seem like such a lucrative offer. I rejected it because the faculty did not have an incentive bonus clause, and I thought it foolish of me to incite their resentment at the outset. In retrospect, at this point in time, as they say, I should have accepted the bowl clause because we were invited to eight bowls while I was head coach."

It would take Butts three seasons to secure a bowl bid, but optimism was high in Athens following his initial campaign. Not from what the varsity accomplished but the rave reviews brought on by his freshman team. The Bullpups rolled over every opponent by such high scores that they were called the "Point-a-Minute-Bullpups."

The Pups scored 68 points versus South Carolina, 65 against G.M.C. and blanked Georgia Tech's freshmen, 33-0, on Grant Field. Only G.M.C. could muster a score, a single touchdown, but was limited to three yards rushing.

The promising freshmen took some of the sting out of the varsity's losing season. The Bulldogs lost four games by a total of 28 points and were shutout four times. Butts' first team did not have much offensive firepower, but that would change in short order.

Tailback Frank Sinkwich would lead a devastating single wing attack in the days ahead. Becoming excited by a bunch of freshman usually is ill advised, but the entire town couldn't hold back. They eagerly concluded this group of players had promise.

Butts, who later would be known as one of the biggest "po-mouthers" in collegiate circles, was excited, too, although he was wise to refrain from optimistic forecasts.

There was one thing, however, that he would wax about enthusiastically, albeit it later in his career, and that was those he hired as his first assistants.

"I was fortunate to assemble what I consider one of the finest staffs any head coach ever had," he said.

Led by line coach J.B. Whitworth, and backfield coach Bill Hartman, whom Butts had coached at G.M.C. and who had backed up the legendary Sammy Baugh with the Washington Redskins in 1938, Butts began to mastermind offensive production that had characterized his prep teams which lost a total of only 10 games in a 10 year career.

Joining Whitworth and Hartman were Spec Towns, the Olympic high hurdles champion who was a very fine end under Mehre, J.V. Sikes, who went on to become head coach at Kansas, and Quinton Lumpkin, who was captain of the 1938 team.

WYATT POSEY, COUNTRY BOY MAKES GOOD

Life on the farm in the thirties was hard work and hard times for James Wyatt Posey, a country boy whose background suggested that he would likely work long hours in hot fields with a modest income, at best, forecast for his future. He likely could expect a hardscrabble lifestyle.

That was the way it was for the majority of rural folk in those days. College football, however, would enable Posey, a native of Headland, Ala., to rise above his austere background. Enrolling in college was out of the question until Posey got off a school bus at a crossroads in Henry County, Alabama, in the spring of 1937.

Wyatt Posey, Wally's Boy who became a Wally assistant

Posey had to take two different busses to get to Newville High School in order to play football which he played well enough to get the attention of the late John Turner McAlister, a Bulldog loyalist and recruiter, who identified a number of capable players who became overachievers at Georgia. Posey was the first.

McAlister thought Posey would perform well as a Bulldog lineman. He phoned a recommendation and scouting report to Johnny Broadnax who was business manager and recruiter. Broadnax went looking for Posey. He found him at that crossroads and offered him a scholarship on the spot to play for the Bulldogs.

"I had never heard of Athens, Ga.," Posey said afterwards. "But it is a place that I will never forget."

To underscore the hard times of that era, Posey's daddy, a struggling farmer, didn't want his son to go off to college without a suit of clothes and sold a bale of cotton for that purpose. Those were the days when a bale of cotton brought a mere $16.00. Think of all the hard work in the boiling sun that it took to generate that much money and you understand why a dollar meant something back then.

The summer before he took a bus to Athens for college, Posey worked at a cotton gin for $1.50 a day. "I made $9.00 a week," he laughed, "and that was good money."

After he arrived at the bus station in Athens, he walked to New College where the football players lived. A new life for a country boy had begun. Harry Mehre was the coach but was let go after Posey's freshman season. Posey was redshirted his sophomore year (1938) and played three years for Butts. "That was good for me," Posey said enthusiastically. He always was a friend to me."

Dan Magill, then a youthful newspaper reporter prior to joining the Georgia staff after World War II, nicknamed him "Tiger." Magill wrote that Posey was the lightest tackle ever to start in a major bowl game when Georgia played Texas Christian in the Orange Bowl of 1942.

Following his senior season in 1941, Posey went off to war and became a distinguished tank commander as an officer. At the Battle of the Bulge at Bastogne his tank destroyed two enemy tanks and helped keep the Germans from breaking out. He was awarded a purple heart and a bronze star for his bravery.

Returning home after the war, he was teaching at nearby Jefferson when Butts called him and told him about a coaching opportunity at South Georgia College. Posey was head coach there for three seasons: 47, 48, 49.

A significant opportunity then came about as the result of a past friendship. At OCS training at Fort Knox, Ky. Posey became acquainted with Tex Rieber, whose father was president of Texaco and a Yale man.

Yale was still a power in Eastern football and was coached by Tennessean Herman Hickman, a clever 300 pounder known for his timely quips more so than for any play he might design for his T-formation offense and his Tennessee 60 defense.

Hickman had lost his line coach, and Tex Rieber recommended his friend Posey. To enhance Posey's interest, Rieber flew him to Manhattan for three days and nights, putting him up at the Roosevelt Hotel. Posey took the train to New Haven for a meeting with Hickman, who didn't offer him a job initially, but later sent a telegram advising Posey to report to Yale July 1st.

The rotund Hickman was a celebrity, a big name in New York, and was a regular guest on a network television show, "Celebrity Time." He would head to Manhattan early on Sundays, taking the train. Posey would drive down later, catch a Broadway matinee, arranged by Yale publicist, Charlie Loftus, and then join the Hickmans for dinner at Toots Shor's famous restaurant. Afterwards, Posey would drive the Hickmans back to New Haven.

"That was a wonderful experience for me," Posey said. "But I was too much of a country boy to stay long." Dewitt Weaver hired him at Texas Tech in 1951, and Butts brought him back to Athens in 1956.

He coached until Johnny Griffith's three year career as the Bulldog head coach came to an end. "I've had enough," Posey said at the time. "I enjoy coaching, but this business is too insecure."

Posey purchased Morris Held Paint Store, and set up his wife, Vivian, to run the business. He became the Southeastern representative for Ridell, the helmet makers, and worked as a college scout for the Chicago Bears on the side.

Football provided him with an education. It took him to big cities with bright lights. The game introduced him to people, some famous, some wealthy. But it never turned his head. He always remained a down home country boy and his life was far different life than what he could have expected when he was growing up in Alabama.

There are plenty of critics of football and some of the criticism is justified. But there is a good side to the game. What happened to Wyatt Posey still happens today. The game continues to provide opportunity for a lot of deserving young men.

Over a century ago, that fact was not lost on Wallace Butts.

VASSA CATE, FIRST WALLY'S BOYS CAPTAIN

Butts' first captain was Vassa Cate, a back with track speed, one who could go the distance.

When Cate finished his career he had played for three different coaches, but the emotional frustration from those changes didn't seem to affect his performance.

As a wingback, Cate worked with the ends but had little interest in blocking. He told Jesse Outlar, "Coach Butts changed my attitude." Cate was referring to his introduction to Butts, the end coach in 1939. Vassa had other recollections about his last Bulldog head coach.

"Spring practice started in January and lasted until the next season. I don't think any squad ever practiced more hours than we did," Cate told Outlar. "There was a little creek beside the practice field in those days, and we would attempt to get knocked into it just to get a sip of dirty water.

"But we learned football. I am positive that every person who played for Wallace Butts came away a better man. He was an offensive genius, a perfectionist in all phases. He was a demanding on the field, but off the field, he would give you his shirt and did. He was a coach who was sincerely interested in helping his players. I know he helped get me a coaching job when I graduated."

Cate was a two sport star for the Bulldogs. He was an all-the-way threat with the football in the open field. His speed allowed for many long runs which caused his coaches to encourage him to participate in track. He became SEC 100 yard dash champion and also won the 220 yard low hurdles. He was the high scorer in the SEC track championship in 1939.

There were many of Butts' players who followed the path that Vassa Cate took professionally. They became high school coaches, and when a good prospect came along, they were quick to inform Coach Butts and to encourage their kids to play for their old coach in Athens.

Cate had curly hair and a wide smile. He seemed always to be in a good mood and had a good word for everybody. Throughout his life, he was always eager to pay tribute to his alma mater and good friend – his coach, Wallace Butts.

Vassa Cate hits the line for big yardage

1940

There was improvement in a number of areas in 1940 for Wallace Butts' second team, which finished 5-4-1. Offensive production went up as the Dogs averaged 20.9 points per game. Only Kentucky held Georgia to less than two touchdowns that season as the Wildcats tied the home team 7-7 Between the Hedges. The Bulldogs lost four games by a total of 32 points, and there was more than mild disappointment in Athens. Expectations were high when the season began, a reminder that even back then, football fans have a way of becoming giddy with their pre-season forecasts.

The town and campus aspired to make that first bowl trip – and Dan Magill remembers that the community was hoping the great freshman class of '39 might be good enough to make that happen immediately – but it was not to be. Wait 'til next year? It would be worth the wait.

Underway With Eye On Point-A-Minute Bullups

Wallace Butts was one of six native Georgians to become head coach of the Bulldogs. When he took over in Athens in 1939 there wasn't much concern about where a head coach hailed from – what everybody wanted, as has been previously stated, was the establishment of a program that could contend for a championship and earn a bowl invitation.

Butts had a reputation for offensive creativity, but you wouldn't know it in that first season, a losing one with a 5-6 record. Only twice (26-0 over the Citadel and 33-7 over South Carolina) did the Dogs score more than two touchdowns and four times they were shut out.

There were close games, however, that could have gone either way. Georgia lost to Kentucky and Auburn by a touchdown and to NYU in New York by a point. Defensively, only Furman scored more than fourteen points, when they defeated Georgia, 20-0, in Greenville at night. It would be the last time Coach Butts experienced a losing season until 1949, when the decade of the forties ended with a 4-6-1 campaign.

But there was good news. Butts, relying on his network of contacts, had recruited a number of versatile and talented freshmen who set alumni hearts pounding to the beat of Glory, Glory to Ole Georgia as they steam rolled over all opponents and lifted spirits for the Butts' second season. Next year? The town couldn't wait.

The War Years Begin, Expectations Dashed

In late summer, 1940, the United States government was troubled by events in Europe. Hitler's German troops had overrun most of the continent, and things were not so stable in the Far East where Japan was planning for war, the confirmation of which was to come a little more than twelve months later.

Most Americans preferred that the nation stay out of the war. That would change soon enough, but for the moment neutrality seemed to be on the mind of a majority of Americans, many of whom were one generation removed from the old countries of Europe.

The "Point-A-Minute Bullpups" would be eligible for varsity action in the fall of 1940. The town was upbeat with the anticipation that those young players might finally bring a championship team to the Classic City.

"We had to wait another year," recalled Dan Magill, "but there were high hopes for the 1940 season."

Only once did the Bulldogs score less than 13 points when the Kentucky game in Athens ended in a 7-7 tie. Butts favored the forward pass while most coaches preferred to run the ball, play defense and utilize the quick kick as a major weapon.

Three of the losses were on the road: Columbia in New York, 19-13; Florida in Jacksonville, 18-13 and

Tulane in New Orleans, 21-13. Ole Miss defeated the Bulldogs in Athens 28-14, the only team to win by a margin of two touchdowns.

The potential firepower of Butts' single wing attack had become recognized, and the town of Athens would get what it had long sought, a bowl invitation, a year later in 1941. Except for the war years of the forties, Butts was to field exciting and dominant teams – three Southeastern Conference championships and six bowl invitations. The foundation had been laid.

SKIPWORTH, CAPTAIN 1940
KILLED IN ACTION 01.17.45

Eight Georgia football players, who played for Wallace Butts, lost their lives in World War II. Nobody paid a greater price that these courageous men.

The first Butts era Bulldog hero to give his life for his country was Tommy Witt, who first played for Coach Butts at Male High. An Army pilot, his plane was shot down during the North African invasion in October, 1942. James Turner Skipworth, Jr., of Columbus was killed in action, Jan. 17, 1945 in the Philippines. He was captain of the 1940 team, Coach Butts' second.

Skipworth attended Columbus High and Gordon Military College before enrolling in Athens. In high school there wasn't an activity or sport at which he did not achieve and excel.

In addition to expertly playing football, basketball, and baseball, he was President of his class and sports editor of the school paper; an officer in the Glee Club, Dramatics Club, and Hi-Y Club; he was a well rounded student, indeed. A steady and dependable right end, Skipworth entered Georgia in 1935 and played his final varsity season under Wallace Butts. Since grade school days he was a leader and nobody was surprised when he was elected captain of the Bulldogs.

"He was an exceptional leader," Bill Hartman remembers. "Additionally, he was a very good blocking end, playing the position very similar to the tight ends of today although we didn't call the position by that name in his years. He could catch the ball well, and on defense, he played the position in textbook fashion."

Eight years younger, his brother, George, followed him to Athens and was quarterback and letterman on the 1944 team. George also played basketball and remembers in January of 1945 after playing Georgia Tech in basketball, the team went into the locker room where Coach Elmer Lampe told George and his teammates that Jimmy Skipworth had been killed in action at Luzon.

George naturally took it hard. "It was tough," he remembers. "I looked up to Jimmy like everybody else. I was devastated."

After a week, however, he did what so many others did at that time. He volunteered himself, joining the Marines. He would have given his life for his country too, but was not called on for that ultimate sacrifice like his older brother.

"That's what we all did. We all volunteered. We expected that of ourselves. We felt it was our duty to serve our country," said George, as he recalled the life and times of his older brother. After the war, George became a dentist, playing two more years of football for Wallace Wade at Duke.

When the news of Skipworth's death reached his friend, Edwin Pope, who was, at the time, sports editor of the Athens Banner Herald, Pope wrote that Skipworth's death could be attributed to the fact that he was "just too brave."

Voted the "Most Popular Athlete" in 1940, the year he captained the football Bulldogs, "Skip" had been in the South Pacific for over three years, winning the silver star for "conspicuous gallantry." What made it so difficult for his family, particularly George, was that Skipworth was about to be sent home from The Philippines.

"When Coach Lampe told me and the team after the game, I was heartbroken because I had looked up to Jimmy all my life. He was an inspiration. He got along well with everybody. Personable, easy going and accommodating, he was somebody I greatly admired."

Pope, in a column for the Banner Herald, wrote of a letter which "Skip" sent to his younger brother, who was advised that two-a-day practices were nothing compared to combat. He further advised his younger brother that "you'll take it on the chin thousands of times in life, George...take it and take it with your chin up."

All of the Butts players who died in World War II were classmates of Dan Magill who wrote about them in his column in the Athens Banner Herald.

On Nov. 22, 1944, Master Sgt. Walter "Chief" Ruark, a native of Bostwick in Morgan county and All-SEC guard on Georgia's Rose Bowl team of 1942, was leading a five-man patrol of the U.S. 9th Division, which was advancing on a German sniper position in a stone house on the River Roer, when a rifle shot pierced his chest. He was awarded the Silver Star posthumously – the second highest honor America can bestow on a fighting man.

In October 1944 Army pilot Lt. Homer Passmore, of Valdosta and center-blocking back at Georgia in 1940, was shot down over France while piloting his B-17 several weeks after the Normandy landing.

At the same time, Army Bombardier Lt. Will Burt, of Macon, a star guard on Georgia's Orange Bowl champions of 1941, was shot down by German aircraft over Italy.

On Jan. 24, Army Captain Winfred Goodman, of Atlanta, a starting guard at Georgia in 1940 and 1941, was reported missing in action after leading his Fourth Emergency Air/Sea Rescue Squadron during the re-capture of the Philippines.

Four weeks later, Feb. 19, 1945, Marine 1st. Lt. Howard (Smiley) Johnson, of Clarkesville, Tenn., an alternate-captain at Georgia in 1939, was killed by exploding shell fragments in the landing on Iwo Jima. He was awarded a second Silver Star, having first earned one in the capture of Saipan in hand-to-hand combat with the Japanese.

In June 1945, on Okinawa in the last battle of World War II, Marine 2nd Lt. Winston Hodgson, of Athens, a running mate of "Smiley" Johnson at Georgia in 1939, was killed while leading his platoon up a mountainside against entrenched Japanese in a cave. He tossed a hand grenade into the cave, not knowing it held the largest ammunition supply of the Japanese. The explosion blew off the top of the mountain and Hodgson died from the concussion. His brave deed significantly hastened the end of the war. These young American heroes did not die in vain.

"LEST WE FORGET."

Across from the Smith Academic Center (the old field house of the Butts era), is a granite statue dedicated to those Bulldog athletes, including Wally's Boys, who lost their lives in World War II:
William G. Burt, Jr. Macon, GA Air Corps (1st LT.) 40-41, **Winfred S. Goodman** Atlanta, GA Air Corps (CAPT.) 39-41, **Winston D. Hodgson** Athens, GA Marine Corps (2nd LT.) 38, **Howard W. Johnson** Clarkesville, TN Marine Corps (1st LT.) 37-39, **Homer S. Passmore** Valdosta, GA Air Corps (1st LT.) 40, **Henry Walter Ruark** Bostwick, GA Army (MST. SGT) 40-42, **James Turner Skipworth, Jr.** Columbus, GA Army (CAPT.) 39-40, **Thomas Eaton Witt** Louisville, KY Air Corps (1st LT.) 39-40

"SMILEY" JOHNSON, BULLDOG AND WAR HERO BY DAN MAGILL

On Independence Day I never fail to remember a poor orphan boy from Clarkesville, Tennessee, who won a football scholarship to Georgia in the late 1930s and made an indelible impact on everyone he ever met, especially his fellow Marines during World War II.

His name was Howard (Smiley) Johnson, a 160-pound freshman fullback at Georgia in 1936 who later starred as a guard under three different Bulldog coaches: Harry Mehre, 1937; Joel Hunt, 1938; and Wallace Butts, 1939, for whom he served as alternate captain.

He was nicknamed Smiley because of his unfailingly pleasant manner, and he was sent to Athens by Georgia alumnus Harold Hirsch, jr., who owned the Coca-Cola Company in Clarkesville and whose father was the renowned chief legal counsel for all of Coca-Cola with headquarters in Atlanta.

In the summer of 1938, just prior to entering UGA as a freshman in the fall, it was my good fortune to be Smiley's assistant caretaker of Georgia's six old red clay tennis courts in front of LeConte Hall. He became one of my boyhood idols.

Smiley never weighed over 190 pounds as a Georgia guard, but he carried about 200 pounds when he played with the Green Bay Packers in 1940 and 1941 – still quite small for a pro lineman. But his great competitive spirit easily compensated for his relatively small size.

He joined the Marine Corps after his 1941 season at Green Bay and was at Pearl Harbor as an enlisted man when the Japanese struck on December 7 that year. A year later he was at the Marine Barracks, Quantico, Virginia, enrolled in the Marines' Officer Candidates' school, and that is when I was reunited with him and saw him for the last time.

Smiley was a most unusual Marine. In addition to being a teetotaler and non-smoker, he didn't cuss and he read the Bible every night. A good example of his Christian charity occurred one evening at Quantico when we went to an off-base café for a milk shake, and in walked an enlisted Marine whom I recognized as movie star Tyrone Power (I had read in the paper that he was coming to Quantico as an officer candidate). But Smiley did not recognize him. This café was the headquarters for taxis taking Marines on liberty to nearby Washington, D.C., and that's why Power was there: to reserve a cab to visit his wife, actress Anabella.

When the taxi manager informed Power that it would require a ten-dollar deposit to reserve a cab, Power said he didn't have his wallet on him. Smiley overheard and said to Power, a perfect stranger, "I'll loan you ten dollars, buddy."

Power snapped to attention when he saw the freshly commissioned 2nd Lt. Johnson, saluted him and accepted the ten-dollar bill. He obtained Smiley's barracks address and promised to repay him that very night, which he did.

"Smiley" Johnson was a Bulldog and a war hero

"I'm surprised you didn't recognize Tyrone Power," I said to Smiley. "He looks just like he does in the movies except his hair is cut shorter." But I should have known that Smiley probably never had seen Power in a movie. Having been a poor country boy all his life, he wasn't likely to throw away his hard-earned money on a movie.

As good a Marine as Smiley was, he had a hard time getting a commission because he was not strong in classroom work. And it must have been fate when he was "saved" by no less than the Commandant of the Marine Corps himself, who had come down from Washington to observe the Marine officer candidates in the field on a machine-gun exercise. He spotted PFC Johnson doing a superb job with his platoon, and commented to the commanding officer of the Quantico base:

"That young man will make a fine Marine officer."

"I'm afraid not, sir," said PFC Johnson's commanding officer. "He is not doing well in his classroom work and is going to flunk out."

"The hell he will," declared the Commandant. "When this class graduates, I will be here to pin the bars on him." And that's exactly what happened on March 10, 1943.

Fifteen months later "Smiley" Johnson won this country's second-highest military award – the Silver Star – for bravery under fire on Saipan. His citation read:

"...When the enemy counter-attacked the flank position held by his platoon, 1st Lt. Johnson daringly directed the defense, exposing himself to heavy fire and helping annihilate in hand-to-hand conflict the Japanese who penetrated the position..."

Eight months later "Smiley" was with the 4th Marine Division (under the command of his old commanding officer at Quantico, Major General Clifton B. Cates) when it landed on Iwo Jima on D-Day, February 19, 1945. Late that afternoon when his unit was preparing defenses for the night – he personally supervising the defenses of his platoon – he was killed by exploding shell fragments when he returned to his platoon command post. His last words spoken to a Navy corpsman seeking to tend to his wounds, were, as he pointed to four other dying Marines: "Take care of my men first."

He received a Gold Star on Iwo Jima in lieu of a second Silver Star, and he was one of nearly 6,000 Marines who died in capturing that Japanese island, which the Japanese considered impregnable and which the United States deemed necessary to take to hasten the end of the war. The Japanese fighter planes on Iwo had thwarted U.S. B-29 bombers in their efforts to bomb the Japanese mainland. After the Marines took Iwo (less than 200 of the Japanese bastion of 20,000 survived the battle), U.S. Army B-29s bombed Japan to smithereens, eventually dropped the atomic bomb, and the Japanese surrendered.

Admiral Chester Nimitz, commander of the U.S. Naval forces in the Pacific, said all the Marines deserved the Congressional Medal of Honor on Iwo Jima, "where uncommon valor was a common virtue."

The Marines did not forget "Smiley" Johnson. There are half a dozen athletic fields at Marine bases scattered throughout the Pacific that are named for the former Georgia Bulldog.

1941

At last Georgia would go bowling. The Point-a-Minute Bullpups were juniors and playing better and better. Only Alabama could whip this team, winning 27-14 in Birmingham. The Bulldogs came back to tie Ole Miss 14-14 between the hedges. Frank Sinkwich broke his jaw in the South Carolina game but kept on playing. Racehorse Davis caught a touchdown pass from Sinkwich with no time on the clock to whip Auburn in Columbus, and the Dogs finally got that coveted bowl invitation, resulting from a 8-1-1 campaign.

The Orange Bowl, anxious to attract winter tourists and sell tickets, were not disappointed as the Bulldogs put on one of the greatest offensive shows in bowl history, defeating TCU 40-26.

From that point on, the town of Athens not only became used to bowl invitations, but also each season began in September with expectations that Wally's Boys would be hearing from bowl scouts when Thanksgiving approached.

Bowl Opportunity At Last

This is pure speculation, but, perhaps Coach Butts developed his "Weepin' Wally" image during the 1940 season.

The "Point-a-Minute-Bullpups" were expected by many to be the "Sizzling Sophs," maybe taking the Bulldogs to the heights that the community had longed for. It didn't happen. The Dogs lost too many close games.

Coming close didn't placate the driven Bulldog coach. Beating Georgia Tech, as Georgia did in Butts' second season, was important, but not only did the fans in Athens expect more from the team, Butts, himself, expected a better record. Butts couldn't "wait til next year" which actually got underway in January.

Spring practice was long and demanding. But that was the modus operandi for those times.

For example, after Tennessee upset Oklahoma 17-0 in the Orange Bowl New Year's Day 1939, Gen. Robert Neyland, the last of major college coaches to stick with the single wing, told his players to enjoy their victory but to "be ready for spring practice Jan. 15."

The General was fond of saying, "A man can live without love but not without work."

That was the view of most coaches in that era, Wallace Butts included. You had to drive your team on the practice field in search of excellence. You could count on your opponents doing just that. You better keep in step, a step ahead if possible.

With Butts there was, perhaps, a more important reason for long and frequent practices. His game was the forward pass, and the margin for error was greater than it was establishing an effective rushing attack with the single wing.

Butts was to learn in later years, it didn't matter how pretty your offense was; you had to produce victory and often to satisfy doting supporters.

Georgia still had not been to a bowl, and expectations prior to his third season were premature. The "Point-a-Minute Bullpups" needed another year of seasoning, which they got in 1940.

All that talent, nonetheless, did not allow the coach to render speculation that would foster high hopes. Butts cried loudly, and often, about personnel deficiencies and missed blocks in practices. "There's too much titty pulling out here," he was wont to say. Too much arm tackling troubled him on defense. There was plenty for Wally to weep about.

However, he began to develop a serious confidence in his team and let on to his coaches, but never publicly, that his 1941 Bulldogs should mature into something special.

Ecstasy enveloped the little town of Athens when the news came that Georgia had been invited to Miami for the 1942 Orange Bowl.

Bowls were fewer in number back then. The Rose Bowl was the lone post season opportunity for many years. The Orange Bowl, which offered vacation sunshine in winter, became established next, and the Sugar Bowl became established about the same time, but that was just about it. The Cotton Bowl originated soon thereafter, but had gained little regional attention.

The Rose Bowl, which had displayed an affection for Southern teams throughout the twenties and thirties, was about to focus its attention on the Midwest although it would invite Georgia to Pasadena in 1942, and later invited Tennessee (1945) and Alabama (1946) to the West Coast.

The Georgia delegation, already at a fever pitch with its 21-0 shutout of Georgia Tech in the final game of the season of 1941, hung out at the old Biltmore Hotel on West Peachtree Street on its trips to Atlanta.

The Butts family always had a corner suite, and after the games it was open house. In addition to the coaching staff which gathered with him and his wife, Winnie, many Georgia supporters and friends dropped by. During his down years, his closest friends came to accept the fact that many who had backslapped him at his own bar in the good times became fair weather critics when the team was not the toast of the state.

Butts came into the midst of the post game party after the Tech game in 1941 about 9:00 p.m. and said softly, "We've just been invited to the Orange Bowl."

Sinkwich in action with mask to protect broken jaw

The reaction almost lifted the roof.

One alumnus who had encountered Butts in the lobby and learned the good news had already sounded off to dozens of anxious supporters. In a matter of minutes the hotel was buzzing with euphoria. Calls went out to Athens and across the state instantly.

Headlines in the Atlanta papers the next day proclaimed: "Georgia Rips Tech; Gets Orange Bowl Bid."

Returning to Athens a couple of days later, the Georgia staff began making preparation for Texas Christian University, a team that used a triple wingback set, something that worried the Butts' staff who had never witnessed live this offensive variation.

It was against the rules in those days to swap film before a bowl game, but someone on the Georgia staff, probably J.V. Sikes, who had Southwest Conference contacts, came up with a couple of TCU game films.

The coaching staff watched the Horned Frogs triple wingback formation in guarded secrecy behind closed doors at night when all visitors and press reporters had retired from the scene.

A week of practice in Florida was intense, and by game time, Georgia was a primed offensive force, which was to peak during the first half. It was devastating. It was obvious Butts had an explosive team, and the excitement of the trip to Miami, all worked to the Bulldogs advantage.

Georgia scored 19 points in the first quarter, 14 in the second and romped home an easy winner, 40-26. The offense gained more yards in the first half than they normally gained in an entire game.

The second half was a time to relax as Butts sent in substitutes and allowed his players to enjoy themselves. TCU then scored a couple of touchdowns and was trying desperately to catch up in the hot sun. Butts became concerned and started sending his front line players back into action. One of the first he screamed for was tackle Harry Kuniansky, who had wandered down the sideline. When "Koon" heard Butts yell, he dashed onto the field with a couple of oranges still in his helmet.

For Butts it was an afternoon he would never forget. He would coach for 19 more seasons and when his career was over, he would look back and remember the first half against TCU as being the finest half of offensive football he had ever seen. Not just the best of any of his Georgia teams, but the best of any team he saw in his life.

It was the closest he ever saw a team come to offensive perfection.

The celebration of Georgia's first bowl win was clouded by the early days of World War II. Eight days after Georgia learned of its invitation to the Orange Bowl, the Japanese attacked Pearl Harbor.

When the team returned home after the game, many of the coaches and players accepted the call to military duty.

There were enough deferments and special assignments, however, for Butts to keep his team pretty much intact the following year, enabling him to develop another outstanding team in Sinkwich's senior season. The Rose Bowl invited Georgia to Pasadena where the Bulldogs beat UCLA, 9-0.

After that game, the war was in full swing in the Pacific and in Europe, and what appeared to be a developing collegiate dynasty for Butts was interrupted. It would never be the same for him.

HEYWARD ALLEN, GEORGIA'S FIRST BOWL CAPTAIN

On weekends and when school let out in the afternoon, the kids in the Southside section of Birmingham, in the mid thirties, could expect a skinny buddy to come calling for pickup football games.

Even in the spring and summer when baseball was in season, young Heyward Allen could be found organizing neighborhood football competition. Mostly two hand touch, but if anybody wanted to play tackle, that was okay with Allen.

He liked baseball, too, and that sport got its share of attention, but every chance he found to organize football competition, he aggressively leaped into action.

Those formative years were to figure prominently in his future. He was to become one of the most widely acclaimed high school athletes in the South at Ramsey High, and his training in the backyards of Birmingham enhanced his athletic development.

Not only did he learn to throw a football with speed and accuracy, he was the kid who was forever coaxing his friends to muster on the playground...three to 11 man squads, even two against two. When he couldn't get up a game, he'd find somebody to play pitch and catch.

Ideal experience for a single wing tailback, which is what he was as a prepster and collegian.

One problem, however. He really wasn't big enough

for the position, although he and printed programs would always proclaim that he weighed fifteen to twenty pounds more. By the time he enrolled in college, he only stood 5-10 and weighed hardly more than 150 pounds.

As a tailback on offense, he was the man who ran the show and faced the threat of bigger men when he ran the ball and set up to pass. As a sideback on defense, he protected against the pass and came up to meet the challenge of hard charging ball carriers who naturally sought out smaller defensive backs whenever possible. If you expect to run over a man in football, you want them to be of the Heyward Allen dimensions, 1939-41. Heyward, however, not only could dish it out, he could take it.

He was a courageous competitor who hustled every play. On top of that, he was a natural leader, captaining Georgia's first bowl team.

"Heyward had a lot of fight and courage. He was an excellent passer," says Bill Hartman. "He wasn't very big, but he could throw the ball hard, and, while he wasn't real fast, he had above average quickness and was a tremendous competitor. Everybody always liked Heyward. He meant a lot to our teams."

His first two years as a Bulldog weren't anything like the great success with which he had been familiar in high school. After his freshman year, 1938, Wallace Butts took over, and in 1939, the Bulldogs finished 5-6.

Coach Butts was first introduced to Allen when the Ramsey team came to Louisville, KY, to play one of Butts' good Male High teams. In that game, Allen completed 18 of 21 passes, and greatly impressed the pass oriented Butts.

In 1940, Allen alternated at tailback with the great Frank Sinkwich, and the Bulldogs finished 5-4-1, but the Georgia program was beginning to reach new heights. The next year, when he was captain, Allen, Sinkwich and the Bulldogs compiled an 8-1-1 record and brought Georgia's its first bowl bid. When Allen died in the spring of 2004, Dan Magill wrote of Heyward's extraordinary athletic talent.

"Butts' love of practicing football the year-around may have kept Heyward from having a major league baseball career.

"He had been a hard-hitting third baseman in high school and had turned down pro offers to play college football. In the spring of 1939 Heyward asked Butts if

Heyward Allen (left) and Cliff Kimsey with Coach Butts

he could join the baseball squad. Butts replied, 'Absolutely not. You can't miss our spring football practice.'

Heyward was the starting tailback in the single-wing formation as a sophomore in 1939.

"As a sophomore he led Georgia to its biggest win of the season (6-2 over Florida). He set up the only TD on a long pass to end Alex McCaskill.

"As a junior in 1940, he shared the tailback job with Frankie Sinkwich, and he threw two touchdown passes to beat South Carolina. Later that season he hooked up on a sensational 65-yard scoring toss to Lamar Davis against Columbia in New York City, and then completed another long pass to Tommy Malone

Captain Heyward Allen strikes a familiar pose

to nip Auburn 14-13."

When he returned from the Orange Bowl, Allen faced Army induction for World War II. He chose the Navy Air Corps over the infantry and was involved with 11 invasions in the Pacific on the aircraft carrier USS Kalinin Bay.

One of the battles he experienced was a surprise dawn attack in the Philippines when the Japanese Navy and Air Force sank seven ships around Kalinin Bay resulting in the loss of 96 men in the battle.

"If it hadn't been for Coach Butts and football, I'd never have made it. You have to have something to pull you through in times like that, and football training was what made the difference with me," Allen said.

After the war, he considered coaching and almost joined Bear Bryant at Kentucky. He chose, instead, the challenge of running an automobile dealership in Gainesville, FL. He was a successful automobile dealer for over six decades in Athens, and his son, Buddy, still owns Heyward Allen Motors.

Heyward Allen was always successful, and it all began with those pickup games in Birmingham in which he not only starred, but was the one initiating the competition.

MO PHELPS – PLAYER, COACH, TEACHER, ADMINISTRATOR

When Morris O. Phelps was offered a football scholarship to Georgia, he anticipated an interesting experience. His anticipation became real, beginning with a mountain excursion through Kentucky and Tennessee with Spec Towns, who could have qualified as a hell driver in his day.

When Towns delivered the Louisville, Ky., native to Coach Butts in January of 1939, spring practice was underway and before Phelps had a chance to see the campus, he was issued a football uniform.

"In those days it was legal to practice the year 'round. I didn't know any better, for if I had, I'd probably have waited until the fall to report. Since I had missed a semester in high school and graduated in January rather than June, I was free to enroll in college," Phelps grinned with raised eyebrows.

The Butts toughness was nothing new for Phelps, who captained the Male High team in Louisville which Butts had left to join the staff at Georgia. That is how the Bulldog coach knew about Phelps and why he invited the Kentucky native to play for the Bulldogs.

Since that time, Phelps has remained in Georgia, except for military duty. He became the director of admissions for the University, a position he held until retirement in 1984.

He left Athens for the Army in 1942, spending three years in the Pacific theatre. Following the war in 1946 he took a teaching and coaching job at Murphy High in Atlanta. He was a football and basketball assistant for Joel Eaves, who was to become Georgia's athletic director.

When Eaves left to take a position with Auburn, Phelps took over the head basketball job at Murphy, producing winning teams each of the three years he coached.

Phelps took leave to begin work on a doctoral degree at Georgia, having received his Master of Education during the summers at Emory University.

After a post graduate year in the Classic City, he continued teaching and coaching at Murphy until he completed doctorate requirements in the summer of 1956. He then went to Stone Mountain as high school principal for three years and returned to Athens for good in 1959 to work in the UGA admissions office. He became director of admissions in 1968.

His appreciation for athletics increased through the years, and he has noted often that anyone who can survive the rigors of sports competition finds the normal trials and tribulations of life routine.

"Without athletics, I never would have gone to college. I have a strong appreciation for athletics, naturally, but also feel I earned everything I got. There are many easier ways to get a college education. Anyone who criticizes the grant-in-aid system doesn't know what he is talking about. An athlete earns everything he gets."

At Georgia, as an undergraduate, he did not restrict himself to football even though spring practice was nearly a January to June requirement. "At nights after football practice in the afternoon, I practiced basketball because I enjoyed basketball very much," he remembered.

A starting guard in basketball, Phelps played behind two great all-Americans in football, George Poschner and Van Davis.

As a freshman, he captained the Point-a-Minute Bullpups, coached by Howell Hollis.

He gave up his final year of eligibility since his draft board was beckoning. Also he was about to marry a University beauty queen, Gregg Yarborough.

Mo Phelps is a classic example of an athlete broadening his horizons and distinguishing himself in other fields. He wanted to be more than a football player, but never lost his affection for a game which nurtured his education.

Leo Costa – First Kicking Specialist Can Now Look Up

Anyone who has ever participated in athletics has surely, at one point or another, experienced some coach's or teacher's admonishment to "keep your eye on the ball," or "keep your head down," but few learned this lesson better than Leo Costa, Georgia's first placekicking specialist.

His coach was J.B. Whitworth, whose cardinal rule was never to follow the flight of the ball after kicking it. Never, ever look up. Not after counting one thousand and one, one thousand and two, one thousand and three – which Coach Whit taught Costa to do.

Like everybody else, Leo tried to please Whitworth – there really was no alternative – who was tough, demanding, cunning, conning and eternally insistent upon obedience to the spoken laws of coaching of that day.

Leo made an effort to please or conform, especially

Leo Costa, first place kicking specialist

if Coach Whit was looking, but like the rest, he'd deviate if he thought there were a chance of not getting caught.

Usually one mistake was enough, and, for Leo, it cost him sixteen pounds and four hours of mental anguish. Whit's punishment, however, made it possible for Leo to forever keep his eye on the ball.

Here's the way Leo remembered it.

"Coach Whit taught me to kick the ball and then reach down and pick up an imaginary silver dollar, which was a blade of grass.

"We had place kicking drills before practice, and he would always be standing nearby observing me kick. One day he was at the other end of the field and I thought that he was busy doing something else and I sneaked a look. As the ball was sailing over the crossbar, I heard him shout, 'Okay, Costa, on the track.' It was about 2:30 and he made me run until 6:30 that afternoon. When regular practice was over, Coach Butts always called the squad together for a few minutes, and when I heard the whistle I was about dead, and couldn't wait to quit. But, just as I came jogging up to the huddle, Whitworth shouted me back and made me run some more. It was the worst day of my life. I lost sixteen pounds, but it sure taught me never to look up again."

Consider the reward of this discipline for the place-kicker. In three years of football when Georgia was going to big bowls twice, Leo's kicks were the margin of victory numerous times, and while thousands of fans and his teammates watched and cheered his performance, he never got to see the results.

"Coach Whit did promise me that if we were ahead in the last game of the season in my senior year, he would let me watch one kick," Leo recalled. "We beat Tech 34-0 and I took a good look on the fifth extra point attempt. I was so excited for this privilege, but the ball went right over the top of one goal post. I thought it was good, but the official ruled otherwise. When I finally got to look, it didn't count."

Born Leonard Jr. to the Athens' Costa family who ran a restaurant in the Southern Mutual building, a favorite hangout for local businessmen and the Georgia coaches, Leo got his start kicking an old bladder football in his backyard.

"I'd dropkick that ball over a backyard fence and started doing it ever since I could remember. I played center for Athens High and made all Mid-South at Baylor Prep, but had no idea I'd ever become a place-kicking specialist."

At Athens High, Howell Hollis used him as a kicker, and he credited this former Bulldog coach (later business manager) with the opportunity to earn a position on some of Georgia's most successful teams.

"Coach Hollis suggested that Coach Butts give me a chance to do the place kicking, and I'll never forget the day Coach Butts asked me to kick for him."

In this brief audition Leo didn't miss, although his holder, Lamar Bryant, was having a bad day. "Lamar hadn't had any practice at holding for me, and he was called in cold and seemed to put the ball down every possible way. This turned out good for me because Coach Butts later commented that if the holder was having that bad of a day and I still kicked it through, then I had the job of place-kicker," Leo remembered.

If any player's role is overlooked as much as the center in a placement combination, it is the holder. Usually holders are backs or receivers, delegated to this duty because of good hands for catching the snapped ball.

Leo's holder was the well-known wingback, Lamar "Racehorse" Davis, and like most successful kickers, Leo always expected his holder to be properly recognized. "All the credit goes to Lamar," he explained. "He had the best hands I ever saw, and he never bungled a snap. I'd mark the spot in the grass with my finger, and that is exactly where he'd put the ball. He'd do it every time, and I can't recall a time when he missed doing his job. I certainly owe Lamar the credit for my kicking success."

While his name does not appear in the record book for one game or season placement records, Leo has one distinction that will keep his name on the honor roll forever. He scored in every game he played, which also happened to be every game Georgia played for the four years he was a Bulldog.

As a sophomore, he got the game-tying point against Kentucky, 7-7, and his kicking provided the margin of victory vs. Auburn, 14-13 and 21-19 vs. Tech. Ole Miss led Georgia 14-0 in his junior season, but the Bulldogs came back to tie the game, and Leo was true in the clutch each time his team had to make its points after to avoid defeat.

As a senior in 1942, Georgia had to come from behind to whip Kentucky 7-6, and Leo was on target with the extra point. Had he missed that one, there wouldn't have been any Rose Bowl trip. After that, Auburn upset the Bulldogs, but in all other games the powerful offense smashed all opponents so convincingly that Costa's extra points were truly "extra."

GREEN KELTNER – WHAT CAN YOU SAY ABOUT AN OLD TACKLE?

Of all the Butts' fraternity of former players I have gotten to know, one of the most enjoyable was Green Keltner.

I didn't meet Green, a starting tackle on the '41 Orange Bowl team until late in his life, and I am not quite sure how the introduction came about. Perhaps through his good friend Heyward Allen.

One experience with Green Keltner made me believe that it would be difficult to hook a fish that fights harder than a 25 pound snook.

One day Green called me and explained that there was going to be a fishing tournament for charity in the Ft. Myers area, and he would like for me to join his team for the "Caloosa Catch and Release Tournament."

We won the tournament, catching the most snook. I told him that was like a caddie winning the Masters. I love a successful outdoor sporting experience, but have no expertise whatsoever. That's why it is good to hang out with those who do.

My fishing experiences with Green Keltner were so fulfilling. We always brought home a good "mess of fish" as they say.

For a few years, I always managed to fish with him, but one day sad news arrived. Really sad. Elaine, his lovely wife, called to say that Green had been diagnosed with Alzheimer's. I went limp as I learned the news.

I began to recall the good times, and it made me flashback to a fishing outing with him, one of those unforgettable experiences.

One December day several years ago when much of Florida was chilly and cold, Green Keltner was out among the mangroves, casting for snook near his high-rise home at Ft. Myers Beach.

It wasn't snook season, but that didn't matter to this one-time Bulldog tackle, who realized a fishing day lost in a man's life would never be regained.

He saw fishing as a cleansing experience, good for the body and soul, and looked on the sport with a philosophy similar to what Arnold Palmer once said about golf. "If you find it, you can hit it, if you hit it, it might go in the hole."

With Green it was a matter of giving yourself a chance. If you are out there casting, something might strike, and if something strikes, you might be pleasantly surprised.

That particular overcast day when I, as his fishing partner, was as inexperienced as Keltner was experienced, got a strike on a backlash. This awkward circumstance had Keltner laughing and me untangling line. Soon the freed up line sang out and the rod bent double, and eventually a 25-pound snook was aboard, the novice not one bit more pleased than Keltner himself, who always took as much delight in the fishing success of his friends as he did his own.

It proved what Keltner has always believed. If you are out there casting, something good might happen.

Part of the reason for the fishing excursion on this particular day was for Keltner to talk about his college football experience at the University of Georgia.

"There is not much to tell you," he began. "You know, I was a lineman. You can't say too much about an old tackle."

Green Keltner, "much" to say about this old tackle

It was obvious he had rather talk about snook fishing, inviting his friend to return later to Florida's west coast when the snook would be biting every day. "That is when life is really fun," Keltner laughed.

Although he grew up in Memphis, far from the good fishing of the Gulf, Keltner's story would be incomplete without a major emphasis on fishing, which occupied so much of his time during his life.

It was an illness that brought him to Florida permanently and opened the door to become a marina owner-operator, turning his business enterprise into financial returns that made his banker smile.

During World War II, a shrapnel injury led to his being stricken with spinal meningitis. It was impossible for him to withstand the cold winters of Memphis where he was in the cattle business with his father and brothers so he would take off for Florida when the temperature dropped.

He and his family would return to Memphis in the spring, but the routine caused problems with his children who had to be moved from one school system to another each year.

In 1960, he moved to Ft. Myers Beach to stay, buying his first marina (he later owned as many as three), taking businesses which were losing money and turning them into profit makers in short order.

Whenever Keltner's conversation about fishing was diverted to football, he wasted no time, enthusiastically speaking out for Coach Butts.

"Football," he said, "is the only way I could have gone to college, and Coach Butts gave me that opportunity. With my background, you appreciated things like a scholarship and you never stop appreciating it, which means I'll always appreciate Coach Butts. If you cared about an education, you could take all those long practices and hard work.

"When Coach Butts took over after the 1938 season, spring practice lasted until school was out in June. I realize now that was too much, and a lot of players didn't like it back then. But I think those who cared about the game and the educational opportunity and stuck it out benefited.

"I will always remember Coach Butts explaining to us why he didn't think he should be soft on his players in practice. 'I've thought about it,' he said, 'and I would be doing you a terrible injustice if you did things halfway. Then you would go through life doing things that way and you'd always have problems.'

"As time went by, I came to realize he was right. If you think about it today, many of the problems we have in society and in business has to do with the fact that people don't really care. They do things halfway instead of making the effort to do it right."

Keltner came to Georgia with his friends Dooley Matthews and Lou Young in 1938. He had offers to join Wallace Wade at Duke and Bear Bryant (then an assistant coach) at Alabama, but followed his friends to Athens.

Keltner was one of those linemen who were "made" in the Whitworth era, learning blocking techniques so well that he became one of the most effective tackles in the Southeastern Conference. Blocking for tailback Frank Sinkwich was a challenge which Keltner explains this way: "Frank was so quick his own lineman had a hard time getting out of his way. Since he didn't have top speed, a lineman might even catch him from behind, but his quickness made him a remarkable back." Keltner and Tom Greene of Macon were the tackles on Georgia's first Bowl team.

During the war, Keltner served as an officer in Europe, seeing action at the Battle of the Bulge, winning the Silver Star, which you often would spot in the lapel of his sports jacket.

He was proud of having served his country just as he was pleased to have been a member of Georgia's first bowl team. To properly express his feelings for his alma mater, he became a major donor to the Butts-Mehre Heritage Hall campaign.

"I'm proud that I was in a position to do something for a building that has Coach Butts' name on it," Green said. "He really helped me when I needed it and contributing to a campaign that involved a memorial to him makes me very happy. I'll always appreciate Coach Butts and the University of Georgia."

LAMAR RACEHORSE DAVIS

Lamar "Racehorse" Davis is a name out of the past – an ole timer he is – but his performances remain unforgettable. Unbreakable, too, perhaps.

Do you think any of us will ever see a touchdown bomb like the one involving him against Auburn in 1941? Not likely. Tailback Frank Sinkwich fades back and heaves the ball downfield. With the ball in the air, the gun sounds, letting one and all know that time has expired. Racehorse runs under the ball, catches it and goes into the end zone for the winning score. Perhaps the most dramatic finish in Georgia football history.

His record for average gain per catch (19 for 542 yards for 28.5 in 1942) is one that may well stand well forever. Even in this era of air-it-out popularity. To break his long standing mark, a receiver has to take a lot of balls to the house.

That's what Racehorse was – a big play producer, one of the best ever to wear the red and black. With

Sinkwich and Trippi in the backfield, he didn't touch the ball that much on offense. But when he did, look out. The end zone is where he most often wound up.

"Although Davis was often upstaged by the aforementioned characters in 1942, he caused as many ulcers to gnaw on the stomachs of opposing coaches as they did," John Stegeman remembered. "Defensive units were implored never to take their eyes off Davis, such lapses often resulting in a sudden six points for Georgia. Already he had tied Don Huton's record of catching eight touchdown passes in a single season, and he had returned kicks for 80-, 90- and 96-yard scores. No Bulldog before or since has ever come close to matching him in the matter of spectacular touchdowns."

Ole timers always recalled Racehorse's catch, with no time left on the clock Nov. 1, 1941, their favorite big play. If it were not the greatest catch and score in Bulldog history, it, for sure, is one of the greatest.

Lindsay Scott's reception from Buck Belue in the Gator Bowl in 1980 has been rated by some as the biggest play in Georgia history because it enabled the Bulldogs to play for and win a National Championship.

But the import of Racehorse's play must be given equal rank in that, as it turned out, it brought Georgia its first bowl invitation. That was something of monumental significance in the early forties.

It signaled that Georgia, under Wallace Butts, was developing into a national power and that his teams would be explosive on offense. Even in those conservative offensive days, a team that emphasized the pass sold tickets and was enormously popular at the gate. Nobody identified with the forward pass like Butts, and he had the horses to do the job, one of them appropriately named, "Racehorse."

Let's revisit that touchdown bomb in Columbus. It was a scoreless tie when the game wound down with Georgia taking possession after an Auburn punt, which Davis recalls, went out of bounds. The Bulldogs took over at the Auburn 40 and needed a score to win. However, you consider the odds in that situation, and even an inexpert observer would know that it was an improbable, if not impossible objective. Something like the hail Mary's of recent vintage, but none of those came when time had expired.

Butts diagrammed his plays to go all the way and firmly believed that if every player carried out his assignment, any play would produce a score.

Pass 2, ends in front got the desired results and brought the Bulldogs victory, 7-0.

Here's how Racehorse remembers it: "The play was designed to put pressure on the safetyman and make him make a decision on which receiver to cover which meant that somebody should be open.

The ends went down and out. As the wingback, I was to head straight downfield. Cliff Kimsey at blocking back was to drift through the line and sprint down the other side of the field.

"When I got downfield, I heard the gun sound. I looked up and saw the ball going to the other side of the field. I didn't see Cliff, so I figured he got held up at the line of scrimmage. Frank Sinkwich put it high and deep and I just ran over to the ball and caught it and went in to score.

"The official came up to me to get the ball. I was so excited. I wouldn't give it to him. Finally, he said, 'Son we've got to kick the extra point.' I've always wondered why. The game was over, there was no time left but I reluctantly gave him the ball for the extra point.

"Later somebody gave me the ball, and I still have it. It is deflated." He could have added, "just like the Auburn defense." – that had to be the way it was for Auburn after giving up such a shocking homerun ball.

It was the biggest play in Racehorse's career! Understandably so, but as a matter of fact, he authored so many big plays that he had a lot to choose from. All the others, including punt returns which went the distance, were memorable and important, but none had the influence in the outcome of the game like the one in Columbus his junior year.

His performance in the Ole Miss game that same year is one which he recalls with special affection. Down 14-0, the Dogs came back to tie the game and Racehorse scored both touchdowns, one on a reverse.

His reputation as a kick returner brought him a lot of attention from the defense. Even so, if he weren't cornered early and reached the sideline, he usually was long gone.

"We practiced punt returns every day," he remembers. "We were good at returning kicks. I got to where I felt like I could take a punt back every time the opposing team kicked. We weren't cocky, we were confident."

There was one incident involving a kick early in his career that he has never forgotten, albeit a negative memory. It came in the South Carolina game, his sophomore year. He fielded the ball behind his goal line and was trapped for a safety.

"We won the game easily (33-2), but I didn't like it that I scored for the other team. I never made that mistake again. Coach Butts didn't have to get on me for that mistake. It embarrassed me and bothered me.

"Nobody I can remember," Racehorse smiles, "ever outran me on the football field. Especially if I had the ball."

It was track coach, Spec Towns, who influenced Racehorse's decision to enroll at Georgia. Basketball was more Davis' sport early in his career.

Davis recently recalled the circumstances that brought him to Georgia. He played football and basketball at Brunswick's Glynn Academy, but had been offered no scholarships. He was invited to play in the state all-star basketball game in Atlanta but suggests that his selection was a mistake or an afterthought.

"Even though the participants were listed alphabetically," Davis says, "the 'D' in my case was near the bottom of the list. Undaunted, I went to Atlanta but when they got down to me, they had run out of basketball shoes and ended up by giving me a pair of football shoes."

Davis started to point out the mistake to his coach, but realizing a football game was also to be played later, decided to hold his breath. "I thought about those three meals a day with a two weeks stay in the plush Henry Grady Hotel," he says, "and kept my mouth shut."

So Davis reported to Georgia Tech's Bobby Dodd, one of the all-star football coaches. Dodd began separating the players into groups according to what they did best, sending the runners, passers, and punters to various sections of the field. Davis was directed to none of the areas and soon found himself alone. "What can you do?" the coach asked. Davis thought fast. "Block," he answered

Dream Backfield: (from left) Frank Sinkwich, Charley Trippi, Dick McPhee and Racehorse Davis

with uncertainly, and Dodd took him at his word.

Davis entered the game as blocking back, blocked nobody, but made a long touchdown run "out of sheer fright" after intercepting a pass. "Spec Towns was in the stands," says Davis, "and congratulated me after the game. He said he didn't know anyone could run so fast while galloping with arms and legs all going in the wrong directions. He offered me a scholarship if I would let him teach me how to run, and I accepted on the spot."

But back to his formative years. Davis' father was a bricklayer who had a drinking problem. His mother divorced him, remarried and moved to California. In the summer before his senior year of high school his mother had settled in Baton Rouge, La. She and his stepfather brought Racehorse to Louisiana and told him he would have to finish high school there.

His high school coach at Brunswick wrote a letter to them pleading for Racehorse to return to the Golden Isles for his final year and they relented.

Now you know the rest of the story.

After the war, Davis played professionally for the Baltimore Colts. Old timers from Davis' NFL era were greatly charmed by Davis' southern personality, his past catching ability and his propensity for making big plays, just like at Georgia.

Following his National Football League days, Racehorse returned home to St. Simons, worked for Sea Pak for years and managed his rental property, which he bought with his NFL money. He has enjoyed a relaxed and unhurried life and always returns to Athens for the reunion of Wally's Boys.

Seldom does a day pass that he doesn't think about the reminders Butts preached to his players each year. "What he told us back then was as sound as it could be. It is still good advice today, especially for athletes."

- **Look a person in the eye when you talk to him.**
- **Hold your head up, don't slouch. Don't let the other fellow think you are beaten.**
- **Get in shape, stay in shape, wear the opposition down.**
- **Your best effort should come in the fourth quarter, a winning effort because you are better in the final quarter.**
- **Smoking is not good for any athlete.**
- **Don't be a quitter.**
- **On game day, get your game face on. Think football, think team, think how you can contribute; be serious, no joking around until the game is over.**
- **Don't take a knee when you are tired; don't let the opposition know you need a breather.**
- **Be loyal to your team and your teammates.**

The last point is one Racehorse took to heart honorably and gratefully. "I don't believe anybody appreciated Coach Butts more than I," he says. "I didn't have a good family situation. I lived with relatives much of my life, and I knew what it meant to have that scholarship.

"Three meals a day was a big thing. There was no way I was going to give up that scholarship and opportunity. No way I was going to quit. I felt that I owed him total loyalty and commitment.

"Over the years I have heard how tough he was. I didn't see it that way. He might have gotten on me when I was loafing, but he never got on me unless I deserved it. I appreciated Coach Butts and will always be grateful to him.

"The practices were long and rough, but we certainly were not abused. I think those of us who played for them back then did all right. Nobody went hungry. Nobody was asked to do more than he could do. And when it was all over with, everybody Coach Butts could help, he did."

When most of those familiar with the forties think of the "Point-A-Minute" Bullpups of 1939, they remember that Sinkwich was star of that popular freshman team. "As good as everybody thought we were," Racehorse remembers, "we still never beat the varsity. They put us freshmen in our place."

Only two players from that group made the starting lineup as sophomores when Georgia opened with Oglethorpe in 1940 – Racehorse and Walter Ruark.

Playing wingback, which was not the glamour position, meant that Racehorse wouldn't get the ball all that often. "If you had been Coach Butts, wouldn't you have designed your offense for Sinkwich and Trippi?" he laughs.

You could say that a backfield, which included two of the greatest backs in Georgia history, provided limited opportunity for him at wingback.

"I never felt left out," Racehorse said. "I got a lot of balls because Coach Butts thought the wingback could contribute to the offense. If he hadn't had that innovative offensive mind, I might never have figured into the game plan. That wasn't the way it was, and I never have had any complaints. I did have a chance to rest up a little, so when I was called on, I was usually fresh."

PART III

FRANK SINKWICH

Heisman In The Making

Left: Number thiry nined goals. Wally gives his star player some tips on the.

SINKWICH

MEMORIES OF A RELUCTANT SUPERSTAR

A country boy from Middle Georgia enrolls at his state university and becomes affiliated with its athletic teams. The association allows him not only to become familiar with the facts and impressive statistics of the heroes of another time, but also to actually become personally acquainted with those heroes and legends.

What he came to appreciate most of all as time went by, with at least one of those greats, was an exceptional and rare example of humility.

It leaves you in an awed state as an undergraduate to be in the company of men like Frank Sinkwich and Charley Trippi. You didn't see them play, but you were impressed with the glowing praise of those who did. Then one day you ask officials of the Orange Bowl and Rose Bowl for copies of old film.

There, in a darkened room with a whining projector, you watch the man they called Fireball and Flatfoot put on a single-wing tailback show in Miami that remains one of the most talked about performances in college football. His record of 382 yards total offense still stands. Some Orange Bowl historians will tell you nobody has ever played a greater game in any bowl.

Overstatement? Perhaps but it would be difficult to find one to exceed that of Frank Sinkwich in Miami New Year's Day 1942. There are other statistics of his fabled career to leave you impressed. There are men like Bill Hartman, who always shook his head in amazement at what Sinkwich could do with the football. He's gone, but Sinkwich's reputation will endure.

Too often those with the untrained eye are given to affection for the spectacular. The long run. The pass we call the bomb. We recognize the home run as skillful hitting, never considering that the pitcher may have made a mistake.

To those who make their living by teaching the game's finer points and developing intricate game plans, there is appreciation for the basic talent of the truly great players. Not just their capability for the spectacular, but their ability to gain the clutch yard or hit with men on base. Frank Sinkwich could be counted on to get his team what was needed. Ten yards, five, four – even one. Didn't matter the number of yards required, Sinkwich came through.

Frank Sinkwich, an All-American, was not without his spectacular moments, but for every long run or pass completion for a touchdown, there were dozens of first downs, stemming from his fierce competitiveness, that kept the chains moving.

Having watched Sinkwich on film, I have some appreciation for his remarkable athletic talent. The respect grows when you hear men who truly knew the athlete's worth, pay him the ultimate compliment. He was, simply put, a team player first. An important measure of Sinkwich is that his teammates were never jealous of him. They knew he earned and deserved every headline. In many respects, they were his biggest cheerleaders.

But there was another side to this reluctant superstar. That is the side I was privileged to know. There has never been one quite like him.

In Georgia's down years, he bought tickets on a game-by-game basis, never having to deal with season tickets. With the turnaround success of the late '60's he was without a priority under a new administration and suddenly was cramped for tickets.

"The only thing we have at this point," I, as Georgia's business manager, told him, "is something down low."

"Fine with me," Sinkwich replied. "I like to sit low." He refused to lobby for better location because of his name and his exalted reputation as the Deep South's first winner of the Heisman trophy.

For years his Heisman Trophy sat in a corner of a

sparsely furnished apartment until he gave it to the University and caused the Downtown Athletic Club in New York to start a tradition of awarding two trophies each year – one to the player voted the best in the country and one to his school.

Sinkwich preferred there be no ceremony. He simply wanted to hand over his trophy to the university without recognition. He had to be coaxed onto the field for the presentation.

When he was asked to participate in formalities which brought those who had their jerseys previously retired, to join in the retiring of Herschel Walker's No. 34 pre-game of Alabama 1985, he asked if his presence were really necessary. His criteria was that if Georgia needed him for anything, he would participate. Otherwise he preferred to stay out of the foreground. He had no need to have his ego massaged.

He was not a man who lived in the past. He never recalled his runs, great or small. He was blessed with fierce athletic pride but he didn't require any stroking or attention for athletic feats of the halcyon days of his youth.

When he made the first major gift to the development of the Butts-Mehre building – prompted out of lasting respect for his old coach – he wanted no recognition. He contributed because he loved his coach. He loved his school and that was reward enough.

I'll remember Frank Sinkwich for what the record book, the box scores and the old game film reveal, but I'll remember most of all his humility, his willingness to give of himself to the University of Georgia without anything in return. Not even a letter of thanks.

He remained steadfast in the belief that it was he who owed the school.

I will always be reminded that Frank Sinkwich was, indeed, a reluctant superstar.

rman Harrison kept Sinkwich's Rose Bowl jersey and later gave it to Georgia in halftime ceremonies at a home game; from left: Harrison, Sinkwich and Coach Bill Hartman

Cliff Kimsey: Make My Block and...

Cliff Kimsey, who roomed with Frank Sinkwich, once offered this assessment of Sinkwich's offensive firepower.

"If I made my block," he said, "Frank would gain at least twenty yards. If I didn't make my block, he only gained seven or eight."

Cliff Kimsey, Bill Hartman's favorite

Truth of the matter, Kimsey's modesty notwithstanding, his blocking contributed mightily to Sinkwich's success, although it didn't take much to set No. 21 free.

Bill Hartman said that of all the players he coached over the years, Kimsey was his favorite.

"He was a hell of an all around back," Hartman appraised. "He played three positions at Georgia – tailback his sophomore year, spinner back his junior year and blocking back his senior year. He was a big contributor to the team wherever you played him. He played defensive halfback, he backed up the line. He was an outstanding pass receiver out of the backfield, and he was an especially good punter. I liked everything about him."

Immediately after graduation, Kimsey reported for active duty. He was handed his diploma, walked a few paces and was given his commission. A couple more steps and an Army sergeant placed orders in his hand for Ft. Benning.

He was a distinguished officer in the Pacific, returned home after the war and began coaching high school football. Coach J. V. Sikes, who had taken over as the head coach at Kansas, called, and Kimsey worked as an assistant to Sikes in Lawrence for five years.

It was an enlightening experience, but the wheat fields of the Sunflower State and the insecurity of coaching made him long for the hills of his native North Georgia.

With a degree in business, he was quite excited when a banking career opened up for him in his hometown of Cornelia. He returned home and just like always, outstanding at whatever he did, he distinguished himself in banking. He never lost his appreciation for what he learned on the football field at Georgia.

"There's no way to understand the type of disciplinarian that Coach Butts was, "Kimsey said. "Spring practice lasted from January until finals in June, most of those days in full uniform. A lot of players quit. I thought about it, but I couldn't have gone back to Cornelia and said, 'I quit.' The fact is, those football players who stayed for the duration under Coach Butts left with a lot of character. I know it especially helped me in the Army. That discipline did a world of good. I don't think there's any question that my experience at Georgia was a key to my success in business."

Broken Jaw Fails to Sideline Flatfoot Frankie

A broken jaw today, in all likelihood, would send a football player to the sideline for the season, even if the injury were suffered early in the schedule.

With Frank Sinkwich, he never missed a game. What's more, a week after the South Carolina game in 1941 when he was hurt, he played against Ole Miss with nothing more than a metal chin strap.

His jaw was wired shut by Dr. Jimmy Allen, brother of his teammate and understudy, Heyward Allen. The week following Ole Miss he played with a protective mask which you can find on display in the Butts Mehre museum on campus.

Sinkwich didn't think it that big of a deal even years later and gave this account of his broken jaw experience to Dan Magill, who recalled that the game

was one of the first played at night in Sanford Stadium.

South Carolina had upset North Carolina the week before, so Coach Butts wanted to make sure his team was ready. They were.

"Georgia was leading comfortably, 27-6, late in the game when Sinkwich broke loose for a long gain and was injured," Magill remembered.

Then Sinkwich described what happened.

"Although that last play forced me to leave the game," Sinkwich told Magill, "I had received a hard lick on my jaw—in the same place—in the first quarter.

"On the handoff to our fullback, I carried out a fake, and the South Carolina end, Nowak, gave me a forearm to the jaw".

"On my last play of the game, though, I faked a pass and ran a good way, almost scoring. Cramps hit my legs, and I buckled. I was run out of bounds, and someone piled on, hitting my jaw again with a knee. I think it was the same Nowak. South Carolina was penalized to the one-yard line, and we scored immediately.

"When I returned to the sidelines, Coach Butts asked what ailed me, and I replied that I had a loose tooth. He commented, 'Oh! That's nothing!'

"It turned out to be a broken jaw. I remember spending the night at the hospital, and the next day Spec Towns (football assistant and head track coach) drove me to Atlanta to see our team orthopedic surgeon, Dr. Joe Boland (captain of the 1929 Georgia team that beat Yale in the Sanford Stadium dedicatory game). Dr. Boland sent me back to Athens to see Dr. Jimmy Allen. Jimmy actually had seen me right after the game and told me then I had a broken lower jaw. Anyway, Jimmy wired my teeth together laterally.

"Now the big question was whether I could play the next week against Ole Miss. The Rebels had one of the best teams in the country, led by a great pair of halfbacks, Hapes and Hovious. They were coached by former Georgia coach, Harry Mehre, and they had beaten us 28-14 the previous year.

"Coach Butts wanted Tennessee's famous trainer Mickey O'Brien to examine me and he recommended a protective helmet. So, early in the week of the Ole Miss game, a well-known Athens pilot, Ben Gunn, flew me to Knoxville. O'Brien telephoned his opinions to Coach Butts, but I don't know what they were.

"When I returned to Athens, our trainer Fitz Lutz and Jimmy Allen designed a protective helmet. However, it would not be ready until the following week when we played Columbia in New York. So against Ole Miss my only protection was a chinstrap of thin metal. I think it was Basham's machine shop in Athens that made it.

"With my teeth wired together, I couldn't eat solid foods. When the fans learned that I was living off soup, I received gallons and gallons of homemade soup from dozens of fans. It was mostly chicken soup. It was much more than I could eat, and the whole team consumed a lot of soup at our dining room in Payne Hall. I also drank of lot of milk shakes. Interestingly, I didn't lose any weight the whole time. I had one missing tooth, in the back, and I sucked soup and milk shakes through a straw."

Heisman voters later took note of the fact that Sinkwich never missed a game. Competing with a broken jaw was a memorable distinction which was forever associated with the legend of Frank Sinkwich.

SINKWICH REMEMBERED RECORD SETTING DAY IN MIAMI

Frank Sinkwich set the Orange Bowl total offense record in 1942 with 382 yards, a record which still stands. He played wearing a mask to protect his broken jaw. Sinkwich, nicknamed Flatfoot because of his unusually flat feet, was a two-time All-America pick. The following are Sinkwich's recollections of Georgia's first bowl game, published by the Orange Bowl (Fifty Years on the Fifty by Loran Smith) on its fiftieth anniversary in 1983.

There's no doubt in my mind – the 1942 Orange Bowl game had a lot to do with my winning the Heisman Trophy in 1942 – the first player from a Southern school to do so.

I never had a better day and doubt very many teams had the offensive execution that Georgia did against Texas Christian University that afternoon. TCU was a good team, but we could have scored as much as we wanted. The only thing that stopped us was the heat.

After 499 yards in total offense, we were completely worn out. Nobody wanted the ball late in the game.

A lot of the detail has faded from my memory, but I'll never forget how sharp we were.

Our ability to move the ball really excited Coach Butts. But I don't bring up the game very often because I don't think people want to hear guys talk about what they once did. What happened to me is something I genuinely appreciate, but the spotlight belongs to others now.

For a kid who grew up in the Depression years, the son of Croatian parents who came to America from another country, what I did as a college football player was truly enriching, to say nothing of the opportunities that resulted from it.

I grew up in Youngstown, Ohio, at a tough time, but I like the idea of toughing it out. Do the best you can and make your own way. My father owned a tavern, and he worked long hours and was attracted to sports. He took me to a game when I was a boy. I liked football; it became natural to me. I learned early in neighborhood pickup games that I had the desire to compete. I'm sure much of that came from the times and my family instincts. When people ask why I succeeded in athletics, I always tell them that I didn't want to get beat.

College football excited me, and I wanted to play in the South. I didn't know anything about the area. I just felt the opportunities would be better. A lot of the Southern schools were recruiting up our way, and one day Coach Butts and his line coach, J.B. Whitworth, showed up at my house and invited me to sign with Georgia. A high school coach had recommended me. I didn't even know which one was the head coach. Butts was quiet and Whitworth did most of the talking, so I thought he was.

My mother didn't like the idea of my going to Georgia – I was her baby boy – but my father said it was OK. My first visit, in the summer, they put me in a house with a dirt floor, and hot as hell. I had never experienced such heat. They were giving me every opportunity to change my feelings about the South.

When practice began, I found out who Coach Butts was in a hurry. He was a little man, but he stood tall on the football field. I didn't know real tough times until his practices. Recruits disappeared without even going by the dorm to get their suitcases. They were afraid some coach would talk them into staying.

I quit a time or two myself, once after the 1942 Orange Bowl when I was told spring practice would begin in the middle of January. But I always went back, and I credit Butts for making a man of me.

The trip to Miami was exciting although many of us had been there when we played the University of Miami in 1940, when I was a sophomore. The Japanese bombed Pearl Harbor right after we got our invitation, and I'm sure a lot of us were thinking that playing football in a bowl was a lot better than being shot at in a foxhole.

In the locker room before a game, Coach Butts could have you so anxious to hit the field that you'd be crying. Before our game with TCU, he impressed on us how important it was to represent the University of Georgia with a fighting spirit in the school's first bowl game. Our performance bore out how seriously we took him. Everything we did went right. We clicked on almost every snap, one of those unbelievable days that you seldom see in a football game.

I played the game with a mask to protect my jaw which had been broken in the South Carolina game. I had played much of the season with my teeth wired shut, but fortunately, enough healing had taken place to where that was not the case in Miami. I couldn't have played in the heat with my teeth wired together.

Flatfoot Frankie gobbles up yardage

We scored the first time we got the ball, driving from our 36 in six plays. The big gain was a 26-yard pass I threw to wingback Lamar Davis, who was called "Racehorse" because of his great speed.

TCU recovered a fumble at our 19, and after pass interference gave the Horned Frogs a first down at the five, they scored, kicked the extra point and went ahead, 7-6. From that point on, however, it was our game.

On our next possession, we drove 85 yards in five plays. I passed to Melvin (Duck) Conger for 61 yards and a touchdown. Late in the first quarter, Cliff Kimsey got open over the middle, and I hit him for 60 yards and another touchdown. Costa kicked his first extra point, and we were up 19-7.

At this point, we began to really notice the heat. It was steaming hot, and in those days we played both ways. No relief. In the second quarter, I threw my third touchdown pass, a 15-yarder to Davis, and Coach Butts took most of the regulars out.

It didn't make much difference. Jim Todd, who played behind me, hit Davis on a 23-yard touchdown pass, and it was 33-7 at the half.

I had never seen a team perform so well, but I was never more tired in my life. We had the game won. I'd have been satisfied to watch the second half from the bench.

Coach Butts had other ideas. He told the regulars to be ready to go. We received the second half kickoff and scored in nine plays. On the touchdown, I dropped back to pass, and when the defense converged, I ducked and ran 43 yards. At that point, our coaches said our offense was so tired from running up and down the field, and their defense was so winded chasing us, that it looked like we were playing in slow motion. I wanted to be tackled, just to rest. I actually did not want to score.

After that Coach Butts began to clear the bench. To its credit, TCU never gave up, scoring three more touchdowns to cut the difference to 40-26.

Butts put the regulars back in a second time, and we drove down to the 7-yard line. In the huddle, I asked who wanted the ball. Almost in unison, everybody said, "Not me." I said, "Well, then we'll throw a pass," which made them all mad because they didn't want to do any running. TCU intercepted.

I gained 382 yards running and passing for the day. I was quite surprised to learn recently that it is still a record. I think all of my records at Georgia have been broken, and I was not aware that the Orange Bowl mark had lasted.

As a kid, I always dreamed of playing in the Rose Bowl, which I was fortunate to do my senior year, but the experience I appreciate most was the Orange Bowl. It was the best.

I don't often talk about the game, however. Even after all these years, I get tired just thinking about it.

RAUCH ON SINKWICH

Although John Rauch did not play with Frank Sinkwich, he met him early in his career at Georgia. Like Sinkwich, Rauch came to Athens as a single wing tailback.

Rauch knew of Sinkwich's legend and has the following recollections of the Fireball.

"His physique didn't look like that of Heisman backs but did give him a unique style. With hips wider than his shoulders and short legs, the Fireball looked squat. This build gave him a low center of gravity and enabled him to lean forward as he ran. He could accelerate, stop, and change directions with extreme quickness, thereby eluding tacklers.

"Above all he had great skills for a single wing tailback. He was very accurate at throwing a football. His punting was superb. I remember Frank suited out for a couple of scrimmages during the 1946 spring practice. He had injured a knee while playing for the Detroit Lions, and he wanted to test the injury.

"He was in full uniform and worked in drills with us. I thought I was pretty quick with my footwork but I had trouble making the hand-off to him. He had the quickest start from a three-point stance I had ever witnessed.

"After practice he put on a display of punting that was unbelievable. He could make a football do whatever he wanted. He kicked for distance (50-60 yards) then kicked to make the ball bounce right, left, or even bounce back toward him. I've seen some outstanding punters but never one that had such control of the ball.

"The injured knee cut short Sinkwich's pro career. He took the head coaching job at the University of Tampa in Florida and quickly made its program respectable.

"Many humorous stories are told around Tampa about Sinkwich, his teams and his players. Frank had fun coaching, and the players enjoyed playing for him. One story is particularly interesting.

"Frank would borrow a school bus the first week in August. He and a couple assistants would drive up to Pennsylvania and Ohio to pick up football recruits. They wouldn't return until they filled the bus. When they made infrequent stops to rest, they slept in the bus. Food was whatever was available at gas stations.

"Maybe the Fireball had visions of finding a Heisman Trophy winner or at least an All-American or two. Many of his 'bus' recruits graduated from Tampa and became successful afterwards."

A SINKWICH PROFILE BY JOHN STEGEMAN

Many stories have been published on Frank Sinkwich, the All-America tailback from Youngstown, Ohio. One of the best was done by John Stegeman, who wrote the following for a Georgia football program a few years before Sinkwich passed away.

Anyone looking for a "picture" athlete on the Georgia Campus in 1939 would have passed the young man by. His shoulders were sloping and he stuck out behind. Closer inspection revealed that he was pigeon-toed and flat-footed as well, an unlikely combination for a freshman backfield candidate.

Still, the 18-year-old youngster had arrived in Athens with something of a reputation. He was proficient in no sport but football, and, even here, he was not exceptional in most aspects of the game. He was a fair punter and fair tackler. He had never thrown a pass in competition. He had been the slowest man in his high school backfield. But once he tucked a football under his arm, everyone took notice. It was an exceedingly difficult challenge to bring him down.

This was Francis Frank Sinkwich, who in the next four years would carry Georgia to the zenith in inter-collegiate football, setting remarkable records that lasted over a quarter of a century.

In 1938, Wally Butts, Georgia's new football coach, received a tip in a letter from an old friend who had seen Sinkwich play in Youngstown. The friend couldn't even remember the player's name but advised Coach Butts to have a personal look. The following summer Sinkwich arrived in Athens where he was put to work doing odd jobs around the campus.

I asked Frank about his first thought when he got to Athens. "To go home," he replied instantly. "I was housed in a basement room on Jackson Street that had no floor – just dirt. I told my roommate that back in Youngstown we at least had wooden floors."

On a later occasion, after he was a star, Frank again had pangs of homesickness and packed up to leave. Coach Butts had no choice but to dismiss him from the squad, but the halfback applied for readmission. Butts put the matter to a vote among the other players and Sinkwich was reinstated unanimously. "Coach Butts knew how to take a smart punk like me and make a man of him." Frank said.

As a first-year player, Sinkwich led the "point-a-minute" freshmen to smashing victories against all opposition. But it was not until late the next year, against Georgia Tech and Miami that he began to run wild. The United Press chose the hard-running sophomore on its All-Southeastern team.

Frank's favorite play was old "Spin 87" in which he received the snap from center (single wing formation), faked to the fullback, and then tore into the center of the line. With the opposing right guard being trapped, while the linebackers were cross-blocked, Sinkwich was in the secondary "like a shot out of a cannon." He gained hundreds of yards on this play alone. "He was undoubtedly the best back that ever played football not to have any more speed than he did," said Coach Butts. "He capitalized on a fast start and a fighting, squirming type of running that made it almost impossible to bring him down from in front."

Coaches realized, however, that defenses would eventually be set for Frank to stop his inside slants, and so he became a passer. Suffice it to say that he threw 325 passes in his college career, completing almost half of them, 30 for touchdowns. Another 30 touchdowns on the ground brought his three-year total to 60.

The Bulldogs lost only one game in 1941, and, for the first time in Georgia history, talk of going to a bowl began to fill the air. Auburn almost put a stop to that. In the annual game in Columbus there was no score on the board with three seconds to play, the ball in Georgia's possession on its own side of the field. "I went back to pass," Sinkwich recalled in the late seventies, "and as I stood there with the ball in my hands I realized that time had expired. I knew that Lamar Davis was running somewhere down the middle so I just threw the ball as far and as high as I could. Davis caught it and ran for the winning touchdown." Old-timers never forgot that one.

Frank's greatest thrill came in the Alabama game of 1942, his senior year. Both teams were undefeated and untied as they met on Atlanta's Grant Field in late season. (Neutral site brought about by gas rationing in war years.) Georgia and Sinkwich were stopped dead as Alabama carried a 10-0 lead into the final quarter.

"We had dedicated the game to Tommy Witt, our former center, who had been killed the first weeks of World War II," said Frank. "When we went into a huddle at the beginning of the fourth period, someone said sarcastically that Tommy must be very proud of us now. I don't remember who made the remark but it was like

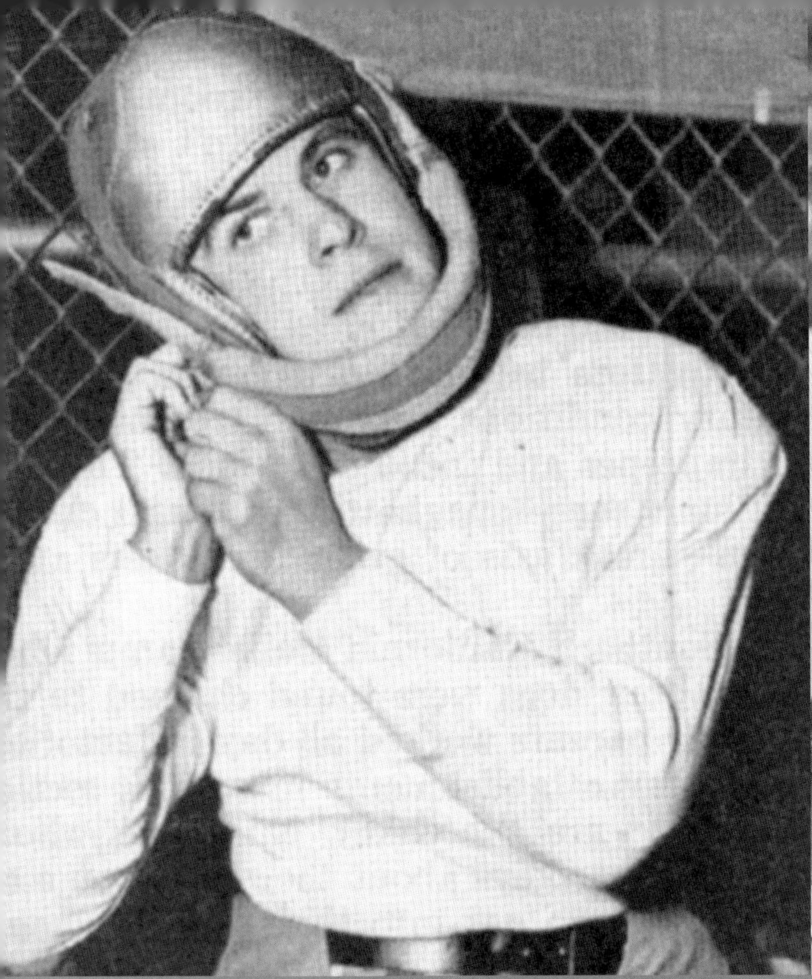

Frank Sinkwich, Year of the Heisman (left) and as a prosperous businessman in his late years

a message from God. The effect was electrical – everyone felt it. We could have beaten any team in the world after that."

Frank himself completed 11 of 13 passes in that great rally. "I'll swear some of those passes were poorly thrown," he says, "but those boys were turning somersaults to catch them. I never saw anything like it."

The winning score came on Frank's throw to his old Youngstown buddy, George Poschner. The Georgia end was hit by two Alabama defenders, one high and one low, just as the ball got to him in the end zone. He turned a flip but made the catch "standing" on his head and one shoulder.

When Georgia beat Tech, winner of all nine of its previous games, in the finale, the Bulldogs were Southeastern conference champions for the first time, and accepted a bid to play UCLA in the Rose Bowl. During practice before this game, Sinkwich sprained an ankle, and later sprained the other one. He walked into the Rose Bowl on crutches.

The game was scoreless going into the final quarter. With sophomore Charley Trippi leading the way, Georgia drove to the one-yard line, but two plays failed to gain. "Sinkwich!" called Coach Butts on the sideline. "Get in there." "What do I do?" asked Frank. "Score!" said the coach. Sinkwich hobbled into the line, his ankles buckling, but he got the nose of the football into the end zone. That was the ball game, and the final play of a great Georgia career.

Statisticians tell us that Sinkwich accounted for more than 2,200 yards in his final season, an unbelievable record for that day. Only one conference player had ever come close to such a figure before, and that was Frank himself during the previous year. He won every honor available to a football player and was recipient of the Heisman Award, presented to the outstanding player in the United States. His name has been immortalized in the National Football Hall of Fame. And his jersey, with its famous "21," has been retired; no other Georgia player will ever wear that number.

After leaving Georgia, Frank became the Most Valuable Player in the National Professional League as a member of the Detroit Lions.

Rose Bowl
ROSE BOWL
ROSE BOWL

PART IV

EARLY FORTIES

Rosebowl, Hollywood, Off To War

1942

The senior class, led by Sinkwich, Racehorse Davis, George Poschner, Van Davis and a cast of quality performers, gained in offensive firepower, with sophomore Charley Trippi becoming eligible for varsity competition.

By the end of the season, following a recommendation by Assistant Bill Hartman, Coach Butts found a way to put both Sinkwich and Trippi into his single wing backfield at the same time.

Only Auburn, when the Bulldogs became mentally flat from its lofty, undefeated ranking, could defeat these Bulldogs. In a remarkable upset in Columbus, the Tigers temporarily derailed Georgia's anticipated invitation to the Rose Bowl.

Alas, Pasadena officials sent word that they would invite the winner of the finale with Georgia Tech. Burning and smarting from the upset at the hands of Auburn, Coach Butts had his Bulldogs, primed and poised for the Yellow Jackets, smashing the cross state rival 34-0 in Athens.

The most coveted bowl invitation of all had Athens buzzing like never before. Eager fans went west by every means possible, more than a few got there by thumb. Georgia defeated UCLA 9-0, but the giddy mood turned foul as the nation went off to war.

It appeared that Wallace Butts was headed toward establishing one of college football's greatest dynasties, but World War II interrupted. Georgia would field teams in 1943-44 primarily made up of players too young for the draft or classified as 4Fs.

Suddenly, all across America, winning a war against the Nazis and the Japanese was more important than winning college football games.

Many football players distinguished themselves in combat. Some returned to campus glory. A number of them, however, paid the ultimate price.

Rosebowl, Hollywood, Off To War

In 1942, war was raging on two fronts, and it was going badly for the United States following the Japanese attack on Pearl Harbor.

In Europe, Hitler was pounding London with his superior air force, the Luftwaffe, but the English stood fast. That nation's collective stiff upper lip withstood the Nazi assault as Hitler began a series of blunders that would eventually cost him the war.

At the time, however, there was little reason for any optimism.

In the Pacific Manila, Bataan, and Corregidor fell. The Marines faced overwhelming opposition at Guadalcanal.

Spirits were lifted some what when Lieutenant Colonel Jimmy Doolittle led a daring raid on Tokyo and the forces of Supreme Allied Commander, Dwight D. Eisenhower, invaded North Africa. Still the enemy had the advantage.

Back home, men and women were volunteering. Gasoline, tires, sugar, coffee, even shoes were in short supply. Rationing stamps were needed to purchase those items.

A tragic fire at the Cocoanut Grove nightlcub in Boston killed 492 people, the big screen hit was "Mrs. Miniver" and the hit songs included "Don't Sit Under the Apple Tree," "Remember Pearl Harbor," "He Wears a Pair of Silver Wings," "I don't Want to Walk Without You," and "Praise the Lord and Pass the Ammunition." The top song, however, was Irving Berlin's "White Christmas."

In Athens, Ga., while Hitler was calling off "Sea Lion," the campaign against Great Britain, and turning his eyes toward Russia, making the same mistake that befell Napoleon, there was worry aplenty about the

Movie star, Ginger Rogers, signs autographs for Georgia players at Rose Bowl

world war, but there was also endearing affection developing for the Bulldog football team.

Coach Butts was perfecting his single wing attack, and his offense was devastating. The Bulldogs were led by Frank Sinkwich, the tailback with a reputation for possessing uncommon quickness, who could explode off traps not only for first downs, but long runs for TDs.

A young sophomore, Charley Trippi, backed Sinkwich up, but Hartman suggested to Butts that they needed to find a way to get both of these remarkable backs in the backfield at the same time.

They first used this alignment with Sinkwich at fullback and Trippi at tailback in the 1942 Tech game. It was Sinkwich inside and Trippi outside. The defense often had no clue what was going to happen.

This team brought Georgia's long awaited championship, the first of four for Butts. The Bulldogs were consensus national champions. Only twice did they score less than 14 points, seven in the opener with Kentucky in Louisville, a hard fought game that Butts' team won 7-6 and 13 against Auburn in Columbus. The upset, 27-13, by the War Eagles was the only loss of the season, a downer for the steam rolling Bulldogs.

Georgia scored more than 40 points in four games and walloped Florida in Jacksonville, 75-0.

After the Auburn game, there was such deflation in Athens, that a good season could only be consummated by defeating Georgia Tech in the final game in Sanford Stadium.

The Jackets came to Athens with a lot riding on the outcome. The word was out. The winner would be invited to play in the Rose Bowl in Pasadena.

Suffering from the sting of being upset by Auburn, Butts had the Bulldogs primed perfectly. Sinkwich,

Trippi and the Dogs blew Tech away, 34-0.

California, here we come!

The team took the train to the West Coast, but many eager fans and friends, like Hartman, who was already on active duty, drove to California. There was limited space on trains, with priority for troops, so many fans pooled enough rationing stamps to drive to Los Angeles.

Hollywood stars and studios made a big fuss over the game, and the Bulldogs mingled and cavorted with stars like Bob Hope, Rita Hayworth, Mickey Rooney, Robert Young, Susan Haywood and Ava Gardner.

Coach Butts underscored heavy workouts as his philosophy dictated, and UCLA was defeated, 9-0, a memorable moment in Georgia football history.

The bad news was that everybody would soon be off to war. The victorious players returned home and reported to their local draft boards.

In 1943 and 1944, Butts fielded winning teams, but America was concentrating on war production and troop training. The Battle of Midway in which the U. S. sank four Japanese aircraft carriers, a turning point in the war, took place in June, 1942, but the U.S. Navy and Marines still faced a formidable challenge. Everybody considered it his patriotic duty to volunteer.

Troops and materiel moved across the Atlantic and Pacific, despite the hazard of German U-boats as Eisenhower and Winston Churchill, Prime Minister of Great Britain, and their staffs were deep into planning for Overlord, the code name of the forthcoming landings at Normandy which was the beginning of the end for the Nazi's.

It also ended what might have been the greatest era in Georgia football.

Through The Screen Door With Kuniansky

A great number of football discussions went on behind a certain screen door in Athens in 1942 – until Harry P. Kuniansky smashed it from its Memorial Hall hinges as he fled from an enraged Wallace Butts, to whom "Koon" had just announced that he wasn't receiving enough publicity.

Anyone who has heard the story previously probably enjoys hearing it again, and those who haven't shouldn't be denied, for it is a classic.

One day "Koon", as he was affectionately known by his friends and former teammates, offered the opinion that his own mother wouldn't recognize he was a Georgia player the way the Bulldogs were publicized – if it weren't for the fact that he was listed in the starting lineup.

"Several players agreed with me and kept suggesting that I complain to Coach Butts." Though scared to death of Butts, (he later admitted that it was ten years after college before he had the courage to smoke in front of his former coach), "Koon" ventured behind the screen door one day and nervously blurted out to his football boss these unpardonable words, "Coach Butts, I'm not gettin' enough publicity."

The colorful Harry Kuniansky

"What?" screamed the Little Round Man.

"He leaped up over his desk and charged me," Kuniansky said of the infamous incident. I started running. Papers flew in every direction, and when I got to the screen door I ran straight through it. I didn't stop until I got back to my room. He never asked me to pay for the door and he never brought up the subject, and I sure as hell didn't bring it up either."

George Poschner, Cheerleader, All-American And War Hero

In the year that this book was published, George Poschner died at 85 in his hometown of Youngstown, Ohio. World War II robbed him of his best years, physically, but it never broke his spirit.

In conversations with friends, he always referred to his teammates who made the ultimate sacrifice, but George was willing to lay his life on the line. And did.

George Poscher, LOOK All American and war hero

It left him with partial paralysis and he had to get about with the help of canes after his legs were amputated.

Those familiar with the circumstances and the extent of his injuries consider it a miracle that Poschner, All American end for the Bulldogs, survived to live a long life.

Poschner, who was inducted into the Georgia Hall of Fame in 1982, went from the carefree life of an All-American college player – the summit – to the nadir of being left for dead on a World War II battlefield.

What happened to him at the time of the Battle of the Bulge would understandably leave most of us bitter. Left for dead after a bullet went through his head, he lay unconscious in sub-freezing temperatures for three days. Frostbite claimed all the fingers on his right hand, and gangrene caused the amputation of both legs just below the knees. The bullet brought paralysis to his left side.

There have been other complications and depressions in his life, and his misfortune could weigh heavily on his mind for George Poschner was once a picture of physical excellence, an All-American football player who had counted on a pro football experience and not the foxholes of Europe. He easily could have bitter if you consider what might have been.

He learned to live with his handicap, as much mental as physical. After getting over the shock of what happened to him, Poschner refused to allow acrimony to cloud his life.

It was 1939 and the country was coming out of the Great Depression. Wallace Butts visited Youngstown, Ohio and signed Frank Sinkwich to play for the Bulldogs. Sinkwich insisted that his lifelong friend be brought along. Butts and the Georgia coaches were not that impressed with the skinny, gangly Poschner who barely weighed 150 pounds and had been out of high school for a year, working in a meat and produce market.

Poschner turned out to be important to Georgia in more ways than one. He became an All-American end (Look Magazine) and kept his buddy Sinkwich from leaving school.

"Frank knew he could get a scholarship at Ohio State at the drop of a hat but I knew that nobody else would take a chance on me. I wasn't about to give up my scholarship," Poschner said.

"Life had been too hard for me, and I was getting three meals a day. It was very seldom that my mother was able to give us more than two meals back home, and I knew if I could get an education there was a chance things would be better for me."

He almost left, however, when his brother John wrote him and told him that creditors were harassing his mother who couldn't pay her bills and that George needed to come home, go to work, and contribute to the family budget.

George will never forget what happened after that letter arrived.

"I was so depressed. I went to see Coach Butts

and told him that I had to go home. My family needed me and I couldn't let my mother down. He asked how much my mother owed and I told him fifty dollars. He took out a checkbook from his desk drawer, wrote out a check for $50.00 and said, 'Here, George, send this to your mother so you can stay here and get your education.' You don't know what that meant to me and my family."

Graduated after the Rose Bowl in March of 1943, Poschner was inducted into the infantry at Ft. Hayes, Columbus, Ohio. He went to OCS at Ft. Benning and was in the same company with Bob Waterfield against whom he had played in Pasadena a few months earlier.

After training in England, he joined the Allied invasion entering the European continent at Normandy. The Allies were advancing rapidly toward Berlin when Hitler struck back with an offensive effort, the Battle of the Bulge in Belgium. The cakewalk turned into a brutal and bloody conflict and the offensive was felt farther away in places like Althorn, France, the location of Poschner's unit.

When it was over, Poschner was one of those who had paid dearly for Allied victory. He came out of the war with a Bronze Star, the Purple Heart and the Distinguished Service Cross, but was a physical wreck.

When he spoke of the sacrifice he made, he minimized his role. "My teammates like James Skipworth and Smiley Johnson made the real sacrifice. They gave their lives for their country. I gave less than they gave."

His patriotism was substantial, his faith ran deep. He never thought twice about the war for he believed in this country's objectives even though there are links to Germany in his heritage. It is even possible that he had distant cousins on that ridge he tried to take in France.

When Hitler began to march through Europe a letter came to his mother suggesting that since he and his brother, John, were born in the Austro-Hungarian Empire, he should go home and fight with the Nazis.

Rose scoffed at the thought and replied that her boy would fight only for America. She had come to this country in search of a better life. It wasn't the way she thought it would be, but she was never confused about her citizenship. There was no wavering or hidden doubt.

George Poschner's patriotism was obvious when he accepted his plaque of enshrinement into the State of Georgia Hall of Fame. He walked to the podium under his own power and said that he was very proud to be an American.

"I'M GONNA PLAY IN THE ROSE BOWL"

When Bob Poss died, I really hurt. We had been friends for years. We partied together, we traveled together and we laughed at endless stories and scenes from the Super Bowl to all the bowl games in which Georgia played.

Possey, a reserve guard on the Rose Bowl team of '42 , was famous for saying that ten years after graduation he made all-conference. Twenty years later he was All-American. "It won't be long," he would quip, "that I'll get the Heisman trophy."

Poss had a sterling career in the food business, principally with barbecue and hash. He manufactured it, he sold it, and he was good at grilling and cooking. For years, one of the highlights of the pre-season was the election of the football captains at his restaurant on the Atlanta Highway.

He loved to laugh, enjoy good food, and party with his friends. He was fond of saying, "if you eat my product, you think about me all night."

"Bobby-Q" was one of his nicknames. He contributed to every cause in Athens, every sports team at Athens High and Georgia. He sold his barbecue at Sanford Stadium for years. He loved Georgia and its people. And when he left this earth, it removed a big heart, the biggest, from the community. But up there in barbecue heaven, he has to be smiling that his son-in-law Mike Williams carried on the barbecue tradition at Pinecrest Lodge.

Possey was proud of his association with Coach Butts and always reached an exalted high when he reminisced about the Rose Bowl!

A colorful raconteur, longtime concessionaire, and letterman on the Rose Bowl squad, Poss was never at a loss for words.

He often bragged that the '42 Georgia team could beat anybody. "I was third string, and I was good," Poss once said.

Many years ago, Poss also pointed out that the reason he did not get kicked off the team that year was that he was smart enough to play poker only when Frank Sinkwich pulled up a chair.

With time running out in the Rose Bowl, line coach J.B. Whitworth, who was always needling Poss ("This week for the Auburn game in Columbus, we are going to take 33 players and Poss."), yelled for the stubby, slew-footed Poss to take the field.

"The referee was looking at his watch and had his pistol stuck in the air," Poss recalled. "I ran by him and yelled, 'Don't fire that damn gun till I get on the field. I'm gonna play in the Rose Bowl.'"

Van Davis – Versatile, Overpowering and Unyielding

With some athletes, recognition seems to come easy – even when it is less than deserved. Likewise there are those unheralded athletes whose peers give them the highest of marks, but their ability and performance fall in the category of "underrated."

Van Davis was one of those players, but that changed somewhat when Davis was elected to the State of Georgia Hall of Fame, 1994. Van didn't play for headlines, but his Hall of Fame selection confirmed what his teammates and coach knew. He was a hell of an athlete.

"I doubt that there has ever been a more underrated football player at the University of Georgia," says Bill Hartman.

"Van was an outstanding blocker, receiver and was just as outstanding on defense," Hartman noted. "As a receiver, he had good hands and could run well with the football. He was a solid overall player.

"He could block the defensive tackle for us as well as anybody who has ever played in the single-wing formation. He also could come down the line and block the offside linebacker.

"Then on defense, nobody was going to run his end. He was tenacious, hard-nosed and tough. He was hard to block, and he was likely to make the play if you ran to his side of the field."

Davis was a big man in his day at 6-2 and 218 pounds. He played his greatest game on November 28, 1942, as Georgia defeated unbeaten Georgia Tech 34-0 with a trip to the Rose Bowl awaiting the winner. It was Davis who scored three touchdowns – a 17-yard pass from Trippi for the first score, a five-yard end around for the second and a 37-yard touchdown pass from Trippi for the third to put the Bulldogs up 27-0. Davis led the team in receptions and minutes played during the season.

In the January 1, 1943 Rose Bowl game; Davis continued his remarkable dominance by catching eight passes.

A California sports writer wrote: "Van Davis stymied virtually every attempt by the Bruins to circle his end." Coach W.A. Alexander, Georgia Tech coach picked Davis as the all time best end at the University or Georgia and Jesse Outlar wrote "for consistency, Davis was the all-time best-ever pass receiver for Georgia."

Davis was one of the all-time greats in Georgia baseball history, too. Playing first base and hitting clean up he collected many base hits and runs driven in on one of Georgia's hardest-hitting teams in 1941, a team that posted a 17-6 record.

Van Davis, Dog's underrated end

Davis became a coach and later a high school principal, concluding his career in Douglas, Ga. where he died in 1987.

Chief Ruark, Breed Apart

Jim Minter, Georgia journalism graduate who rose to the lofty position of editor of the Atlanta Journal and Constitution is a devoted aficionado of World War II history. In the following profile on Walter "Chief" Ruark, Minter poignantly addresses the attitude and courage of men who returned home from the glamour of the Rose Bowl and willingly laid their life on the line on the battlefield

Chief Ruark, so named as a result of Native American ancestry, was one of the best linemen to play before the war, and Dan Magill says Chief Ruark was probably the best guard ever to play for Coach Butts.

There are conclusions to be drawn from a study of young men who wore the mantle of stardom and then too soon were required to meet death on whatever terms offered.

They died before their time, but the honors they won and the deeds they performed are cherished forever. They were of a breed apart, possessed of a great

Coach Butts with Sinkwich (left) and Chief Ruark

courage, which reflected on both the playing fields and in sterner battles of life and death. Most certainly, they were also men of a great faith.

There was Smiley Johnson, an orphan who lived by the Bible and died a hero's death on Iwo Jima; Joe Jordan, who knew no compromise on a basketball floor or on a sickbed.

They had something extra, and it showed when they lived and when they died. They stand as a testimonial to athletics, to youth, to courage, and to their faith.

Walter Ruark belongs among them, for his was a life which fits firmly in the pattern.

He came from Bostwick, GA and he first played football at Morgan County High, as a halfback. Then he went to old Monroe A&M to quickly establish himself as one of the finest athletes in the state.

From the time he arrived at the University of Georgia until he graduated with the Bulldogs' 1942 Rose Bowl team, he was a pillar in the strong forward wall which sprung Frank Sinkwich and Charley Trippi to fame and the Bulldogs to national acclaim.

He was all-Southeastern Conference in his senior year, and alternate captain of the Sinkwich-led Rose Bowl team. But Ruark was a guard, and when a Sinkwich is running and throwing, you don't read much about a 198-pound fellow in the middle of a line.

As those who played beside him would have expected, Walter Ruark died a hero's death. After the Rose Bowl, The Chief joined the army, and as the luck of a guard would have it, wound up in the infantry.

He was soon working at his old job, invited by Fort Benning brass to play with their football team in the fall of 1943. But when the Allied forces hit Normandy, they needed infantrymen more than Benning needed football players.

D-Day the 6th of June found him on the way. He had little infantry training when he joined the Ninth Division in Belgium but Americans and Germans alike soon discovered he needed none.

The Chief already had one Purple Heart and the stripes of a master sergeant on November 22, 1944. His company commander, fresh out of stateside officer candidate school, made no bones about it: The Chief was the man he called on when the chips were down.

November 22, 1944, was generally a good day for Allied forces hammering through Europe. The Germans were digging in on their own soil, and GIs had just gotten their Thanksgiving Turkey.

With the Ninth, it was different. The Germans were entrenched in the homeland along the Roer River, and defending Aachen with ferocity.

The night of the 21st. Sgt. Ruark led a five-man patrol into high ground held by the Germans. He soon saw an attack the next day would be suicide, but the order was to attack anyway.

Sgt. Ruark was in the lead when the battle began, and when his men bogged down in knee-deep mud he led them on, yard-by-yard, tree by tree.

Soon the shattered platoon was cut off and pinned down by German sniper fire. One by one, Sgt. Ruark saw his men die, even as he tried desperately to drag them to cover.

When he could stand it no longer, he took a rifle

and started into the open in search of the sniper. His commanding officer ordered him back, but The Chief stalked on toward his unseen foe.

The German lay hidden in a stone house near the bank of the Roer, and The Chief, fully exposed and hampered by an arm almost immobile from an old football injury, never had a chance.

A single rifle shot pierced his chest.

He was awarded the Silver Star, second highest honor America can bestow on a fighting man. From the battlefields of Europe, and from many post offices in the states, comrades wrote of the way he lived, fought and died. A family he met in Belgium visits his grave until this day.

There is, perhaps, a lesson to be learned and a goal to be set from the short lives of these stars who died before their time.

They were no more than mortal men. They were brave and scared alike. They were not necessarily men of great physical strength, and they did not necessarily seek the glories they won.

They merely accepted whatever came their way, and made the most of the moment.

Terrible Terry

In the beginning the Georgia coaches really didn't hold Joe Tereshinski Sr. in high esteem as an athlete. Just too small to play college football, they estimated. In the end, they came to realize the problem with their evaluation was they could not see his oversized heart.

However, they were put in a position to where they really couldn't refuse aid to the Glen Lyon, Pa. native – all because of an alumnus who had previously sent them capable players.

Harold "War Eagle" Ketron, a Coca Cola bottling franchisee in Wilkes Barre, Pa., had arranged for Charley Trippi, among others, to sign with Georgia. As a favor to Ketron, Bill Hartman and J. B. Whitworth, who were on a recruiting trip to Pennsylvania, simply couldn't refuse to sign the 165 pound Tereshinski.

This the way Hartman remembers the story. "I believe Howell Hollis was on the trip with Whit and me. Mr. Ketron took us to meet another player who was highly regarded, George Tepo, a big lineman. We thought he was an excellent prospect, and he later signed with us. When Mr. Ketron drove us to where Joe lived, he said with exaggeration: 'This boy is about 185 pounds, not very big, but he is a fighter.'

"He kept emphasizing the word fighter. He blew his horn, and Joe, who was very passionate about the idea of playing college football, came out of the house with a vest, a sweater and a big coat. Even so we could tell he didn't have much size.

"Mr. Ketron called him over to the car, Joe stuck his head inside to meet us, and Ketron said again with exaggerated emphasis. 'This boy is a real fighter.' With that we had no alternative but to take Joe. We said, 'Come on down to Athens, and we'll give you a scholarship.'"

Recruiting has never been an exact science. The can't miss prospects often times do, in fact, miss. Certain players, not highly recruited, surprise everybody and turn out to be outstanding and productive. A serendipitous story? Joe was one of them. "It didn't take us long to realize that Mr. Ketron was right, Joe was a real fighter," Hartman concludes.

"In all my years of coaching, I don't think I ever knew a player who appreciated a football scholarship more than Joe. He worked exceptionally hard to prove he was worth it."

Not only did Joe repay his alma mater with heartfelt emotions through the years, he sent his two sons to play for Vince Dooley. Additionally he scouted football talent in the Washington D. C. area and recommended a number of players to the Bulldogs.

Throughout his life Tereshinski has remained one of the most loyal and supportive former players ever. He was always quick to express his love and appreciation to Coach Butts. He has forever been grateful for that scholarship.

Even before his sons signed to play at Georgia, he was always finding reasons to return to Athens, which, you could say, has become the land of the Tereshinskis.

"The name originally was Taraczinski, and I don't know what it means except that 'tara' means land," says Joe Sr. After Joe played for Georgia, next came Joe Jr., who has been known forever around the Coliseum and Butts-Mehre as Joe T. Then followed Joe's brother, Wally, and in 2002, Joe Tereshinski III, joined the Bulldogs to play quarterback.

The youngest Bulldog Tereshinski would play anywhere for that matter and has. He'll line up at any position that helps the team. Always the team comes first. That tradition began with his grandfather.

The first thing you learn about the Tereshinskis' is they are intensely loyal. Loyal to their heritage, to their families, to their friends and especially to the University of Georgia. The eldest Tereshinski set the pattern, and it passed on to his sons and grandson.

Joe's father came over to this country at age 12 from a small town in Poland – Juzefu which is near Lublin. He took passage on the boat with friends and wound up in Charleston. From there he wandered on to Mobile and New Orleans but eventually settled in Pennsylvania.

The immigrant's son took to football eagerly growing up, and impressed the cagey Ketron the first time the sage old Bulldog saw him play. "Joe didn't have much speed," says Hartman. "He had unlimited desire, however. He was lanky and skinny but we were all impressed with his heart and desire."

An interesting development took place on the practice field one day that reveals something about the Tereshinski heart and pride. His name was not easy to pronounce. One day Coach Butts made mentioned of that and suggested that his name be changed to Terry.

Joe's pride was stung seriously and he remarked, "Coach Butts, if you let me keep my name, I'll make you proud of it." He did, indeed, and later played seven years with the Washington Redskins for whom he coached nine years.

John Rauch, too, remembers Joe Tereshinski with deep admiration.

"Joe also was a member of the Rose Bowl team of 1942 before entering military service, returning early in the 1945 season. He immediately made an impact on the Bulldogs with his constant hustle and dedication. For his actions on the field he was called 'Terrible Terry' by his teammates.

"Off the field he was a good student, a kind and considerate man who often volunteered his time to campus and charitable organizations. Terry was the prototype player and person who Wallace Butts sought for his teams.

"When Coach Butts designed a play, it was diagrammed to go all the way if everybody carried out his assignment.

"If the play (29-H) went to the right, the left end was to block the last man in the defense, the safety man. This was no easy assignment but Coach Butts demanded it be carried out, and Terry, more often than not, obliged him. When the varsity would scrimmage the junior varsity safety men would often claim they were injured – if Terry were in the lineup.

"If they weren't injured, they would be hurt after a couple hits from Terrible Terry. In one scrimmage a fast but small member of the B-team volunteered to man the injury riddled safety position. This little fellow gave Terry a problem because his quickness and speed made it difficult for Joe to put a hit on him.

"Terry was soon in a rage chasing this little fellow all over the field. When the ball was snapped and Terry came toward him the smallish safety would turn and run for his own goal line thinking he would escape Terry's punishment. Not so, Terry would have chased him into the stands if necessary because blocking the safety was what Coach Butts assigned him to do."

MORE WALLY LORE

Ken Keuper came to Georgia from Wisconsin. He had good size 6-1, 200 and lettered 1940-42. "He ended up playing blocking back. He started out as a fullback and was a factor in our spin series, which our opponents had difficulty stopping. He was red headed and was a fiery competitor," says Bill Hartman. "Elmer Lampe was from that area of the country, and he was the one who recruited Ken to Georgia. Ken was a good solid back who was a tough, solid performer, especially on defense."

Clyde Ehrhardt was an outstanding linebacker at Georgia, lettering in 1941-42. "He was extremely good at backing up the line," Bill Hartman says. "He and Bill Godwin were a great pair. Godwin probably was better against the run, and Ehrhardt was especially good on pass defense. With Sinkwich and Trippi in the backfield, we were quite explosive on offense, but, like all championship teams, we were very good at other phases, particularly defense. One of the reasons we were so capable on defense was having linebackers like Godwin and Ehrhardt.

Hartman is right. In 1941-42, the defense allowed only 135 total points in the regular season, for an average of 6.7 points allowed per game. The Bulldogs shut out 10 opponents during these two years.

Gene Ellenson was a native of Chippewa Falls, Wis., a river resort and brewing community, but later became an all-state tackle at Miami (FL.) High. He came to Georgia in 1939, a member of the "Point-a-Minute-Bullpups." And subsequently a regular at tackle on the Orange and Rose Bowl teams.

Interestingly, he is one of the few football players to earn a degree in Journalism, but where he, perhaps, distinguished himself the most was in action at the Battle of the Bulge where he was decorated with the Silver Star, Bronze Star and Purple Heart. He also received the Russian Medal for Valor.

After Coach Butts retired as coach, Gene was a finalist for the job, but when Johnny Griffith was named to succeed Butts, Ellenson spent the rest of his career at the University of Florida as a coach and administrator. He developed something of an Erk Russell style personality with the Gator players. He was beloved and revered.

Richard Lee was three years younger than his brother, Ryals, and had similar athletic potential. Only 16 years of age and playing on the varsity team as a freshman, Richard was outstanding. He intercepted a pass in the season opener in 1945 and returned the ball 35 yards – two more plays and he ran the ball in for a touchdown. As veterans returned from service Richard saw less and less playing time. Richard had misfortunes similar to that of Ryals – he also played the same position as Charley Trippi. After several injuries he was advised to give up playing football. Richard graduated from Georgia and had a successful career in the banking business.

William J. "Sleepy" MacKenna arrived in Athens to play for the Bulldogs in 1942 following an impressive career at halfback for Darlington Prep School. As a defensive back, he was a member of the '43 team which played L.S.U. in Baton Rouge and was called for pass interference on a pass by the Tigers' immortal Steve Van Buren. Sleepy didn't agree with the call and with the passing of years lost none of his antipathy for what he considered ill judgment on the part of the official.

His football career was interrupted by World War II, but poor eyesight also contributed to his having to eventually give up football, but he considers his vision a damn sight better than that of the official in Baton Rouge when Georgia lost a close game 34-27.

Following the '43 season, MacKenna volunteered for the American Field Service and was a member of an ambulance team which was overwhelmed with trying to remove wounded and dying soldiers to a field hospital during the battle at Anzio where Allied casualties were severe.

"There was brutal fighting," he recalls. "I was happy to survive, but I had a lot of classmates at Georgia who didn't. What I will always appreciate is that everybody volunteered. They thought it was their patriotic duty. Because of my eyesight, I could have stayed home, but I felt that since everybody seemed to be willing to volunteer and go off to war that I could volunteer for some area of the service."

When the war was over, he returned to football and became a manager. He also ran the mile and two mile in track, earning letters in both sports. "During my track days, Dean William Tate often came to track practice. He was especially fond of track since it was his sport, but he was an inspiration to me because he loved the University so much. All of my family attended Georgia, and I am proud of being a Bulldog."

MacKenna was very successful in his business career and has always been a generous contributor to Georgia athletics.

The rules for college football changed in the forties, due to the war. Freshmen were eligible, starting with the 1943 season, until the fifties which meant that while most players played both ways, specialists were efficiently utilized – like with place kicker

George Jernigan. Jernigan lettered four years, beginning in 1943, rules allowing him to go into the game only to kick extra points. Field goals were pretty much unheard of in that era. **Leo Costa**, for example, Georgia's first kicking specialist, could only go into a game once a quarter.

Billy Rutland (lettered 1943-44) captained the last war year's team. "He was an excellent halfback, very efficient on the dive play," Bill Hartman says.

Furman Bisher, sports editor of the Atlanta Journal, once visited Rutland at Cypress Gardens and wrote:
"As halfbacks go, Rutland wasn't even big for those hard-pressed times. He couldn't have weighed over 165 pounds, but he is remember as the kid you describe as 'tough as a pine knot.' If his body got hurt, his head had never seemed to get the message."

After Georgia, Rutland, while coaching high school football in Sarasota, Fl., organized a circus for the school. It became a major attraction in a city where many popular circuses wintered. He moved on to Cypress Gardens where he produced and promoted water skis when that community was renowned for water skiing championships.

1943-44

With the team breaking up after the Rose Bowl, Wallace Butts set about changing his offense to the "T" Formation. He stuck with the single wing through the '43 season but by '44 he was experimenting with the "T."

Bill Hartman doesn't recall with whom Butts consulted and does not remember him having any contact with Clark Shaunessey of the Chicago Bears, who is credited with originating the "T." Practically all colleges went to the "T" in the post war years. Tennessee's Gen. Robert Neyland never gave up on the single wing, but he was about the only one.

Hartman wasn't discharged from the service until April, 1946, but it didn't take him long to understand why the "T" formation intrigued and captivated Coach Butts.

"He loved offensive excitement, and the 'T' offered such great flexibility. It is a perfectly aligned formation. All three backs behind the quarterback could hit every hole on the offensive line. It was the beginning of the spreading of the field which appealed greatly to him."

Butts' biggest challenge during the war years was getting up a schedule. The Bulldogs, in 1943, lined up against Presbyterian (twice), Howard, Tennessee Tech and Daniel Field, which had enough service players to win 18-7. Bernie Moore, his coach at Mercer, had taken over at LSU and played Georgia twice, winning 34-27 in Baton Rouge and 27-6 in Columbus.

In 1944, the Allies gained a foothold on the European continent with the D-Day landings at Normandy. Things eventually would be looking up with the war but the Bulldogs were playing football with 4F's and teenagers too young for the draft. Nevertheless they won seven games. The losses were to Wake Forest (14-7 in Athens), LSU (15-7 in Atlanta) and Tech, 44-0 in Athens.

Some normalcy would return to college football in 1945, but draft boards remained active. Even with the war ending, college age young men were still being drafted.

Ken McCall, starting quarterback in 1944 for example, was drafted for two years after the 1945 season and returned to finish his eligibility in 1948.

Considering the circumstances, Wallace Butts rendered an outstanding coaching job to win as many games as he did in the war years with his motley, rag tag teams.

Sam Bailey Paid The Price Before He Met Wally

Sam Bailey, who started the financial ball rolling to underwrite the production of this book, also had the idea to found and put in place the annual reunion of Wally's Boys. Nobody admires Sanibel Sam more than John Rauch whose profile follows.

To play football for Coach Butts a player must be ready to sacrifice.

In Sam Bailey he found a young man who knew everything there was to know about sacrifice. Sam's parents and grandparents were early settlers of Sanibel Island, now referred to as Sanibel. The first bridge was constructed from the mainland [Fort Myers, Fl.], during the 50's.

The Island was remote and pristine, and after the bridge brought rapid growth the island is still to some degree pristine, as I would imagine the Islands in the South Pacific.

Sam and his two brothers worked with their parents to farm the land and operate the only store/post office on the island. They enjoyed great hunting and fishing opportunities as recreation as well as for food.

When Sam started his schooling he had to travel about three miles across the bay waters to Fort Myers. A ferry with an infrequent schedule or rowboat was the mode of travel. He fell in love with sports and that presented a problem – practice and games at school conflicted with his transportation schedule.

Sam made a big sacrifice. He chose to find lodging on the mainland and return to the island on weekends where he worked long hours. No rest for the weary became a way of life for Sam.

He did odd jobs at a boarding house for his room and board during the school year to be able to play all sports. Sam was a good athlete, who succeeded via guts and determination.

Sam graduated from high school May of 1942 and accepted a football scholarship to Hampton Sidney University in Virginia. Soon thereafter Hampton Sidney cancelled its athletic program because of World War II. Sam dropped out of HSU and returned home to Sanibel Island.

Sam Bailey, Wally's Boys founder

He didn't accept the fact that a war would keep him from playing sports. He tried to enlist in the military but was turned down because of a hearing defect.

He wouldn't give up nonetheless and wrote to several colleges and universities offering his services. His narrative: " I am 6 feet, 2 inches tall, weigh 190 pounds. Played the tackle position in high school, but will play any position the coach needs a good man."

Coach Butts must have liked the sincerity in that letter for he had assistant coach Carroll Thomas, wire Sam to come to Athens. Sam made his way to the Classic City as fast as the bus could take him.

While lettering at Georgia 1943-44-45, Sam played several positions on the football team and ran track.

I have so many great remembrances of Sam Bailey and here's the one I like best.

We had a week off between the spring and summer quarters of 1946, and I was really looking forward to going back to Yeadon, Pa. Sam asked if he could make the trip with me and I was glad to have him come along. He was always great company.

The summer baseball league had already started, and I was asked if I would play a game. I said, "Sure, if you let my friend Sam play also." The manager had only one uniform left for Sam and it was a couple sizes too small. That didn't bother Sam; he wanted to play so badly he would have worn a bathing suit.

With his chest bulging out of the shirt and knees showing between the pants and stockings – he was an awful sight. The game was quite exciting considering that we were amateurs.

The score was tied in the last inning, and Sam had not played. We had a man on first with two outs when I reminded the manager to put my Bulldog friend in the game. The crowd questioned the move with a buzzing reaction when Sam strode to the plate. He made a mighty swing, but missed on the first pitch, and was caught watching for a second strike. On the next pitch he hit a "blue darter" between left and center field. The ball hit the ground and ran like a rabbit all the way to the fence. Before the ball was returned to the infield Sam had rounded the bases for an inside the park homerun.

There was jubilation in the ole town that night. The town folk asked me for my friend's name, and I jokingly said " Ozark Ike." To this day when I go home someone will ask " what ever happened to Ozark Ike?"

Sam played professional football for four years with seven different teams. When Frank Sinkwich became football coach at Tampa University, Sam joined him as line coach. A great ability of Sam's is managing multiple duties. While at Tampa University Sam was line coach, trainer, ticket manager, sports information director, baseball coach (their field is named "Sam Bailey Field,") basketball coach, athletic director, alumni fund solicitor, and assistant to the president. Sam was instrumental for much of the athletic development and tradition at Tampa.

Sam returned to Sanibel and works with his brother operating Bailey's Shopping Center. The Bailey family has donated many acres of land for a Wildlife Sanctuary and a shell museum. They are very active in civic and environmental activities in the area.

The University of Georgia Chapter of the National Football Foundation and Hall of Fame honored Sam Bailey during the 100th year of college football celebration, April 1992.

"Sanibel Sam" has paid the price for success. He is the most persistent, dependable, hard working, and honest person I have ever known.

TECH GAMES DON'T COUNT

Throughout the country in the war years, training programs were organized on the college campuses, most of them designed for officer education which meant they often enrolled in classes on campus.

The military brass has always appreciated athletics, particularly football, so as these officer candidates from various parts of the country were billeted to a college town, they attended class and played football.

There was one exception. The Navy pre-flight school in Athens attracted outstanding athletes from various sections of the county, but they were assigned to Athens for training only and did not attend class.

At Georgia Tech, for example, it was different. Many football players from other colleges came to Tech where they were enrolled in class. This made them eligible for football.

As a result Tech fielded strong teams, and won many games by lopsided scores including games against Georgia in 1943-44.

Dan Magill, when he became Publicity Director in 1948, told Coach Butts that he was not going to count those games in the records. "They were not true Georgia-Georgia Tech games," Magill said. "The players Tech had were not Tech men, they were outsiders who had initially enrolled to play football at other colleges. Tech had the Vanderbilt captain, the Alabama captain and players from other sections of the country. Georgia lined up with 4Fs and players too young for the draft."

It rankled Magill, whose antipathy for the arch enemy was and is supreme, that anybody would count those games in the ancient series with Tech.

Georgia does not count those games for that reason all owing to Magill's sense of history and his fervent feelings about his alma mater and, of course, Coach Butts.

MIKE CASTRONIS, ONE KIDNEY, GREAT BIG HEART

When the Georgia team broke up after the Rose Bowl, New Year's Day 1943, every able bodied male volunteered for war. Only those too young for the draft and 4Fs were around to keep football ongoing in Athens.

One of those who helped hold the team together was Mike Castronis, a son of Greek immigrants, who located in Jacksonville. He lost a kidney in a softball game on campus and that kept him from military duty.

The Armed Forces didn't want a man with only one kidney. In fact, playing football was not advisable, but Castronis was determined. So determined that he was an inspiration to everybody on the team.

Coach Mike, everybody's friend and hero

Lean and mean when the action began, charming, generous and altruistic off the field, Castronis was a dogged and hard edged competitor. A lightweight tackle at 185, he may have been the smallest tackle ever to make All America after 1940.

A longtime counselor for the YMCA, assistant coach and, in his final years, cheerleader advisor, Coach Mike touched a lot of lives. An inveterate jogger and pickup basketball player, there is an annual 5K health run in his memory, that takes place every spring. His loving memory endures.

When Castronis was growing up in Fernandina

Beach and Jacksonville, he developed a passion early in life for football, but his Greek-born father thought such activity ridiculous.

The senior Castronis believed a man should work. Work long, hard, hours and earn your bread by the sweat of your brow. Playing games was for young children, not a growing boy big enough to help out at the family restaurant when he wasn't in school.

"Oh, Mike, he's playing foolishness," John Michael Castronis was always lamenting to his wife, Helen.

The son tried to convince his parents that if he played his foolish game well enough, that some school might offer him a scholarship, and he could get an education for free.

In heated family discussions, which were always in Greek, the father lectured his son that nobody, not even in America, the land of opportunity, would pay money for his education if he played "that foolish game."

When it came time for college after a highly successful prep career at Andrew Jackson High, it appeared that the father's logic was accurate. No college was willing to pay for young Mike's education.

"Even in those days, 185 pound tackles were not what they were looking for," Castronis said. Certainly not the University of Florida where he preferred to enroll. The Gators had just hired Tom Lieb, a Notre Damer, whose team beat both Georgia and Georgia Tech (which was a first) and caused an abundance of excitement in Gainesville.

Lieb, Castronis remembered, announced that he was going for size and that he would recruit out of state in order to achieve his objective.

Some of Mike's friends who were Gator backers appealed to Lieb to give the Andrew Jackson star lineman a look, just a chance, but the Gator coach was too preoccupied with the size factor.

Three of Castronis' friends – Ivan Alsobrook, Clarence Heyn and Carl Crosby – earned scholarships to Georgia. On a spring visit to Athens, they told freshman coach Howell Hollis about their skinny friend back home.

"Coach he will really work hard," they advised. "All he wants is a chance to try out. Can we bring him back with us when we report in August?"

Hollis was happy to have another "try out" join the team, a move which was to prove fortuitous and lasting for the Bulldogs.

Castronis arrived in Athens in the summer of 1942. He was given a bunk in the attic of Payne Hall where the Georgia athletes lived. There were 30 others just like him in the heat soaked attic where they shared one shower and one toilet.

"That didn't bother me," he remembered. "I had an opportunity to play football and that was all that mattered."

Castronis mattered on the field where his tenacious spirit and old country work ethic soon caught the eye of the Georgia coaches who issued scholarship aid to any players who made the team, a fact with which Castronis was not familiar.

When the freshman team played the South Carolina freshmen in Columbia before fall classes began, Hollis gathered the team at a downtown hotel for the game plan the morning of the game. He first announced the starting lineup and Castronis, to his great surprise, was one of the starting tackles.

"I didn't know what that meant other than I'd be starting," he remembered. "After the meeting I asked Coach Hollis if I would have a chance to earn a scholarship. He told me I was on scholarship then, which was the greatest news I'd ever had. I couldn't want until the game was over so I could tell my parents."

John Michael and Helen were pleased with the news, not so much for the football status, but that their son would be getting an education and that it would be paid for by the University of Georgia. They were happy he had proven them wrong.

Suddenly, the game of football was not so foolish.

Johnny Cook - First To Score Four TDs In A Game

Johnny Cook was a freshman on the 1943 team, a 17-year-old talent, who stepped right into Coach Butts' single wing formation as the starting tailback. Johnny had a super year and was selected on the All-SEC team, leading the conference in the following categories: 1,007 yards passing and 1,368 yards total yards. He scored 72 points, second best in the league. Johnny entered the service shortly after the season and returned to Georgia three years later. His timing was his misfortune — there was overwhelming depth in the backfield. He finished school on the GI Bill and became an outstanding SEC official.

He scored four touchdowns against VMI in 1943, the first Bulldog back to accomplish that feat.

1945

The war was over. Finally. Our boys came home and overran college campuses. Football in Athens, Georgia, began with a flourish. The team had the makings of a good one and could only become better as the boys in uniform returned. Charley Trippi, the greatest all-around player in Bulldog history, would be wearing silver britches by mid season. No telling how far these Bulldogs would go.

The first four teams—Murray State, Clemson, Miami and Kentucky—were blown away by an average of 36 points per game. Then Trippi was back for the LSU game in Athens. What an ignominious homecoming! Georgia was blown away, 32-0.

There even had been Rose Bowl talk after the steamrolling start, but the LSU defeat and a loss to Alabama in Birmingham, 28-14, spoiled the hopes for a trip to the West Coast. A bowl bid was to come, however. Georgia won nine games and defeated Tulsa in the Oil Bowl at Houston, 20-6. Trippi was at peak form after the Alabama game as the Bulldogs tallied 33 points or more in the final four games.

In the Oil Bowl, Trippi returned a punt for 68 yards which was proclaimed the greatest punt return of all time. "He completely reversed his field and ran over two Tulsa tacklers who had him trapped near a sideline," Dan Magill wrote.

Carl Sanders
Quarterback To Governor

Carl Sanders is, perhaps, the former Wally's Boys who rose the highest after graduation.

He was elected governor of the state and then became head of one of Atlanta's most prestigious law firms, Troutman-Sanders. He was always an enthusiastic leader and pace setter in a number of associations and decisions, which have benefited his alma mater, and has never failed to credit football for helping stimulate his success.

Georgia has always been on his mind, and he spoke with fervor and commitment when any project or activity, regarding his state university, came about. Occasionally, he would pick up the phone and call friends in Athens to check on things. Progress in any area excited him. Problem? How could he help? He wanted to know what was going on. He wanted to keep up.

In 2003 he made a seven-figure gift to the Law School which didn't surprise anybody who knew of his feelings and commitment to the University.

Sanders was always been keenly interested in athletic association affairs. When Vince Dooley became Georgia head coach, it was important to prospective athletes and their families to know about the status of athletic residence halls. The big thing at that time was to develop dormitories for athletes. Dooley felt that Georgia should have one. The competition, led by Bear Bryant at Alabama, had such facilities.

Georgia got one owing to the able assistance of Gov. Sanders. Bulldog backfield coach, John Donaldson, a teammate of Sanders, paid the governor a visit and helped sell him on the importance of such a facility for athletics.

The point is that the governor was willing to step forward and bring momentum toward initiating the project. Anything to help his alma mater.

At Georgia Sanders experienced the hard knocks of the college game of the mid-forties, good for the scrimmaging and tussling that comes when you enter politics, wouldn't you say?

Sanders served the state of Georgia as its governor from 1963 to 1967 during a time of spectacular social and economic change. In his capacity as governor, he was chairman of the rules committee at the 1964 Democratic National Convention and a member of the executive committee of the National Governors Conference.

Prior to becoming governor, he served one term in the Georgia House of Representatives and three terms in the Georgia State Senate, serving as President Pro Tem of the Senate from 1960 to 1963.

In 1965, Governor Sanders received the Golden Key Award, the highest award given by the National Education Association for contributions to the advancement of education. He was elected into the Georgia Athletic Hall of Fame in 1968 and served as president of the University of Georgia Alumni Society in 1969 and 1970.

When it appeared that the old American Football League was about to put a team in Atlanta in the early sixties, Sanders recommended to Commissioner Pete Rozelle of the National Football League that the NFL expand into Atlanta. When the subject of who would own the team came up, Sanders suggested his classmate, Rankin Smith, Chairman and principal owner of the Life Insurance Company of Georgia. Rankin Smith did become the owner as a result of his friend, the governor, arranging the introduction with Pete Rozelle.

When his political days ended, Sanders concentrated on the practice of law and has enjoyed a distinguished legal and business career.

Today, the former governor, is trim and lean – like he has always been. As head of one of the biggest law firms in Atlanta, he keeps a full schedule but works out weekly with emphasis to remain fit.

He is eager to recall his days on campus and reminisce about Georgia football. Any conversation reveals a generous testimony to the value of his football scholarship enhanced university education, which was followed by an accomplished political career.

An incident worth recalling, took place after he was elected governor in 1962 when his former coach paid him at visit at the state capitol.

In Sanders' campaign against Marvin Griffin, Coach Butts had supported Griffin. He had long been friends with Marvin and chose to endorse his old pal. The coach picked the wrong horse.

"One day my secretary came in and said, 'Coach Butts is here to see you,'" Sanders remembers. He told her to send his old coach into his office. Immediately a sheepish Wallace Butts apologized for not supporting his one time quarterback.

"I never held it against him," Sanders says. "It was easy to be his friend because he was man enough to come see me, say he was sorry about his decision. In my book it takes a pretty big man to do that.

"Although I regretted the hard times he experienced in the fifties, I always appreciated the good teams that he had. When he offered me a scholarship, I was grateful and enjoyed my time on the football field. Always, I have said that I was proud to be one of his players and to have been coached by Wallace Butts."

If he were given to emotional outbursts Sanders would be a foot stomping, back slapping advocate of the values of football. "The main thing," he said, "is that the game taught me perseverance. I learned in my career that perseverance sometimes will succeed when ability won't. The smartest guy doesn't always succeed,

Gov. Carl Sanders (right) joins the traditional Senior Parade

but, most often, the one who perseveres does.

"Football taught me discipline. It taught me that when you get knocked down, you don't stay there. I deeply appreciate the values of football."

Sanders arrived in 1942, but did not make the trip to California with the Rose Bowl team. He was an outstanding back, starring in the single wing and Notre Dame box formations at Richmond Academy, making the All-GIAA team in 1941.

He had graduated from high school at sixteen years of age in the years when the high schools ended after eleven grades. In 1943, he lined up like every other able bodied, patriotic male – he volunteered for the military.

In Atlanta, he underwent a physical exam to join the Naval Air Corps at age 17. The officer in charge told him he had passed the examination but that he had a problem.

"What is that," Sanders asked?

"You've got to go home and get your parents' permission to join," was the reply.

He returned home to Augusta and subsequently showed up at nearby Daniel Field where he enlisted in the Army Air Corp. He successfully completed training to become the chief pilot on a B-17 bomber and was ready to join the action when the atomic bombs were dropped on Japan.

The war soon was over, he was discharged and returned to Athens for more football and a law degree. He was a backup quarterback on the 1945 Oil Bowl team, but he correctly foresaw that nobody would beat out John Rauch. Further, he wanted to accelerate his school work toward completing requirements for a law degree.

"Back then," he says, "if you chose to work overtime, you could get complete your three year requirements in two years. I was able to do that and passed the state bar before I actually graduated."

His legal career was off and running. Soon he would enjoy a spectacular political opportunity. He achieved elected positions to the Georgia House and Senate, which were followed by his election as governor.

One of the highlights of the '45 season was that he and his brother, Bob (Blaze), both lettered for the Bulldogs. "I don't know how many bothers lettered on the same team, but I bet there are not many," Sanders says. "We were the best of friends, and I always appreciated his heart and courage. He was an athlete with a great heart."

Sanders met his wife, Betty, while on campus. She was studying art under the renowned Lamar Dodd and became an accomplished artist. The Sanders remain active and supportive alumni.

PEACETIME FOOTBAL RETURNS

In the fall of 1945, the world war had ended and with that long awaited relief came great enthusiasm for life to return to normal. The mood on college campuses was upbeat. Enrollment across the country would immediately explode. The G.I. Bill meant educational opportunity, and veterans were eager to enroll.

Saturday's heroes in Athens would no longer be 4Fs, not with returning players, fresh from military duty, seeking to pick up where they left off.

At the University of Georgia, Wallace Butts in August began preparing what would become his third bowl team. Optimism began to spread that the '45 team might have that old magic that took his '41 team to the Orange Bowl and his '42 squad to Pasadena.

Following a strong start, the Bulldogs got Charley Trippi back from the Army. Spirits soared, but collapsed when LSU shut Georgia out 32-0 and Alabama defeated the Bulldogs 28-14. Georgia recovered with four closing

Celebrating at the Oil Bowl

wins in which the Dogs averaged 34.0 points an outing and limited the opposition to a total of 7 points, a per-game average of 1.7.

The 1945 Bulldogs were, in many respects, one of Wallace Butts' best teams, but even with a 9-2 record, featuring a 20-6 victory over Tulsa in the Oil Bowl (later to become the Bluebonnet Bowl), the Bulldogs experienced notable disappointment.

At one point during the early season it was anticipated that this team would bring Georgia a second Rose Bowl invitation and perhaps challenge for the national championship.

After getting off to a fast 3-0 start including shutouts over Murray State in the opener and Clemson the following week, the Dogs began SEC competition against

Kentucky in Lexington where Charles "Rabbit" Smith, a 150 pound halfback from Palatka, FL, made old Stoll Field a memorable playground. He scored from 85, 61, 7 and 3 yards out, to tie a Georgia record of four touchdowns in one game. It was set by Johnny Cook in 1944.

Smith was rated as one of the best backs in the SEC. Rabbit played in the College All-Star game and briefly with the World Champion Chicago Cardinals in 1947, but said, "I was really too small to play professionally."

At Georgia, however, nobody worried about his size. His quickness, as Bill Hartman once pointed out, was tailor-made for the "T" formation.

In a reunion story for the Georgia football program, several members of the '45 team reflected on Butts' first post war team.

The captain was Charles "Beefy" Eaves, a native of Elberton. Eaves suffered a broken back in the first game and was out for the season. "At that time, they didn't know much about broken backs," said Eaves. "I remember coming off the field and then blacking out. I woke up in St. Mary's Hospital. I don't remember much about the games themselves because of my time in the hospital, but I did make the Oil Bowl trip to Houston.

"We were a close group who had a lot of fun and won a lot of ballgames," Eaves said. "We were mostly 4F's or returning veterans from the war. There was a tremendous difference in our ages. Johnny Rauch, our quarterback, was 17 years old, and some guys were 27 or 28. We were the nucleus of the '46 team that won the SEC title and Sugar Bowl.

That 17-year-old quarterback – John Rauch – learned quickly in the Bulldogs' new "T" formation. "I was really amazed at becoming a starter so soon," said Rauch. "There were still many great athletes on campus at that time and I felt very honored to have earned Coach Butts' confidence.

"We had a great camaraderie on that '45 squad," Rauch said. "That feeling for each other has carried over through the years. We get together often and especially have a great time each G-Day when we return to Athens for the lettermen's barbecue. That 1945 team was a very important part of my life."

Mike Castronis, an All American tackle, was a great admirer of Beefy Eaves. "Beefy Eaves was one of the most loved and respected players Georgia ever had. He was tough. Even when he broke his back he ran off the field. We all remember that," Castronis said for a story in the Georgia football program.

Castronis remembered that after the blowout against Kentucky, there was Rose Bowl fever in Athens. "We had beaten everybody, and we played pretty well while Charley Trippi was still in the service. The next week was homecoming against LSU and Trippi was getting out of the Army. The whole town was buzzing about Charley returning to our team."

The whole football world was aware that Trippi was trading in his khaki for silver britches. Charley was back home and now there was no stopping the Dogs. That is what many thought. But it was a rude homecoming for Trippi and Dog fans. LSU whipped Georgia 32-0.

"I remember when Charley came home and all the hoopla about us going undefeated. When LSU beat us so bad some people started talking about us getting jealous of all the publicity going to Charley, and we just laid down and quit. Well, that's the biggest bunch of bull I ever heard. We tried our hardest but just got beat. Some folks down at the pool room started that talk and even though that was several decades ago, when I think about it today, it makes me sick at my stomach," Castronis said in that program story.

"That first game after getting out of the Army was a strange feeling," Trippi remembered. "I felt a little awkward and was very ineffective. I probably should have just played defense that day.

"Going to the Oil Bowl that year was a good reward for a fine season," added Trippi.

It was in this game that Trippi made what is still considered by ole timers to be the greatest punt return of all time, a 68-yard jaunt that featured a spinning, field reversing and adroit broken field effort by the Bulldog left halfback. "Simply unbelievable," said Dan Magill.

BILL HARTMAN
BULLDOG COACH AND LEADER

There are so many good and decent things about William Coleman Hartman Jr., to appreciate, such an extraordinary and unselfish man. What follows does not do him justice. He is, in fact, worth a book all by himself.

There is deep and abiding pride in what he achieved in athletic competition. He does talk about his glory days but it is never offensive. Never any braggadocio, nor vanity, nor self-serving monologue. Crass and irritating ego are not in his makeup. He has always been a man of goodwill, good humor, honor and service.

His is a modest, unselfish and charitable personality.

For a man who has achieved and accomplished to such an enviable extent, there is not a trace of arrogance. Such a rare trait in the athletic world.

When I think about his long and productive life, built on an objective to live uncomplicatedly in his beloved Athens and make a lasting contribution to his University, I think about the old 4-H Club motto, "Service above self." He was and is that in the purest sense.

With his name and reputation, he could have amassed considerable assets but that was never a motivation. Simply put, he did not have the drive to accumulate.

His goal from the start was to enjoy life in the college town where he experienced so much undergraduate pleasure. He starred in football, and developed enduring friendships. He married a beauty queen. They enjoyed the theatre, the arts and Saturday afternoons in Sanford Stadium. A few scotches and water and a thick steak from the grill most weekends of the year.

The well rounded description of what we traditionally expected of the college man, is what Bill Hartman was when he was a student, and he carried the concept into his post graduate life when it came to service to alma mater.

There are many who profess to believe in the following preachment but can not measure up – the one that says there is no limit to what a man can accomplish in life, so long as he doesn't care who gets the credit. Hartman actually could have written that. Certainly, he has lived it.

His hallmark is unending respect. Of all the Georgia men I have ever known, none have engendered the respect that he and Dan Magill have enjoyed historically.

And for one refreshing reason. What they did was not for themselves, but for the University of Georgia. They are perceived as putting the school ahead of any personal interests. The perception is eminently correct.

Having known the two of them for nearly a half century, I can attest to the fact that such a notion about these two remarkable Bulldogs, without question, hits the mark dead center.

For years, he was the unpaid chairman of the Georgia Student Educational Fund. In fact, he didn't want to be paid. He felt that he should be a volunteer chairman.

Keep in mind he lived good, but he was never a wealthy man, although many perceived that he was better off financially than was actually the case.

What did living good mean for him? To take up residence near the campus in an old home with charm and a front porch swing where he could idle away in late afternoons in the spring and summer. Coffee and the newspaper in the morning at a relaxed pace.

To the office, five minutes away whenever it suited him. Coffee mid morning at the National Bank of Athens (now SunTrust) where business gossip, good humored banter and reminiscing about the Bulldogs, past and present, were the order of the day. Lunch at the country club with an insurance client or friend of the University. In the old days, golf which eventually gave way to tennis, and ultimately a swim at the Y.

After he turned 80, his physical activity decreased as his mobility, with the passing of time, became impaired, but his adroit mind and his remarkable memory remained as keen as ever.

He, in his 90th year, the year of the publication of this book, still enjoyed Saturday lunches at the Athens Country Club with friends who not only take delight with being in his company but appreciate his conversations, spiced with remembrances and colorful and insightful lore of another time. In all those recollections, there is a propensity for remembering details exactly. His acute mental powers have never diminished.

His greatest setback came in 1995 when his wife, Ruth, died. They had enjoyed life to the fullest, but typical of Bill, loyal and devoted, he grieved and mourned but moved on, remarrying and making the best of the situation.

When he was playing football at Madison High School, Hartman took serious note of what Wallace Butts was doing at Madison A&M. Butts, only 23 years old, established himself over night as a special talent when it came to coaching.

Success at G.M.C. followed his noteworthy record at Madison A&M, and Butts recruited Hartman to play at the nationally regarded military school.

Hartman admired Butts from his teenage days and developed long lasting respect and feeling for the man for whom he began working after a year of professional football in 1938.

Even in Butts' toughest days in the fifties, he was never criticized nor second guessed by Hartman, who always could overlook any man's faults by pointing out the good that he had done or the plusses that he saw in his fellow man's makeup.

Some of that was Hartman's good and generous nature. Much of it was his intense loyalty. He has always been loyal to his friends. He can offer a critique of performance and has, but in reality he has never criticized anybody. Certainly not maliciously.

Nobody ever took greater delight in poking fun at Hartman than John Terrell Jr., as good a friend as the Bulldog coach ever had. The record book shows that after Hartman returned the second half kickoff against a favored Tech in 1937 for a touchdown, he missed the extra point that would have brought victory in a game

Bill Hartman, Quintessential Bulldog

which ended in a 6-6 tie.

Hartman was winded from the 93-yard run, the regular kicker in those limited substitution days was not in the game and it was a wayward snap.

Didn't matter to Terrell, whose antipathy for Tech set the standard. He has never let Hartman forget that missed point after.

Hartman's remarkable memory sets him apart. He can remember who made the blocks on Spin 87 that led to a Sinkwich touchdown. He knows the down and distance in every significant scoring situation in the time that he coached.

He remembers pre-game conversations with the quarterbacks, like Zeke Bratkowski, and can describe players' abilities succinctly and graphically to perfection – but without rancor nor sarcasm. He can appraise saliently and graphically.

Whenever he talks about John Rauch, he always compliments the Hall of Famer for his great discipline. "If you told Rauch," Hartman said, "that you were going to come in there when he was in the pocket and hit him in the head with a hatchet, Rauch would still stay in the pocket."

He might describe a running back as having "good track speed." Translation: the back was a straight ahead runner.

With an ability to remember dates, facts and figures that confirms he owns an incomparable memory, Hartman, carries on throughout life without reactions which trip most of us.

He might analyze any of us who have known him can say with deep conviction and accuracy that he never has said a bad word about anybody.

A classic example of the remarkable respect he commanded came when he was called to testify on behalf of Butts in the Saturday Evening Post trial. He answered truthfully the questions asked of him, but he never impugned the integrity of either Butts or the University of Georgia.

Like most everybody else I know, he couldn't bring himself to believe that Coach Butts would actually be a party to fixing a football game. On the other hand, he realized that his long time friend's discipline had broken down amid acrimony and dissent. He longed for a better circumstance. For his friend and for his school. Throughout his career, Hartman has wished for and sought the best for the University of Georgia.

When Vince Dooley came aboard, three years removed from Butts' last season as coach, Hartman extended a helping hand. He didn't deal in the speculation that Georgia might have made a mistake, hiring an unknown freshman coach from Auburn.

He considered it his mission to assist the new coach, both as an alumnus and as Chairman of the Georgia Student Educational Fund. Dooley's success, in part, had to do with Hartman's advice, support and generosity of GSEF funds.

Bill Hartman has been a Bulldog all his life.

Most southern schools were interested in recruiting Hartman and several of his teammates from G.M.C., but Georgia had always appealed to Hartman, dating back to his seventh and eighth grade years in Columbus. He saw his first Georgia-Auburn game in 1926 and always had a "basic desire" to enroll in Athens.

The thing that really sold him, the clinching circumstance, was the offer of a summer job with the Coca Cola company, a practice allowed in those days.

Harold Hirsch, the general legal counsel for Coca-Cola and a Georgia benefactor, sent a representative to meet with Hartman and three of his teammates – Walter Troutman, Stooge Davis and Clayton Wilhite. They were advised that they would be given summer jobs with Coca Cola in New York, $75.00 a month salary and $6.00 a day expenses.

Believe it or not, Hartman says that he ate on $1.50 a day and that $3.00 would cover room rent. However, he made a better deal.

He arranged for a suite at the Shelton (now the Marriott Eastside behind the Waldorf) for $90.00 a month. He and his roommate each were paid $180.00 a month in expenses which meant there was an attractive net after bills were paid.

On top of that, he and Troutman bought a Model A Ford for $65.00 and drove it all summer, making money on mileage in Manhattan and out to Long Island. When it came time to return to Athens at the end of the summer, their pullman fare, paid for by the Coca Cola Co., was $60.00. He, Troutman and two others who worked for Coke drove home in the car, which meant that after they shared expenses, they were able to turn a handsome profit.

"It is easy to understand why those of us who played back then have always been partial to Coke," Hartman says.

When he put down roots, Hartman put them down so deeply that he became a fixture almost as well known as Athens landmarks like the double barrel cannon, the tree that owns itself, the chapel bell and Sanford's famous hedges.

The Veterans Return

The Butts magic picked up after the war ended, and championship football returned. Hopes were deflated in mid-season 1945, but the Little Round Man fielded his only undefeated team in 1946.

A quarterback and letterman on the '45 team, Carl Sanders would later be elected governor of the state. There were some players, holdovers from the war years, who made a significant contribution to the post-war success.

With the war over, veterans returned and campuses all across the country literally exploded as everybody sought to enroll in college.

Some returned but had lost that step of speed. They never regained their old form but a few, Charley Trippi being a great example, picked up where they left off before war broke up the Rose Bowl team.

Twin Towers of the Forties
By John Rauch

Jack Bush: Offensive tackle, defensive end, 1946-48. Jack spent his early years in Cordele and Brunswick. At age 13, his family moved to Jacksonville Beach, FL. where Jack grew bigger than other boys his age. He wasn't a bully; he demanded respect, however, one of the qualities he has carried through his life. He was very good at charming people, yet in competition he was meaner than a snake. He took the measure of many opponents on the handball court as well as the football field.

He knew how to succeed in business, using those competitive instincts to establish several successful car dealerships.

Jack, like so many others in our time, had an unusual path to the University of Georgia. He was awarded a scholarship to the University of Florida in1942, but transferred to Georgia that same year. He entered the Marine Corps in January 1943.

The Marines assigned Jack to study transportation at Duke, and he eventually was shipped to Hawaii where he often played handball with Ted Williams, the great Boston Red Sox slugger. Jack did such a good job he was put in charge of a unit in China transporting supplies. That was actually where Jack began his business career. He bought, sold and traded pearls. When he returned to Georgia he brought a sack of cultured pearls home with him. He heard of a Philadelphia jeweler who would pay top dollar for pearls; so when we went to Philadelphia to play Temple University early in the 1946 season, Jack carried the sack of pearls with him. I remember sitting in the lounge on the train where Jack counted pearls in the sack.

Jack sold his pearls for a lot of money. He enrolled

in the business school, and following graduation, he became an enterprising businessman.

With all his success Jack and his lovely wife Sue have remained down to earth people. They have entertained Jane and me so generously we could never repay them [sometimes we feel like they have adopted us]. They are devout Dawg fans and tirelessly support the University of Georgia. Jack and Sue in April of 2002 purchased a five-bedroom home next door to Coach Vince Dooley. They frequently offer accommodations for their friends for important athletic events. They always reserve a room for the Rauch's. We're grateful.

Garland "Bulldog" Williams: Tackle, lettered 1942, 1946; hometown Forrest City, Arkansas. Bulldog was a remarkable football player. At 6-4, 235 lbs., he was the other tackle opposite Jack Bush. I looked at them as Twin Towers. They were awesome.

Coach Hartman drove Bulldog and Bill Godwin from Arkansas to Athens, where they finished high school and enrolled at the University of Georgia. Bulldog was a country boy and looked different from the locals with curly, unkempt hair and high cheekbones. He was smiling or laughing most of the time.

Just as you can not tell a book by its cover, you couldn't determine Bulldog's smarts by his looks. He was much smarter than you might think if you didn't look beyond his "aw shucks" style. He would win you over with his smile, laughter, sympathy, tears, or just because he seemed so sincere and honest.

Bulldog was truly an unforgettable character, and there are so many stories to tell about him. A favorite of mine took place on November 30, 1946, Georgia Tech in Athens. On Tech's first possession from the Jacket's own 15 yard line, they marched to the 40 mostly with the aid of four offside penalties called against us. Tech pulled a surprise by employing a shift that caught the Bulldogs off guard, causing an eager lineman to charge before the snap of the ball.

The first three penalties were called on Bulldog. Captain Charley Trippi called time out to calm the team down. When we formed the huddle prior to the next play Herb St. John [who lined up next to Bulldog and didn't say a dozen words his four years in Athens] said, "Bulldog, if you jump offside again I'm going to knock you alongside your head." Bulldog didn't say a word.

We lined up, Tech shifted and St. John jumped offside. Bulldog wore a big smile on his face. The good news is we solved the shift and we solved the Yellow Jackets that day by the score of 35-7.

Coach Hartman deserves a medal for "kidnapping" Bulldog and Bill Godwin and bringing those two Arkansas boys to Athens.

RYALS LEE

Ryals Lee, a successful businessman in Tallahassee wrote John Rauch a letter about the generous attitude and spirit of Coach Butts:

"I was witness to a historical incident that exemplifies Coach Butts' keen sense of judgment as well as his innate sense of fair play. Georgia was to play Florida State in Tallahassee on a Saturday night in the early 50's, and Coach Butts asked me to take him to the Florida A&M game, played in Tallahassee that afternoon," Ryals wrote.

"The legendary Amos Alonzo Jake Gaither coached the A&M team and sent Coach Butts tickets to his game. Since Georgia was to play FSU at night we went to the A&M game in the afternoon. At the end of the first half, as the players were heading to their dressing rooms, Coach Gaither walked up into the stands and thanked Coach Butts for taking time to attend his game.

"Many years later, as I was visiting with Coach Gaither at our favorite sausage-grinding store, I mentioned how much Coach Butts appreciated his taking the time to come up in the stands to welcome him.

"Coach Gaither said, 'I don't know of anybody that could move me to take time away from my team at that moment, except Coach Butts'.

"He then told me how much he came to respect and love Coach Butts over the years, not only for his keen football mind, and his willingness to share his knowledge, but also for what Coach Butts did for him many years ago. When Coach Butts was either President-elect or President of the American Football Coaches Association he called Coach Gaither and asked if he would serve on the AFCA board of directors.

"Coach Gaither, very passionately, told me how much it meant to him for Coach Butts to recognize him in such a way. He knew that Coach Butts wanted him on the board for what he could contribute to the coaches association. Coach Gaither expressed how proud and honored he was in that he knew his nomination came from Coach Butts' heart. As he put it, it was not 'popular' at that time to name a black coach to such a high position."

PART V

JOHN RAUCH

Four Memorable Years

RAUCH

JAMES WALLACE BUTTS
MY FATE IS IN YOUR HANDS

James Wallace Butts – my fate is in your hands. That is how I felt when I reported to Athens for football practice in the summer of 1945.

While I wasn't sure of my fate, I always had positive feelings about my future. If it didn't work out in Athens, I would find another opportunity. Yet, I always wondered if I could be a successful football player. Could I start for a winning team? How would I respond in tough situations? My dreams turned out the way I wanted, and I've always been grateful.

Let me tell you how I put my fate in the hands of James Wallace Butts after an interesting detour.

In 1945 I was a senior at Yeadon, Pa. High School. It was the month of May. I had just returned to school from three days at the University of Tennessee in Knoxville. This trip was paid for by the Tennessee athletic department. It was arranged through my high school coach, Ed Kirschner. Coach Kirschner had recommended a Yeadon player to Volunteer coach John Barnhill the year before.

The player's name was Oscar "Ozzie" Meneses. He was awarded a scholarship and was a second string wingback his freshman year. His career was short because he entered the service immediately after the 1944 season. The coaches in Knoxville must have been making a last call for players. They phoned Coach Kirschner with the hope he could send them another "Ozzie" Meneses.

He gave them my name, and a few days later a train ticket to Knoxville arrived at his office. I had never been further from home than Washington, D.C., and that was for a relative's funeral. I was apprehensive about going that far away to school. Coach talked me into it, saying "You have the ability to play college ball. You owe it to yourself and family to take this opportunity."

It was sound advice. He was a great person, one of my favorite people. He played an important part in shaping my future. When I arrived at Knoxville I was met by assistant coach Ray Graves. Graves was a star player at Tennessee, who also coached for the Philadelphia Eagles, Georgia Tech, and Florida; and is a member of the Collegiate Football Hall of Fame. I liked Coach Graves and the University of Tennessee.

The next day was Friday, and Coach Graves, along with a couple other coaches, worked me out for about 45 minutes. I was in sweat clothes. The workout was running, passing, catching the ball, punting. There didn't seem to be much to it. I couldn't tell whether I did well or bad. The coaches didn't give me any indication.

Saturday, they issued a full uniform. Five other players were present, also in full uniform. This workout was much tougher. We blocked and tackled in addition to running, passing and kicking. Again nothing was said, no evaluation. Sunday morning Coach Graves drove me to the train station. He made sure I had my return ticket to Philadelphia.

Before saying good-bye he said, "if you come down here for fall football practice in August you will go on football scholarship." Nothing in writing, however. I wasn't sure if they wanted me or not. Nonetheless, I had a certain feeling. I would play college football. If not Tennessee, some college. *I would play football.* My confidence was encouraging.

It was only a few days after my return from Knoxville that my basketball coach, John Naegli approached me. He had met an alumnus from the University of Georgia at a wedding in Old Forge, Pa. over the weekend. This man owned some Coca-Cola franchises and was a supporter of Coach Butts and the Bulldogs.

He told Coach Naegli he would send me a train ticket to visit Athens. I wasn't too thrilled about that.

My understanding of geography told me that Tennessee was closer to home than Georgia. Coach Naegli, another favorite person in my life, gave me the same advice as Coach Kirschner. Off to Athens I went.

The train pulled into the station well into the night, midnight to be exact. It was very dark except for one light hanging in the center of the platform. I was the only passenger to disembark. The train whistle blew and was off, leaving me in the middle of nowhere. I had been very sleepy but this unfamiliar circumstance had me wide awake.

The station itself was little more than a wooden shack. I started to walk around the station to see what was on the other side. Good luck for me – there was a car parked at the curb.

As I got closer to the vehicle I could see a man at the wheel. It was a taxicab. I hoped the driver was only asleep, but I wasn't sure. I tapped on the window. He woke up, rolled the window down and asked, "Where you going?" I didn't know what to tell him because I had no instructions, just a train ticket.

When I finally mentioned football, he said, "Milledge Annex, that's where all the players live." We headed for the campus.

Milledge Annex was almost as dark as the train station. We got out of the cab, and I took some money out of my pocket to pay him. He refused to take any money saying, "If you going to be a 'Jawga' football player, the ride's on me."

He walked in the dorm, knocked on the first door we came to, and told the sleepy occupant he had a football prospect. The occupant was very obliging. He told us where the linen room was and then slammed the door. This cab driver got sheets, blanket, and towels. He found an empty room, helped me make the bed, and when he was sure I was settled in said, "Good luck, kid," and was gone.

That night I slept sounder than a baby. I woke up about 8:00 o'clock with the sun shining in my face. Before I could get out of bed, the door opened and a head peeked in. We introduced ourselves, and he told me the coaches were out of town for a couple of days.

The players were to work out on their own in the afternoon. He also informed me that I had missed breakfast. A couple of them were going uptown and suggested I go with them. I don't remember their names, but as we walked to town I found out each of them had been on campus for only a week or so. They were waiting for summer quarter to begin. Meanwhile they lived at Milledge Annex and practiced football. Two in the group were from Pennsylvania.

They were a happy-go-lucky bunch, and I felt very comfortable with them. We ate at D. Jones Café, shot pool at the Q Room and ate again — at the Varsity – two chilidogs and a "squirt." It became my favorite meal along with Poss' barbecue.

We then went to a movie. At 2:30 we ran through the campus to Memorial Hall. The equipment man reluctantly gave me equipment. Then it dawned on me, nobody knew who I was. The equipment consisted of shorts and a tee shirt. The workout was a game of touch. We had a great time. After dinner we went to another movie theater.

Georgia football players didn't have to pay at the two theaters in Athens. This was great. I was really enjoying Southern hospitality.

The second day was about the same as the first except I went to class with a couple guys. I didn't understand what was going on in the classroom, but I had my first experience with college classes. The third day started out the same as the second until it was time for the touch football game.

We had been playing for an hour when a car pulled up to the end of the field. I was playing the tailback position taking direct snaps from Mike Cooley, sophomore center from Atlanta. I was the quarterback in the huddle calling the plays which wasn't much more than, "you go over there, you cross over here, and I'll hit you down the middle." It was all passing, and I was throwing pretty accurately.

Mike Cooley told me the men in the car were coaches and one of them was Coach Butts. The game went on for another half hour before the men got out of the car. They were dressed in business suits.

We stopped playing as the coaches walked onto the field. The shortest, Coach Butts, came directly to me and asked my name and where was I from. I felt like he didn't know about my being on campus until I told him I had received a train ticket from a Mr. Harold Hirsch, Jr. He took me aside and asked me some more questions about the position I played. I was a single wing tailback which was the system ninety-nine percent of football teams used.

Coach Butts informed me he would be using a new system called the "T" formation. "I want to see you take some snaps from center," he said and called Mike

Cooley over. The other coaches kept the players busy while Coach Butts, Mike, and I got the center/quarterback exchange down pretty good. Then the coach called everybody up and directed the players to form a line. One at a time they would run down field as pass receivers. Mike would snap the ball to me. I would drop seven yards deep and hit the receiver with the ball. My percentage of completions was pretty high.

As it got dark one of the coaches produced white tape. He wrapped two rings of tape around the ball so the receivers could see it better. It was almost 6:30 p.m. when Coach Butts said, "That's all." The players ran for the locker room. Coach Butts grabbed me by the arm and said, "Let's talk." He asked if I had any plans for college. My answer was, "Yes, Tennessee." He then made a very bold statement.

He said, "If you come to Georgia you could be my starter next year." He then turned to Coach Whitworth and instructed him to go to Philadelphia with me and bring me back as soon as I graduated from high school. All of this happened so fast I could hardly understand it. Going to Tennessee was still in the back of my mind. I was afraid to tell anybody but my parents what Coach Butts told me. How could I believe he would be true to his word. Maybe he just wanted to keep me from going to Tennessee.

The thought of being a first string player on a major college football team was blowing my mind. He must have meant it or he wouldn't have sent Coach Whitworth home with me.

My problem was to decide if I should put my fate in the hands of James Wallace Butts. My decision was "Yes, he looked like an honest man."

He was much more than that. He was staunchly loyal, a leader, a motivator, a friend to me and every player he coached. I started every game for Coach Butts for four years. He made my dreams come true.

Big Time Football Underway

The University of Georgia June 1945. I'm on my way to big time college football.

After I was graduated from Yeadon High with 46 other seniors, we had a informal dance. Coach Whit waited in the car around 10:30 p.m. while I kissed my high school sweetheart, Jane Livingston, good-bye at her front door.

We both knew it would be a long time before we would see each other again. But going to college was something I had dreamed of for a long time. Since my parents, Lillian and Walter Rauch, could not afford at that time to send a child to a university it was a godsend that Coach Butts offered me a full scholarship. We all were on an emotional high.

The plane ride the next morning was uncomfortable and bumpy but without incident. We landed at the Athens airport sometime in the middle of the afternoon. Coach Carroll Thomas met us at the airport and drove me to Milledge Annex. Coach Thomas got linens, blankets, towels, etc. and a key for me to a room on the second of this three story building.

The dining hall was in the basement. When Coach Thomas left me, I sat on the bed trying to collect my thoughts. I knew I had a great opportunity, and wondered what the future would be like.

Someone else occupied the room already, and it wasn't long before Godfrey "Goot" Steiner came bounding through the door to introduce himself as my roommate. When he found out I was from Pennsylvania, he gave me a nickname, Coal Cracker. It seemed everybody had a nickname. Mine didn't last very long when he found out I never saw a coal mine.

Then I was known as "The Kid," probably because I was younger than most of the people living in the dorm. Goot was a great guy. He took me under his wing like a big brother. Soon others came by the room. Many were from Pennsylvania. They had a special camaraderie about them. We talked about our hometowns and summer football practice which started the next day.

Soon a bell rang. It was very loud like a fire alarm and startled me. I watched the others to try to figure out what to do. Someone said "chow down" and we all filed down the stairs to the basement and picked up our food, moving through a cafeteria line. I was hungry until I examined the food on my tray. There was fried catfish, grits, okra with stewed tomatoes and cornbread. I had never eaten any of that stuff before, and it certainly didn't look very appetizing.

Pitchers of milk were on the tables. I tried the cornbread with milk first. At the first swallow I gagged. It was buttermilk, which reminded me of milk of magnesia that my mom used to force down us when we were sick.

Finally, I found the pitcher with regular milk. Thank goodness for the strawberry shortcake. It kept me from starving.

We just shot the bull around the dorm for the rest of the evening. All the athletes were very friendly. They introduced themselves and wished me luck. Coach Thomas lived in the dorm with us. He told me to be in Coach Butts' office the next morning at 8:30 a.m. I had a hard time sleeping that night. I had the upper bunk of a double bunk bed. I lay on my back for hours staring at the ceiling. Occasionally, a door would slam. I finally went to sleep exhausted.

A bugler blowing revelry woke me the next morning. It was still dark. An Army V-12 unit was making formation in the courtyard between Milledge Annex and their quarters, Milledge Hall. I watched with interest because in two more months (August 20th) I would have to register with the draft board. Everybody had to do that. We had the Nazi's and the Japanese on the run, but draft boards remained active, processing recruits.

Goot took me over to Memorial Hall which was on the other side of Milledge Hall (V-12 barracks). Most people scurrying around at that hour were military – Army, Navy, Marines, Wacs, Waves, all kinds of service personnel. In Memorial Hall we climbed a couple of flights of stairs to Coach Butts office. He was at his desk when Goot knocked on the screen door. He barely looked up as he said, "Come in."

As we approached his desk he said, "John, see the secretary for a voucher. Go up to the academic building and get enrolled. Practice is at 3:00 o'clock." Goot said, "I'll take care of him."

Coach Butts put his head back down and started writing. Looked like he was making out the practice schedule. Goot and I stood silently for about a minute. Goot grabbed me by the arm and we left through that screen door. I still wasn't sure if Coach Butts knew who I was.

As Goot and I walked through the main campus, he pointed out the buildings and their names. It was a pretty campus. I was more interested in the Magnolia trees, the dogwood, azaleas and gardenias than the buildings until he pointed out the law school, Harold Hirsch Hall.

That made me stop and reflect because that was the name of the man that sent a train ticket to my high school for me to visit Georgia for a tryout. Later I learned that the building was named for the father of Harold Hirsch, Jr. who had sent me the train ticket.

Goot went to class. I went to register. First to the purser's office with my voucher. Then to five or six tables where I enrolled in a college and selected the courses I would take. Since I was late enrolling, most courses were filled, and I took whatever courses they assigned me.

When I walked out of the registrar's office on my way to the bookstore, I studied my course assignment sheet. I was enrolled in the College of Arts and Sciences. My courses were: French, algebra, European history, and an elective in astronomy. I felt academically ambitious.

That schedule lasted just two weeks when one of

Rauch one time coach of the Bills

the assistant coaches suggested I transfer to the School of Education. The load was much lighter there. I was happy to graduate in five years with a BS in education. Suddenly, it was high noon. There was a big line waiting on the stairs for that loud bell to ring again. It was a warm, sunny day. Most windows and doors were open. I trudged upstairs to unload my new books. Almost every room had a radio blaring. They all had the same station. It was country music like they play at a square dance.

Then a voice came out of each radio and said,

"Hello everybody, this is Eddy Arnold coming to you through the courtesy of your local Purina dealer."

Guys were lying on their beds, sitting in chairs or lounging on the floor. The Eddy Arnold Show was a half hour show, and the players acted like they were in church. Such reverence! When the show finished, there was a mad dash for the dining hall.

Goot came and sat next to me. He missed the radio show, and I told him about it. He said, "Let me give you some advice, never, I mean never, interrupt a guy while he's listening to Eddy Arnold or Roy Acuff."

Goot and I got along very well. He went out of his way to help me get adjusted. He was a tough talking guy but seemed to have a soft side about him. His temper was short and he was ready to fight at the slightest provocation.

He was very conscious of his appearance. I think he went to the barbershop every week. His short hair wasn't exactly a crew cut. It might have been called a brush cut.

He wore a clean pair of denims everyday. We didn't call them jeans in those days. Dungarees were the most common name. Just about everybody wore them at Milledge Annex, but Goot's were different. His were laundered with light starch and pressed like a military uniform.

A white tee shirt and a pair of loafers rounded out his normal attire. The loafers were so brilliantly shined they looked like a mirror. Another interesting thing about him was that when he went to bed, he turned out the light and would kneel down beside his bed and silently say his prayers.

He also worshipped Coach Butts and would jump into a raging fire if Coach Butts asked him to. He had a brother who was a star player at Alabama named Rebel Steiner, but Goot was proud to be a Georgia Bulldog. I was completely surprised at our first practice. Goot was competing for the quarterback position along with about eight others. He knew Coach Butts' system and I didn't. He helped me learn the system. I often wondered if Coach Butts had Goot sacrifice himself to look after me.

Coach Butts worked us hard. After two days of a single practice, the schedule evolved into two practices daily. Not many, if any, players had afternoon classes. Our schedule: 2:00 p.m. meeting; 3:00 to 5:00 p.m. practice; 6:00 p.m. dinner; 7:30 to 9:00 p.m. practice.

It was grueling. The coaches were having a hard time keeping the players from quitting. Almost every day five or so players would escape but five or more new faces would show up. In the quarterback group I started in the middle of the pack. Nobody in the quarterback group had played the position at Georgia previously. The quarterbacks ahead of me had been on the 1944 team but now played other positions. They were ahead of me because they knew the system. The ones behind me were new faces like myself.

On Saturday we had one practice. It was a full scrimmage starting at 1:00 p.m. and finishing whenever Coach Butts was satisfied, which was always about four or five o'clock p.m. Saturday night and Sunday we were free. I got to see more of Georgia's great campus each weekend.

The first tour was Ag Hill which was mostly occupied at that time by the Navy Pre-Flight School. Most buildings were new and built by the government. The pre-flight athletic department had a field house with locker room space much larger than we were using at Memorial Hall.

The university ROTC had facilities there, also. The ROTC unit was originally a cavalry unit. At one time horses were stabled on Ag Hill. The cavalry mechanized tanks were later parked at the stables. It was fun to see people in the military riding horses along with a couple of tanks rambling over the fields.

On another tour Goot got us a ride out to Coordinate Campus five miles west of main campus. This was where the freshman girls lived and attended class. The rules were very strict for the girls, and, as with the football players, leisure time was welcomed.

The favorite meeting spot was a cafe-bar type place that had booths, a dance floor with jukebox, and food and drink at reasonable prices. The big problem was curfew. I remember the girls had to be in by 9:00 p.m. on weekdays and 12:00 p.m. on weekends. The campus was pretty. The girls were pretty. But the distance from Milledge Annex and the early curfews didn't allow a lot of time for socializing.

Inside Memorial Hall there were the athletic offices, a ballroom, bookstore, swimming pool, two or three locker rooms, training rooms, exercise rooms, and a narrow little room that had wooden benches along the walls. This room had very little lighting. One door opened from the interior of the building. The only other door opened to the north side of Sanford Stadium, a 32,000-seat stadium which didn't have a bad view anywhere.

The stadium was named for Dr. S.V. Sanford, long-time professor and chancellor of the University of

Georgia. It was through his leadership that this historical structure was built. I had never played football in a stadium before. Back in Yeadon, we played on open fields, never more than a hundred people in the bleachers. I was anxious for the opportunity to play in Sanford Stadium.

The most impressive things about it were: the playing area which was a soft, thick mat of grass, and a shoulder high hedge, neatly trimmed, separated the field from the stands. Anybody who played against Georgia knew what is meant by getting caught between the hedges. It was only a few weeks at UGA before I could recite all the big games and all the great players that made history there. Coach Butts had won most of his games between the hedges. I longed to help him win more.

Just west of the stadium was another field, the kind I was used to playing on. The grass was sparse, the surface very hard, and had exposed tire tracks. It was the practice field of the Georgia Bulldogs. It was also a parking lot during events in the stadium or at Stegeman Hall, the huge indoor swimming pool built by the Navy. The stadium, the parking lot (practice field) and Stegeman Hall were all in a valley separating the main campus and south campus.

At the east end of the valley and stadium was a train trestle. During big games a special train would park on the trestle. The passengers had an excellent view of the game.

To the west end of the valley, beyond Stegeman Hall was the main thoroughfare, Lumpkin Street. Across Lumpkin Street was the American Legion Hall and swimming pool. The Saturday night square dances and Sunday afternoon leisure hours at the pool made us forget about our tired, sore muscles. The football players referred to the valley as Death Valley. If the practice didn't kill you, the sprints up the hill to the Memorial Hall locker room would.

A well remembered incident took place at the end of a series of sprints up that hill, during a 1945 practice. Our tongues were hanging out from exhaustion. Some were literally crawling to their lockers.

The equipment manager had made a grave error. He had Donald "Chub" Jenkins and Garland "Bulldog" Williams in lockers next to each other. The lockers were narrow and the space on the bench in front of their lockers even narrower. These were the two largest men on the team. They both possessed aggressive personalities, particularly under miserable practice conditions.

Bulldog said, "Move your fat ass over." Chub said something like, "go take a flying leap." A fist came down on Chub's head. Chub, a southpaw, came up with a left hook from the floor that splattered Bulldog's face. The two stood toe-to-toe alternating smashes to the other. We all moved back. This was like two animals out for the kill.

With an aggressive roar from his throat, Bulldog reached out and put an arm lock around Chub's head. Chub stopped punching, his arms went limp and before long his face was turning a little gray. From out of nowhere came the savior. It was C.T. (Charley Trippi). He shouted for Bulldog to let go and got no response. With a volley of jabs that were as quick as a lightning bolt, CT convinced Bulldog to let go.

Chub dropped to the bench gasping for air. Bulldog stood dazed against the lockers. The rest of us were scared to death. In a minute or so everything calmed down and we went on our way. Nobody got killed, nobody got hurt, nobody mentioned it again. We all just griped about those damned sprints up the hill from Death Valley.

Negative things were building up within me by this time. I wasn't making much progress on the football field. I was pulling D's or F's in all my classes and August 20th was not too far off - draft registration day.

There were fights all the time on the football field and in the dorm. I saw two guys start fighting on the third floor one day. It was like something you would see in a movie. Their fists would flail away at each other. Then they would wrestle a little. They rolled down the stairs to the second floor. More fisticuffs, more wrestling, down another flight of stairs to the lobby.

There was a lot of blood. Shirts were torn to ribbons. One guy went flying through the screen door and landed on the lawn in front of the dorm. The other guy was in hot pursuit. A big crowd had gathered and was cheering them on. Then that loud bell rang and everybody ran for the chow line. The fight was over and the two guys actually sat side by side and ate their dinner. Nobody bothered to find out what they were fighting about.

It became apparent that the dormitory was now 50% Yankees and 50% Confederates.

There were some hard feelings brewing. Eating habits helped smooth the relationship, however. When we were served cornbread and strawberry shortcake we each got one piece on our tray, no more. The Southern boys would put their cornbread into a bowl, and they would pour buttermilk over it till it filled the bowl.

The Yankees thought that tasted like milk of magnesia poured over corn flakes. So a mutual friendship came about. Southern gentlemen traded that delicious strawberry shortcake to us "Damn Yankees" for a piece of cornbread. And they were convinced they were taking advantage of us.

I came to a very significant conclusion. With all my frustrations plus being homesick and missing my girlfriend, Jane, very much, I decided I, too, would sneak off like so many others had. Goot was still in class. It was about 11:00 a.m. and only a handful of players were around the dorm. I hastily put my few possessions in my little suitcase and laid a suit coat over my arm so it could hide the suitcase and nonchalantly walked down the stairs.

Just as I hit the lobby, Coach Carroll Thomas walked past me and said, "Hi, John, where are you going?" I replied, "taking some clothes to the dry cleaners." Mike Castronis, a senior lineman, was sitting in the lobby reading a newspaper. Two or three other players were also in the lobby. My heart was pounding.

Once outside the door I felt I had made it and walked briskly toward the train station at least a couple of miles away. I couldn't call a cab because that would give my escape away. Plus, I had just enough money with me to buy a one-way ticket to Philadelphia.

Circling around the campus and town so I wouldn't run into anybody, I came to a red brick schoolhouse with a short wall in front. I was a little tired, and it was hot. I sat on that wall to rest a couple of minutes.

The train from Atlanta came through at 1:30 p.m. so there was plenty of time. I no sooner sat down when two cars came around the corner with tires screeching. They pulled up in front of me and three coaches got out. It must have looked like cops catching a robber.

They circled me and started firing questions about why I was leaving. I answered them as honestly as I could and they assured me things would get better. All the players would have a week's break between summer and fall quarter. I could go home for a visit at that time, and I was advised I should register for the draft in Athens, asking for a student deferment.

They really poured it on about how well I was progressing on the football field. It did make me feel bad when they told me how hurt and disappointed Coach Butts would be if I left.

Finally, one of them said, "Come on, give it a little more time. Everything will work out great." I am forever indebted to those coaches – Whitworth, Thomas and Ken Keuper.

We drove back to the dorm just in time for that loud bell to ring for lunch. The lobby was crowded and there were all kinds of needling remarks shouted at me as I picked my way through the players.

Later, at practice. I discovered how the coaches found out about my attempted escape. Mike Castronis went to Coach Thomas and asked, "Do you know where John's going?"

Thomas replied, "He's going to the dry cleaners." Mike laughed, "Coach, have you ever seen anybody carry their dry-cleaning in a suitcase." With that Coach Thomas was out the door. I'm grateful to Mike, the informer.

Things did get better. My interest in class improved. The thought of preparing myself to be a teacher and coach was a big incentive. I did register at the Athens draft board and got a student deferment for the fall quarter. I moved up in the quarterback derby. Only because some others managed to escape. A few gave the game up. Goot went back to playing halfback and fullback. We were now down to three quarterbacks and I got more repetitions.

However, more quarterback candidates were on the way. The war was winding down. The military influence on the campus rapidly disappeared. There was a mass enrollment of veterans which more than doubled the student body. Some returning football players made the team stronger. It was sad to see those who failed to make the team because they had given so much of themselves toward winning World War II.

Coach Butts was the most sympathetic to that situation. He was caught in a bind. He was loyal to those who stuck it out during the war years and yet he welcomed the returning vets with open arms. He gave them every opportunity to win back the position they had before leaving for the military. I was very fortunate. I can think of only two returning vets who had played "T" formation quarterback at Georgia before entering the service. Billy Hodges and Ken McCall were quarterbacks on the 1944 team, Coach Butts' first "T" formation team.

Billy was an excellent athlete. He played backup quarterback in 1945, but later he dropped football to concentrate on his studies. Ken moved over to halfback. When two platoon rules came in, he concentrated on defense. He was an excellent safety man and punt and kick-off returner.

As the 1945 season got underway, more veterans were returning. Trippi joined us in time for the fourth game of the season. Unfortunately, it was against a good LSU team, and they laid it on us by a score of 32 to 0. The next week we lost to Alabama 28-14. It took two weeks for Trippi to get the feel of "T" formation football after having played the single wing. It took the rest of the team two weeks to get used to Trippi because he had so much ability. When he saw an offensive opening he took it.

It appeared to many in the stands and press box the team was standing around watching Charley. We were completely sold on his ability, but we were confused as to where he was going. This two week period had to be some of the greatest coaching by Coach Butts and his staff. Butts got Charley and the team on the same page.

Also, in that short period of time he formulated one of college football's most productive and versatile offenses. Together with a strong defense and kicking game, Coach Butts' Bulldogs cruised along to seventeen consecutive victories. Charley Trippi most definitely made the difference.

There really never was a real problem with the North and South players. There was some kidding about Rebels and Yankees. Maybe a few discussions about the Civil War. Those of us from above the Mason Dixon line appreciated the opportunity we had at the University of Georgia. Not many of us were offered a scholarship from a northern school that played big time football.

The players, professors and university employees, along with the people in Athens, and around the state – were extremely hospitable toward us. We were Wally's boys, and that was good enough for them. How could a Yankee not like southerners like Captain Beefy Eaves, Dan Edwards, Sam Bailey, Rabbit Smith, W.L. "Dub" Hiers, to name a few.

They were country boys and you had to appreciate them for being humble, hard working, thoughtful people. It was great to hear them talk. The words seemed to have sweet syrup coming out their mouths. "Y'all come see us, you hear."

Coach Butts moved me up to the starting quarterback position. Suddenly, I was feeling great. The team was developing on schedule. The promised week off came, and I had a chance to go home. I never thought of not returning to Georgia. I had even acquired a taste for southern cooking.

My girlfriend, Jane, was prettier than ever and best of all she was glad to see me. She had another year of high school remaining. We didn't want to make any commitment on our relationship but we did agree to get serious after her graduation. With all these good things happening to me I felt so lucky, my fate was leading me in the right direction.

Off To A Good Start

The 1945 season started minus Captain Charles Beefy Eaves, a fine football player and a finer man. A back injury ended Beefy's career but he was always around to lend moral support. J.P. Miller adequately filled the role of on-the-field captain for the year.

With the war winding down, players were returning and Coach Butts had visions of developing an explosive "T" formation offense. After all, he would get Trippi back and the offense would click. But it didn't fall in place overnight. Quinton Lumpkin, had returned from Navy duty and was responsible for teaching the centers to direct snap the ball five yards deep to the halfbacks. They learned their lessons well. None became as good at making the direct snap as Coach Lumpkin but his teaching and training made our centers more than efficient.

Coach Butts had devised foot positions for the quarterback in order to integrate and disguise the direct snap. It took many hours of painstaking repetitions by the centers and quarterbacks to make this maneuver efficient. Coach Butts' Bulldog tenacity made it work.

With Trippi's return Butts constructed that explosive offense he envisioned. Trippi could pass to any back or end – even the quarterback. The quarterback often lateraled to a back who passed to an end or another back. It was so diverse. But we had to work hard to make it click. We ran plays over and over again.

Whether football is imaginative or boringly simple, you must get in those repetitions. It has to become second nature.

After the 1945 season, I took an Army physical at Fort McPherson in Atlanta. I passed the physical and was on stand-by to be drafted.

Later, I went home for a physical after a notice from my draft board. I didn't tell any of the coaches.

This physical was much more stringent than the one I took at Fort McPherson. At the end of my physical I was called into a doctor's office. He reviewed the results of my examination and said, "You have torn cartilage in your left knee. You also have a heart murmur." He read further and noted that I played football at Georgia. "My advice to you," he said, "is to forget about football. You would be a medical risk in the Army. You are classified 4-F."

My heart sank. I felt like a failure. They processed me out and gave me a cab fare home. I felt rotten but my parents rejoiced after getting over the shock of my quick return. That was a different era.

My dad had a talk with me that night. He advised me to forget about my disappointment with the Army physical, go back to Georgia and get the knee taken care of. As for the heart murmur, they knew I had had that for a long time. In fact my high school doctor wouldn't let me play sports until the 10th grade – and only if I didn't exert myself.

Jane wanted me to return to Georgia, which was very important in my decision. I hung around for a couple of days, wrestling with my decision. My dad gave me money for a train ticket back to Athens.

Back in Athens, after a brief trip home, I picked up where I left off, enrolling for the winter quarter. Then my knee was operated on at Crawford Long Hospital in Atlanta. It was my first time under the knife and not a pleasant experience.

A month after the operation we started a grueling spring practice. The knee didn't bother me. Trippi was playing baseball and didn't participate. With Trippi as our leader we never doubted our ability to win. He was the greatest football player I have ever seen. He excelled in all sports. He played baseball with the Atlanta Crackers after graduation, before playing in the NFL. This was unheard of in that day. As a football player he was the best in all phases: running, passing, catching, punting and defense. He was a complete player.

Many people who saw both of them play try to compare Charley and Frankie Sinkwich. As far as I'm concerned they were both great. Many also compare the 1942 team to the 1946 team. The way I see, it with Trippi and Sinkwich in the same backfield, the 1942 team has to win that argument.

However, the 1946 team has one big distinction – those Bulldogs were the first undefeated, untied team in modern times to represent the University of Georgia. It was also the only undefeated, untied team in the nation in 1946.

The 1946 season was the most memorable of my career. Ours was an unusually good-natured group of athletes. Maybe the returning war veterans made us relax. They were older and more mature. They had more money since they received subsistence from the government to continue their education. I don't know how much they received, but it was a lot more than my ten dollars a month laundry money.

We had some very enterprising players on that team. Trippi would come around to the dorm the middle of the week always in need of tickets. Each player received two tickets for each home game. Most of us young players from far away states didn't have family or friends to give the tickets to. We were happy to sell our tickets.

The tickets were 40-50 yard line seats, but we didn't know, at first, people would give sizable amounts of money for those well located tickets. The enterprising Trippi influenced us to take advantage of the market for our tickets. He taught us a lot about ticket commerce.

My roommate at Milledge Annex that year was Dan Edwards, a very good football player and great friend. We called him Eddards. His enterprise was the whiskey business. Whenever we made an away trip he would take a very large suitcase with him. Since Clarke County was dry, Dan would purchase several bottles of liquor at these visiting cities, and bring it home. He'd stash it away for resale.

Dan would store his purchases in his closet, putting the contents under special lock and key. At dances and fraternity parties, Dan was close by and for a premium he could come up with any kind of beverage the buyer preferred.

However, he lost most of his profit the day after the Tech game, the last game of the regular season in 1946. Training rules were off until further notice and most of the boys were doing some unwinding.

Dan's brother was in town for the game and my father and brother came down from Pennsylvania. Our visitors left Sunday afternoon, and Dan and I went to our room to relax. We were lying on our bunks reading the accounts of Georgia's big 34 to 7 victory over Georgia Tech when about a dozen of our player friends entered the room. They were pretty far gone and wanted us to join their party.

There was one little problem; they had run out of booze, but they were sure their buddy, Eddards, had plenty to donate. When Dan refused to open his closet, half of them held us down while the other half pried the door off of Eddard's whiskey vault.

As they broke open a couple bottles Dan said, "If

they're going to steal my booze we might as well drink with them." We pitched a real humdinger in the dorm that night. Ole Eddards drank a lot of his booze to keep the others from taking it. Around midnight Dan had had it but couldn't get up the stairs to our room.

We carried him up to the room and threw him into the upper bunk. The party was over. The next day I felt very sorry for him. He was hung over, and his business was bankrupt until the next out of town trip.

Coach Butts made great motivational talks to the team but was down in the mouth with the press. He wasn't going to let anything he said end up on the opponent's bulletin board.

One memorable speech I can recall was given before the first game of the season. The first 22 or so players on the team were issued brand new equipment the day before we kicked off. The new equipment was sparkling, from headgear to shoes. We looked great. Everything was tailor made.

We sat in that little ready room in the bowels of Memorial Hall, when Coach Butts began his pep talk. He began with how good the new uniforms looked. But, he shouted, "That doesn't win games; you are the only ones that can do that."

He named each piece of equipment from the helmet to the shoes and even stated how much each piece cost. Then he shouted again, "But, the equipment doesn't have a heart – you are the ones that are supposed to have a heart." He finished up with strong emphasis, noting "we can give you everything in God's creation, but if you want to win a football game you have to pay the price." After a slight pause he bellowed, "If you think you are ready, let's go."

With that, a mass of bodies poured through that little door leading to the stadium. The door was torn from its hinges and trampled on. So was our first opponent, Clemson, by the score of 35-12.

The second game was played in Philadelphia against Temple University. Many of our players came from Pennsylvania and Coach Butts built up that fact to get us motivated. Thousands came from the coal regions of the state to see Charley Trippi and his Pennsylvania teammates.

My girlfriend and three members of my family came to see John Rauch. Coach Butts made a very shrewd move. His starting lineup was all from Pennsylvania. The enormous publicity about Georgia's Pennsylvania players must have charged up the Temple Owls because it was 7-7 at half time. It would have been 13-7 in favor Temple if they hadn't fumbled the ball away at our one-yard line just before the half.

We all were sure Coach Butts would skin us alive for playing so poorly. It turned out just the opposite. The Little Round Man knew when to excite your emotions and when to calm them. He went to several players at half time and quietly made corrections and suggestions. It paid off big. The final score, Georgia 35, Temple 7.

He was truly a genius at handling men. We had tough games against Kentucky and Alabama. The rest of our opponents were never in the ball game. Even so, Weeping Wally never let up on the routine of building up each opponent and playing down his own team.

Bowlmaster Butts had to be disappointed he couldn't take us to the coveted Rose Bowl. The granddaddy of all bowls in Pasadena, Ca. had entered into an agreement to match the Pacific Coast Conference champion against the Big Ten champions. The Bulldogs were happy to accept the Sugar Bowl invitation to play North Carolina since we couldn't play in Pasadena.

While most students at Georgia were home for the holidays, we stayed in Athens and practiced. The weather was cold and wet. Milledge Annex was the only dorm open on campus. As Christmas day neared, the players gathered decorations. First, they came in with a big tree and added the lights, the same type of lights that were displayed on the streets of downtown Athens. We were very proud of our decorated tree.

The dreary weather turned worse. In fact it turned to a sheet of ice. The lights went out. We had to use candles. It was getting very depressing until we were told our evening meal the night before we left for New Orleans, would be at the Georgian Hotel.

To our joyful holiday surprise the townspeople of Athens gave the team a Christmas party. Every player got a gift. It put us in a good mood. My mood was so good that night I went to a telephone booth in the lobby of the hotel and called my girlfriend, Jane. I didn't have much money to pay for this call so I quickly asked her to marry me. She accepted and set the date for the wedding on January 11, 1947. I was floating on air.

We left on our trip to the Sugar Bowl Christmas day. Busses took us to the train station in Atlanta for the ride to New Orleans.

Typically, Coach Butts wanted us to stay in a spartan frame of mind. The game was almost a week away. The French Quarter might be too tempting for his Dogs.

We boarded busses and headed east to Biloxi, Mississippi, a little town on the Gulf of Mexico. At that time there wasn't much in or around Biloxi except an Air Force base, Keesler Field.

This was a perfect set up for Coach Butts and staff to put the finishing touches to his Sugar Bowl game plan. It was all work and no play. The only thing I can remember besides football practice was walking the beach in front of our motel.

The day before the game we bussed back to New Orleans. Our first stop was Tulane Stadium where the Sugar Bowl was played. We had a brief workout.

We expected to see what New Orleans was like. Were we ever so wrong about that! We were treated to a tour of the Tulane University campus that ended at the gymnasium. This would be our headquarters until after the game. Army style cots were set up in rows on the gym floor. The school cafeteria was close by. It might have been the only building open on this campus because everybody was off celebrating the New Year.

After dinner in the cafeteria we retired to the gym, and that's where this mighty Bulldog team stayed until they let us out the next morning for our pre-game meal. The isolation bothered some of the players, but most of us read magazines or books, played cards, or just rested. It had been a tiring week, and who would want to be walking around the French Quarter on New Year's Eve in the cold rain?

The game itself was as exciting as forecast. The North Carolina Tar Heels, coached by Carl Snavely, was well prepared. Each team had a great player with the same given name. North Carolina was led by Charlie Choo-Choo Justice, a 165-pound scat back who could do it all from the single wing tailback position.

Georgia, of course, was led by our great back, Charley Trippi. The players celebrated our 20-10 victory when we were bussed from the stadium to a nice hotel close to the French Quarter. The Sugar Bowl committee put on an elaborate banquet for the two teams. After the banquet, we were free to do whatever we wanted. We deserved the right to celebrate.

My plans were to get home to Yeadon as fast as I could to make sure Jane hadn't changed her mind about our wedding plans. Coach Butts knew I was leaving early the next morning. He told me to call him at his room before I left. The Georgia trainer, Fitz Lutz, had taken his car to New Orleans and was driving to Pennsylvania to visit relatives.

He invited me to make the trip with him. With all the plans in my mind I couldn't let myself celebrate too much. I did see some of the French Quarter, however. The Bulldog players and fans had pretty much taken over all the joints. I felt it was time to go to my room when midnight came. Before leaving I was on stage with Mercedes at Pat O'Brien's bar. She played the piano and I was singing.

Fitz Lutz and I were up and ready to go by 7:30 a.m. the next morning. I called Coach Butts' room as he had requested. The phone rang a long time before his sleepy voice was heard. He told me to join him in his room, where he gave me a short talk against marriage.

Actually, it was more about responsibilities than anything. He said he didn't have time to buy a wedding gift, and he handed me some money. As we walked to the door he said, "Good luck, get back to Athens as soon as you can."

Fitz Lutz had a nice big car. I did most of the driving. We made it to Athens late the night of the first day. The next day we drove the rest of the way to Yeadon. Fitz was a grand person. He was one of the best trainers in the business. It was uncanny how he patched players up and kept them on the field. He was very up-to-date on new medical procedures. He devised protective equipment for injured players like Frank Sinkwich's jaw brace in 1942 and my facemask when I had my cheekbone crushed. More on that later.

C.W. Jones was the team doctor and trainer when I first came to Georgia. Doc Jones had lost a leg but was very active despite his artificial limb. At one time he was a boxer of note. Doc Jones was a gentle man and spoke very softly. His favorite message to players suffering from injury was, "You have to suck 'em up, sonny," meaning if you have any guts keep on going. "You gotta play hurt" is a term, I think, that originated in pro football, but we knew what it meant at Georgia in the forties.

Jonesy gave his favorite advice to me many times. One day at practice I dislocated four fingers on my left hand. While running the ball in a scrimmage I was hit. I bounced off the tackler and ran for a few more yards and went down in a pile. Upon getting up, there was no football in my hand. In fact, it was like there were no fingers on my left hand. They were all laid back to my wrist. It didn't hurt so much but it sure looked ugly.

One of the coaches grabbed me and rushed me over to Doc Jones. He took my wrist with one hand and the laid back fingers with his other hand and said,

"Look the other way, sonny." With that he snapped those four fingers back in place. After he checked for broken bones, he admonished me to "suck 'em up, sonny," and I was back in the scrimmage.

Dr. Marion Hubert returned from service prior to the 1946 season. You could not find a better doctor, person or friend than Dr. Hubert. The combination of Fitz Lutz and Dr. Hubert had to make up the best medical staff any university had at that time.

Neil Alford, from Indiana, served as assistant trainer. He played football at Indiana in the early 1940s, transferring to Georgia soon afterwards. There was some question about his playing eligibility so Coach Butts asked him to stay on to assist the training staff. He eagerly learned from Doc Jones and Fitz Lutz and became a respected trainer as well as a good friend. He went into private business a few years later and was very successful.

Sam Richwine was another player who had questionable eligibility when he returned from service. He, too, joined the training staff. He progressed rapidly and was the head trainer at Georgia for many years.

Jane and her parents, Anna and Chester Livingston, had made all the plans for the wedding before I got home. Relatives and friends packed the Methodist church in Philadelphia for the event. Jane's long time minister conducted the service. After a joyful reception Jane and I were two happy kids riding the train to Athens. Her mother and father upgraded our tickets to a compartment so we could have privacy for our first night of wedded bliss. How thoughtful!

It didn't take long for Jane to fall in love with the University of Georgia and its people. She quickly developed a southern drawl and learned to cook all kinds of southern dishes. To this day we yearn for black-eyed peas, butter beans, yellow squash, turnip greens with barbecued beef and pork. Fried chicken is always welcome. We haven't attempted Brunswick Stew or chicken mull at home, but when friends serve it we like it.

The two of us were very happy and content. Being married and living in Athens and playing football for Georgia was an unforgettable time in our lives.

I was very fortunate to escape any injury that kept me from playing during my four years of eligibility. The closest I came to missing a game was in the middle of the 1946 season. As I returned the kickoff at the start of the second half against Oklahoma A&M, a tackler hit my legs, and I fell forward to the ground as an opponent came down with his knee to the left side of my face.

With no mask for protection, I knew immediately that knee did some damage. It was not an intentional thing, just one of those things that occurs in the heat of battle. When I got back to the huddle, I felt blood running down my face. I asked my teammates what it looked like, and they said it was some skin off my cheek and nose. It didn't hurt that much, and I played the entire second half on offense and defense without any noticeable discomfort.

After the game a trainer applied a disinfectant and powder where the skin was torn. That made my face sting. There was a rule that all players had to meet and eat at the dining hall after a game. I was starting to feel nauseous as I sat down for my meal. The first time I bit down on food the pain was horrible. I quickly left and went to my room. I was really hurting.

My roommate, Dan Edwards, brought Fitz Lutz to the room. Fitz gingerly pressed around my face. He stood up and said, be downstairs in ten minutes, "I'm taking you to Atlanta." He drove as fast as he could to Ponce de Leon Infirmary where the doctors operated on my face early the next morning. The cheekbone was broken close to the nose. The rest of the cheekbone was pushed in from the skull.

Instant swelling prevented it from revealing the actual damage. They performed a new technique that eliminated cutting on my face. Under x-ray observance wires were pushed through my cheek. The wires had tiny hooks that grasped the main part of the cheekbone. By pulling and maneuvering the wires they reset the bone. Except for the break at the nose, it was not a serious injury.

They kept me at Ponce de Leon until Wednesday morning to make sure no infection set in. Upon arrival back to Athens I was taken directly to the field house. My face was messed up by all the missing skin. There was no white in my eyes, just red. My nose was raw meat, which brought on a new nickname from my teammates. Would you believe "Rose Nose?" I had to put up with silly remarks like, "California has its Rose Bowl, we have our Rose Nose." You had to hang loose around these guys.

Already Fitz Lutz had prepared a helmet with a very wide mask attached. The mask was spring steel covered with a thin piece of leather. I had one and a half inches from the front of the helmet to the mask to see through. The mask covered down to the chin. Fitz's work was a masterpiece. I got great protection as well as publicity from that mask. I got a kick out of it when they would print pictures of me in the mask with the caption, "the man in the Iron Mask."

Only one problem. Every time the mask got jarred it would rub on my nose. The raw meat had a hard time healing and "Rose nose" went on for much of the season.

After the Oklahoma A&M game and my stay in the infirmary in Atlanta, I dressed out for Thursday's practice.

Furman was next on our schedule. Coach Butts told me he wasn't planning to play me unless he felt it necessary. I stood around observing for most of the practice. When we came to the teamwork period, Coach Butts told me to go in. Teamwork was like a scrimmage, but the defense wasn't allowed to hit the quarterback. I felt comfortable with the situation, but the first three passes I threw were considerably off the mark. Coach Butts slowly came toward me. He grabbed hold of that facemask and said, "You're not going to lose your guts are you?"

The challenge worked. My passing improved. At the pre-game meal in Greenville, Coach Butts announced the starting lineup. My name wasn't on it. I understood. After the warm-up Furman won the toss and elected to receive. I had always been on the kickoff team, but now I was standing beside Wally on the sideline. As our kicker placed the ball on the tee, Coach Butts looked at me and said, "Get in there." He kept my string of starts alive. We had little trouble winning, 70 to 7.

There are two things to be conscious of when you have reached the top in football: 1) your opponents will work harder to dethrone you and 2) complacency and the turnover of players will weaken the team.

We had a big turnover of players going into the 1947 season. Without Trippi we were without a dependable game breaker, a player who could make the big play when we needed it. We lost a couple men through injury. We also lost some valuable players for breaking Coach Butts' team rules. They were sent packing. The players left over from the 1946 team were not good enough to carry the young players coming up. There was talent on the team, but the transition challenge after 1946 was too great.

Once again, Coach Butts and staff had to adjust. We discarded the direct snap that worked so effectively with Trippi, and rule changes eliminated the quarterback from catching a pass beyond the line of scrimmage.

The total number of players on a team was increased to make room for platoon football. Players could specialize as offensive or defensive players. This gave more people a chance to participate. All the schools had improved their programs because there was more talent available following the end of World War II.

The 1947 team limped through a 7-4-1 season but kept Coach Butts' bowl string in tact. We were invited to play Jim Tatum's Maryland team in the Gator Bowl. The game was a thriller down to the last seconds. With the score tied at 20 points, Georgia was threatening to score but could only reach Maryland's one-yard line when time ran out. I never thought much about that game until Georgia played in the Gator Bowl years later. A sports reporter from Athens called for comments of the January 1, 1948 game.

Rauch, passer extraordinaire

He asked a very sensible question. Why didn't Georgia kick a field goal in the last seconds to win the game? I was at a loss for words. I hurriedly thought, "yes, we had an excellent kicker in Joe Geri." But then he had never kicked a field goal in his Georgia career. In fact nobody ever kicked a field goal while I was at Georgia. To give this reporter an answer I stupidly said, "The coaches didn't call for it."

That was a terrible statement because I was putting the blame on the coaches. If there was any blame for not kicking a field goal it was mine. I called all the plays.

There were no messengers, or signals from the sideline. I had the responsibility of calling the plays. I had the responsibility of running the offense on the field. Geri was in the game. Our regular holder, Ken McCall, was a defensive player and on the sideline. I was the back-up holder, and it frustrates me to think I didn't make the right decision.

A notable incident from the 1947 season was a shellacking we suffered in Lexington, Ky. by Bear Bryant's Wildcats. They tore us apart. I played so poorly that Coach Butts took me out of the game at the end of the third quarter. My teammates and I were not only beaten badly by the Wildcats, we were embarrassed and physically hurt. I had a deep bruise on both thighs. My legs hurt like hell. I could hardly walk.

Defensive linemen were always taught to rush the passer with their hands up in an effort to deflect the football. If they couldn't block the pass, their arms caused vision complications in the passing lanes for the quarterback. Their final effort was to inflict pain on the quarterback by slamming their arms down on his head. Believe me, this maneuver is very effective in making a quarterback ineffective.

Kentucky pass rushers used a different technique. They didn't go for my head, they went for my legs. Every pass I threw that night I was hit by one or two Kentucky linemen in the legs. I had no defense for it. I was a pocket passer in our reorganized offense and couldn't move fast enough to avoid the rush. I thought to myself, is this what they mean by paying the price? Coach Butts regrouped us for our next opponent – Oklahoma A&M at Stillwater. This should have been exciting to me for I had never been further west than the Mississippi River and New Orleans. A damper to this excitement was my hurting legs. I saw very little practice during the week. I spent many hours in the hot tub. Coach Butts announced that he was looking for another quarterback, but I did manage to make the traveling squad.

In those days if you couldn't practice, you didn't play, and if it was an away game, you didn't make the trip. It was an exciting trip indeed. This was the first Georgia team to travel by air. We left from the Athens airport loaded in two DC-3s. This was the workhorse airplane of World War II. The seats were metal plates that pulled down from the side of the plane. We sat facing each other from across the isle. I could envision paratroopers sitting in those seats waiting to jump for battle.

The two workhorses carried us smoothly to Dallas, Texas, where we all boarded one larger airplane and made our way to Stillwater. I was fond of Cowboy movies when I was a kid. So when we arrived at our hotel, I thought we were on the set of a Cowboy film production.

The hotel looked old; the whole town looked old. We didn't see any horses but our hotel had a wood railing on the roof and a wood railing at the front entrance just like the hotels in the movies. The railing at the front entrance was to tie up your horse. It was emotionally fulfilling if you liked old cowboy movies. And I did.

We had a light practice in the stadium. All the players were in a lively mood. They were aware of the pressure to win this one. Coach Butts put me in at quarterback. I ran about five plays and fouled up all five. Coach Butts stopped the practice and shouted, "If you can't play, get off the field." With my head down I slowly walked away to our locker room. I could hear the spirited yells from the team as they returned to work, and I felt so helpless. Clegg Stark met me as I walked in the locker room. He said, "Let me help ya, Mr. John."

He knew I was hurting and he also knew Coach Butts had sent me in. He had seen enough situations like this to know exactly what was taking place.

When I discarded the uniform down to a pair of shorts Clegg said, "On the table." Clegg rubbed both of my legs with hot stuff until they were crimson red, really hurting, burning intensely. When he finished rubbing, he took a folding chair and sat it in the shower. With his huge hands he unscrewed the showerheads of two showers. He then bent the shower nozzles so the streams of water were directed straight to my legs. He turned on the hot water till it was hotter than I could stand. I thought Clegg was going to finish my playing career at Georgia.

By the time the team came in from practice, I was dressing. They knew I felt bad and nobody spoke to me. That night my legs not only ached, they felt scalded. The next morning we went downstairs for a meeting in the ballroom. As I took each step down the stairs I waited for the pain. Surprisingly, there was none. So I walked faster, then faster. Amazingly my legs felt fine.

The ballroom was the exact replica of the bar rooms in cowboy movies, but I had other things to think about. I waited till Coach Butts finished the meeting, and I went to him with the news that my legs felt fine. He remarked softly, but firmly, "I'll think about it." We went for our pre-game meal, which was something else. We had never seen such huge steaks and baked potatoes. Waitresses in old style gowns served us bowls of vegetables and bread. It was like a scene out of the old west.

When we warmed up, Coach Butts stood close by. I could tell he was trying to make a judgment if I was well enough to play. When we came to teamwork, he had me in the lineup. Coach Butts once again saved my starting string, getting a great big assist from Clegg. The Bulldogs had plenty of life that afternoon. We headed back to Athens with a 20-7 victory.

Perhaps, this is a good time to pay tribute to Clegg. No one has accurately pinpointed the exact time of his arrival on the scene. I understand it was during Coach Harry Mehre's head coaching era. Clegg must have been an outstanding athlete in his younger days. His body still showed signs of muscle tone and fluid movement through the 1940s and 1950s. It was said that Clegg was an exceptional baseball pitcher. Good enough to make a name for himself in the black minor leagues and the Caribbean leagues.

Unfortunately, black men like Clegg weren't allowed to play in the lily white big leagues at that time. I've heard stories that Clegg performed with and against the great Satchel Page who was a baseball legend who did make it to the majors late in life. I can attest that Clegg had baseball skills.

Coach Butts allowed me to join the baseball team after two weeks of spring football practice in 1948.

Clegg would pitch batting practice, and he was better than those electric pitching machines that came about. He had perfect control and never seemed to tire – the Lord only knows how old Clegg was in 1947. He loved baseball, but his greatest love was Georgia football and Wally Butts.

Clegg was not paid a large salary by the athletic department. However, he did supplement that salary many fold by greeting and entertaining lettermen at any gathering. It made us feel good to have Clegg remember us by name and recall a story of our time on campus. His stories were more than slightly exaggerated and worth at least a five dollar donation when he finished his review of a player's memorable moment.

With no formal education, I'm sure Clegg never got past grade school. He spoke in the vernacular of the day for those with his background. His grammar may not have been correct, his slang words highlighting every phrase, but his heart was all for Coach Butts and Georgia. What a rapport he had with Coach Butts! We all loved Clegg very much because he loved us.

Clegg and Wally were very close. That was refreshingly obvious. Clegg managed many chores around the Butts house, and I know Coach Butts felt he was an important member of his staff.

In the 1950s the coaches were in the middle of a meeting when Clegg stuck his head in the door one day. He apologized for interrupting and told Coach Butts he had to talk to him immediately.

Wally told him to come in the room and state whatever was important. In front of all the coaches Clegg proceeded to tell about how he was cited for ten traffic violations. Some of his comments were pure comedy. Coach Butts was enjoying this show but kept a stern look on his face. He allowed Clegg to be the center of attention.

Clegg finally summarized, "The po-lice says if I don't pay the fines they'll take my car away. If they does that I won't be able to run all your errands. Let's get together and pays them off."

The entire staff went into hysterics. Clegg and Coach Butts not only were close friends, they were in business together.

When Coach and Winnie Butts were out of town Clegg kept watch on their house. Lawn cutting, dog feeding, trash hauling were but a few of his chores.

The Butts' had a large bar in their basement. This bar was decorated in traditional red and black colors and was perfect for entertaining guests.

A Georgia fan from South Georgia gave Coach Butts an oak keg of moonshine. In those times, that was a libation to be treasured and consumed conservatively. It was also reserved for special occasions. Before leaving on their trip, Coach Butts had opened that keg to give a couple northern guests a sample. This hardly lowered the level of the cherished liquid.

The day after the Butts returned, we were all sitting in the coaches' locker room when Clegg came in. Coach Butts confronted him with, "Clegg did you clean up the bar while I was gone?"

"Yes sir," was his answer. "Did you notice anything wrong with the keg on the bar?" "No, sir," was his reply. "Half the moonshine has disappeared out of it," Coach Butts said with a questioning voice. Cleggs' quick and logical response was, "Well, Coach, you knows how fast that stuff evaporates."

In 1948 more changes surfaced in collegiate sports. Until then rules were generally policed by conference officials. All conferences were flourishing with bigger and better facilities and more athletes. Competition was stronger than ever.

To control programs, rules were set and enforced to regulate off season practice, recruiting and financial aid.

It was an eerie feeling for those who were freshmen in 1945. Over four years we saw a lot of players come and go. We saw a lot of changes in football rules and the style of play. The players had more free time in the spring and summer instead of practicing football year round.

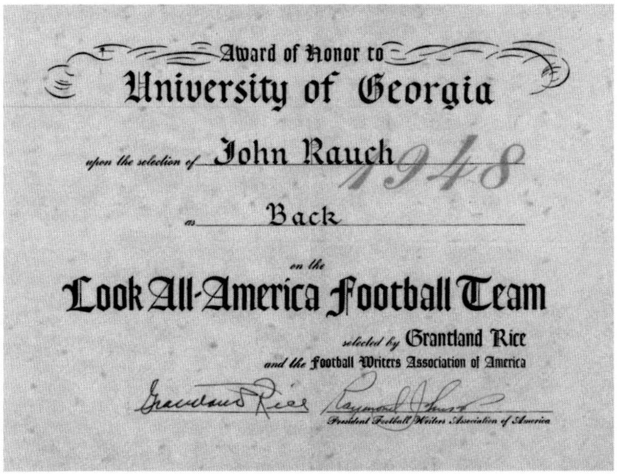
Award of Honor to
University of Georgia
upon the selection of John Rauch 1948
as Back
on the
Look All-America Football Team
selected by Grantland Rice
and the Football Writers Association of America
President Football Writers Association of America

There weren't many of us to survive the entire four years. I can think of a few – John Donaldson, Weyman Sellers, Tommy Pope, Floyd Reid, Jerry Deleski and Hamp Tanner were among those who stayed for the duration.

John Donaldson was earmarked to be the next Georgia All-American but injuries his junior and senior years slowed him down. He did make a noteworthy contribution to the Wally Butts era and later had a very successful high school coaching career in his hometown of Jesup.

Weyman Sellers had four outstanding years with the Bulldogs. He later coached the Athens High Trojans, winning state championships and coach of the year honors. Tommy Pope was small but a very respected guard. He later became a successful in business. Jerry Deleski and Hamp Tanner also joined the high school teaching and coaching ranks upon graduation. I would say at least 75% of the players who played under Coach Butts at this period of time became successful coaches, teachers, or professional football players. They had embraced the concept of paying the price.

Each and everyone would give Coach Butts the credit for molding his life. Those who became coaches used his methods and teaching to become championship high school coaches.

By late summer 1948, we had a collection of outstanding players. We were tuned into Coach Butts' platoon style of football and were ready for action. The result was a 9-1 record, good enough to present Coach Butts with his third SEC championship and sixth bowl team.

This time it was back to Miami and the Orange Bowl, ironically the same site he started Georgia's Bowl fever back in 1941. The lone defeat of the regular season schedule was to North Carolina.

Carolina could match our personnel and go one better. They still had their Charlie from the January 1, 1947 Sugar Bowl game. Charlie Choo Choo Justice was the Tar Heel star who rocketed his team to the number three position in the national polls. He was the icing on the cake that the Bulldogs didn't have. In a hard fought game, the Dogs came out second best. It was close. The score: Carolina 21, Georgia 14.

Without a so-called star player we managed to defeat the other nine opponents. Coach Butts had us working harmoniously. It was a team that shared great respect. Everybody wanted to contribute, to do his part to win a championship.

We could never forget the embarrassment Kentucky laid on us in 1947. There were no vows of revenge, just long silent practices in preparation. Weeping Wally would have sent us packing if we ever gave an opponent a propaganda edge. We never gave out interviews before or after games back then.

The Georgia players were told the Bear was receiving scouting help from Georgia Tech in preparation for the game. The Wildcats came in a day early, not to Athens but to Atlanta, which gave credence to the story. I'm not sure it mattered a hill of beans to us. We just didn't want to end up with another embarrassing score. If

Tech gave help, it didn't prove any advantage: Georgia 35 - Kentucky 12.

The 1948 Alabama game was played in Birmingham. The Crimson Tide had lost the great Harry Gilmer and several other players who were responsible for two of Georgia's defeats in the past three years. However, Alabama wasn't at low tide when it came to personnel. It was another well-coached team, ranked high in national polls, but the Bulldogs dominated as the final score indicated: Georgia 35, Alabama 0.

Alabama had five passes intercepted, one by the Bulldogs Joe Jackura was returned 80 yards for a touchdown. I needed some special assistance in this game. It was the closest I have ever come to being knocked unconscious.

Early in the third quarter I called a screen pass to the right halfback. To execute the screen pass I would first drop back seven yards deep and set up the same as I would to pass downfield. The right halfback would assume a blocking position in the backfield, then after a delay of four counts, release behind the line of scrimmage while the offensive linemen released in front of him. Everything was looking good except I had put the offensive team in the wrong formation.

A big Alabama defensive end was not accounted for in our blocking scheme and came roaring in like a raging bull from my left side. As I turned to the right to throw, the untouched rusher hit me between the shoulder blades, simultaneously bringing both fists to my face. I saw a ball of fire and went to my knees.

Everything seemed to be spinning around. I could hear voices but I wasn't in any shape to communicate. Things cleared up in about thirty seconds, and I managed to stagger off the field. Incidentally, the pass was incomplete.

Ray Prosperi took over at quarterback and played a great game. Buck Bradbury spelled me on defense that day as he did most of the '48 season. We had more than enough talent to compete with the best, and Coach Butts was platooning his talent expertly. It didn't matter who was in the game; we had depth and we could play. The traditional visit to Jacksonville for our matchup with the Florida Gators was next, and Coach Butts was mindful of a possible upset. His team was at full throttle, and he knew we were ripe to be surprised. It was the time for some good old fashion emotion.

We worked hard during the week until Thursday. The practice was light that day and the assistant coaches conducted the practice. Coach Butts was missing and the assistants were not giving out any information about him. We boarded the train for Jacksonville after dinner and arrived the next day around noon. The team bused south of Jacksonville to a plush resort club, Ponte Vedra Inn, where we lunched and afterward dressed in sweat clothes for a light workout on the golf course.

Hundreds of people were there to watch us work. Most of them were Georgia alumni or fans. They all wore bright, expensive, golf attire. I made a vow. "Someday I will belong to a club like this." Later in life I realized that was not so important, but I was quite impressed with the plush amenities at Ponte Vedra.

At the evening meal the assistants told us Coach Butts had been ill. They didn't know how serious his illness was, but he would make every effort to be with us for the game the next day.

If the rest of the players were thinking like me they were thinking we had a problem. We had never gone into a game before without Coach Butts.

We began to adjust mentally to the crisis but were still hopeful he would get well enough to join us. The next day we bused to the stadium, dressed, and warmed up. Still no Wally.

We were all seated on stools in front of our locker. No one moving, complete silence, when the door opened. Coaches Whitworth and Sikes held Coach Butts by his arms and cautiously helped him to the middle of the room.

There was pure emotion flowing from every person in the locker room. Coach Butts in a very weak voice said, "Fellows, I'm thankful to be able to get here for the game but I will not be much help to you in this condition. You have everything it takes to win this game. Do it in true Georgia tradition."

Tears filled most players' eyes and Coach Whit was unshamefully crying. It was very warm inside the stadium, yet Coach Butts wore a long, heavy, winter coat. He also had his traditional felt hat pulled snug to his head. He truly looked like a very sick man. The team sat silently until an overly emotional reserve jumped off his stool and shouted, "Let's beat the hell out of them for Wally."

Before he could say another word a senior next to him gave him a shove that sent him into a locker and then said loudly, "Let's go."

It was a very tough game but the spirit of Wally Butts prevailed, Georgia 20, Florida 12. In the locker room after the game Coach Butts had shed the coat and hat. He happily moved around the locker room shaking hands. That victory must have been a medical miracle, or was it an emotional act that kept us from being upset that day?

There was one game left on the season's schedule and it was a big one. Georgia Tech was having a sensational year by winning its first seven games. The experts predicted Tech would win the SEC title for sure. Some thought they could be national champions. However, the engineers' express ran out of steam in the eighth and ninth games.

For the Bulldogs of 1948 and their platoon of warriors, this game was an opportunity to regain state superiority. Tech had squeezed out a narrow 7-0 victory in 1947 and the Bulldogs were treated like second-rate citizens for the whole year. We also were eager to keep the Bowlmaster's string going. Four bowls in four years would certainly make Coach Butts happy. To say nothing about the countless Bulldog fans over the state.

The game was played in Sanford Stadium, witnessed by more than those who were in possession of a ticket. The train was parked on the trestle and those without seats found standing room somewhere. In some cases, they were hanging from trees outside the stadium.

It was a hard fought game with many unusual plays. The kicking game was instrumental in the outcome. Georgia used its infantry of running backs early in the game to establish a 14-0 lead. Joe Geri, John Tillitski, Floyd "Breezy" Reid, and others were hammering the Techs while captain Bernie Reid, Jack Bush, Howard Johnson, Joe Jackura and Porter Payne were winning the battle up front.

Gene Lorendo, Bobby Walston and Weyman Sellers were catching timely passes and defending the defensive flanks with superiority. But the Tech players wouldn't roll over and quit. Tech's George Matthews broke through to block a punt deep in the Dogs territory and George Broadnax, an outstanding player for the Black and Gold, picked the pigskin up and raced into the end zone to narrow the gap 14-7.

The defenses took control of the game. Georgia's Al Bodine and Gene Chandler were plugging holes and knocking down passes from their linebacker posts. Ken McCall, Buck Bradberry and Spafford Taylor threw a blanket over the secondary. Tech had little success through the air.

The Tech defense had found a way, however, to stop the hard charging Georgia backs in the second half. They shut the door at their own three-yard line to stop a Bulldog drive as the fourth quarter began. The two teams were battling on even terms now.

Then Red and Black lightning struck. Tech punted from its own end zone. It was a lengthy kick that spiraled into the arms of return specialist Ken McCall at the Bulldog 46. Ken gave a couple Charley Trippi type fakes then headed for his right sideline. The wall of blockers had formed.

With a burst of speed Ken utilized his blockers and sped all the way into the end zone. It was a great run enhanced by beautiful blocking. Geri kicked his third extra point of the day and the score read Georgia 21, Tech 7. Tech came back to score a touchdown with five minutes remaining, but the point after was blocked. It was all over. The Dogs ran the clock out and the Georgia alums claimed state superiority, once again, 21-13.

It was a glorious ending for the seniors of 1948. The Bulldogs were SEC champions for the second time in their careers. The Orange Bowl invitation would be their fourth consecutive bowl appearance.

Coach Butts had led his teams to three SEC titles and six bowl appearances in the forties. The Bulldogs had won 36 games, lost 7 and tied one, following the '44 season, a record that would compare favorably to any coach's in the country. To sweeten those statistics, he was 74-21-3 since he started coaching at Georgia in 1939. Even with the war years of 1943 and 1944 he only had one losing season, his first in 1939. Eleven players off his 1948 team went on to play professional football. They joined 25 that already played for pay.

Although Coach Butts and his assistants deserve the credit for Georgia's football success, they always gave credit to the players. We appreciated that.

The season wasn't over, however, for the seniors. The Orange Bowl invitation was immediately accepted after the Tech game. We had a few days off from football and enjoyed the chance to relax. Marriage was the popular thing at that time. About fifteen players on the 1948 squad were married. Most had children or one on the way.

Jane and I had a daughter, Nancy. The married players and wives got along great. There were picnics, school activities and just plain socializing that gave us a common bond.

We took advantage of the University's food processing plant. Groups of us would take to the fields. With supervision from the agricultural staff we gathered corn, tomatoes, squash, beans and other vegetables for our kitchens. We picked peaches, apples, pecans and berries when in season.

The manager of the processing plant instructed us in preparing for canning or freezing our harvest. We stored our frozen foods in freezers, which we rented. It was a lot of work but our families ate well. The manager was a devoted Bulldog fan who assisted us in many ways.

There were all kinds of food being processed at the plant, and we were allowed to purchase the surplus and store that with what we harvested.

Several of us got together and bought a side of beef. The manager had it cut and wrapped, the contents marked and put in our lockers.

The cost of the locker and food was not inexpensive for our budgets and the manager let us run a tab but we were expected to pay it off by the end of the school year.

Through the year I would often go to my locker and find vegetables or meat that I hadn't ordered. I was worried my bill would be so high I'd have to float a loan from the bank. When I told the manager about the mysterious food in my locker, he gave me a story about surplus and leftovers in lockers and for me to go ahead and use whatever is put in my locker – no charge. That was the way the community treated Bulldog football players.

They appreciated us and made us feel warm and welcome. They wanted to help us. Years later I often think about how generous people were toward us. I'll never forget that generosity.

At the end of the school year I estimated I owed the plant around forty dollars. Money was a little scarce at that time, but I scraped up enough and headed to the plant to close out my account.

After cleaning out the locker, I told the manager I wanted to settle my account. He looked at me sheepishly, went over to a file cabinet, leafed through several rows of files and came back with a good story. He said I had paid off my bill a month ago. When I disagreed with him he said, "Look if there is no bill in the file – it's paid, y'all come back and see us, you hear." What hospitality we received!

Henry Rosenthal was the owner of a shoe store in downtown Athens. He was a prominent business leader in the community. He was also a staunch fan of the Bulldogs. Two months after our daughter was born, the two of us passed in front of Mr. Rosenthal's store carrying our baby, Nancy. He saw us and ran out from his store to congratulate us.

After making a fuss over our daughter, he asked us to come into the store. He sat us down and insisted that he put the first pair of shoes on Nancy. He did likewise when our son was born. What a generous and thoughtful man he was. So many people in Athens were generous and considerate. Georgia football was important to the community.

When we began our preparation for the Orange Bowl, Coach Butts thought we had lost too much in the way of conditioning. The first practice was devoted to a long period of wind sprints. He was right about our conditioning, for most of us left our latest meal on the field.

The Orange Bowl committee was having a problem

From left: Rauch as head coach of Oakland Raiders; with Hall of Fame plaque and Coach Vince Dooley; instructing Bulldog quarterbacks as Wally assistant

finding an opponent for us. I don't know why but two or three teams had turned down the bowl opportunity. The press made it sound like nobody wanted to face the mighty Bulldogs.

The Texas Longhorns were 6-3-1 during the regular season. Our only mutual opponent was North Carolina who beat them 34-7. The press pounced on Texas as being a third rate team. The more bad things they said about the Longhorns, the more they set this game up for a burnt orange upset.

Even Weepin' Wally couldn't get them to listen to his worried song. The pre-game activities were magnificent. As a team we were more relaxed than any Georgia bowl team before us. We were even allowed to bring our wives along. This was another first for a Georgia football team.

Everything seemed to be in place for us to take another bowl trophy back to Athens. There was a lively crowd of 60,000 on hand. The Longhorns had just as many supporters in the stands as the Bulldogs. It was a colorful sight to behold. Georgia scored early when Al Bodine intercepted a wayward pass and galloped 73 yards for a touchdown.

The sportswriters stuck out their chests and said, "I told you so." But the Texas Longhorn band cranked up and played, "The Eyes of Texas are Upon You." You could tell Texas was not going to throw in the towel.

The Longhorns responded by rushing over the double strip twice to take a 13-7 lead. Minutes later Joe Geri powered the ball into the end zone and kicked the extra point and Georgia regained the lead 14-13.

But here came that damned Texas band again. They made the speedy Texas backs seem even faster and Texas led at the half 20-14. The third quarter was a defensive battle until the Texans pulled a razzle-dazzle play that completely fooled the Georgia defense.

Longhorn quarterback Paul Campbell dropped back to pass. As he raised his arm like he would throw a pass, Perry Samuels, a small 9.7 sprinter, circled behind the Campbell from his wingback slot and the defense yelled, "Reverse," it appeared to be the old Statue of Liberty play.

The defense went into pursuit, and we were completely fooled when Campbell kept the ball and threw down field to an uncovered Ben Proctor waiting near the goal line. Great execution and the Longhorn band played louder. Score Texas 27 - Georgia 14.

Georgia wasn't finished, however. Our band played loudly, too and inspired Geri to put seven more points on the board, closing the gap to 27-21. Minutes later a Bulldog lineman, Nick Feher, recovered a fumbled punt at the Texas 34. Three plays and the quarterback's pass was on the mark to Bobby Walston in the end zone. Geri's kick was perfect and we regained the lead 28-27. Once again the Texas contingent rose in unison as the Texas fight song blared forth once again.

The Longhorn rushing attack, led by Tom Landry, Billy Pyle, Perry Samuels and Randall Clay made a track meet out of things, running to score: Texas 34 - Georgia 28.

We had one last shot with three minutes left. A holding call penalized us and we couldn't get out of the shadow of our goal line. On fourth and seven from our own 15-yard line I attempted a desperate pass that was broken up by Texas. They hurriedly scored the final points to embarrass us 41 to 28.

It was a big disappointment for our team. More so for Wally Butts who lost his first post-season game. The hardest thing for the seniors to accept was ending our college careers with a loss.

How true the words of Coach Butts sounded forth at this moment.

If you want to win in football, you must pay the price. We had played well but not well enough.

RAUCH'S FINAL THOUGHTS

Not sure, come to think of it, what prompted me to put on paper my thoughts and feelings about Coach Butts and my teammates. I have always wished I had gone up to him late in his life and personally thanked him for including me on the teams of that fabulous era.

Coach Butts was asked to address a joint session of the Georgia Assembly in 1960. It was an unprecedented occasion since no other football coach had ever received such an invitation. Wally spoke from his heart when he told those legislators football is the most democratic game in the world.

It makes no difference where you come from, what your race or religion is — there's only one way to become a good football player, and that is through hard work. There are no short cuts. You have to pay the price to be successful. His choice of words at that session is very meaningful to me. I had many dreams of successful plays, winning games, winning championships, but they were only dreams until I played for Wally.

With him to motivate me, teammates to rely on, and a lot of what I call fortunate fate, I realized my dreams.

CHARLES TRIPPI, Georgia '46
All-SEC LHB 1945-46
All-Pro LHB 1947 with Chicago Cardinals

PART VI

CHARLEY TRIPPI

Worth Four Scholarships Today

Charley Trippi

Trippi Could Have turned Pro In '45

The Sugar Bowl has been the final collegiate game for many Georgia players through the years, most notably Charley Trippi and Herschel Walker.

In the case of Trippi, he stayed on following the '45 Oil Bowl to lead the Bulldogs to the Southeastern Conference Championship in '46 and a 20-10 victory over North Carolina in the '47 Sugar Bowl.

After spending time in the military, Trippi could have signed with a professional team following the Oil Bowl.

A member of both the college and pro football halls of fame, Trippi, following his junior season, could have told his coach he was not returning in '46. Understandably, Butts wanted to make sure there would be no complication with Trippi completing his eligibility for the Bulldogs.

Following the Tech game in '45, Butts announced in an emotional display in the locker room that Trippi would be team captain the next fall. A teammate, John Donaldson, remembers well that scene. "We all appreciated Charley," Donaldson said, "and we were pleased that Coach Butts wanted him to return.

"We knew what Trippi could do, and we wanted him to be with us in 1946. I was his teammate, I respected him, and wanted him to stay. I think most of the team felt that if he came back, we could have a great year and that is exactly what happened."

The Bulldogs went undefeated and were ranked No. 1 in several polls.

Then, Trippi led the Chicago Cardinals to the NFL Championship in 1947. An All-Pro selection, Trippi distinguished himself playing offense and defense for ten years.

In the mid fifties, Trippi returned to Athens from professional football to work as backfield coach for his old friend of many years and former coach.

Trippi and I became friends, much to my great pleasure. I knew his legend. I was aware of his competitive reputation and enjoyed being around him. He was clever and delightfully cynical. He was engaging and disarming.

He often took me on recruiting trips. His invitation went something like this: "Wanna go to Atlanta with me Friday night to see a game? Beer and expense account steak?" Naturally, I enjoyed his company and always thought I could learn something about football with one of the greatest ever to play the game. And that expense account steak was a fulfilling treat, for sure, for a college kid on partial scholarship and pretty much working his way through school.

Trippi has many fine attributes, and those who played with him will tell you that they seldom played with a greater competitor. Once, when I worked with a national television network as a spotter for a Bulldog game, the color analyst was Paul Christman who played with Trippi when they were teammates with the Cardinals. "I've never played with a better back than Trippi," Christman said. "He could do whatever it took. In short yardage situations, nobody was better. When you needed a big play he was your man."

Growing up in Wilkes Barre, Pa., life was a challenge for Trippi and his family. His dad, Joseph, was an anthracite coal miner, and had it not been for football, chances are that Trippi would have taken up employment residency in the mines. He wanted a better life, but he respected men, like his father, who labored for their families.

In his formative years in Pittston, Trippi wore overalls. He had two pair. One for school and one for play. He would have gotten a serious whipping if he had played in his school overalls.

He owned only one pair of shoes which meant that

when he wanted to go out for football, he could not afford to buy cleats for competition. His father told him that the family had no money to buy football shoes. "You got no business playing football," his father said. "You'll get your leg broke. And when you do, I'll break the other one," Trippi recalled.

One day on the school playground Trippi, who had borrowed a football, started booming punts in his street shoes which got the attention of coach Paul Shebby of Pittston High. Shebby immediately invited Trippi to football practice, but Trippi told the coach that he didn't have any shoes. Shebby took care of that, and the next fall Trippi became the team's No. 1 punter.

Charley Trippi didn't take a knee except for the photographer

He was also the starting center except in punt formation although there are many who would suggest Trippi was good enough to snap the ball, run get it, and soar off a punt before the defense could collar him.

In the third game of the season a low snap resulted in Trippi chasing down the errant ball. He then zig-zagged his way for an 80-yard touchdown which put him in the backfield to stay.

A life altering development took place in Trippi's junior year at Pittston. He got to know a former Bulldog football player, Harold "War Eagle" Ketron, who owned the Coca-Cola Bottling Co. in nearby Wilkes Barre. Ketron gave Trippi part time jobs and later sent him to LaSalle Academy on Long Island. At Pittston the college scouts didn't pay Trippi all that much attention, but after a sensational prep career, every recruiter wanted to sign him to a college scholarship.

One of the things Trippi learned from his daddy other than hard work, was to keep his word. When the scouts started coming around, Trippi told them he was not interested for one simple reason: "I had given my word to Mr. Ketron that I would sign with Georgia."

An interesting sidelight developed involving Trippi, Ketron and Coach Butts. In the evenings after a few shooters, Ketron was given to calling Butts and touting Trippi. "Wally, he is the slickest halfback you ever saw," Ketron would say.

One night, Butts, in a light hearted response, said, "Well just how slick is this guy Trippi?" To which Ketron replied, "Wally, he is slicker than owl sh_t in the moonlight." For those who know anything about owls understand that Trippi was, by that description, a very, very slick runner.

Trippi was a remarkable halfback at Georgia, and later in the National Football League. His slick ability to evade tacklers made him one of the most competent runners in college and professional football. On top of that he performed expertly on defense, punting and returning kicks throughout his career. In college football today, it would require four scholarships to do what Trippi did at Georgia.

Making all-conference for Trippi was as easy as brushing his teeth. The only group to pass over him was the Heisman committee, which awarded its trophy to Glenn Davis of Army in Trippi's senior year. You remember the great Army backfield combination of (Doc) Blanchard and Davis? The Heisman voters, predominately Eastern based, and biased, chose to honor Blanchard one year and Davis the next.

"We could have told you what was going to happen on the voting before the season started," Coach Butts once said about the Heisman vote of 1946. Butts, like many others, always regretted the Heisman injustice involving Trippi.

Trippi was a far better runner and defender than Davis. Or anybody else for that matter. When you consider all-around ability, it wasn't even close.

He had the instincts to make defenders miss, but when the situation called for him to lower his shoulder, run through a tackler and leave him in his wake, Trippi could do that, too. And with the best of them.

Additionally, Trippi threw the ball better than most quarterbacks in the country. He returned punts with a flair and style that made him the most dangerous kick returner in college football. He also punted expertly for his team, and he played safety with such a focus and grasp for the position that, to this day, old timers say he was the greatest safety in the history of the Southeastern Conference.

But he experienced the misfortune of playing football in a region where his heroics were primarily chronicled by the provincial southern writers of the day. If the New York press decided you were the best, then you were. If not, forget it.

When asked what he thought he was best at, Trippi said, "Defense." Why?

"Well, I took a lot of pride in playing defense. It is a different type of challenge. I never thought anybody could go by me or complete a pass over me."

Could he be as great today?

"Well, I'm not sure about that, but I think it would be a lot easier. I played both ways in college, and now, with the specialization, I could have devoted all of my energies to one phase of the game, either offense or defense. Playing both ways takes a lot out of you. They don't hit any harder today than back then. You only hit one way, as hard as you could. When you hit someone, you're getting rocked, too, and that defense took its toll on a player who also played offense."

In Trippi's prime with the Cardinals, the legendary Jim Thorpe while watching Trippi play one Sunday, remarked, "Trippi is the greatest football player I have ever seen."

Bobby Dodd, longtime coach at Georgia Tech, said Trippi was the greatest safetyman ever. Dodd further stated that because of Trippi's offensive ability, he was the best all around football player he ever saw.

It was Bill Hartman who suggested to Butts that it would be overwhelming for defenses to put Trippi and Frank Sinkwich in the backfield at the same time.

In late 1942, Hartman, who had been backfield coach prior to military duty, was an officer in the Army Counter Intelligence Corp stationed in Atlanta. This enabled him to scout Georgia Tech, the Bulldogs main opponent, on weekends. He would consult with Coach Butts and the staff and had an occasional opportunity to meet with them.

He recommended to Butts that it would enhance an already explosive offense if the Bulldogs lined up with Frank Sinkwich at fullback and Trippi at tailback. At the start of the season Sinkwich was the starter at tailback and Trippi backed him up.

Hartman reasoned, along with Butts, that Sinkwich was more of an inside threat while Trippi's skills made him dangerously competent at plays to the outside, always a threat to go all the way.

The Maxwell Award goes to Trippi

"We were using the single wing, "Hartman says. With Sinkwich at fullback, he had many productive options with his ability at that position. Harvard, which still had a viable football program nationally, had developed the spin series where their fullback would spin as he went into the line and developed a variety of plays off the spin. We had a number of those plays, and we had a number involving the half spin.

"Sinkwich was a natural at spin plays. With his remarkable quickness, he could explode past the line of scrimmage on traps. He was so good, so explosive on inside plays. Against Tech in '42 he made a half spin and handed off to Trippi going wide and Charley went 80 yards for a touchdown.

"We would have had the two of them in the backfield for the Rose Bowl, but Sinkwich had two sprained ankles and could not play very much."

Sinkwich did get into the game and scored Georgia's only touchdown from the one yard line. It was a big day for Trippi as he rushed 27 times for 115 yards and received the Helms Award as the game's outstanding player. Trippi was later named to the Rose Bowl's all time team at halfback.

After returning to Athens from the pros in 1958, Trippi coached the Bulldog backs until 1963 when he returned to the Cardinals, who had moved to St. Louis, to coach the running backs. There was a lot of controversy surrounding Butts at the time, and Trippi didn't want to be a part of the skirmishing involving his old coach who had given up coaching but had remained as athletic director. So Trippi rejoined his old pro team.

When Trippi left, he knew he would come back to Athens after a few years coaching in the pros. Athens had become home, and he had accumulated considerable interests in real estate.

Trippi always had excellent real estate instincts, and he had money to invest in the fifties and sixties. After his playing career at Georgia had ended, he signed a $100,000 contract with the Cardinals which Georgia Business School Dean, George Benson, said would be worth at least a million dollars today. On top of that, Earl Mann of the Atlanta Crackers, paid Trippi $10,000 to play a season of minor league baseball. After a season with the Crackers, Trippi reported to the Cardinals, and Chicago won the NFL Championship.

In all likelihood, Trippi could have been the first player to make it in the NFL and the big leagues as Deion Sanders and Bo Jackson did later. Those who should know suggest that Trippi was a much better all around athlete than Sanders.

Trippi, who always believed he could have made it in big league baseball, had no interest in playing two sports. "It would not have been fair to either team," he said.

And that is something Trippi always had, something that many Johnny-come-lately superstars, seemed not to have – loyalty to the team.

Trippi never put himself ahead of his team and his teammates.

WHEN TRIPPI MET CHOO-CHOO

For the Georgia football programs, John Stegeman recalled the memorable matchup in the Sugar Bowl between North Carolina's Charlie and Georgia's Charley.

The paths of two great all-time halfbacks crossed when Georgia met North Carolina in the Sugar Bowl on the bleak New Year's Day of 1947. No dazzling heroics developed in the duel between the two stars, but the game itself was as thrilling and as bitter a struggle as the New Orleans classic has ever seen.

Charley Trippi had led Georgia to its second Southeastern Conference championship. He was the All-Everything for the Bulldogs: a quadruple-threat, great runner and punter, fine passer and the best safetyman in the conference.

Four years before he had been voted the outstanding player in the Bulldogs' Rose Bowl victory over U.C.L.A.; then after a stint in the Army, he had crushed Tulsa in Houston's 1946 Oil Bowl game. But the game Captain Trippi wanted most of all was the one coming up, as a victory would give Georgia's its only perfect season in modern football history.

At North Carolina, Coach Carl Snavely had one of his finest squads, champions of the old Southern Conference and losers only to Tennessee. The Tarheels' super-star was a freshman named Charlie Justice, already well known to the football world as "Choo-Choo". Though a bit flamboyant when compared to the quiet, unassuming Trippi, Justice was no brash youngster. Like the Georgia star, he had played football for a service team and was already 22 when his Carolina career began. He was not the passer or defensive star that Trippi was, but once he tucked the ball under his arm there was no better runner anywhere.

When the teams lined up, the day was cold, drizzly, foggy and dark, becoming more so as the game progressed. But for the Georgians, the chill wasn't all due to the weather. The Bulldogs were being stomped, but good. In the second quarter a Trippi pass was intercepted, and Justice and Walt Pupa combined to bring Carolina a 7-0 halftime lead.

When the second half began, the Tarheels drove to the Georgia 34, and the Bulldog fans shuddered in silence. Pupa went back to pass, but Joe Tereshinski, Georgia end, intercepted the ball and passed it off to Dick McPhee. Carolinians maintained for years the "lateral" went forward, and even the staunchest Georgia fans admited it was close. At any rate McPhee ran 56 yards to the Carolina 13, as Georgia followers came to their feet for the first time. The livid Tarheels screamed in futile protest and at the end their fans chased Referee Alvin Bell off the field. But the play stood, and Georgia had its spark. Trippi carried the ball to the one-yard line, and John Rauch, the quarterback, sneaked it over. George Jernigan's extra point tied the score.

Then came the crossing of paths. Justice took the kickoff, broke into the clear, and only one man stood between him and the goal. "I could always fake one man," Justice said later, "and I was sure I had a touchdown. But when I saw it was Trippi my heart sank. No one could fake Charley Trippi . . . He nailed me."

Carolina lost its touchdown but got a field goal, Bob Cox hitting from the 17 to put the Tarheels ahead, 10 to 7. But the lead lasted only 90 seconds.

Two plays after the kickoff, with Georgia at its 34, Trippi shot his famous jump pass to Dan Edwards. The rangy end took the ball only 10 yards over the scrimmage line, short of midfield, and tore off toward the Tarheel goal with the swift Jim Camp in pursuit. Three times Camp seemed to overtake Edwards, only to have the Georgia end change directions to throw him off stride. Finally Camp took a dive at the Bulldogs' heels. Edwards stumbled, regained his footing, and crossed the goal. Georgia was ahead to stay.

Late in the game Trippi and his mates marched 80 yards, Rauch again getting the touchdown, to bring the final score to 20-10. When it was over, Trippi was still on the field, having played 60 minutes. He was tired, wet, dirty and a little peeved at himself for not doing better in his last game. But a happy smile flashed across the muddy face. Charley Trippi's Georgia Bulldogs were the only unbeaten and untied team in the nation.

Trippi's Greatest Play?

The play in "John Stegeman's book" that was the greatest Trippi ever pulled off came against Alabama in Athens in 1946.

"When his quick-kick was blocked by the visiting team, the ball bounced toward Georgia's goal. A number of Tide linemen followed it, anticipating a certain touchdown. But Trippi had turned around and now he outran the Tidesmen to the ball, recovering at his one-yard line. Since it was a third down play, Georgia still had possession. From deep in the end zone, Trippi punted over everyone's heads. It was one of three punts he made from behind his goal, and he averaged fifty-one yards per kick."

Trippi vs. Harry Gilmer

In the 1946 Georgia-Alabama game in Athens, it was Trippi against (Harry) Gilmer, two of the SEC's highly touted players.

Big plays well chronicled in Bulldog history, include:

First quarter, linebacker Dick McPhee intercepted a Gilmer pass, lateralled to John Donaldson who raced 50 yards to the Tide 13 to set up Trippi's scoring pass to Dan Edwards.

Georgia's second score came when Trippi swept right end for 40 yards, tight roping down the sideline to the end zone.

On that play, Dan Magill, made a memorable run, too. Here is his story: "I happened to be holding the chain on the sidelines along with the Alabama chain holder, a distinguished lawyer from Birmingham, the late Borden Burr, a scatback for Alabama in 1893-94. He was past 70 years of age.

"Well, when Trippi ran past me on his touchdown run, I got so excited I pulled up the chain and ran down the sidelines with him, dragging Mr. Burr, who was cussing me from 'Here to Kingdom Come.'

"I really didn't abandon my post because I was still holding on to it. Nevertheless, my deed was perhaps the main reason that the rules were changed so than only a bona fide official, wearing a striped shirt, could hold the chain on the sideline."

Trippi's Rose Bowl Remembrances

In the nineties Charley Trippi sat down with Loran Smith to recall his memories of the Rose Bowl. Following is Charley's story.

All of my dreams came true. In my career there were plenty of honors, and I am grateful, but I am always quick to point out I had a lot of help.

Whatever you achieve in athletics, you realize that without your teammates, it would have not been possible. I played on championship teams in both college and professional football, and when I look back over my career, the thing I appreciate most of all was taking the

Trippi, Theron Sapp and Sinkwich when when Sapp's jersey was retired; Trippi's Hall of Fame Plaque and making remarks when honored by the Rose Bowl

field in the Rose Bowl with more than 90,000 fans cheering. The attendance at the Rose Bowl that day was four times the population of my hometown of Pittston, Pa.

What an opportunity to play in the granddaddy of all bowls! If there were a moment I would like to relive, that is the one I would pick.

We ran the single wing and Frank Sinkwich was a senior in 1942, my sophomore year. As early as the Ole Miss game they had begun talking about playing Frank some at fullback and when they tried it late in the season, we really had an awesome offense.

Frank's quickness was unbelievable. I couldn't have scared anybody at fullback, but Frank's quickness was so devastating, that you could not imagine a more effective inside runner. His inside running opened up the outside lanes for me. His quickness was simply overwhelming.

In all my years of football I think Frank was the quickest off the ball that I ever saw. His acceleration was remarkable.

We stayed three days in California after the game. Movie stars invited us into their homes. At official functions, each player sat between two movie stars. I drew Susan Hayward and Barbara Britton. Errol Flynn, Rita Hayworth and Bob Hope – all the top stars – were our hosts. Through the years I often saw Bob Hope at charity golf tournaments. Without the Rose Bowl, I would have never met celebrities like that.

Sinkwich had come into the game with badly sprained ankles, and he didn't play until very late. I had played for 58 minutes as I recall but when we got in scoring position, Coach Butts sent Frank in. That didn't bother me. In football the object is to win. It doesn't matter who scores the points.

After all, it was Frank who got us to the Rose Bowl. I thought it was great tribute to him, a senior in his final game.

Rauch on Trippi

Charley Trippi – I cannot say enough about Charley's athletic or coaching ability. He was extraordinary to say the least. I have often compared him to superstar Michael Jordan of the NBA Chicago Bulls. No two players I have seen in my life could dominate a sport like Trippi and Jordan.

On the playing field Charley had grace similar to Joe DiMaggio, the New York Yankees baseball legend and a friend of Charley's. Joe and Charley both had that suave Italian appearance which made me think of dignity and respect. They were private men who carried the star label proudly.

Charley's ability to needle his teammates and friends was and is as keen as his football ability. He could dish out those zingers with the best of them. If he came across something funny or unusual about you, he would playfully agitate you with it.
You had to be alert around Charley.

Charley Trippi was a very big influence in my early coaching career. His knowledge of the game and ability to demonstrate any phase of football was instrumental to the maturity and development of the Georgia backfield men during the late 1950s.

He was an outstanding coach but I don't think he aspired to be a head coach. He told me once, "I can make more money standing in front of the Varsity for fifteen minutes than I make from coaching in a month."

He was a wise businessman.

22
65

PART VII

LATE FORTIES

Undefeated, Untied, and Sugar Coated

1946

This was Wallace Butts only undefeated football squad. You would have to go back to 1896 for Georgia's first undefeated team. The coach of that team was the legendary Pop Warner, and the Bulldogs only played four games. The 1920 team, under H. J. Stegeman, lost no games, but was tied by Virginia at Charlottesville, 0-0.

The '46 Dogs finished 11-0 and were declared national champions. The fewest points scored all year were the fourteen against Alabama in which Trippi and Tide great, Harry Gilmer were matched in a much ballyhooed contest. Georgia won 14-0, and Gilmer didn't complete a single pass.

That was the closest encounter of the year, but Georgia was never in any real danger. What a powerhouse team! The celebration ended in New Orleans, where North Carolina was defeated 20-10, Trippi outshining the Tar Heel's heralded Charlie "Choo Choo" Justice. Carolina actually gave Georgia its stiffest test in '46, but Trippi, playing his last game as a Bulldog, was too much for the Tar Heels.

Herb St. John
Send Me a Ticket

Mike Castronis aspired to play football at Florida, and when it didn't work out, he not only became an All-American lineman at Georgia, he influenced another player to turn his affections from the Gators toward Athens. He, too, would earn All America honors.

On a trip home to Jacksonville, Castronis informed Herb St. John he believed that he could influence the coaches to work something out for Herb to try out with the Bulldogs.

"Send me a ticket," St. John replied.

Castronis told Coach Butts who had a ticket at the bus station waiting and St. John in short order was practicing with the Bulldogs in January of 1944.

The decision turned out favorably for both St. John and Georgia. All it took was that bus ticket.

St. John played on three straight bowl teams: the '45 Oil, the '46 Sugar, the '47 Gator.

Florida had indicated that he had a scholarship waiting, but cooled on Herb as he finished high school. St. John thought they had forgotten about him when Castronis arranged that bus trip to Athens. Later on Herb learned that, more than likely, Florida's fading interest had to do with the fact somebody talked to his draft board in Jacksonville and learned that Herb was about to be drafted for military service.

Turns out that St. John became classified 4F, after he had reported to Georgia for football practice. He developed a tailbone infection which resulted from awkwardly fitting hip pads, and while he wasn't seeking to avoid the draft, the examining doctor rejected him for military duty.

Nobody knew it at the time, but the war would be over in little more than a year, and following his freshman year in 1944, St. John would become a mainstay in the Bulldog line for the next three years, which included not only those three bowl teams, but also the SEC championship and national championship team of 1946.

Herb was a big man for his day, weighing 195 his freshman year and muscling up to 215 by his senior season. "I don't think anybody was bigger except for Jack Bush," he recalled. "Can't remember bouncing off too many people until we played Maryland in the Gator Bowl my last year. Physically Maryland was big, very large and tough."

When it came to excellence in the trenches, St. John was one of the best ever at Georgia. The 1947 media guide offered this assessment: "St. John is built like a fireplug and is twice as tough. He has been the bulwark of the Georgia line for the past three years."

You don't make All America if your team doesn't put up headline-producing offensive numbers. Respect from your opponents enhances your reputation, too. Georgia could move the ball and opposing team scout reports suggested that he dominated on offense because it was tough to run his way on defense. That was the era when you played both ways, and teams that excelled were those that could dress out tough, hard nosed linemen like St. John.

"Herb was a quiet type," Charley Trippi remembers. "I used to call him 'Gabby' because he said so little. He led by example. I thought he was small at 5-9, but he was quick and aggressive. Our line was very capable and we got a lot accomplished because of players on our team like Herb."

When his college career ended, Herb played two years of professional football with the Brooklyn Dodgers and Chicago Hornets. Then the Pittsburgh Steelers got his contract, and he retired from football. For one simple reason. "I just didn't want to play in Pittsburgh," he says.

He earned $6,500 playing professional football, and when he retired to begin a lifetime of coaching and teaching, he made $2900 his first year as the head coach at Manchester High. He later was head coach at Perry, where he started football, for 16 years. Certainly, he didn't accumulate wealth in education, but life was rewarding in other respects.

For Herb, there was more to winning games as a coach. "It was the deep satisfaction of being able to help young boys get the most out of their ability, to develop a serious interest in getting an education," Herb says. "Then, when they come back and say thanks, that is the greatest reward there is in being a teacher and coach.

"There is great disappointment when one of them fails to take advantage of opportunity which athletics provides. A coach hurts when he fails with a kid, even if it is not the coach's fault."

THE RABBIT
BEST EVER ON THE DIVE PLAY

Charles H. "Rabbit" Smith wasn't very big. Only 155 pounds. Not a power runner, mind you, but if you perused the statistics after a game (without knowledge of his physical dimensions), you might conclude otherwise.

He was a very productive halfback, and his specialty was quick hitting plays. Like the dive play, the simplest rushing play of all.

Bill Hartman says that Rabbit was the best he ever saw on the dive. "He could hit the hole as well as you could want," Hartman remembered. "He could see the blocking as it developed and could squeeze behind the blocking. He was uncanny at making something big out of a simple dive play.

Rabbit Smith could take a dive with the best

"A lot of time when the dive back gets to the hole, there is a lot of congestion like a traffic jam at a cross roads intersection. Rabbit's instincts enabled him to veer to either side in tight quarters, and a lot of times, when he would slide to the outside, there would be daylight. If I remember correctly, the four touchdowns he scored against Kentucky were all on the dive play."

The records reveal that Rabbit's scores in that game came on jaunts of 86, 61, seven and three yards. "To score on the dive play in short yardage situations expresses just how good Rabbit was. Down close inside the ten, it really gets tight at the line of scrimmage."

Hartman was eager to talk about Rabbit's offensive halfbacking, but was just as generous when he brought up Rabbit's ability on defense.

"He played pass defense well, he was an expert tackler, and I always thought he was a great competitor. Rabbit liked to play, and he enjoyed the competition of football."

At Georgia, Rabbit was Charley Trippi's roommate on the road, but a little known fact was that he was Trippi's teammate in the National Football League.

They played in the College All-Star game in Chicago in 1947 and joined the Chicago Cardinals to win another championship, the NFL title of 1947.

"I was really too small to play in the NFL. I got beat up pretty good and knew that I wouldn't last long up there. I went back to Athens and Coach Butts helped me get into coaching," Rabbit recalled.

"Coach Butts was like a father to me," Rabbit said. "He taught me a lot of leadership principles which I used as a coach. In fact I tried to emulate him as a coach."

JOHNNY GRIFFITH, MEMORABLE RECORD SETTING RUN

Johnny Leonard Griffith was born in Crawfordville, GA, the home of Alexander H. Stephens, vice president of the Confederacy. Johnny's father moved the family to Atlanta when he was a boy.

At Boys' High, Johnny played for a coaching icon, R.L. (Shorty) Doyal, who recognized that Griffith's speed dictated that he be shifted from guard, his original position, to halfback. This turned out to be a wise move. Griffith developed into an outstanding runner with his sprinter's speed. He won the state 100-yard dash and became a star player in football.

Following high school, Griffith spent three years in the U.S. Navy (1943-45), enrolling at Georgia after being discharged.

As a freshman, he was a substitute halfback on Georgia's undefeated, untied team of 1946.

Against Furman that season, Johnny set the Georgia school record for a rushing touchdown – 89

The unbeaten, untied Bulldogs of 1946

yards. That record is yet to be broken, although Tim Worley, Georgia's then sophomore running back, tied it in Jacksonville in 1985.

"That run came late in the game over at Furman," Griffith said of his record dash. "I recall that the play was 48-tear. I was playing right halfback and it was an end run to the left, I got by the defensive end and kept cutting back until I finally broke clean and staggered into the end zone. That was the last score of the day and locked the game up," he once joked.

The final, Georgia 70, Furman 7.

Griffith, who died in 2003, was surprised that the record held up so long, but enjoyed seeing references to the run throughout his life.

Another former Bulldog lineman, Homer Hobbs, then head coach at Furman, hired Griffith as his backfield coach in 1955, but he stayed only one year.

In 1956 Butts asked Johnny to return to Athens as varsity defensive backfield coach and head up the recruiting program. In 1959 and 1960 he was assigned head freshman coach/director of recruiting duties.

As a recruiter, Griffith made many friends working with Georgia people throughout the state, which brought him a lot of support for the head coaching position when Butts retired following the 1960 season.

Johnny's stock rose when it became quite obvious that President O.C. Aderhold and the athletic board preferred to hire someone on the staff, or at least a coach who would not resort to wholesale firing of assistant coaches.

It was not the best of times when Johnny Griffith became Georgia's 19th head coach. Turmoil had intensely clouded the football program, and unfortunately for Johnny, a Georgia man and a good man, Bulldog alumni chose sides. Some supported Johnny, but many clamored for a coaching change.

Yet, Johnny soldiered on. He tried to be nice to everybody, but as many came to realize, he never really had a chance. There was simply too much dissention for anyone to be successful under the circumstances.

In 1962, following a libelous story by the Saturday Evening Post, Coach Butts resigned as athletic director. In December of 1963, President O. C. Aderhold hired Joel Eaves as athletic director, and following the Tech game, Johnny resigned, and Eaves replaced him with Vince Dooley.

You cannot review Johnny Griffith's career without addressing the turmoil which made his task so overwhelming. But too few are aware of his remarkable reaction following his severance from the Bulldog program.

If you went through what Johnny had gone through, would you not be bitter? Certainly most of us would. Johnny Griffith, however, never showed any bitterness. He remained a loyal Georgia man right up on to his death. He recalled his days as coach with fondness for the program and the alumni he knew. Johnny had a lot of friends, and it helped make him a very successful businessman.

I have often told this story, which demonstrates a fine example of Johnny's special qualities. Vince Dooley was hired as head coach, and when he got to town, Johnny took him on a recruiting trip. Griffith introduced the new Bulldog coach to those he felt could be of assistance to the man in charge of Georgia football. Know any other coach who would do that?

Chick Gatewood
Made Choo Choo Go Right

When he came along, not many high school athletes enjoyed a better reputation than Jim "Chicken" Gatewood.

If there were ever a "can't miss" prospect, it was Gatewood, who grew up on a farm near Americus.

Gatewood enrolled in Athens in late summer of 1942 when there was a plethora of tailbacks in camp. In addition to Sinkwich, there were Charley Trippi, Joe Geri, and Ryals Lee, all of whom were capable and talented performers. Sinkwich and Trippi were superstars.

Coach Butts took a number of players to the Rose Bowl even though they were not likely to play. Gatewood was one of them. His future was very bright. But World War II would change everything in Gatewood's football life.

Like many athletes when he returned from the Navy in 1946 Gatewood expected to pick up where he left before the war. Many athletes did not come back successfully from four years of football inactivity. They had lost a step.

That was not Gatewood's problem, however. He was still considered a can't miss prospect. In addition to that, he had distinguished himself with his play in service ball.

At the Naval base in Bainbridge, Md., his team was a powerhouse. He was the left halfback on a team which included the great North Carolina All-American,

Charlie "Choo Choo" Justice. This was the early days of the "T" formation, and coaches generally agreed that you put your best back at left halfback. This meant that Justice had to play right halfback because he couldn't beat Gatewood out for the left half position. Bainbridge didn't lose a game in two years.

A number of professional teams tried to entice Gatewood to forego his college career and sign to play professionally, but he chose to return to Georgia where his luck ran out on him.

In 1946 he was competing with John Donaldson for a starting position when he was hurt in practice one day, suffering an injury that ended his football career.

"The coaches had a rule back then that when you ran a play from scrimmage that you ran until you heard the whistle. After I broke through the line on this particular play and went down field for several yards, I heard the whistle. Naturally, I let up," Gatewood remembered.

"Then the lights went out. I was hit from behind by Bill Chonko who really barreled into me. What we realized later was that Bill had impaired hearing from the war and never heard the whistle. He was sick when I was hurt, but that is the way we played back then – all out. Bill just didn't hear the whistle."

Billy Henderson Wanted to be Like His High School Coach

For years, even after he had seen his 60th birthday, you could always find Billy Henderson jogging down Milledge Avenue in Athens. The long time high school coach was always young at heart, wearing a crew cut long after it had gone out of style.

He was an old fashioned coach who eventually changed his hairstyle. He adjusted successfully to the changing of mores and times. "You had to if you expected to succeed," he said prior to his coaching retirement in 1996.

Henderson is one of the many Wally's Boys who entered the coaching profession, and his record ranks him as one of the most successful coaches in Georgia high school history.

He wanted his players to enjoy their high school experience realizing that only a very small few will ever enter a game in college competition. A much smaller percentage will ever line up in the NFL. In fact, only one high school athlete in 12,000 ever plays a down in the NFL.

That is why high school football is so important, which is why Henderson stayed in the profession for so many years. A person can learn so much during that time in life, when he is playing a sport like football in those formative years.

Coaches, on the high school level, don't make big bucks. They get no huge television contracts. Nobody pays them to wear their shoes and caps. Nobody asks them to endorse anything or make commercials.

Even so, the hours are long, the work a challenge, the headaches many. High school aged kids are too frisky, too full of themselves and multiple and complex problems surface daily. Yet men like Billy Henderson know that coaching is worth it. And that is why he made it his career choice.

Billy Henderson coached like he played—outstanding

Henderson, a two-sport standout for the Bulldogs in the late 1940s, earned a total of eight letters. He was member of the 1946 and 1948 SEC championship football teams and was MVP in baseball. Following graduation, he was drafted and signed by the Chicago Cubs. He spent two years in the Cub organization before embarking on a teaching and coaching career.

Chub Jenkins

After World War II, Chub Jenkins, who knew first hand what it was like to be shot at, came home from the South Pacific and, somewhat by accident, played football at Georgia. That gained him an education, but he didn't consider the experience in Athens as rewarding as playing baseball in the Ogeechee League for Wrightsville for three years.

"I made $125.00 a week and expenses. In 1947 that was good money. Real good," Chub says. A lefthander, he was cleanup hitter for a team that, in its first year, won 40 of 47 games including the playoffs. "We won the fight against Glennville, too," Chub laughs.

A pitcher got upset, the manager got upset, and before you knew it, the fans got into it. "They'd pull a knife on you in a snap. There were some ornery people involved," Chub remembers. "Their players were trying to protect us, but some of the meanest of the lot really came after us. Somebody got smashed over the head with a Coca Cola crate. We were worried about some fool brandishing a pistol. Somehow or other we got out of there alive."

Small towns throughout the country identified passionately with baseball after the war and into the fifties. This was before the televising of baseball proliferated and eventually ruined minor league baseball at that level.

"Everybody in town enjoyed our team," Chub says. "My wife and I rented the upstairs of an old house in the summer, and the local football coach rented it the rest of the year. People couldn't do enough for us. They would bring us vegetables from their garden and were always giving us things. I thought I was in heaven. Born and raised in Atlanta, I really took to the small town of Wrightsville. You knew everybody, and the people were so nice and accommodating. We became good friends with Ralph Jackson, Sr., who owned the team. Life was good with people like him involved."

Before he could finish high school, Chub was off to the Navy in 1943. When he was discharged, he returned to Atlanta and somebody on the staff at Alabama had sent him a bus ticket to Tuscaloosa, the common recruiting practice of that era.

But he never took the trip to the Crimson Tide campus. He was sitting on his front porch one day when Dick Jones, Georgia recruiter, rode by and saw him. Jones stopped, picked him up and drove Chub to Athens, where a funny thing happened on the practice field where he reported immediately.

"You have to remember I had been shot at in the Navy, so when a plane flew over the practice field, I automatically ducked. I was with the linemen and Coach J.B. Whitworth was talking, and when I ducked, he got mad and yelled to me to look him in the eye when he was talking. I didn't like being yelled at after what I had been through, and I told him.

"He said, 'if you had pads on, I'd work you over.' I told him I didn't need any pads. Somebody gave me a helmet and I began scrimmaging in sweat pants right on the spot."

Whitworth was impressed, but Chub soon realized he had gotten off on the wrong foot with the Georgia line coach. "From then on," Chub says, "it wasn't a good relationship. It wasn't bad, but it wasn't good either, if you know what I mean."

He stayed around and lettered on the undefeated SEC championship team of 1946. A bout with tonsillitis kept him sidelined much of the '47 season, and his relationship with Coach Whit didn't improve so he decided to give up football with a year of eligibility remaining.

"I never had a problem with Coach Butts. We always got along," Chub points out. "He really liked baseball and always let me practice baseball after we finished football. A lot of people don't know this, but Coach Butts was the best batting practice pitcher I ever saw.

"When the Braves came to Atlanta, he used to call me and we would go to games together. I always appreciated his friendship. He was good to me."

With a degree in education, Chub taught and coached until retirement. One of his fond memories was driving to New Orleans in 1996 for a reunion of the Sugar Bowl teams of '46, Georgia and North Carolina.

"I played behind Jack Bush, so I didn't play all that much," Chub says. "But I remember the Sugar Bowl with so much appreciation. I just didn't think somebody my age who had been through a war could have that nice of an experience. When I drove down for the reunion and saw my old teammates again, it warmed my heart and made me appreciate Georgia and the education the University gave me."

After waxing sentimental, he grinned and began reminiscing further about his long ago life in the Ogeechee League.

"Boy, I'd like to go back to those times," he says. "People didn't have that much, but they enjoyed what they had."

1947

With so many outstanding players departing after the undefeated and national championship season of '46, it was a rebuilding year in 1947. Even so, the Bulldogs finished 7-4-1 and made it to another bowl, the Gator Bowl in Jacksonville. Georgia and Maryland played to a 20-20 tie, with the Bulldogs poised to score the winning touchdown at the Terrapins' goal line when time ran out. One more play and victory would likely have been notched. Not counting the war years, Georgia had been invited to five straight holiday bowl games. Coach Butts became known as the bowlmaster.

The lack of offensive production in close games was the Bulldogs' downfall in '47. In the four losses, the Bulldogs scored only 14 points total.

Rebuilding

In the spring of 1947 the atmosphere was tentative, to say the least, as it related to Bulldog football. Georgia had some talent, some capable players returning like John Rauch, Dan Edwards, Jack Bush, Joe Geri and John Donaldson.

But Charley Trippi was gone. Everybody knew it was to be a rebuilding year. But the Bulldogs lost two games by a touchdown (North Carolina in Chapel Hill 14-7, Choo Choo Justice and the Tar Heels getting revenge for the Sugar Bowl defeat), and to Georgia Tech in Atlanta 7-0.

Alabama won 17-7 in Athens and Kentucky 26-0 in Lexington. That was hard for Butts to take, being shut out twice and only scoring a single touchdown against North Carolina and Alabama. He was accustomed to more offense than that.

Had John Donaldson been healthy, it would have made a big difference since he was counted on to take Trippi's place.

A pulled hamstring followed by calcium deposit buildup didn't keep the swift South Georgian out of the lineup completely, but he was never at full strength.

"He could have really helped us if he had been well," John Rauch remembers. "John was versatile; he could catch the ball, and he had that all important speed, the kinds of assets you need in the backfield. John was a do it all type player who had talent similar to Charley Trippi."

A healthy Donaldson might have meant there would have been more touchdowns scored that year, and that could have elevated the Bulldog's status.

He could have complimented the play of Joe Geri, a player of exceptional skills also.

Nonetheless, Wally's Boys were invited to the Gator Bowl in Jacksonville and were on the Maryland goal line when time expired. One more play and that game would likely have gone Georgia's way. As it was, the fifth bowl invitation for Wallace Butts ended in a disappointing 20-20 tie.

If you are truly rebuilding, however, then something good should be coming your way. In 1948, the chapel bell would ring nine times. Another championship was in the making.

Dan Edwards

From Gatesville, Texas, to Athens, Georgia, the distance is 924 miles, which makes one wonder how distant it must have seemed to a young boy in 1944 with a world at war and his only means of travel being by bus.

"Or thumb," laughed Dan Edwards, who was not the least bit concerned that he had to negotiate all those miles for a free education; a degree did not come without a price – grueling year-round practices with the Georgia football team.

My conversation with him took place at his oil jobber's office in Gatesville, Tx. in the mid eighties.

His decision to play football for Georgia was easy, however. Edwards was the last of six children whose parents had experienced the hard life, eking out a living by working long hours at low-paying jobs, allocating household duties and chores in the so-called free time in their daily lives.

"I saw opportunity," the former Bulldog All-America end said when I looked him up in the spring of 1993. "Besides, no school in this area had anything much to do with me except Texas A&M, and I was not interested in their mandatory military program."

An interesting story, however, reveals that Edwards might never have enrolled in Athens had it not been for military influence. A former Bulldog player, Lee McKinney, was stationed at nearby Fort Hood. McKinney thought Edwards a good prospect and sent word to Coach Butts who forwarded a bus ticket to Edwards for a recruiting visit solely on McKinney's recommendation.

What influenced Edwards as much as anything was that McKinney gave him a pair of military shoes from the Fort Hood PX. Times were so hard that a pair of shoes to Dan Edwards was an overwhelming gift. "I couldn't believe it," he says. "Nobody had shoes like that, and I'll never forget how I felt about Lee's generosity."

When Edwards got to Athens, where the days were long, the Spartan practices seemingly endless and many football players considering alternatives by the day, he was a perfect fit. He had grown up so tough that he found the practices to be only an extension of what he was accustomed to. But there was a joyous benefit for all that practice field labor. Edwards was the recipient of three square meals a day and a free education. To him, those demanding practices were a breeze.

Edwards played on three bowl teams, including the 1946 undefeated squad which was proclaimed National Champion by the Williamson rating system. He was captain of the 1947 team which tied Maryland in the Gator Bowl, 20-20, and was drafted No. 1 by the Steelers, which led to a nine-year professional career in the NFL and the Canadian Football League.

Bill Hartman considers Edwards one of the two most underrated ends in Bulldog history, the other being Van Davis.

Edwards' career was characterized by big plays. The one for which he is best remembered occurred in the 1947 Sugar Bowl. He caught a 67-yard touchdown pass from Charley Trippi.

In 1950 with the New York Yanks, Edwards caught 52 passes for 775 yards and six touchdowns. Those are

Captain Dan Edwards takes a pass downfield

big time numbers. He was a star in the first Pro Bowl game, played in Los Angeles.

He looked back on his football life as a pleasant experience, but with no inclination to live in the past. Perhaps his attitude can be expressed by the fact that his parents were not impressed when he made All-American.

"It was no big deal to them," he said. "But going to college and getting a degree! That was a very big deal to them."

George Ford

George Ford, fullback from Lowell, Mass, was another football prospect to arrive at UGA in an unusual way. He was recommended to Coach Butts by Coach Frank Leahy of Notre Dame.

Ford arrived in Athens, Ga. via a train ticket supplied by the same Coca-Cola representative who gave me a ticket to visit the Classic City. George was so talented he couldn't decide what direction he should go after graduating from Lowell High School. He first entered Notre Dame. In short time he didn't feel like he fit in at South Bend and returned to the family turkey farm near Lowell. He later applied to the Naval Academy in 1944 and was sent to the Navy prep school at William & Mary.

Then military duty came about. As the war was winding down, he was assigned to a destroyer as a repairman. He sailed around the world, being assigned to an escort ship of the USS Missouri at the time the Japan armistice was signed. After his discharge from the Navy in January 1946 he went to work at the Coca-Cola plant in Lowell, and hence the train ticket to Athens.

George Ford made a big impression on everyone the first time he set foot on the football field. Coach Butts knew he'd be outstanding based on Coach Leahy's recommendation. At 220 lbs. and built like a bull, he ran over people like a bowling ball knocks down pins. He wasn't very maneuverable; he just ran over any opponent who got in the way. He had one speed — all out all the time.

If he had a weakness, it might have been alerting the opponents when he had the football. Every time he carried the ball, he would make a shrill sound, like a locomotive letting off steam. George had the ability to be a star football player, and with that, he also was a fun guy, which happened to lead him to misfortune.

During a break from studies in 1947 George was involved in a very serious automobile accident involving alcohol. He was close to death, but his strong will and physical strength helped him survive. He graduated from UGA and gave 20 years to teaching and coaching at the high school level. He counseled young people to avoid the misfortune that can destroy their dreams. Although he was not driving when the accident happened, George, nonetheless, felt his good fortune in surviving warranted his encouraging young people to refrain from drinking and driving.

Upon retiring from teaching and coaching George was elected city councilman in Powder Springs, Ga. – J.R.

Bob Greer

Bob Greer thought he was doing well in practice in 1948. He had been elected captain of the '47 freshman team, and in addition to giving a good account of himself in fall scrimmages, some of the guards had gone down with injuries. He saw opportunity.

The coaching staff considered holding him out, but he let it be known that he preferred to play. The first road game was against L.S.U. in Baton Rouge, and when the travel list was posted, his name was not on it. He was livid, his emotions were fractured, and his pout was intense.

His roommate, Wilbur Newman, told him he was leaving Georgia. He was going to enroll at South Carolina. Greer knew deep down he didn't want to leave Georgia, but in his depressed state, he said, "I'm going with you."

When he left the dormitory, his fate was decided in favor of the Bulldogs. He bumped into Coach Quinton Lumpkin, who asked him where he was headed. "I'm going to South Carolina with Wilbur," Greer said.

Lumpkin looked at him with steely eyes. "You aren't going anywhere," the Bulldog assistant coach said. With that, he gave the troubled lineman a ten dollar bill and told him to go to a movie and settle down. The ten dollars was nice. It meant that he would enjoy a good meal, which was a big thing in those days, after the movie. But he was still mad and burning as the silver screen came to life. It wasn't long before a card flashed up down front, saying, "Bob Greer report to the Field House immediately."

He didn't know what to expect, but felt there was an appeasement session awaiting him. When he got outside, a cab driver signaled for him to get in. "Bob they are waiting on you, they are taking you on the trip to LSU."

Without a toothbrush or a change of clothes, he was hustled to the airport and flew with the team to the LSU game. The Bulldogs stayed in New Orleans, and when they arrived at the hotel, trainer Sam Richwine, told him that Coach Butts wanted him to go buy some clothes.

"I bought a suit, and that excited me," he says. "When I went to Georgia I didn't even own a suit of clothes. That made me feel good."

When the team took the field for warm-ups, Greer still had no indication of what was to come. He still thought he was along for the ride. He would enjoy himself, but did not expect to play into the game. "When Coach Whitworth started giving me hell, it dawned on me that I would be starting the game." From a pout at the movie to Tiger Stadium in Baton Rouge, La.—Bob Greer was suddenly into Southeastern Conference football competition.

It wasn't a memorable start. "I was fired up, I was going to take the head off the guy lined up in front of me. When I blasted across the line, he sidestepped me and I felt like a fool. I got up and went back into the huddle and John Rauch simply said, 'Block him.' John called the same play, and I took a step back to let the LSU lineman make the first move. I unloaded on him, hit him right in the mouth. Then I settled down and played football. Did okay from that point on and played a lot of football for Coach Butts after that.

"For the rest of my life, I have been grateful to Coach Lumpkin. If I hadn't bumped into him, I would have left Athens, which would have been bad. I never wanted to go anywhere but Georgia. I visited other schools like Florida and Auburn, but I was just having fun. I knew where I was going to enroll."

Taking advanced ROTC ("for the money"), he spent two years as an officer in Japan ("up North where it snowed for months") and returned home to coach after he was discharged from military service.

He had a great run at Southwest High in Atlanta, taking over a program which won only a single game in two years. He lost his first five games and tied the next three before winning his first. "After we won the first game, we were off and running," he says. "We won the region championship almost every year and played for the state championship one year."

In recent years, he has remained an avid Bulldog football fan, holding season tickets and often travels to out-of-town games. "I'll always love and enjoy Georgia football," he says.

MORE WALLY LORE

Gene Chandler – A four year letterman from 1946-49, Chandler was an end in the Van Davis tradition—hard nosed, fundamentally sound and physically competent to the extent that he usually left crumpled bodies in his wake.

"I remember that he came to us as a center," Bill Hartman says, and he was an outstanding end for us. He was a tough player, and very sound fundamentally. Physically, he was what you look for in a player. He could block and he was a superior tackler on defense. The thing that I recall most about him was that on punt returns, he could take out that first man down on the kicking team."

Homer Hobbs (46-47-48) – Hartman remembers recruiting him, a big country boy from South Carolina. When he paid a visit to the Hobbs home, Homer was out back and his mother called for him in a distinct Southern drawl, "'Hoomeerrr,' come heah." It turned out that Homer Hobbs was typical of so many country boys who went to college and bettered themselves.

What happened to him in football took place often. He showed up as a fullback, but found a home in the offensive line. He didn't quite have the speed for the level of competition at Georgia, but at guard, it was different—he was very quick and fast for a lineman.

Hartman was acutely aware of the practice of moving big, strong backs to the line. It could have happened to him. When he came to Georgia, he competed with Pete Tinsley for the fullback position. He was a step faster than Tinsley who became an outstanding guard for Harry Mehre.

Buck Bradberry, an Athens boy, played at Georgia (letterman 44-48), but spent his life coaching and working at Auburn. As a player Bill Hartman remembers him for his tenacity and courage on defense where he performed best. Hartman also recalls the Orange Bowl game with the lamentable irony of Buck standing on the sideline at a crucial juncture. "I recall that Texas had a third down and about 13 situation and lined up in short punt formation which was a formation often used at that time. Tom Landry got the ball and threw a pass for a completion and Texas drove on in to score late in the game. On the sideline, I was trying to get Buck into the game on defense. If he had been in there I am sure the pass would not have been completed and that would have stopped the drive. With Buck in the game, we might have won the Orange Bowl."

Reid Moseley (letterman 43-46) was a sure handed receiver. Hartman's scouting report on the Huntsville, Al. native, who, interestingly, lettered in tennis: "Elusive, he could always get open. He had great hands, he could jump and if he were playing today he would be what they refer to as a 'go to' receiver. He wasn't very big which meant that we couldn't rely on him to consistently block the tackle. We had to use him selectively. He was effective enough that he made our short passing game work. If we got the ball to him, you could rely on him catching it."

Pat Field (lettered 48, 49, 50) was caught in the unfortunate rules changes of the fifties. An outstanding punter, he couldn't be inserted into the lineup just to kick. "When we got him in the game," Hartman says, "he could do the job as a punter."

John Tillitski (lettered 48, 49, 50) only lacked one thing as a football player and that was speed. "Nobody gave greater effort," Hartman says. "He was adequate on defense and he was a hard runner. We always felt he was dependable and productive. If determination and effort would get the job done, then John could always be counted on. He tried hard and when a player has that character on the field, coaches try to understand what he can do and utilize him based on what he can contribute to the team."

Bobby Walston (lettered 47-50) was an athlete with remarkable skills and competency. An agile receiver, he could make the big play and often did. An indication of his exceptional talent is that he played safety on defense. "He played it well, too," Hartman says. "And that was because he was such a fine athlete." In addition, Walston could kick field goals and extra points. When he became a receiver for the Philadelphia Eagles, he was also the team placement kicker and at one point was the NFL career leader in scoring. Hartman remembers an incident, when line coach J. B. Whitworth in a fit of rage kicked a coal bucket in the locker room, thinking it was empty. It was not and he almost broke his toe. Walston thought that was funny. Whitworth didn't. Walston further raised the line coach's ire, when he remarked: "When we get on the goal line, we ought to put Coach Whit in, he's ready."

J. P. Miller (lettered 1941-42, 45). He was alternate captain in 1945, a steady reliable and well respected guard. "I remember him as a very hard worker," Bill Hartman says.

Sam Richwine came to Georgia as a lineman in 1942, practicing with the Rose Bowl squad, but he did not make the trip to California. Soon he was off to war, like everybody else, returning to try football again in 1946, but his body was not up to it. "I spent three years on the USS Colorado, and that's not a good way to keep your athletic skills from deteriorating," he says.

Football was not over for him, however. In 1947 he became a member of the team's training staff. When he became head trainer, he started out with little more than adhesive tape, a whirlpool and analgesic balm.

A sign hung above the whirlpool: "You can't make the club in the tub," apropos for the tough minded Wallace Butts. "They talk about playing hurt today," Sam says, his voice trailing off and punctuated by a hard laugh. "Back then, if your leg wasn't broken, you had better find a way to get on the field."

He had a pleasant disposition, monitoring activity of the athletes in Payne Hall where he lived with his wife, Doris, and three sons, Sammy, David and Joe.

When the players filed into the dining room for breakfast, Sam was always there, reading the morning paper and kibitzing with the players. Good natured banter was a staple of his personality, and the players always enjoyed the fun loving Richwine.

Who was the toughest player he ever "doctored"? "Well it would be hard to find one tougher than Theron Sapp. Anybody who can play after breaking his neck, really is tough. But I tell you one who you couldn't keep off the practice field or out of a game was Ed Greenway. It didn't matter how bad he was beat up, he would somehow or other be out there when the whistle blew."

When he left Georgia in 1963, he went into business but wound up as a vocational rehab counselor for the state correctional institute for boys at Alto, anchoring in retirement in Cornelia.

His Alto experience, working with wayward boys, he says, tongue-in-cheek, was not a challenge. "I had good training from living in Payne Hall," he laughs.

1948

Let the good times roll. This team claimed a third SEC title for Coach Butts. Only North Carolina took the measure of the Dogs with a 21-14 thriller in Athens.

Georgia opened with a 14-7 victory versus Chattanooga, scored only 14 points when the Tar Heels came to town the next week, but from that point on, the 'Dogs averaged nearly 27 points per game and dominated all opponents—although the final game with Georgia Tech in Athens was a nail biter.

It took a punt return of 54 yards by Ken McCall, a swift, fluid and classic broken field classic run, to defeat Tech 21-13 in Athens. It was back to the Orange Bowl but disappointment prevailed; underdog Texas blindsiding the Bulldogs, 41-28.

Georgia was such a heavy favorite that the sportswriters kept calling Texas a third rate team. That got under the Longhorns' skin, and they took psychological advantage.

John Donaldson, Outside Runner, Outdoor Aficionado

Few athletes, perhaps none, have obeyed the rules better than John Donaldson, who wore the greatness-to-be label until a pulled hamstring sidelined him.

John always lived the clean life, forever disdaining alcohol and tobacco and choosing a healthy diet. Even if there had been no team training rules set forth, that still would have been his choice.

It was that way when he played, earning four letters under Butts; it was the same as a coach, both in high school and college. When he finally retired to his hometown of Jesup, his lifestyle never changed.

Donaldson had speed, and he could run and catch. Throw the halfback pass, too, if needed. Much of his college career was hampered, however, by the hamstring complications which sidelined him late in the championship year of 1946.

On one of the many fishing outings I had with Donaldson, he recalled his college career with one, and only one, regret. The fact that he was not at full strength.

A pulled hamstring is something which can require extended time to heal. Even today, with new and advanced medical treatment and training procedures, a pulled hamstring can sideline an athlete indefinitely. The injury ruined the last half of Donaldson's sophomore year, pretty much all of 1947, and in his senior season, the championship year of 1948, he remained handicapped.

After a while, calcium deposits formed. It was disappointing, debilitating and plagued him right on into professional football with the Los Angeles Dons. The muscle's enervating condition actually forced him to give up the game.

Yet he finds nothing to complain about. "I had a good career, playing on two championship teams and four straight bowl games. Naturally, I would like to have played at full speed, but that didn't work out. When that happens, all you can do is try to make the best of it," Donaldson says.

He was leading the conference in scoring in 1946 but Charley Trippi overtook him with four TDs in the final game with Georgia Tech.

Donaldson remembers exactly how the pulled muscle took place. Because of his speed, Butts put in a reverse, sure to trap unsuspecting opponents. With Donaldson flared out wide to the right, Trippi would sweep in Donaldson's direction with the ball. All defensive eyes were always on Trippi. He was a ball carrier who attracted a lot of attention.

When Trippi got to the corner, he would hand off to Donaldson coming back the other way on a deep reverse. It would fool a lot of defenses. In practice one day when Donaldson geared up to top speed on the reverse – he always went all out in practice – the muscle

John Donaldson, quick on his feet, quicker at setting the hook

popped. He heard it and he knew what had happened.

The hamstring is one in which virtual immobility results when it loses its elasticity. Tie a knot in a broken rubber band and you gain something of an appreciation for what an athlete deals with when a severe hamstring pull takes place.

Donaldson realized he would be sidelined but never dreamed it would be so difficult to return to the lineup. He was the shell of his old self by the time of the Sugar Bowl, and will always be grateful for Coach Butts' consideration to let him play in the game.

"It was late, and there wasn't much I could do for the team. I had taken a shot of Novocain and they bandaged my thigh. But I still hobbled on the field. Coach Butts wanted me to get in the game for a few plays, and I'll always be grateful to him. Trippi played great, we won, and I was a member of a bowl championship team. I appreciated that."

Donaldson grew up a Georgia fan and always wanted to play for the Bulldogs. Frank Sinkwich was his hero, and when he told Coach Butts he would sign with Georgia (following his Navy stint), it was a decision that could be taken to the bank.

Other schools, nonetheless, persisted and tried to sign him. Don Faurot, the founder of the Split T offense and for whom Donaldson played with the Jacksonville Naval Air Station, offered him a scholarship to Missouri. The United States Military Academy at Anapolis sent an admiral to make a pitch. The Philadelphia Eagles drew up a contract for $12,000.

None of that mattered. He had given his word to Coach Butts and Athens is where he would continue football.

Following his campus days and a brief period with the Los Angeles Dons of professional football, Donaldson became a successful high school coach, winning state championships at Jesup in 1954 and 1959.

Throughout his life, Donaldson has been an outdoor advocate. He spends much of his time on the inter-coastal waters and marshes of Georgia's coast. Early in life, he identified passionately with the outdoors. He longed to fish, even being attracted to an assistant's position under Ray Graves at Florida because of bass fishing opportunities near Gainesville.

College coaching appealed to him, but he really didn't like working against his alma mater, which he had to do not only in Jacksonville each November, but in recruiting south Georgia.

Donaldson would have preferred to have been in Athens, and when Vince Dooley gave him an opportunity to return in 1964, it was "like manna falling from heaven."

While at Georgia, as a coach, Donaldson spent his holidays and down time with a rod and reel.

With the productive fishing grounds of Shellman Bluff, less than an hour from Jesup, Donaldson grew up fishing on the coast and later built a second home right on the marsh. His freezer has always been stocked with a variety of fish, and right on into his late retirement years, you could find him eager to cast for trout and spot tail bass, which are prevalent in the area.

"I love to breathe the salt air," Donaldson would say when he got out on the water. He believes salt air is healthy.

Fortunately, I have often been invited to fish with Jesup John. I don't think I can ever remember, unless the conditions were absolutely unfavorable, that we didn't come home with a cooler of fish or our limit of marsh hen in hunting season.

Here is what I once wrote for the Athens Banner Herald on a trip down to the coast to fish with him:

For one eager fisherman it is a four-hour drive from Athens, maybe a little more, to the coastal village of Shellman Bluff where you don't have to lock your doors at night. Radio is a nice companion on a trip like this, but sometimes it is better to travel with your thoughts, thinking about life and the past. Ponder those questions which float into your mind when you are caught up in vehicular solitude.

It's suppertime when you arrive at Shellman Bluff where John and Anne Donaldson have prepared a low country boil, to be accompanied by fresh crab which await steaming.

This is a couple retired from a lifetime in education. He was a long time coach in Jesup, plus a couple of college stops, and she taught art. Pace has always been important to them. Outdoor living has been given the highest priority.

They fish together, they shrimp together. His art is in the understanding of the marshlands and the factors which determine when the fish bite and where. Casting is also art with him.

He painted an unforgettable picture one memorable autumn day. High tides and muddy waters were not the most favorable time to fish, but nothing ventured, nothing gained often motivates him to try his luck, even when conditions suggest it is not likely to be productive.

"Let's cast a couple of times along the beach here," he said, as it was time to head home, after a half day of trying our luck. "Water's clearing up, you never know," he smiled.

Soon he was watching line spin off his reel, having hooked something too big and strong for his lightweight equipment. A 26-pound spot tail bass had taken his bait and only finesse would bring the quarry home. Power and force would lose this battle. Tiring out his prey, with the velvet touch, gained him the catch of the fall.

I had just seen man and nature in perfect harmony, but the story is not over. There will be another day when I'll make that drive down through those small towns again. I will sit down to a stuffed bass supper in which Anne's cooking artistry will match his in landing the bass. We'll hold hands while he says grace over supper. The moonlight will reflect off the waters of the marsh, the salt air will sensitize my thoughts and I'll think to myself as I retire for a restful night.

"What man is richer than the one who is in a harmonious step with nature?"

JOE GERI'S STORY, BEST WE KNOW, THE ONLY ONE.

Joe Geri the versatile Pennsylvania back who was sent to Athens by the late War Eagle Ketron, played as a freshman in 1942 on Butts' first SEC championship team. Then he was off to war but returned to star with the '46 and '48 teams, which also claimed SEC titles.

"There may be somebody else who started as a freshman with me in '42 and was still around in '48, but I don't think so," the steely-eyed Geri, once told me. I asked Bill Hartman, and Hartman says Joe was correct.

The ideal tailback, Geri could pass and run with aplomb. Tough to bring down. He could kick, too, first learning the art of punting with the other immigrant children he grew up with in Phoenixville, Pa.

Geri found Georgia something special when he first arrived. "Mr. Ketron told me that he would buy me a bus ticket to Athens and back if I wanted to take a look at Georgia. I thought that I had nothing to lose. Coach Whitworth and Coach Hollis met me at the bus station and immediately showed me to the campus.

"I saw all those pretty coeds, who smiled and said, 'Hey, how you,' and I thought they were all talking to me. Coach Whit, who was a charmer himself, knew that impressed me, and I'm not so sure that he didn't have people staked out around the campus to speak to ol' Joe. I know that I was sold on Georgia as soon as I got on the bus to return home."

Of course, his mother had to be sold and all that took was learning that there was a Catholic church in Athens. "Coach Whit took me to St. Joseph's while I was in town and that made it okay with Mama. She wouldn't let her boy come to Georgia unless he could go to Mass.

"Everybody was Catholic where I grew up. Our neighborhood was full of Irish, Polish, Italian and Hungarian immigrants. We all were Catholic and wanted to play for Notre Dame. Most of our fathers and grandfathers had come over from the old country and worked in the steel mills. My dad came from Poland. I was the fifth of nine children. My mother thought it was something special that I got to go to college on football scholarship and play professional football."

On that first trip South, Geri was introduced to Butts-style football immediately. After a few minutes at practice, he asked somebody, "Who is that little man in the huddle who does all that talking?"

He would soon find out. Once when he crossed Butts, he was advised: "Joe you are going to run that play over and over again. You are going to be a great football player because I'm going to make one out of you and you're going to do it my way or else."

Geri would never forget the circumstances. "It happened when I first returned from the service and I thought I was pretty good and that I could loaf my way through. I was older and felt independent. Looking back, I realize what a favor Coach Butts did me, by making me do things right. Had he not coached that way, I could not have done the little things correctly, and there is no doubt I wouldn't have been the player I became.

"When I got to the pros, I realized I had been taught things a lot of the players had not been taught. I felt it gave me an advantage, and I'll always appreciate that practice field lecture that turned my career in the right direction."

In 1949, Geri was rookie of the year with the Steelers and then all-pro in 1950. He was the last of the triple threat tailbacks. He finished out his career after five years with the old Chicago Cardinals, where he was a teammate of his one time Georgia backfield partner, Charley Trippi.

John Rauch had a high regard for Geri, his fellow Pennsylvanian, who, after retirement, moved to Athens and was employed part time in sales by his former teammate, Frank Sinkwich:

"He was trim and athletic looking with hips slightly wider than his shoulders. I mistook Joe Geri for Georgia's 1942 Heisman trophy winner, Frank Sinkwich. Joe never won a Heisman, but he made a big contribution to Coach Butts' teams the next three years. Joe always gave 100% effort on the football field.

"We considered him a "game player". By that I mean he was more productive on game days than on the practice field. I know Coach Butts took a liking to Joe, but several times he would appear to be upset with him at practice, and he would tell Joe to get off the field.

"At first we felt sorry for Joe, but when we finally reached the locker room, Joe was dressed and kidding us about the long hours we were putting in. There never was any fuss about being sent off the field from Coach Butts or Joe. Could this have been Coach Butts' psychological way of saving Joe's legs for game day

Joe Geri could do it all

while not letting the team think he was getting soft?

"An unfortunate auto accident started Joe into physical decline. He healed of the injuries to his body but not his mind. He was diagnosed with Alzheimer' s disease which robbed him of a normal happy-go-lucky, witty, and carefree personality.

"In two years it was so bad, Joe's doctor signed the papers to admit him into a private Alzheimer home in Athens. After the 2000 Wally's Boys reunion, Jack and Sue Bush, Sam Bailey, my wife and I, made a visit to the home, and we were shocked by what we saw. We never imagined how cruel this disease can be to a human being. Joe vaguely remembered us but in conversation our reminisces seemed to be able to revive memories for him.

"Shortly afterward Joe was admitted to the Alzheimer ward at the Georgia War Veterans Home in Milledgeville, Ga. This move was much better for Joe, and when my wife and I made a visit the next year, Joe remembered us. We had a great time letting him dominate the conversation.

"He told us about his football injuries, his family, how good the food was at the home. When we were leaving, Joe wanted to see us to the car. A nurse on the floor escorted us down the elevator to look after Joe and this led to a funny story I'll never forget. The nurse asked me, 'What kind of football player was Joe.' And I answered without exaggeration. 'He was a triple-threat star. He could run, pass, or punt or kick with the best players in the country.'

"I looked at Joe and he had the biggest smile on his face. He might have been remembering his glory days at Georgia or Pittsburgh, so I continued. 'Joe gave 100% every time he was on a football field, he was a game player and I'm proud to have been a teammate of his at Georgia.'

"Joe was pumped up. It looked like he was ready to play. The nurse then asked Joe, 'What position did John play?'" With a burst of boyish laughter Joe said, 'He was my substitute.' We all had a great laugh, and I think we left Joe with a pretty good feeling about himself. I know it made me feel good."

Ken McCall Broke Up A Damn Good Football Game

The story of the '48 Tech matchup in Athens was the punt return by Ken McCall which iced the game for Georgia.

It was one of those games that was like an arm wrestling contest, in that it could go either way. The Bulldogs were leading 14-7 with Tech seemingly having gained the upper hand late in the game, but McCall's punt return of 54 yards settled the issue.

Later on, following graduation, McCall had a conversation with a Tech player whom he knew through business. The Tech alumnus told McCall what happened on the Tech sideline during the punt return.

The Tech coach, about to make a substitution on the exchange following the punt, watched dejectedly as McCall weaved his way clear for the touchdown scamper.

Said Bobby Dodd, "That kid just broke up a damn good football game."

Here is how John Stegeman remembered the return.

"A lazy punt floated downfield with good Tech coverage. At least one faint-hearted Georgia fan hoped that McCall would not try to field the ball, but play it safe to avoid a fumble. McCall, however, had no such ideas. Racing up into the very thick of the action, he caught the ball on the dead run, fought his way past the first wave of Jackets and veered to his right toward the sideline.

"Suddenly, at midfield, he cut back toward the Tech goal, behind the blocks of Al Bodine, Joe Jackura, and Hamp Tanner. Then, in the next instant, there was a common awareness on the part of fifty thousand onlookers – the realization, all at once, that the game belonged to Georgia. McCall was in the clear and there was no one on the field that could catch him from behind. In the flash of time it took him to cover the last fifty yards, every Georgia heart knew the Bulldogs were champions.

"Tech received the kickoff and marched to a touchdown, but McCall's run had salted the game away, and Georgia gobbled up an invitation to spend New Year's Day in Miami."

The passing of time has brought about a dimming of the memory of McCall's return. It, for some reason, has not made any all-time lists. It has not gotten the ranking it deserves. Yet, the Tech skirmish has always been the big game with Georgia partisans, the most important one on the schedule.

The Dogs were playing at home and it was a game that well could have gone the other way. It clinched the SEC championship and sent the Bulldogs to the Orange Bowl for the second time.

When you review past games with Tech in which there have been many great plays by both teams, McCall's punt return ranks as one of the outstanding performances in the long series with the Yellow Jackets.

If you deliver the play that makes the difference in the game that brings a championship and a big bowl opportunity and takes place against your main rival, then it deserves upper echelon status as one of the biggest plays in the series with Georgia Tech.

After he scored, Butts ran out on the field and put his arm around a startled McCall. "I had never seen him do that before. When he did that, I was surprised but I will always appreciate it. Most of us just never saw that side of Coach Butts."

McCall, who grew up in Orlando, was inclined to play for Florida, but his father, who owned an citrus packing plant, had customers all over the South and suggested they take a tour of several SEC schools.

They visited the Florida campus and then drove north to Athens, their second stop on the tour. That would be the last. Ken made up his mind after arriving in Athens and meeting Coach Butts.

His first impressions were convincing although McCall and his dad had planned only a half day visit. After meeting with Coach Butts, the Georgia boss asked when they would be moving on and McCall remembers his dad saying, "After lunch."

Ken McCall in action versus Tech

With that, Butts exclaimed, "Oh no. We are having a party at my house tonight, and I want Mr. McCall to join us." The McCalls stayed three days. The younger McCall was comfortable and at ease meeting the Bulldog players and working out with them.

Butts told him that if he came to Georgia, he would be a starter that fall. "That got my father's attention. Mine, too," McCall remembers. Though brief, it turned out to be such an encouraging stay. When they got in the car to continue their tour, probably to Tennessee, Ken recalls his father asked, "Well, son, have you made up your mind about where you will be playing college football?"

"Yessir," the son replied. Ken's association with the University of Georgia had begun.

The promise that he would start in the fall was not idle talk. McCall did start at quarterback. Georgia was switching to the "T" formation, and even though he wound up sharing the quarterback's job with Billy Hodges and George Skipworth, McCall was versatile enough that he would always have a job. He lettered in 1944, then spent two years in the military and returned for the '47 season.

"I think they appreciated my defensive ability more," McCall said. A change in rules his senior year allowed for platooning of offensive and defensive players. They were not required to play both ways.

In fact, Spec Towns the long time football assistant and head track coach, told him he would be playing defense exclusively. (McCall and Spec developed a warm friendship, one that lasted affectionately until Towns' death in 1991.) He told Ken, "Since you are not going to play offense, I'll get you out of spring practice."

If you were a football player in those days and heard that news, it was, understandably, the kind of message that ensures a lasting friendship, but that didn't mean Ken could slough off on the track.

A sprinter and a pole vaulter, McCall was never the lazy, unmotivated athlete. But Towns always kept him on his toes by often saying to him, "Ken wonder what is going on in spring practice?"

An indication of the type athlete that McCall is comes from the fact that he didn't take up golf until age 32. He became a scratch player and was senior club champion at the Orlando Country Club four times and also was club champion four times at the Highlands, N.C. Country Club.

A long time track official for the Florida Relays, McCall has been elected to the Central Florida Hall of Fame.

When his father died at age 47, Ken took over the business and the work ethic he learned on the practice field at Georgia kicked in. His hours generally were 7:00 a.m. to midnight. He became successful in business early on and later got to the stage where his working hours were less intense.

This gave him more time with the family and also made it possible for him to take up golf.

Just like it was against Tech in '48, when he needed to come through – with the match on the line – he usually did. That is why he became club champion and today is one of the leading senior golfers in the state of Florida.

JACK BUSH, HOME IS ATHENS

Jack Bush was always overjoyed to call Athens home.

To be abundantly correct, Jacksonville was home for most of his life, but since he played for the Bulldogs, home, at least emotionally, was unquestionably Athens.

Though business interests kept him in Atlanta and Jacksonville for years, Bush always thought that he would prefer to live in Athens.

He even bought a home at the mountain resort, Sky Valley, near Clayton, so he could visit Athens more often, especially in the fall when the Dogs kicked off in Sanford Stadium. He eventually moved to Athens, becoming Vince Dooley's next door neighbor.

Born on a farm in Irwin County, Jack ultimately enrolled in high school in Jacksonville and then wore the football colors of both Florida and Georgia.

"My case is a little unusual," he chuckles, "but since I was from Georgia or had spent most of my life in the state, I originally planned to enroll at the University of Georgia. When I finished high school, a lot of Florida alumni put pressure on me to go to Gainesville. I was dating the daughter of one of the men involved and gave in, although I had reservations because of my Georgia background."

He actually took residence in Gainesville in January of 1942 and lettered in freshman basketball. Recruiters had told him he could finish high school there and would be eligible for football in the fall.

"At practice in September, one of the coaches came up to me and told me that they were wrong; that I would not be eligible for football and that I could transfer. I finished practice, walked off the field and called Coach Butts. He told me there would be a ticket at the bus station by 10:00 p.m., and I headed to Athens, one of the happiest moments of my life. I'll always appreciate what Coach Butts did. He could have told me he didn't need me at that point. After all, he tried to get me to sign in the first place, and I turned Georgia down."

Jack's father, Matthew Jackson Bush, was in the produce business and moved from time to time. Jack's early years were spent in Cordele, and he first began football at Glynn Academy in Brunswick.

"Lamar Davis and Vassa Cate were older players on the team when I first started," Jack says. He returned to Cordele for the 1938 and 1939 seasons and then to Jacksonville where his mother lived.

When he enrolled at Georgia, he had to sit out the '42 season as a transfer and practiced against the team that would wind up in the Rose Bowl.

Jack knew what was coming next. It was time to serve his country like everybody else. He was sent to Duke, participating in the V-12 program, which meant that he played a year of tackle (1943) for the Blue Devils before receiving his commission and ordered to the Pacific.

When the war ended, he was stationed at Pearl Harbor. His next orders were for China, but he was discharged in time to return in August of 1946 to Athens, where Butts, Whitworth and Hartman were putting together another championship team.

Jack Bush, forever grateful to Wally

"When I got back to Athens," he says, "I walked into old Memorial Hall where the coaches offices were. Nobody knew I was in town. I walked in on Coach Whit, who had his feet up on the desk. He looked up at me and grinned, 'Do I have a place for you!'"

The place was left tackle. Both ways for Jack as it was for all players in those days.

Jack was a starter for the SEC champs of '46, a team that went undefeated and whipped North Carolina in a comeback in the Sugar Bowl. He started again in 1947, playing mostly offense and then again in 1948, when the Bulldogs won the SEC title once again.

John Rauch remembers that Jack grew to be bigger than the other boys. "He wasn't a bully; he just demanded respect, one of the qualities he carried through his life. He was very good at charming people, yet in competition he was meaner than a snake. He laid many opponents out on the handball court as well as the football field. He evidently is just as tough in the business field because he was extremely successful in that arena.

"The Marines had Jack study transportation while at Duke, and he eventually was shipped to the Philippines. His greatest accomplishment there was playing handball with Ted Williams – the great Boston Red Sox slugger.

"He did such a good job in transportation they put him in charge of a unit in the Far East. This is where Jack began a business career. He bought, sold, traded, or confiscated pearls. When he returned to Georgia he brought a sack of cultured pearls back with him.

"He learned of a jeweler in Philadelphia who would pay top dollar for pearls; so when we went to Philadelphia to play Temple University early in the 1946 season, Jack carried the sack of pearls with him. I remember sitting in the lounge in the Pullman train where Jack counted the number of pearls in the sack. Jack sold his pearls for a lot of money.

"From that business venture, he enjoyed success in business throughout life. What I like is that he was always generous with his alma mater."

Jack spent most of his postgraduate life in the automobile business, primarily in Jacksonville although there was a brief stint in Atlanta. But wherever he has been, Georgia has always been on his mind.

After moving to Athens, Jack and his wife, Sue, have become avid fans of all sports. You can see them at basketball, gymnastics, baseball and tennis competitions. If a red and black uniform is involved, you can expect them to be in the stands, dressed appropriately.

Jack's affection for Coach Butts is enduring, and he has always found that one of his greatest pleasures through the years was making excursions to Athens. "I don't have to make any more trips to Athens," he said in the spring of 2004; "I'm home now."

Hugh McCarley

It was the Bulldog coaching staff that stimulated Hugh McCarley's commitment to the University of Georgia. But in the back of his mind he foresaw exceptional educational opportunity.

"From the beginning I believed that I could get an excellent education in Athens, and I did. Even back then, Georgia offered a quality curriculum. All you had to do was apply yourself."

Paying the price on the football field was a rewarding trade off in McCarley's opinion. He sincerely believed that then and has not moved away from that premise with the passing of years.

His memories are treasured, and, like so many of his teammates, team reunions and get togethers never lose their appeal. "Nothing like a gang of old players having an opportunity to reminisce," he says. Some of his recollections that remain indelible and worthy of a whimsical chuckle began when he was being recruited.

Line Coach J. B. Whitworth, a charmer if there ever was one, turned it on whenever he was in McCarley's company. "He would always put his arm around, hug me and tell me what a great player I would be at Georgia. I was quite affected by all that," McCarley affectionately recalls. When he got to Athens, however, McCarley soon realized the atmosphere had suddenly changed.

After the Bulldog team returned from the '45 Oil Bowl and McCarley had enrolled early, he saw Coach Whit on campus, yelled out to the coach and ran across the street to greet him. McCarley said, excitedly, "Coach I'm here. I am already attending class."

Whitworth nodded without emotion and said, indifferently, "I'll see you at practice." The let down was for McCarley the confirmation that football would require an intensely serious commitment that was not discussed when the hugs and the backslaps of recruiting were extended.

A practice field incident later in his career confirmed, too, that Coach Butts, whom he admired greatly, had a split personality. One day in a rugged scrimmage, McCarley went down in a heap with a neck injury. He couldn't get up. It turned out to be a pinched nerve but after he lay there for a while and the scrimmage moved to another area of the field, an ambulance was summoned. There was fear that his neck might be broken.

When he was examined at the hospital, the attending doctor explained the diagnosis, but suggested that he not leave the hospital and remain for observation. That circumstance would not have been unwelcome, even with the most dedicated of players.

Following practice, Coach Butts paid McCarley a visit to the hospital. Out in the hall he could hear the conversation between his doctor and his coach.

Now in a concerned mood, fearing McCarley

might have a serious neck injury, Coach Butts kept repeating to the doctor that Hugh was such a nice young man. "We know, Wally," the doctor said. "We understand and we will do everything we can to make sure he is comfortable." Coach Butts reminded the doctor that his player was to receive the very best of care.

As the conversation continued, McCarley began to feel that his coach had suddenly experienced an infusion of uncommon sympathy. Then he heard the doctor remark to the coach that the player should be able to practice the next day.

With that, Butts wheeled and charged into the room and berated McCarley for an act of malingering. "Don't you lie here. You get your ass back over to the dorm and be ready to practice tomorrow." All of that is amusing to McCarley today. He laughs about the incident, understanding without any acrimony that was the way it was in those times. Your father applied the belt if you got out of line, your teachers' authority at school was never questioned, and if you played football and no bones were broken, you could expect to scrimmage without relief.

Playing on a championship team remains something McCarley holds dear. "How many people can say they played for an SEC championship team? That I can, means the world to me," he says. "A championship means that you are separating the sheep from the goats."

Football in autumn has always been uplifting for McCarley, whose wife, Marsha (McKinney), was a cheerleader during his days as an undergraduate. They especially enjoyed strolls through the campus with the turning of the autumn leaves. "It was so soothing emotionally," he says. "I've always enjoyed every season, but I don't think there is a more uplifting experience than to walk a college campus in the fall of the year. It is downright enchanting."

The rivalry in his time with North Carolina further defined his feelings. "Their campus and ours are similar, and we always played them in October. I loved those trips to Chapel Hill and the setting in Kenan Stadium. It was such a rewarding experience to play against their stars like Charlie "Choo Choo" Justice and Art Weiner. I wish that rivalry had continued."

McCarley said Butts was "grossly misunderstood. He was tougher than nails on the field. He wasn't the type who complimented you. But he would do anything in the world for you off the field. He was a great person.

"Coach Butts made winners out of us. In business, since then, I've always felt like I was going to win. I would always find a way to win. That's what I received at Georgia – a spirit and the will to win. In business, that's essential."

Bernie Reid

Hamilton, Ohio, is a suburb of Cincinnati, which is why it was only natural that Bernie Reid would begin college football at home. If you can find scholarship aid close by, that usually is too alluring to pass up.

But a funny thing happened while Bernie was playing for the Bearcats. Georgia came to town in 1942 and waxed his team, 35-13. The Bulldogs were on the way to the Rose Bowl, and Bernie watched in awe as Frank Sinkwich, Charley Trippi and Racehorse Davis ran roughshod over his team.

Drawing up a play, perhaps? Weyman Sellers (left) and Bernie Reid

He was amazed at the passing precision Wallace Butts' team displayed. When Sinkwich connected with Davis on a 90 yard touchdown completion, Reid thought to himself, "those guys are special football players."

Little did he know that in due course, he would be wearing the silver britches of the Georgia Bulldogs. It wasn't, however, a direct route to Athens. First, after a year of football at Cincinnati, he spent nine months with the Merchant Marines.

He had his eye on playing at Notre Dame, but Coach Frank Lehay informed him that he was short math credits which resulted in the Irish coach placing a call to his good friend Wallace Butts, who sent assistant, Tom Nash, to offer Reid a scholarship.

With a decision in place, he enrolled in Athens and lettered at Georgia in 1944. Then Reid was drafted into the Army for two years. Finally, he was back in Athens in time to start the '47 season.

He and Weyman Sellers were co-captains of the Orange Bowl team and Reid not only played on the SEC championship team in '48, he got what he came for – a degree in education which meant that he could coach, an objective since high school.

In recalling his collegiate career, he says that he played his finest game against Alabama in 1948 when the Bulldogs thrashed the boys from Tuscaloosa in Birmingham, 35-0. He was given the game ball, which he has since given to his alma mater.

"Georgia meant a lot to me," he says. "Still does, and I thought that I should offer the ball to the school as an expression of appreciation for what I gained from having played for Coach Butts and the Bulldogs."

The highlight of his career, however, was being named captain. "There can be no higher honor than to be elected captain by a vote of your teammates," Reid says with emphasis.

After coaching successfully at Albany, Reid took an assistant's position at Maryland. When Lou Saban became head coach of the Denver Broncos, he invited Bernie to join him. "My family situation was such that I just didn't think it was wise to pick up and move them that far away at that time. I asked Lou if there were a scouting opportunity and he said, 'yes' and hired me in 1957."

He worked for the Broncos for 25 years, scouting the eastern section of the U. S. "It was a good decision," he says. "Everything worked out okay."

While he was an assistant for the Terrapins, he learned about a quarterback from Beaver Falls, Pa., by the name of Joe Namath, who signed with Maryland.

Namath had a poor academic record in high school, pretty much owing to the fact that effort in class was lacking. Homework was out of the question. When he saw that Namath would not be admitted at Maryland, he called coaches at Georgia to alert them about the availability of an outstanding player. He didn't qualify at Georgia either, but Alabama found a way to admit the quarterback who shocked the NFL Baltimore Colts in the third Super Bowl, Jan. 12, 1969, by the score of 16-7.

"Joe wasn't big on going to class, but he was some football player, and if we couldn't get him in at Maryland, I wanted Georgia to have an opportunity to sign him," he smiles.

Bernie didn't say it this way, but what we see here is a man who sincerely appreciated the educational opportunity he had at Georgia and was always seeking to repay his alma mater.

WEYMAN SELLERS

Weyman Sellers (lettered in 45-48, co-captain with Bernie Reid). If you were to draw up a rock hard, granite jawed, unyielding and unmovable football player that is what you would have in Weyman Sellers. Even past his prime, when he was in his last years as the football coach at Clarke Central, he filled out a tee shirt better than his biggest and strongest linemen. He had a Charles Atlas build and coached like he played. Tough and unyielding.

Fran Tarkenton is Sellers' most accomplished player from the old Bulldog end's high school coaching days. It was from Sellers that Tarkenton learned fundamental football. It was at Athens High, Tarkenton's education as a quarterback began. It was with Sellers that the NFL great-to-be discovered that while he didn't give off a tough appearance or countenance, he was as tough as the next guy.

"At age 13, I learned every fundamental in football. Weyman Sellers knew fundamental football and he knew quarterback fundamentals. He learned it from Coach Butts," Tarkenton says.

Football under Weyman Sellers was tough, and you can underscore tough. He won a state championship with only 21 players. Most kids couldn't take it. Tarkenton could and he pointedly says that after high school, football was a breeze.

He'll never forget what his high school coach taught him and the regimen he had to endure. Here is the NFL Hall of Famer's recollection:

"Let me tell you how he started his practices," Tarkenton says. "The first thing we did was run four laps around the football in full uniform. Then it was calisthenics, which were followed by up/downs or what many coaches call, 'grass drills.' Next we practiced which was always live contact work. After that we lined up at the 50 yard line and ran through our entire playbook. We ran every play in our book and ran it for a full 50 yards. If anybody let up on any one of those plays, if they didn't grind their hardest to the goal line, he made us start all over again from the beginning of the play book.

"We had to be the best conditioned team in the world. If we played lousy on Friday nights, at least in his opinion, we had to scrimmage on Saturday morning."

Tarkenton, in looking back, realizes that Sellers played end at Georgia, but learned quarterback fundamentals from his exposure to the offensive system at Georgia under Butts.

"He had to mirror what Coach Butts taught," Tarkenton adds. "He was the toughest, most disciplined coach I ever played for. It was the way he did things and only a few of us could manage or accept it. I appreciate it now. When players quit, I never once weakened. There was no way he was going to run me off. I was going to be a football player, and I was going to be successful.

"One of the reasons I was successful was the fundamentals I learned under Weyman Sellers, who learned those same fundamentals under Wallace Butts."

HAMP TANNER

In the days before football players became big as dump trucks and the side of the house, Lanier High School in Macon had the biggest manager in football – bigger than any of the football players. It was a great source of embarrassment for the manager. He wanted to play, not stand on the sidelines.

But there wasn't much Hamp Tanner could do about his predicament. At 270 pounds, he probably would be the biggest lineman in the state, but when his stepfather told him he couldn't play football, there wasn't much Hamp could do except burn with frustration.

In those days, your parents' word was final, no questions, no exceptions. It was a case of worrying about injury and Hamp's parents couldn't deal with this possibility. In those days, kids played the game without school insurance. You got hurt, your family had to bear the medical costs, which could be an overwhelming financial burden.

Eventually, his parents relented – after Hamp forced the issue – and Hamp took to the game with great commitment and determination.

He had watched Tom Greene, who became a Georgia star, practice under the legendary Selby Buck, longtime Lanier coach. He had longed to be in on the action, and when his opportunity came, he was eager and grateful. Here's how it came about.

Hamp was watching practice one day, bothered by his role as a manager. "I just couldn't take it any longer," he recalled. Hamp threw the equipment keys to an associate and dressed out, figuring that he could hide his football activity from his parents.

But Sam Glassman, sports editor of the Macon Telegraph, wrote a story about a 270-pound manager coming out for football. Hamp hid all the papers he could find, but a neighbor called his parents with congratulations after reading the sports pages.

It was only after a family conference that he was able to convince his parents that he should be playing football. Approval came reluctantly. Eventually, they would be pleased, however. He would be offered a college scholarship and later briefly play professionally with the San Francisco 49ers and the old Dallas Texans.

BILL BRADSHAW

Bill Bradshaw (47-50) – A rangy center-linebacker with good speed, Bradshaw enrolled at Georgia in 1947, lettering his first year as a Bulldog. In the sixties, he became a member of the Athletic Board and served the University well in that capacity. He was very successful in business.

Like so many others, he wasn't eager for all that scrimmaging and head knocking during his days on campus. However, when he saw his business career advance favorably and productively, he was quick to note that the perseverance he learned on the practice field at Georgia was invaluable to him in business.

His personal introduction to Wallace Butts was memorable and lasting. As a high school player he came to Athens on a recruiting visit. When he was taken in to meet Coach Butts, he saw the Georgia coach at his fidgeting best. The man couldn't sit still; his nervousness made Bradshaw conclude that Butts might literally jump out of his clothes.

"Anybody who wants to win that bad, I want to play for him," Bradshaw recalls thinking. Many high school prospects felt the same way and the highlight of Bradshaw's career was playing on an SEC championship team in 1948. Bradshaw got considerable encouragement from his dad and says, "being a Bulldog was just was in my blood."

There was a side to Boys High graduate that was as worthy as his ability to compete successfully at his favorite sport. When he enrolled at Georgia, he fully intended to earn a degree. It never crossed his mind that he would give up football, no matter the practice field rigors. And it was the same in the classroom. He expected to leave in four years with a degree, and he recalls competing with his teammate, Hugh McCarley, for the highest grades in the courses they took.

At the end of one spring, a professor told Bradshaw and McCarley that they were the only two football players in his class. "You made the highest grades," they were advised. It was a high moment of Bradshaw's college years.

When Bradshaw entered business, he applied the discipline of football and his classroom experience to his profession. When National Services Industries bought his company, he retired, but not for long. Soon he was back into a successful venture. Success, like before, followed substantially, bringing about a second retirement as the second business venture was taken over by his sons.

Bradshaw later became a member of the University athletic board and had a strong influence on Georgia's hiring Joel Eaves as athletic director in 1963—an auspicious hiring at a critical juncture in Bulldog athletics.

Barry Phillips

Among the many Wally's Boys who owe allegiance to assistant coach, Quinton Lumpkin, is Barry Phillips, a Valdosta native and now a prominent Atlanta attorney who considered himself fortunate to have been awarded a scholarship.

Soon after he went through a summer of practice, Phillips realized that he could expect long hours on the practice field, but he would not likely experience much playing time.

That did not deter him. He had a plan. He aspired to become a lawyer, and if his scholarship paid the bills, he would gladly take what was dished out on the practice field. He remained focused and motivated to achieve his objective.

"Quinton Lumpkin is the father of the academic assistance program for athletes at UGA," he says. "In the Fall of 1948, Lumpkin was the freshman football coach at UGA. He and his wife, Mary, and sons, Jack and Jimmy, lived in an apartment in Milledge Annex (later expanded to become Payne Hall) behind Milledge Hall. Milledge Annex was then the athletic dorm, and which primarily housed athletes on football scholarship. I enrolled at UGA on football scholarship in June, 1946, just out of high school in Valdosta.

"Coach Butts had practice all summer of 1946 so he could evaluate the many football players who were coming out of the service at the end of WWII. I enjoyed summer school and Coach Lumpkin and Coach Butts let me continue in the summers of 1947,48 and 49 so that I could graduate in August and start law school in September 1949.

"Georgia played Texas in the Orange Bowl on January 1, 1949. I was not a good football player, but always had a good relationship with Coach Lump and we talked a lot about a variety of things. While we were getting ready for the Orange Bowl in Miami (which was the only trip I made), Coach Lump and I agreed that I would not play out my last year of eligibility for the 1949 season. Instead, he asked me to work with him on the academic assistance program which he was starting.

"This involved checking with teachers on grades, arranging for tutors for students needing help, holding study hall for those on probation and assistance on course selection and registration. These were all Coach Lump's ideas, and I helped to implement them. I am not aware of any other schools which had similar programs at the time. Georgia did not have such a program until it was developed by Coach Lump. His program not only helped to keep players eligible, but stressed the importance of the academic program. It improved the graduation rate.

I was privileged to work with Coach Lump on his academic assistance program through all three years of law school, with all of the benefits of a full football scholarship. Thus, I had a seven year scholarship which was only exceeded by the 30-plus year scholarship which one of my law professors said that former mayor Bob McWhorter jokingly said he had. (McWhorter was a longtime member of the law faculty when he made that statement.)

"Hurley Jones was an outstanding center and Phi Beta Kappa from Jesup who practiced medicine in Brunswick. I learned several years ago that Hurley established a scholarship fund in Coach Lump's name. We need to see that scholarship materialize. There are many former players who have degrees because of the scholarship assistance program developed by Quinton Lumpkin."

1949

After a 2-1 start, Georgia scored a total of 30 points in the next five games. A trend was taking effect although nobody would have predicted the downturn that was on the horizon. What the '49 season forecast was that in the days ahead, the Bulldogs would often field inconsistent offensive teams, a far cry from the past. In addition, Georgia developed a heart wrenching habit of not being able to win close games.

On top of that, a missed extra point allowed Georgia Tech to defeat the home team between the hedges 7-6. From that point, there would be an excruciating, humiliating eight straight victories by the ancient enemy. After the great heroics of the Forties, Georgia would experience hard times in the Fifties as Coach Butts began his second decade as the Georgia head coach. The '49 Dogs went 4-6-1, the first losing team for the Little Round Man since his start in 1939.

Billy Payne on Porter

Billy Payne, All-SEC end for Vince Dooley, is the man who brought the Olympics to Atlanta. If you know about the seemingly insurmountable odds in accomplishing that mission, you have to say that it came about in large part because of Billy's Bulldog tenacity. His determination was like the ant moving the rubber tree plant, the high hopes of achievement coming about because he never considered that it couldn't be done.

After all, it was for the year 1996, the 100th anniversary of the games but there was great sentiment over the world to return the Olympics to Greece, where the games originated.

When the announcement was made, Billy's biggest challenge began, the challenge of keeping the greedy and politically self-centered forces from derailing the goals and objectives of the organizing committee he had put together.

It was graphically akin to the story of the Little Red Hen who planted the grain, cultivated and harvested the wheat, baked the bread from what she had sowed and not one member of the barnyard offered to help. When she sat down, however, to eat the bread, everybody was ready to join her for a meal.

Billy had to skillfully maneuver, placate, compromise and underscore flexibility to pull it off. That he did is a testament to him for never giving up the dream, forever underscoring second effort, doggedly pursuing his goals and objectives.

His connection to Wally's Boys? His father, Porter, who captained the 1949 team. Billy's success as a player at Georgia and his professional achievements are linked to the advice and counsel of his late father, who was notably influenced by Coach Butts. Billy's tribute to Porter and Coach Butts and his recollection of his days in Athens follow:

My memories of Athens and Coach Butts date back to the time I was eight or nine years old and would go to Athens in the spring when my dad would officiate scrimmages and the G-Day game. After Georgia, my dad entered the insurance business, but like a lot of former players who did not play in the National Football League, he wanted to stay close to the game and did that by becoming a Southeastern Conference official. He was proud of his time spent officiating in the SEC.

One day in Athens, I remember sitting on Coach Butts' knee and he began to tell me about my parents and how they had quite a challenge in going to school and raising two small children, my older sister, Patti, and me.

Those, apparently, were austere times for my parents. Coach Butts began to tell me how he helped them out. He said he slipped my dad a key to the dining hall and told him he could go in after hours and take food home for the family.

He sounded very pleased that he could provide that assistance to a player and his family who had no money to live on. I am sure that Coach Butts helped other players in one fashion or another, and I always appreciated his benevolence and altruism. I know that my dad was one of his former players who would literally fight you about Coach Butts. He never forgot Coach Butts' consideration for our family when times were hard for us.

Porter Payne—captain, SEC official and father of Billy

Bill Hartman remembers that when he and his wife, Ruth, purchased a new refrigerator, they gave my parents the old one. It was the time in my life when I was on a bottle, and I can imagine how important it was for the family to have a means for keeping milk refrigerated for their baby.

Naturally, I don't remember those days, but it is not lost on me that Coach Butts was good to his players and did what he could to help them through tough times.

When I would go to Athens with my dad and watch those scrimmages, I was always impressed with the size and strength of college football players. I was too young to know very much about the game, but I do remember how intense the scrimmages were. I was quite impressed with college football. I knew that I wanted to play the game.

As a high school senior, my dad told me that I could choose the college I wanted. He did not insist that I enroll at Georgia, but I have to believe that when I signed with the Bulldogs that he was a very happy man. Making all those trips to Athens as a kid, I think, made me aware, subconsciously, where my heart was.

One thing that was important to me when I got there was that I was going to give it my best in the Georgia tradition I was familiar with, I was going to enjoy the college experience and I wanted to carry into life multiple friendships like my dad.

I can say that I have never known any man who had so many close friends as my dad. Everywhere he went, somebody was spending time with him, reminiscing about Georgia and Athens. I was fascinated by all that and came to realize later that friendships are so valuable and emotionally fulfilling in life.

He enjoyed his experience at Georgia, he appreciated all those friendships, and I always felt that he was successful in business because of friends. But if Coach Butts had not extended a helping hand at a critical juncture in his life, he might not have made it through college.

I remember my dad's advice coming along. Persistence is most important, he always said. "Don't ever let anybody tell you that you can't do what you want to do!" I'll always remember that.

When he died, on a weekend, there was only a small squib about his death in the paper, but on the day of the funeral there were thousands who showed up for the service. Our family was stunned. His legion of friends and teammates got the news by word of mouth, and they came to pay their respects. I was overwhelmed.

Indirectly I am a Wally's Boy and very proud of it. My father tried to pass on to me what he learned and experienced under Coach Butts, and I am grateful for that influence in my life.

LUKIE BRUNSON

His name is Stephen Lewis Brunson, but everybody calls him "Lukie."

When he was growing up, a playmate couldn't pronounce Lewis. It kept coming out, "Lukie."

He has been called by that name ever since. "Nobody knows me by any other name," Lukie says. In his hometown of Florence, S. C., you mention "Lukie," and anybody can tell you how to find this former Georgia halfback. When you ask him why he chose to enroll in Athens, he says, matter of fact, "I just liked the Dogs."

An All-State, All-Southern halfback (5-10, 170) halfback with speed "and shiftiness," the football brochure said of him in the fall of 1948. He lettered for four years and was a factor in the running game throughout his career.

His affection for Georgia evolved into an early commitment to play for Coach Butts. A friend, Charlie Womack, drove him to the Sugar Bowl in 1946. "Hey, that was something," he says. "I remember the drive was a long one. Back then there were a lot of two lane roads between here and New Orleans, but when you are young, you are fascinated by the experience. I don't remember too much about New Orleans, but it was the first time I had been west of the Mississippi, and I appreciated the opportunity to go that far away, enjoy a wonderful travel experience and see a big time bowl game."

Georgia played North Carolina, a school that wanted him to enroll at Chapel Hill. He could have played in the same backfield with Charlie "Choo Choo" Justice. That didn't change his mind. "I was going to the Dogs," he laughs.

When the Bulldogs played the Tar Heels in the second game of the season in Keenan Stadium, Justice returned the opening kickoff and Lukie tackled him. "You remember things like that. Justice was a great back, but I had seen the greatest there ever was in the Sugar Bowl, and that was Charley Trippi. I really loved watching him play and enjoyed a few conversations when he spent time in Athens while he was playing in the NFL."

Interestingly, he doesn't remember too much about the games he played. He doesn't remember scoring plays, big plays. "When I left, I pretty much left football behind me. I loved my time in Athens, but when it is over you need to move on."

What he remembers most is the Downtown Varsity. "I fell in love with Varsity hotdogs," he says, "and I would go out of my way now to get one. I was really sorry to learn that the Downtown Varsity closed. That was a great place for me while I was at Georgia."

With a degree in education, Brunson returned to his hometown and began a career in insurance. When he could get away, he would drive over to Murrell's inlet on the Carolina coast and fish for flounder, becoming an expert.

"I'm not just talking, not bragging—but, I don't mind telling you I can grill the best tasting flounder you ever put in your mouth."

A better tasting meal than a big thick pre-game steak? "You better believe it," he laughs.

BRYAN WHITWORTH

Bryan Whitworth didn't play football for his father, the highly regarded Wallace Butts' assistant. However, he benefited well from the teachings and philosophy of his father.

"We had many conversations about life. What he taught his players helped me, and that is, never give up. Regardless of how dark things appear, you don't quit. As long as you make an effort, as long as you try, you've got a chance to make it."

In Bryan's opinion his father, Jennings Bryan Whitworth, was happiest when he was in Athens. He and Coach Butts enjoyed so much success in the Forties, and that glorious comeback in 1959—the year the two old friends were reunited. "It is vivid in my memory," Bryan says. "He was so pleased to be back in Athens, and I don't think he ever enjoyed coaching more than that season. He had a special fondness for the players on that team. He felt that they were over-achievers. My mother, (Virginia) enjoyed Athens so much, and pretty much lived out her life there. Athens meant a lot to my parents."

Before Coach Whitworth took over as head coach at Oklahoma A&M, he got a call from Bobby Dodd. The Tech coach made an attractive offer to Coach Whit. "When he talked to the family," Bryan remembers, "he said, 'I just couldn't do that to Wally. I just have too much respect for him to take a job at Georgia Tech.' He enjoyed working with Coach Butts. He was very appreciative of Coach Butt's football mind. He always said he learned a lot of football from Coach Butts."

DOWN

GEORGIA
VISITORS

PART VIII

THE FIFTIES

Lean Years Surface

1950

What a year this could have been. Georgia opened the season against powerhouse Maryland, which had moved to national prominence under Jim Tatum. The Bulldogs were decisive in a 27-7 victory between the hedges. But gloom settled over the campus when quarterback, Billy Grant, with a knee injury, was lost for the season.

The team posted a 6-3-3 record, and the Bulldogs were invited to the first and only Presidential Cup in College Park, Md., where they were defeated by Texas A&M, 40-20.

Ole Timers, long time observers, believe that with a healthy Grant, Georgia would have enjoyed Chapel Bell ringing success. Tying three games and losing twice by a touchdown took the luster out of a promising season: 7-7, St. Mary's in San Francisco; 0-0, North Carolina in Athens; 13-13, LSU in Baton Rouge; 7-14, Alabama in Birmingham; and, depressingly, 0-7 to Tech at home.

That would be Georgia's last bowl game until 1959. Hard times were ahead, but not immediately.

How Did He Hang On?

With circumstances so unfavorable in the Fifties, there was that inevitable question of how did Wally Butts, who fielded all those championship teams in the Forties, hang on when the down times seemed so overwhelming?

First of all, he was so beloved from the success of the Forties that he not only lastingly endeared himself to Georgia partisans from that championship era, but also he had a generous personality which brought him great affection in return. He had built up a deep reservoir of good will.

Alumni, fans and friends felt that he truly loved the University of Georgia. They believed that he gave of himself and that he cared for the school. He was a man's man. Furthermore, people saw heart, courage and fight in his makeup.

Think about it in this perspective. In the fall of 2005, it will have been 25 years since Herschel Walker led the Bulldogs to the National Championship. In the midst of Butts' toughest days, the mid-Fifties, he had fielded the only undefeated major college team in the country just ten years prior. Most loyal Bulldogs refused to give up on him.

It was hard for the Georgia people to forget what he had accomplished as a coach, and most of them had faith that with improved recruiting success, he could regain the winning edge. They were willing to hang with him, and he, with the SEC title in 1959, followed by the Orange Bowl championship, justified the long standing faith of those loyal Dog supporters.

There were critics, indeed. He, himself, was far from satisfied and unending frustration set in, affecting his ability to develop a championship team. In the end he became embittered and tenaciously fought back at his critics, but resigned as coach after the 1960 season and as athletic director in 1963.

Dick Yelvington

There are those who have followed the Bulldogs over the years who remember Dick Yelvington, but if you were born after World War II, you'd have to be a bit of a historian or a researcher to know much about him.

Yelvington is not one who lives in the past, and he has never been given to returning to campus for reunions and lettermen gatherings. It isn't that he doesn't appreciate his experience in Athens: he just never got into homecomings. Further, he has forever disdained the hassle of travel, and it is a long way from Lake Charles, La. to Athens.

A three year Bulldog starter at offensive tackle, 1949-51 (he was a reserve on the 48 team), Yelvington also started immediately as a rookie with the New York Giants, a team for which he played productively for six years. He owns an NFL championship ring from the Giants upset over the Chicago Bears in 1956 in the title game in New York, the highlight of his professional experience.

That was the game, if you are up on your NFL history, when the Giants eschewed their cleats for tennis shoes, for the frozen conditions thereby gaining traction and the advantage over Bears who chose soccer cleats for the frozen Yankee Stadium turf.

His winner's share was $4,000, but as Yelvington

Dick Yelvington when he was a Bulldog

has noted Indianapolis Colt quarterback Peyton Manning makes that much in the time it takes him to tie his shoelaces for a workout.

When it was over, when he was done as player, Yelvington became a narcotics agent. That second career ended in early retirement when he suffered a brain hemorrhage.

When he met me after I pulled into his driveway, he remarked with an easy smile, "You can see that I have lost my football build." We sat in his den, where several treasured photos are displayed, and reminisced. He has not distanced himself from his past because of any ill feelings. He holds no contempt. It is simply a case of choosing to be anchored at his home on Barbe St. which backs up to a quiet bayou.

"I just don't want to go through the hassle of travel," he repeated. "I lived in New York, I worked in foreign locations, but I just want to stay home. I would return to Athens more often if I could just be there and not have to travel. Under those conditions, I would probably say okay." That not only is an honest opinion, it literally defines him.

When his old professional team held a reunion of the '56 players for a Giant game, he stayed home. "I know I would have enjoyed seeing all those guys, but I just couldn't make myself make the effort the trip required."

Yelvington lives quietly with his wife, Peggy, a high school friend whom he married at age 65 after her husband had died. It was his first marriage and they enjoy a peaceful life in the state known as "Sportsman's Paradise," which he only knows about by reading the outdoor page in the newspaper. "You can't live much quieter than we do," he smiles.

Yelvington played on the '48 Orange Bowl team, backup to Porter Payne, the Bulldog captain. He can recall the subsequent disappointment like it happened yesterday. "I've always felt badly that we didn't enjoy more success the three years I was a starter," Yelvington says. "I am disappointed that I didn't play better, too.

"Over the years, I have thought about it, and I don't think anybody can put their finger on what went wrong. I have always felt that we scrimmaged far too much. I felt that I played a lot of great games on the practice field. You could sense Coach Butts' frustration.

"While I don't believe in spells or voodoo, I often think about the Orange Bowl. Texas was considered a third rate team. They were ready and we weren't, and what I remember is their band playing 'The Eyes of Texas Are Upon You.' That damn band played so loud and hard, and I can remember that we felt like it gave their team a big lift.

"Things for Georgia just seemed to go down hill after that. I've thought about that a lot, and if you check the record you'll see that things were never as good after the Orange Bowl. Especially when you compare it to the great success of the forties.

"I blame our problems on the Texas band. It was like the band caused a hex or a spell to envelop Georgia's program."

FRANCIS MARION CAMPBELL
THE SWAMP FOX

Marion Campbell, the Swamp Fox, spent his life in football. A look back reveals that he was successful at what he knew best, but there were some bittersweet times.

At Georgia, for example, he did not make All-America but was a better player than many who did. "Some of that had to do with the fact that the teams he played on in 1949-50-51 were not as successful. The '50 team could have been a major bowl team if we could have moved the ball better on offense," says Dan Magill, an admirer and friend.

The Bulldogs gave up a total of 65 points, an average of 5.9 points per game for the regular season of 1950. What did the team in were three tie games in which the points scored totaled a mere 20: 7-7 vs. St. Mary's; 0-0 against North Carolina and 13-13 with LSU. On top of that, Georgia could not score against Tech in Athens and lost a close one, 7-0. The 65 points allowed by the defense remains the fewest of any team at Georgia, playing an eleven game season.

Frustration reigned supreme for both coaches and players. "We were so close, but we just lacked the edge we needed in tight games," Campbell says.

It was Dan Magill who named the Bulldog tackle for a sly Revolutionary War general. Campbell distinguished himself at Georgia and later in the National Football League, first as a player and later as a coach.

In the late 1950s and early '60s the Philadelphia Eagles could've changed their name with the great number of Bulldogs on the roster.

At one point or another at least half dozen Bulldog players had signed to play for the Eagles. Theron Sapp and Riley Gunnels joined Bobby Walston and Campbell in 1959 and soon to follow were Dave Lloyd, via a trade, and Pete Case.

The Eagles won the world's championship in 1960 which made them the toast of the city, and nobody on that team was more popular than Campbell, all-pro defensive end. Campbell had started his pro career with the 49ers after leaving Georgia in 1952.

He was All-SEC for the Bulldogs three times and went from player to coach immediately after his playing career ended.

Those who knew him were not surprised that he chose to become a coach, and certainly were not surprised that he soon established a reputation of enduring respect.

In coaching, there is no magic formula. Some use one approach, others choose another. With Campbell, he established the philosophy early in his career that players counted more than coaching. He never changed his view. "You can always find a coach," Campbell said. "But finding players who can get the job done is the trick."

After the 1960 NFL title game, when the Eagles defeated Vince Lombardi and his upstart Packers, Campbell decided to play one more year. "To make the big money," he laughs. The big money then was $17,500. His winner's share from the championship game was $5,200.

Marion Campbell, the Swamp Fox

But he learned something from that experience. "Naturally you want to make the most money you can," he says, "because that is your profession. But you don't really play for the money. I didn't. My teammates didn't, and you know something, that is the way it is now," he said in the late Eighties, when he was Falcons head coach. Campbell's view on that subject will never change. "The pro athlete plays because of the competition. He wants to improve as a player. He wants to play on a championship team. That is more important than anything," Campbell believes.

Following his NFL playing career, Campbell coached for two years with the Boston Patriots of the American Football League. He then joined his old teammate Norm Van Brocklin, who had quarterbacked the Eagles to the title in '60, at Minnesota where Campbell began an NFL coaching career that lasted for nearly three decades.

He was a head coach of the Eagles (1983-85) and twice with the Falcons (1974-76 and 1987-89). The head coaching years were not the best of times for him. Campbell never campaigned or politicked for any head coaching position, thinking that if management wanted him, they could seek him out. A self-promoter, he never was, but there were many who were quick to recommend him.

His genial rapport with the players and those around him, made him a popular choice, and those who know him and his abilities believe he would have been more successful had it not been for the poor timing – catching teams in decline with ownership expecting quick results. Remember what he always said. Winning comes when you've got the players.

When the Los Angeles Rams lined up the "Fearsome Foursome" of Merlin Olsen, Lamar Lundy, Roosevelt Grier and Deacon Jones on defense, Campbell was their coach. He ran Norm Van Brocklin's defense at Minnesota, and he was the defensive coordinator for Dick Vermeil when the Eagles made it to the Super Bowl in 1980.

I had an opportunity to visit with him in all of those NFL stops, and watched him work. He had a smooth teaching style and he taught with an accent on the positive. He was never blatantly critical. He never put down a player, but rather simply elevating his status, based on performance.

"When I got into the league," Campbell once said, "People appreciated my background when they found out I had played at Georgia. You can't imagine the respect that the coaches in the NFL had for Coach Butts. He threw the ball as much, sometimes more than a lot of teams in pro football.

"Any coach knows that to move the football you need more than passers and catchers and schemes. You gotta have a few linemen, and I think that helped me when I entered the league. They felt I had come out of a good background for pro football.

"I played mostly defense in college and wound up on defense in the NFL, but I know it was to my advantage to have come out of a college system the pros respected."

As a head coach at Philadelphia, and twice in Atlanta, though, it was the lack of enough capable players which led to his dismissal each time, due, in part, because he did not have enough time to build his teams into contenders.

Nonetheless, it was a good life. He saved his money, he developed a handsome NFL retirement, and when he finally had enough, he could sit on his dock at Lake Lanier, tie fishing lures and plan his next outing to Alaska where familiar rivers yield an abundance of salmon and steelheads.

He settled in at St. Augustine in 2003, where there are inter coastal outings to suit his mood. Go when you feel like it, grill what you catch and never worry about a blitzing linebacker to dump your quarterback and kill a drive that might have been the difference in a game.

Never on Sunday? That is almost always his decision on watching the NFL on television. He had been in Sunday combat so many years, that when he retired, he left the game to others. "I appreciate my time in the league, and I have a lot of friends still coaching, but when you retire, you'd rather play golf or wet a hook—especially if the fish are biting."

When he finished Georgia and was discharged from the Army, he signed with the 49ers and suspects Coach Butts figured into his early success at San Francisco. His Georgia coach told the San Francisco head coach, Buck Shaw, that Marion was the "best offensive tackle he ever coached." Campbell laughed and told Shaw, "but did he tell you I never played offense at college."

Campbell didn't stay on offense very long but that is how his pro career began. Shaw's offensive left tackle had quit and he pressed the Swamp Fox into action, and was encouraged by his conversation with Butts. "When I began my professional career," Campbell says, "there was great respect for Coach Butts. He had a reputation for working hard. Everybody in the league respected his offensive knowledge but he was appreciated, too, for the work ethic. I know it helped me as a player. He did for me what needed to be done. I learned a lot at Georgia, and I don't think I would have had the NFL success I enjoyed had I not had the experience of playing for Coach Butts. Even today, with all the changes you see in football, the teams that are successful are those which are fundamentally sound. Fundamentals haven't changed and won't. That was the way is was at Georgia with Coach Butts. It was at Georgia I learned fundamental football."

Campbell remembers that Shaw was influenced by Butts with the design of the 49er uniforms. "He told me that Georgia was always a sharply dressed team. He liked the way they looked when they came on the field. The only significant difference is that Georgia wore silver britches and the 49ers wore khaki pants."

AL THOMPSON

Nancy Butts, the youngest of Wally's and Winnie's daughters, has always espoused deep affection for her late father. She was a Georgia student in the mid-fifties when his teams struggled. She was a cheerleader and she defended and stood up for her father – fiercely and doggedly.

She knew the head of the house to be one of compassion and humility. If he, ever the competitor, coached his players tough and underscored physical tenacity, relentlessly, on the practice field, she naturally assumed that was the way football was coached and played in those years. His on-the-field habits, to her, were hearsay.

What she remembered most about her father, were his gentle ways, his concern for others, his insatiable generosity and warm affection for people. Wally Butts around the house was a lamb. If he were a lion on the field, she knew nothing about that.

When she married one of his former players, Al Thompson, she often told him about Coach Butts' personality on the home front. Al soon begged for forgiveness for being confused. "Soon after we were married," Al laughs, "Nancy would talk about how nice he was. I heard her quoting him all the time, using the baby talk for which he was famous for with the family, and I was amused to say the least.

I never knew about that side of Coach Butts, so one day, I stopped Nancy (in conversation) and said, 'I don't think we are talking about the same person.'"

It was a light hearted conversation, and, without question, both are right. Like John Rauch said, "When Coach Butts trotted on the practice field and pulled his ball cap down tightly on his head, he became a different person."

He wanted the best for his players, but practice field conditions were to be Spartan. "I think all of us," Thompson says, "had some encounter with him off the field which revealed that he had a tender heart and concern for others. That is the man that Nancy knew best, and it was the man many of us knew about, too. But she never experienced his drive for perfection on the practice field.

There are two memories from his playing days that Al especially enjoys recalling: Coach Butts often told him to run one more lap when he was getting in shape for the season. "That last one," his coach said, "does you the most good."

In 1948, Al charged across the line and tackled LSU's Y. A. Tittle for a loss on the first play of the game. "I saw the center tighten his grip on the ball, which meant he was about to snap it. I got the jump on the guy in front of me and got to the quarterback as he was backing away from center. I watched Tittle in his great pro career and often wonder how many people ever sacked him. It is the kind of thing that becomes unforgettable."

Just like Nancy remembering the baby talk around the house. "Me Butts told me to do this, me Butts sent me out to run an errand, me Butts told me to wash the dishes. Whatever me Butts tells me to do, I do."

MIKE MEROLA
PERSEVERANCE PAYS OFF

When Mike Merola was discharged from military service, following World War II, he went about the business of college education much more seriously than the average G.I, but, nonetheless, there were more applicants that billets available on college campuses.

He sought to enroll immediately but so did thousands of other discharged veterans. His first choice – a college in the East – wasn't possible without a six to twelve-month's wait.

A friend had been accepted at Georgia – where there was more space – without a wait and Merola applied immediately. With the first hurdle cleared, it was his intention to try out for football. He had received scholarship offers from Columbia, Dartmouth and Oregon following high school, but the anticipated six-month wait convinced him it wasn't worth determining if aid might still be waiting for him at one of those schools. He chose to explore other options.

After all, he had G.I. bill benefits and could support himself reasonably well if there were no football scholarship assistance available. All he wanted was a chance to play the game. Simply put, Mike loved football.

Mike Merola overcame all obstacles to become a Wally's Boy

But who could have blamed him if he had given up. Nothing went right. To begin with, the overflow situation after the war caused Georgia officials to send him to Savannah where there was an off campus setup at the military base. He then realized that while there was no wait time to enroll at the University, it could be a year before he could schedule classes in Athens where serious college football was available to ambitious veterans.

In Savannah, a physical education teacher named Wendell Wilson was impressed with Merola's skills in physical education classes, including touch football, and asked if he had ever thought of trying out for college football. "That is why I came down here," Merola told him and then explained how disappointing things were going.

Wilson got him an early exit and arranged for him to enroll in Athens in January of 1948. Nobody in the athletic department knew anything about Merola.

Touch football was to benefit him again. During a pickup game in the quadrangle formed by Memorial, Reed and Milledge Halls and Hooper Street, Coach Howell Hollis saw him catch a long pass. He yelled out to Merola from his Memorial Hall office that he should consider coming out for spring practice. Merola did just that, and in one week was issued a scholarship.

What Wallace Butts' staff liked about the tough Italian from New Jersey was his tenacious and rugged style. When they threw him into the everlasting head on tackling drills, Merola showed his mettle immediately. It was survival of the fittest. He took to contact work as if it were second nature.

It was too much for a lot of guys who had had enough of the tough life fighting a war. Many passed on football's demanding routine. The rugged Merola loved the game too much to become discouraged by a three-hour scrimmage. With a scholarship and G.I. bill benefits, he was living a very good life. Football was hard work, but the benefits were well worth it.

Merola lettered for Georgia in 1949 and 1950, being named captain of the 1950 team which was one of Georgia's outstanding defensive squads. That year the Bulldogs allowed only 65 points for the eleven game season, holding opponents to an average of 5.9 points per game. Yet the Bulldogs lost three games and were tied thrice, much of it having to do with a sputtering and inconsistent offense.

On that defensive team with Merola at right defensive end were Marion Campbell and Hamp Tanner at tackles, Art DeCarlo at linebacker and Claude Hipps in the defensive backfield. A couple of touchdowns here and there, and the Bulldogs would have been posted a championship record. As it was they finished 6-2-3 and lost to Texas A&M in the first and only Presidential Cup Bowl 40-20.

After his final year, Merola played in the Senior Bowl and gained the attention of several pro scouts, but the National Football League never excited him. First, he looked at it practically and realized that he was not likely to make it as a pro, at least for any length of time. Most of all he didn't want to interrupt his schedule for graduation which would come in the summer of 1951.

He never returned the scouts' phone calls even though he had no idea exactly what he would do when he completed requirements for his degree. All along he had thought about coaching, and in late summer he saw a note on a bulletin board at Stegeman Hall which advertised the availability of a head-coaching job in Sandersville, which then played Class B football.

The interviewing committee found favor with him and he liked the looks of things in the community. That is how Mike Merola became a head coach just a few weeks after college graduation.

Merola developed a solid program at Sandersville, but realized that if he were going to stay in the coaching and teaching business he needed to find a system where the pay and benefits were better.

So he packed up his wife, Virginia, who was from Deepstep, Ga. a rural town in Washington County and returned home to New Jersey. First he coached in his hometown of Newark, then nearby Linden and finally Parsippany. Six years of head coaching was enough and he resigned to concentrate on athletic director responsibilities. He wound up his career in administration, taking early retirement in 1983.

All along he and his wife, Virginia, thought of returning South. She spent her summers at the family spot on Lake Sinclair and two of their four daughters enrolled at Georgia, and were awarded degrees.

Picking a place to live when they returned to Georgia had one overiding priority. They wanted to locate near Athens. Mike wanted to be around college football. Watching football and playing golf were his main recreational interests so he returned to Athens where a lot of his old teammates and friends lived.

"Makes for a happy retirement," he says.

LAUREN HARGROVE

Lauren Hargrove, named the "Fabulous Phantom From Fitzgerald," by Dan Magill was the first Georgia prep star to be named All-America. His reputation, as a player in Fitzgerald in the late Forties, was as sensational as any in history of high school football in the Peach State. Even Herschel Walker, three decades later, did not enjoy greater tribute, relatively speaking, than Hargrove, who, like Herschel, had a propensity to go all the way from any spot on the field.

Hargrove entered Georgia in the fall of 1949 after leading Fitzgerald to the state championship his senior year. He scored two touchdowns in the Purple Hurricane's 20-19 victory over Decatur.

Many ole timers remember his reputation as a touchdown maker, but most probably have forgotten that he kicked two extra points, which were the margin of victory.

"Honors are nice, but I don't think it would have happened for me (making high school All-America) if it hadn't been for Dan Magill. He was a tremendous promoter of high school athletics when he wrote sports for the Atlanta Journal, and I am one of the many who benefited from his work," Hargrove says.

When Hargrove got the handoff, often for sweeps and plays designed to get him outside, his speed would leave would be tacklers in his wake. Long distance touchdown runs became his specialty.

Lauren Hargrove, Fabulous Phantom from Fitzgerald

He remembers, during his Georgia career, he would often be summoned to the old field house (where the Rankin Smith Student Athlete Academic Center is today) to race visiting high school prospects.

"They would measure those prospects against me, trying to determine how fast they were," Hargrove says. He recalls there were some close finishes, but nobody ever beat him. If you were able to out sprint Hargrove in those days, you had speed to burn.

Growing up in Fitzgerald, Hargrove's dad owned a shoe shop, and Lauren fashioned together his own football cleats. He took a pair of brogans, heavy duty work shoes, and nailed thick strips of leather to the bottom of the shoes, which meant he was the only kid in town with cleats. The shoes were as heavy as they were unique, but Hargrove believes they made his legs stronger.

After playing sandlot football all his life, Hargrove expected high school to be a breeze, which it was to a large degree. He became so serious about the game that he wouldn't drink Coca Colas or eat candy during the season. But that was after he had a run in with his coach. He cut practice one day and was informed that would be running one hundred laps. Hargrove told the coach that he would not run the laps.

"He shoved me up against a locker and told me that I had a choice. I would run the laps or I could turn in my uniform. That changed my attitude which was a good thing for me. When I finished at 9:00 o'clock at night, I never talked back to a coach again."

At Georgia, he enjoyed outstanding games, but did not experience the overall success as in high school. Against Auburn in 1951, he ran 79 yards for a touchdown and gained over 167 yards in the first half alone.

Framed on his basement wall is the front page of the Atlanta Journal Constitution in the Fifties that reads: "Georgia Whips Maroons, 27-0 As Lauren Hargrove Stars." Played underneath that account of the game with Mississippi State was a headline which revealed, "Truman and McArthur Meet on Wake Island."

That famous conference between the President and the commanding general of the Far East was subordinated to the story of Georgia's Saturday afternoon football game. The importance of and the passion for college football is not a latter day circumstance.

Today, Hargrove lives in a picturesque setting on the side of a mountain in Hiawasse, near the North Carolina border. As a hobby he builds bird houses in the shape of churches. He dresses in red and black every Saturday for Georgia's afternoon game.

He freely admits that he did not agree with the hard scrimmaging style of coaching in Athens during his time, but remains loyal to Georgia. The fact that he doesn't attend games in Sanford Stadium is due to his suffering from emphysema. "I'd be there if I didn't have to climb those steps to my seat," he says.

After his time at Georgia, he was twice signed to play with the Green Bay Packers. Before the first training camp was concluded, he entered the Army for two years, a time in which he did not play service football. There was no football competition on the bases where he served.

Following two years of active duty, he was again signed by the Packers but says he had missed too much football. His playing career had finally come to an end.

He chose a job in sales, becoming a district manager for a steel company and retired to his mountain home where the Phantom enjoys a fabulous view from any direction any time of the year.

Giuseppe Scichilone!

Italian to the core, a Bulldog football letterman in 1950, 1951 and 1952. I had heard about Joe, but didn't know this colorful character, and who truly loved his coach, Wallace Butts. When I met him at Cape Cod, he constantly talked about his football experience under Coach Butts at Georgia.

A running back when he showed up in Athens, he became a college graduate via the G.I. Bill and football scholarship. When he finished in Athens, he was drafted by the Chicago Cardinals, where he was a training camp teammate of Charley Trippi, who was finishing his pro career.

Scichilone returned to Athens to play in the G-Day alumni game in 1991. When the mustachioed, big girthed former letterman – with the four-lane-wide-smile took the field, the crowd roared with delight.

His jersey was too small for his protruding stomach, and when he jogged on the field, he was at top speed. He didn't make a dazzling play, but Scichilone was a happy former Bulldog.

"Even at my age, I felt young again," he smiled. "To put on a uniform and to go on that field, to line up between the hedges, makes an old man proud. To line up as a Bulldog again, even in a spring game is something I'll never forget."

In 1988, the U.S. Open golf championship was played at the Brookline Country Club in Boston. I made arrangements to attend the tournament and stay with friends Jonnet and Howard Holladay, who lived on Beacon Hill, which overlooks the Boston Commons. But, first, I decided to take a side trip out to Cape Cod and visit Joe Scic.

It was a delightful experience. At that point, he was a big time caterer on the Cape. The social elite, including the Kennedys, did business with Chef Giuseppe, Bulldog alumnus.

Joe took me fishing with his son, Ray, a member of the local police force. Ray was also a body guard for Rose Kennedy, and he drove me to the Kennedy compound. I stood in the famous yard where the late President initiated those well publicized touch football games.

I walked up to the front porch where Rose and her nurse sat in rocking chairs, enjoying the sun and a breeze off the bay. He explained I was a guest, but I was not allowed to take a photograph.

Joe took me to the best restaurants on Cape Cod. He arranged the best table, ordered for me, and when the check came, I asked if I could pay? He seemed insulted. "You are my guest. You are a Bulldog, you were a friend of my coach, Wally Butts. You think I would let you get the check? You can forget that!"

There was unmatched hospitality throughout my stay. Every time he introduced me to his friends, he presented me as though I might have been the governor. All because I was a Bulldog and a friend of Wallace Butts.

He autographed his authentic Italian cookbook, "Food for Thought with Chef Giuseppe." That is a special cookbook to keep.

You may not be aware, but actress Sophia Loren's last name is Scichilone. A cousin of Joe's, she called him a few times when she came to New York.

BILLY MIXON

Billy Mixon could play – a back with speed who grew from 175 pounds in high school to 195 at Georgia.

Mixon was a highly regarded halfback in Tifton. He made the 10-flat club. And if you had 10-flat speed, you quickly got the attention of the college recruiters. Although the measuring stick became a player's time for 40 yard sprint, in Mixon's day your reputation was based on what your speed for 100 yards.

While Mixon could play the game well and had people in Tifton waxing eloquently about his abilities on the football field, he shied away from Georgia because he was worried about the disciplinarian style of the Coach Butts. "The best way to say it," Mixon said, "is that I was afraid of Coach Butts.

So afraid, that he would not sign with the Dogs until Spec Towns came and convinced Mixon that he could make it at Georgia. Even with his older brother, Ray, in school in Athens, Mixon was reluctant to report in the fall of 1947. He had what most folks sought in those days – a scholarship. But he could not overcome his reluctance, based on the fear that the style of "Little Round Man" in Athens was too hard nosed.

None of that bothered his parents, who packed his suitcase late one summer day, put him in the car and drove him to Athens. When they got to the dormitory – Milledge Annex – Mixon's father put his clothes out on the curb and said goodbye. Billy knew what that meant. If he were going to get along with his father, he'd have to enroll at Georgia and get on with the business of playing college football.

It wasn't long before Mixon fit in very comfortably in those campus days of hitchhiking and walking. He eventually had his own car on campus. Mixon's father was a mechanic and Billy's '34 Chevy was the best running car in Athens. A Saturday hero with wheels in those post-war years never suffered for lack of friends, dates and attention.

Billy lettered three years, starting for the Dogs in the 1949 Orange Bowl versus Texas. Playing on the SEC championship team of 1948 remains an achievement he is proudest of, although Mixon is one of those players whom you would have to peruse old scrapbooks to get any information about his career.

In the 1949 game with LSU, it was Mixon who scored the winning touchdown. The game, which was played at night, was a defensive battle from the start. Neither team could score through the first three quarters. Early in the fourth quarter, Eli Maricich returned an LSU punt to the Georgia 45-yard line to begin Georgia's winning drive. Three plays later, quarterback Ray Prosperi connected on a screen pass to Bob Walston, who took the ball to LSU's 17. A couple of plays later, Mixon leaped over the goal for the winning touchdown.

COL. CHARLES BECKWITH

Unlike most Georgia alumni, Charlie Beckwith's line of work prevented him from returning to campus following graduation in 1952, but it didn't keep Georgia off his mind.

A letterman, 1950-51, Beckwith became a professional soldier, one of the best this country has ever produced. When he was engaged in brutal fighting in Vietnam and in training this country's Delta Force, the anti-terrorist unit, he often reflected on the value of his football experience.

Beckwith, who died in 1994, was a study in commitment, and if there ever was a no nonsense, tell-it-like-it-is proponent, it was this Atlanta native who was willing to die for his country and did indeed put his life on the line a number of times.

That is why he evaluated his college football experience as important in what he accomplished in life. But he was quick to speak his mind on the things he didn't like about football, even after years had passed.

"A lot of boys got beat up during spring practice, which lasted far too long in my opinion. Some of what we did in the spring was not necessary. It didn't make sense, but I appreciate the good things that I learned from football.

"I like the way Vince Lombardi explained it. The players had to know what their jobs were and they had to understand what unity was all about and cover for their buddies. Love your mates. Really respect and love them. And develop self-discipline. I think those things are very important. Football taught me a lot of self-discipline and that was significant in my business."

Charlie Beckwith's business became the business of fighting for his country. Twice he volunteered for duty in Vietnam. He saw men die because other men didn't possess the proper leadership instincts and skills. They were not properly prepared, nor did they make the right decisions under the pressure of combat.

Charlie Beckwith demanded of himself that he be different, that he be the exception, the one forever prepared. That commitment to be the best officer he could be saved lives and, not coincidentally, his own.

He took a machine gun bullet right through his stomach in The Vietnam War and the field doctors determined he would not make it. Beckwith, lying on a cot dying, overheard a doctor say that the operating table could be better used on a solider who had a chance to pull through.

Beckwith heard that comment, and it was the doctor who almost didn't make it as Beckwith reached up and grabbed him by the neck and told the physician in no uncertain terms that he would make it and that the doctor better "get the hell to work."

The stories about Beckwith's commitment and hell-for-leather style are legendary in U.S. Army circles, and anyone appreciative of one man's commitment to his country would do well to spend a couple of evenings with Beckwith's book, *Delta Force*, an account of his military career. It offers vivid details of why his commando unit, which he had worried and sweated into what he believes was the best anti-terrorist unit in the world, failed to get to Tehran and rescue the American hostages in 1980.

In his book Charlie spares no punches, taking on the media, the military bureaucracy, the ego czars of the Pentagon and the miserable, lamentable hippie protestors who threw whiskey on him and other Nam veterans when they walked through the San Francisco Airport.

Beckwith was an eye-for-an-eye-and-a-tooth-for-a-tooth combatant, who wanted to be the best at something. He entered the Army with no family tradition for the military, expecting to serve his two years and move

Charlie Beckwith as a hard nosed lineman and later as a decorated soldier

on to something else.

In fact, with a college football background, he was asked to play and coach football, but he never got to that. By the time his first military contract was ending, he got a call one morning from a Col. Robert L. Linvill – a man he came to admire and appreciate – advising him he had two pieces of paper on his desk. One to apply for a regular Army commission and the other to resign from the Army altogether. "You are not going to leave until you sign one or the other," said Linvill.

That became a turning point in Beckwith's career. He did not think that he was good enough to become a regular Army officer, but once he gained the confidence, there was nothing to stand between him and becoming the best. He evolved into a soldier who spoke his mind and "kicked ass" to get the job done. "I never accomplished anything with tact," he said candidly. "I never cared about that. I was always just interested in getting the job done. Consequently, you will find my name to be the subject of a lot of controversy in Army circles."

Did that bother him? "Hell, no because I have the satisfaction of knowing that I did the best that I could do, and that, during my entire Army career, I never asked anybody to do anything I wouldn't do or hadn't done or wasn't prepared to do," he said after retirement from the Army.

When Beckwith organized Delta Force for the United States, he worked night and day for years. His men were special and if his unit should be called on, he knew it would be ready.

When the Iranian students overran the U.S. Embassy in Tehran in 1980, Beckwith and his anti-terrorist unit developed a plan to rescue the hostages. He met with President Carter, two Georgians dealing in international high stakes, and laid out his plan at the White House Oval Office.

As we now know, the mission failed and with it went a big piece of Charlie Beckwith's life. The interesting part about the aborted mission was that Beckwith stuck with the game plan. The plan called for six helicopters to go from the rendezvous in the desert to the outskirts of Tehran, and while it pained Beckwith to the utmost to call the mission off, he stuck with the plan. He refused to risk the lives of his men by going in with five helicopters when the plan called for six.

Beckwith was not going to do anything foolish, and he had a backup plan for every move. When a busload of Iranians happened to surprise Beckwith and his taskforce at the rendezvous in the desert, Beckwith knew the best decision. "We were going to fly them out of the country until the mission was over, then fly them back. I'd given my word to President Carter that I was not going to go maliciously kill people. I had told him that I would kill every s.o.b. in the Embassy that had a weapon if God gave me the strength, but we were not going to maliciously shoot innocent people. That's not the way we do business."

In the end it was helicopter failure that caused the aborted mission. It was Beckwith's decision on whether or not to proceed when he was told that only five helicopters would be available for the trip into the outskirts of Tehran. Beckwith said, "We're going back to the (aircraft carrier) Nimitz."

A simple accident had wrecked the plan. The most experienced helicopter pilot made a mistake, lifting off and bumping into a C-130 loaded with fuel, causing rockets to explode. Eight men died and made Beckwith the sickest he had ever been in his life. The mission had to be aborted, the unfortunate accident made it appear that the Americans didn't know what they were doing. It was a bitter experience. From the beginning Beckwith knew it was a 50-50 chance of success operation. "It was a risky operation," he says, "but I felt that we could handle it."

He remained confident throughout his final years that had his task force made it to the Embassy, which it would have with enough helicopters to handle the assignment, they would have brought the hostages home. "No question about that. Where we were vulnerable was getting there," he always maintained. When it was over and the publicity had subsided. Beckwith quietly retired from the Army and settled in Austin. He had no regrets. He was proud that patriotism seemed to be making a comeback at the time of his death. One thing was certain – if his country ever needed him, Charlie Beckwith would not have hesitated to answer the call.

This former Bulldog lineman was always ready whenever America needed him, whatever the assignment. Life in the trenches is very much a part of the football lexicon, but in the truth, nobody's life is ever on the line.

Charlie Beckwith, a loyal Wally's Boy a great American, who distinguished himself in real combat, often put his life on the line.

CLAUDE HIPPS

Against Florida in the old Gator Bowl in 1944, Georgia had the ball, and when Claude Hipps leaned forward and heard quarterback Ken McCall call his number, his heart began to pound harder and harder.

It was for a pitchout. Hipps turned the end, got outside and scored. His heart pounded even harder, not so much from the exhilirartion of scoring, but from the awareness that his family was in the stands, having driven down from Waycross for the game.

"You always want to play your best, just for personal pride reasons," Hipps says. "You want to please your

Wally and Captain Claude Hipps

coaches and help the team, but when your family sees you perform and you do well, you gain an extra amount of satisfaction."

Georgia defeated Florida 38-12, but the headlines were more about World War II, and Hipps was soon off to war when he became of age. He had made a four year commitment to the Marines in order to have some voice in his military assignment, wanting to serve with his twin brother, Francis.

He would play service ball while on active duty but believed his college playing days were over. When he was discharged in 1949, he returned home to Waycross, where Vassa Cate, Coach Butts' first captain, was coaching. Cate ran a men's store on the side, and when Hipps walked in one day, the first thing Cate said was, "What are your plans about football?"

Hipps had not given a return to college football any thought, but Cate immediately called Coach J. B. Whitworth. Soon thereafter Hipps was on a bus to Athens. He would letter as a regular at halfback in 1949-50-51 and was voted captain his senior season. He was one of those returning veterans who appreciated his scholarship to the extent that he would have postponed marriage if his coach failed to give him permission.

"He (Coach Butts) had a no marriage rule," Hipps laughs. "At least you had to have permission. Even after four years in the Marines, I was quite in awe of Coach Butts and a little afraid of him. I went down to see him at his restaurant downtown, 'The Huddle,'. Bette waited in the car, wondering what the decision would be.

"When I walked up to his table and asked for permission, I thought I was whispering, but all of a sudden I sounded like the loudest person in the restaurant. He looked at me and said, 'Well, you are old enough to know what you are doing.' I was quite relieved because I was not going to give up that scholarship. When I returned to the car, the smile on my face gave Bette the good news of his blessing for us to get married."

Later, the coach helped the young married couple find an exclusive apartment but at a rate they could afford, reminding the player that his coach was always doing things for those who came his way.

After receiving his marketing degree, Hipps played two years with the Pittsburgh Steelers and will never forget Coach Butts' advice: "Work hard and you will make it. If they ask you to run 50 yards, run 100."

That is the same philosophy he underscored when Hipps signed on with a career with Frito-Lay. He retired from there but later joined Tom's Foods for eight years.

Moving about with Frito Lay caused Hipps to give up his season tickets, which he started buying immediately after graduation. When he returns to Athens, he is reminded that "memories of your college days stay with you forever. Times have changed, Georgia has changed, but the look of the main campus still is familiar. I have good feelings when I go back to Athens."

When he talks about being elected captain, you hear a familiar refrain, but one which reflects heartfelt thanks. "Is there a greater honor than to be elected captain by your teammates?"

His answer to his own question is obvious. "I certainly don't think so."

1951

The '51 Bulldogs broke even, 5-5, but lost three tough outings: 0-6 to Mississippi State in Starkville; 0-7 to LSU in Athens and at home to Alabama 14-16. In six games, Georgia scored but 34 points and only claimed victory in one of those games, a downing of Florida in Jacksonville, 7-6. The Bulldogs' offensive inconsistency would linger on.

Zippy Morocco

In this day of specialization, playing both college football and basketball is pretty much out of the question. It wasn't exactly easy in Anthony Morocco's day either.

We're talking about the years 1948-53. His half-backing was often flashy and his basketball scoring was so productive that he set the Southeastern Conference single season scoring record. It was on the basketball court that he acquired his nickname, Zippy, which characterized his stop and go style. He zipped about with remarkable aplomb.

Even so, he had to go from the bumps and bruises and muscle tightening of football right into basketball, a non-stop action when his muscles needed to be loose and relaxed. Not an easy transition but Morocco was a quick, fluid and graceful athlete.

Perhaps the toughest challenge was that he was caught up in a day-to-day grind the year 'round. He was late for basketball practice, even in those years, by the time football season ended. When basketball concluded with the annual Southeastern Conference tournament, he was late for spring practice, which seemingly lasted forever.

"I remember finishing the SEC tournament one week and playing in the G-Day game a couple of weeks later and then practicing football until school was out," he recalls. When everybody took off for home for Christmas holidays Zippy remained behind, almost in isolation, in Milledge Annex, for basketball workouts and games.

Playing sports and completing degree requirements under those circumstances were far more suitable than his other option, which was to return to his hometown of Youngstown, Ohio, and find work in the steel mills. "After my senior year in high school I worked in the mills, and I knew then if I could do something else, I would," he says. The University of Georgia afforded him that opportunity, but he had to wrestle with acute homesickness his first year in Athens.

He reported with over 100 freshmen in the summer of 1948 and it was obvious that it would be a classic case of the survival of the football fittest. The freshmen recruits were housed in the basement of old Memorial Hall. Bunk beds were arranged barracks style.

"You could hear those suitcases being stuffed and slammed shut in the middle of the night," he laughs. "You knew in about three days who would stick it out and who wouldn't. I was homesick form the start but I wanted to play for Georgia, and with Coach Quinton Lumpkin's encouragement I settled down and soon became adjusted. Once that happened I fell in love with Athens and realized I had made the right decision. I never wanted to leave after I gained the confidence that I could make it at Georgia."

Born the son of an Italian immigrant who spent his life in those steel mills, Morocco was taken by athletics early. For any competition that took place in the streets and on neighborhood playgrounds, he expected to be included.

Youngstown, situated in Eastern Ohio near the Pennsylvania border, has spawned many accomplished athletes. A number of them have worn the red and black of Georgia including Morocco, Art DeCarlo, George Poschner, Al Bodine, Nick Feher, Al Perl and

Heisman Trophy winner, Frank Sinkwich.

"I met Frank on that first visit to Athens which was special since I knew about his career," Zippy says. "Frank was very popular back in Youngstown, and Georgia was a big name there because of his career and the great teams that Coach Butts had produced. Frank's association with Georgia had a lot to do with my wanting to come to Athens.

His initial visit came Thanksgiving weekend 1947. He made his first plane flight from Akron to Atlanta and remembers riding a bus to Athens with a Barberton, Ohio athlete named Bob Toneff, who would wind up at Notre Dame although he signed with Georgia first.

Zippy Morocco excelled in two sports

"Toneff was a great All-American in college and played many years with the Washington Redskins. He was ruled ineligible for Georgia because he had signed with Tennessee. By signing with two schools in the same conference he couldn't play with either and that is how Notre Dame wound up with him."

Zippy developed into an outstanding punt returner for the Bulldogs and was rated by Coach Butts as one of the best he ever coached. By the end of his football career Butts also named Morocco the best pass-receiving halfback he had coached.

"Zippy's quickness and leaping ability were exceptional," says Bill Hartman. "Today, he would likely play the position of wide out, and he would excel. He had great hands. He probably had as much pass receiving ability as Lindsay Scott although he was not as fast.

In basketball, he ripped the nets so often in his career that he set the all-time SEC single season scoring record of 590 points. It took a big man, a center, Bob Pettit, who was almost an entire foot taller and positioned close in at the basket where tip-ins and rebound scores gave him considerable advantage, to break Zippy's mark.

The SEC coaches voted Zippy the most valuable player in the league. No trophy was awarded, and the only thing tangible he has for that honor is a collection of faded newspaper clippings.

As a senior Morocco led the SEC in scoring with a 23.6 average and scored 39 against Tennessee in Knoxville, leading the Bulldogs to an 87-86 win. Gus Manning, the Vols Sports Information Director, called Furman Bisher, sports editor of *The Atlanta Constitution* and told him, "Zippy Morocco gave the greatest performance I have ever seen on a Tennessee court. I've never seen anything like it."

After his final collegiate season, the Minneapolis Lakers drafted him for basketball and the Philadelphia Eagles for football. He played in the 1951 North-South Shrine football game in Miami, which was to influence his choice in regard to pro football or basketball. The South coach was Douglas Clyde (Peahead) Walker, who advised Zippy he should consider Canadian football.

Peahead offered him $1,000.00 more in salary than the Eagles plus a $5,000 bonus. Zippy, always one to keenly appreciate top dollar, took the higher offer.

Five weeks into the season he was drafted into the Army and finished his career playing service ball. A badly torn hamstring muscle hastened the end of his football career.

Returning to Athens, Zippy tried the restaurant business and a couple of other ventures before qualifying for a real estate license. Success in business allowed time to pursue tennis and golf.

"I feel good every time I think about my association with Athens and the University," Morocco says. "I've been very fortunate in business and it was because of my affiliation with Georgia athletics. I got to know a lot of people and people who remembered me from my days at Georgia.

ED GREENWAY

In 1950 Georgia lost to Alabama, but Ed Greenway, an indefatigable guard, born at Rock Branch in Elbert County, was named the outstanding Bulldog lineman.

That was a big deal and is easy for him to explain. "The winner got a pair of new shoes from Lamar Lewis Shoe Store. If you had grown up in those times, you would consider it a big deal, too," he laughs.

Those times were when the work ethic was way underscored and people made do. A penny saved was, indeed, a penny earned. If you were an appreciative football player on scholarship, your basic keep was covered. Any bonuses like the gift of a pair of shoes or some clothes meant that your parents could devote their energies and finances in the direction of the remainder of the family.

For many of those who played high school football in the Forties and early Fifties, college was often out of the question unless there was scholarship aid.

"Certainly, in my case," says Greenway, whose parents owned a grocery in Athens' Five Points where Ed was expected to pitch in. In the summers he worked the better part of the day at the store, then headed down Lumpkin Street to practice football.

"We all expected to work, and when I look back on it," Greenway says, "I realize how important that was. We have a lot more today, but life was never better." A grateful Greenway often reflects on that good life of the past.

Everybody had responsibilities at home, each member of family expected to handle a variety of chores. An ice cream cone was a big treat. A free movie pass, which the football players were entitled to, gave the athletes a much appreciated entertainment option. Ed remembers a chili dog at the Varsity cost only a dime back then. There were both train and plane rides to distant cities for the football team, a learning experience that became more appreciated with the passing of time.

"To go to college on football scholarship, get an education, play between the hedges, wear those silver britches, travel out of town for games and hang out at the Varsity were wonderful experiences," he remembers. "Today I treasure all that."

With a degree in education, Greenway chose a career military opportunity which enlarged his geographical exposure. He lived in places like Morocco, California, Viet Nam, Montana, and Nebraska. But when his Air Force days were winding down, he knew what he would do.

"I always wanted to return to Athens where I grew up," he says. "I knew the quality of life, and wanted to return home. It was a rewarding experience, living other places, but I never considered living anywhere else when I retired."

Ed Greenway, the smile of a well shod lineman

You would expect that of a lineman, a trench alumnus who maintains an appreciation for the training and exposure on campus which stimulated opportunity. He often reflects on the values he learned from toughing it out as a lineman.

"We didn't worry about the headlines," Ed explains. "We just wanted to do our job and help Georgia win. Victory on Saturday was our objective and we were willing to work to get it. Everybody had a job to do and Coach Butts expected us to do our job. Quite frankly we expected it of ourselves, and we learned never to let up.

"I can remember taking out three men on a play in a game, and Coach Butts never even acknowledged it. But when I missed an assignment, he was all over me.

"Years later in the military, I appreciated what he taught me. You don't expect praise when you do your job. But when you make mistakes, you are put on notice. When you make mistakes in the field, somebody might lose their life. There is no greater reward than the satisfaction of knowing you did your job to the best of your ability. I learned that from Coach Butts."

LOUIS TROUSDALE

Following the Tech game in 1951, Louis Trousdale, an emissary for industrialist, Louis E. Wolfson, called on his friend Wallace Butts.

He joined Coach Butts for breakfast in his suite at the Biltmore Hotel in Atlanta. Georgia had been dominated by the Yellow Jackets the day before, 48-6, which should have enhanced Trousdale's mission.

Wolfson, a 1931 Bulldog football letterman, had accumulated considerable wealth and was anchored in the Washington, D. C. area. A group of influential Baltimore citizens sought an NFL franchise and asked Wolfson if he would consider ownership of the team.

The Bulldog loyalist was, in fact interested. He would buy the team for his brother, Sam. There were eleven principal points to be considered to consummate the deal. The first ten had to do with business matters, but the eleventh was the most critical. To own an NFL team, his good friend, Wallace Butts, would have to agree to coach it.

It was, indeed, an attractive opportunity. Trousdale explained to his long time friend that he would be fixed for life, financially. In essence Coach Butts could pretty much write his own ticket if he accepted Wolfson's offer.

The offer included 40% ownership of the team. Sam Wolfson would have a 50% stake and Trousdale 10%. "Selfishly," Trousdale smiles, "I wanted him to take the job. My ten per cent would be for my sweat equity putting the deal together for Lou."

After explaining the details, Trousdale pushed the documents across the breakfast table, graphically confirming the golden opportunity. To Trousdale's shock, the Bulldog coach didn't even scan the paperwork, which he immediately pushed back in Trousdale's direction, politely declining.

"Afterwards I kidded him about what he did to me financially, but I was not too bothered since I knew how much he truly loved the University of Georgia. A part of me wanted him to stay at my alma mater," Trousdale says. Wolfson later said, "We made Coach Butts an offer which we did not think he could refuse."

There was another offer which Trousdale thought would be near impossible for his favorite coach to refuse, and that came from Florida governor, Fuller Warren. If Coach Butts would take over the Gator program in Gainesville, he would be given a home, cars, free education for his daughters and the use of an airplane for recruiting. In the Forties, having a plane at a coach's disposal for recruiting was an unheard of perk in the business.

"Coach Butts didn't even respond on that overture either," Trousdale notes. "What is so interesting to me about all this is that he did not leverage his opportunity with Georgia officials. I don't think there has ever been anybody more loyal to our University than Coach Butts."

Trousdale got to know Coach Butts in 1938. He was a member of the Bulldog freshman baseball team, and Coach Butts coached the freshmen, one of his responsibilities in addition to serving as an assistant in football.

"I admired Coach Butts so much, I loved his tenacity and his fighting spirit, and when he gave me an opportunity to work in the business office and assist in recruiting, I considered that one of the greatest days of my life."

That was in the winter of 1941, but Trousdale's official affiliation with Coach Butts and Georgia would be interrupted by World War II. Trousdale became a Marine aviator, seeing action in the Pacific for fourteen months. During his time as a fighter pilot, he flew during one period of his assignment with the famous aviator, Charles Lindberg. After the war, he rejoined Coach Butts again. His job? "To do anything Coach Butts wanted me to do."

In the fall of 1949, their mutual friend, Lou Wolfson, offered Trousdale an opportunity he could not refuse. He spent the rest of his professional life associated with Wolfson, the one time Bulldog lineman and Wally Butts aficianado, whose horse Affirmed is the last thoroughbred to capture horse racing's Triple Crown.

1952

The '52 Bulldogs won seven games but were shut out twice, by Maryland in Athens 37-0 and Florida in Jacksonville, 30-0. Georgia won big against N.C. State 49-0, Pennsylvania 34-27, and Miami 35-13. It was an up and down year, but, unfortunately for the 'Dogs, that was the day when seven victories would not bring a bowl invitation. What was on the horizon for the combative Wallace Butts? Gloom would settle over Athens as he would field only one winning team in the next six years.

Harry Babcock By Dan Magill

Wallace Butts called Harry Babcock his best pass-catcher and also his best blocking end. And he thought Babcock, who was the San Francisco 49ers' first choice in the 1953 college draft, would be a big success in the NFL.

But extremely tough luck, especially in the injury category, cut short his pro career and also kept him from setting more records than he did in college.

Charley Trippi was indirectly responsible for Babcock's coming to Georgia. Rocco English, a former high school coach in Babcock's home area who had served in the army with Trippi during World War II, told Trippi Georgia should "look at" Babcock. So, Babcock reported Sept. 1 as a candidate for the Georgia freshman team.

Being Georgia's SID in those days, I well remember Harry. He was a six-foot, 174-pounder with crew-cut light brown hair – an exceptionally alert-looking boy who eventually was 6-2, 196 in his prime.

He had been a blocking back on a single wingback team in high school at Pearl River, NY. Because Georgia used the T-formation and Babcock had no ball-carrying or passing experience, Coach Butts immediately switched him to end.

Coach Butts drilled his freshmen mostly on fundamentals. The SEC permitted freshmen to play only three games, and Babcock did not catch a single pass in any of those freshman games. But he did make the first team at right end, and his freshman coach, Quinton Lumpkin, termed him a "good, all-round football player."

Babcock began the 1950 Varsity season as the second-string right end, but he earned a starting assignment in the third game against North Carolina. Although Georgia had several fine receivers at end, led by Bob Walston (later a star with the Philadephia Eagles), Georgia was not a passing team: they had no passer! The no. 1 QB Billy Grant was lost for the season (injury) in the opening game against Maryland.

Harry played well as a sophomore, though, never failing to carry out his blocking assignments and always hustling on pass routes. His receiving record showed eight catches for 77 yards, with two more catches for 22 yards against Texas A & M in the first and only Presidential Cup game in College Park, MD.

Big Jim Whatley was Harry's end coach as a sophomore. Whatley, who had played right tackle next to the immortal Don Hutson at Alabama, often remarked that Babcock was the best blocking end he had ever seen. Coach Butts raised Jim one with this praise: "Babcock is the best blocker I have seen at any position".

Babcock, in the 1951 spring practices, really began "coming into his own," and that fall he did everything one could expect of a truly great offensive end. In ten games he caught 41 passes for 666 yards to lead the SEC. He received more votes in the balloting than anyone else except two All-America backs — Kentucky's Babe Parilli and Tennessee's Hank Lauricella.

Harry had a new end coach in 1951, Perron Shoemaker, who had been an All-SEC end three straight years at Alabama from 1936-38. Shoemaker further polished Babcock's play.

Perhaps Harry's finest performance was against

powerful Maryland in the fourth game. He caught nine passes for 114 yards and thoroughly pleased his parents, who had come down from Pearl River to see him play for the first time at Georgia. They had hoped to see Harry catch a TD pass. If they had been in Athens two weeks later, they would have witnessed him snagging two TD passes against Boston College, one for 76 yards, and the other for 53 yards.

Harry Babcock, one of the greatest to play for Wally

At the beginning of Harry's senior season, Sept. 6, 1952 he was injured in an automobile wreck in Athens. He sustained a cut lip requiring 23 stitches, also a bruised knee and badly bruised chest bone. He was unable to practice for the opener against Vanderbilt Sept. 20, but he begged to play; although he started, he could last only eight minutes. He did catch one pass for eight yards. The next week at New Orleans he led Georgia to victory over a strong Tulane team, catching eight passes for 58 yards.

It was three weeks later when Harry had fully recovered from his injuries. Against LSU in Baton Rouge, he caught three passes for 59 yards in a 27-14 Georgia win.

Tough luck again hit Babcock the next week against Florida in Gainesville. Early in the game he was ejected for fighting. Actually, he was "held" by a Florida linebacker while covering a punt. Babcock tried to free himself, and the official ruled he was slugging his opponent.

The next week at Alabama Harry came back with a super performance: eight catches for 106 yards. Alabama players unanimously picked him on their all-opponent team.

The next week against Pennsylvania in Franklin field in Philadelphia, QB Zeke Bratkowski and Babcock put on a fabulous All-America passing and receiving act. Harry caught four of Zeke's passes, two for TDs (44 and 32 yards). Penn players named both Zeke and Harry as the two best players they had met all season.

It was at Franklin Field that Harry so impressed Andy Kerr that he invited him to play in the East-West All-Star game in San Francisco. In his last two games at Georgia against Auburn and Georgia Tech, Babcock was at his best blocking.

"We were in great danger against Auburn in the fourth quarter, trying to protect a 13-7 lead," said Coach Butts. "We had just stopped Auburn at our 4-yard line and did not want to give up the ball by punting. Zeke knew our best chance to keep the ball would be to run plays over Babcock's position. On six straight rushes, featuring Babcock's blocking, we gained 46 yards and kept the ball long enough to assure victory. And the man Babcock had to move was big Bill Turnbeaugh, Auburn's 270-pound All-America tackle."

Georgia scored early in the game against undefeated Georgia Tech with FB Bob Clemen's ploughing over from the four behind Babcock's blocking. But Harry's hard luck continued. Early in the second quarter he received a broken cheekbone colliding with Tech's safetyman Jakie Rudolph. Harry missed the remainder of the game and also the final against Miami the next week. And it cost him the SEC receiving title for the second straight year. Teammate Johnny Carson edged him, 32 catches to 31.

Harry was great in covering kicks, too. He made a bone-crushing tackle on Tech's fleet Bill Teas, stopping him in an open field. It broke Teas' collarbone.

Coach Butts often said that Babcock was the best decoy he had ever seen, always drawing at least two defenders to cover him, making other receivers wide open. He was selected to two All-America teams after his final season: Saturday Evening Post and Collier's.

Four weeks after the Tech game, playing with a mask protecting his fractured cheekbone, Harry was a standout in the East's 21-20 victory over the West in San Francisco. Switched to left end, he caught seven passes, tying the record for that classic. He scored the first TD, catching a pass from Tommy O'Connell (Illinois) while almost lying down in the end zone. He also cleared the way for the winning TD run by Bill Reynolds (Pittsburgh).

In the pros with San Francisco the fans saw in Babcock the most graceful receiver in football. For short passes, he was absolutely unconcerned over the defenders bearing down on him. On the run, he caught the ball over either shoulder, resembling a fast outfielder racing down a ball.

In fact, Babcock was quite an outfielder. He made the All-SEC first team at centerfield his junior year, and the 49ers were anxious to sign him after the '52 season, thinking that if he played his last season of baseball at Georgia in the spring of '53 that baseball scouts would sign him.

Harry was "snake bit" in pro football, too. He played two years with the 49ers, injuries ending his career there. He tried a comeback in the Canadian season, but injuries forced his retirement after one year. It wasn't in the books for him to have a long life either. He died in 1996 at age 66.

AN UNSUNG HERO GLYNN HYDE

Doesn't matter the war—in the Butts era—Georgia football players answered the call: World War II, Korea and the Cold War. One, Jack Cox of Waynesboro, lost his life in Viet Nam.

The cold war was not a shooting war, but it kept America on its toes militarily. Although fighting never broke out, times were often tense and apprehensive with America and Russia in an atomic arms race. The United States government was greatly concerned about the expansion of Communism, and one of the important missions of the Air Force was round-the-clock surveillance. When the U-2 spy plane was put into operation, the general public was unaware of the existence of the aircraft until Francis Gary Powers' plane was shot down over Russia.

For security reasons, Americans were unaware of U-2 missions. A U-2 pilot who lost his life in an accident was Glenn Hyde of LaGrange. Hyde came to Georgia as an outstanding high school lineman, but had to give up football, on medical advice, after suffering a head injury.

Eugene "Tiger" Methvin, 1954 letterman, who was also an Air Force pilot, recalled for the Georgia football programs his knowledge of the U-2 and what is known about Hyde's fatal crash off the coast of Florida. The title of the story for the program was apropos: "An Unsung Hero. Glory Evades Hyde in Football, but Finds Him Later." Here's Methvin's account of Hyde's fatal crash.

"The U-2 flew on the edge of the stratosphere, where the air had a density of only about three percent of that at sea level. The winds there were still much of a mystery. Every aviator knows he risks such devils lurking in the sky with every liftoff, just as every football player knows he risks crippling injury every time he leaves the sideline.

"One former CIA supervisor of U-2 reconnaissance missions once told me, 'that plane took many lives. A lot of good pilots were killed in it. It was difficult to fly properly at altitude or close to the ground.'

"The U-2 presented an extraordinary hazard in that it flew in air so thin it was always on the edge of a stall and spin. And yet because the speed of sound was lowered to near the U-2's cruising speed in the thin air, the 'sound barrier' presented the ever-present threat of buffeting, a vibration that could tear the plane apart.

"Thus the U-2 flew in a very tender 'throat' between twin disasters. The margin between stall and mach buffet was about four knots. At least three pilots training over the U.S. tangled with those hazards. They lost control of their planes which came apart, but they ejected and survived.

"So every pilot who took a U-2 up on a reconnaissance run over hostile territory was a hero. And that is what Capt. Glenn Hyde, ASAF, did. After the Cuban Missile Crisis, the U.S. sent U-2-s over regularly to check on Soviet and Cuban installations. Glenn flew just such a mission on November 20, 1963, two days before President Kennedy's assassination. Typically, the U-2 pilots took off in the middle of the night and climbed to altitude in darkness so they would arrive over the target zone in the first hour or two of sunlight. The long shadows helped the photo interpreters decipher what they were seeing.

"Glenn was flying a new model of U-2, with a more powerful engine and more critical center-of-gravity characteristics than the earlier U-2s. Just before he began the long 'coast-out,' when he could begin to power back and start a slow descent to safety, Glenn's autopilot failed. He had to hand-fly the aircraft homeward. He lost control and entered a flat spin, from which the plane never recovered. Glenn tried to eject, but the ejection seat failed. SAC radars were tracking him on their radarscopes as he exited Cuba that morning, but at 10:32 a.m. the blips vanished 16 miles Northwest of Key West. Eight minutes later, a pilot in the area saw an oil slick.

"The wreckage was recovered, but there was no sign of Glenn. He was presumed to have attempted a manual bailout but failed to make it. Accident investigators speculated his unfamiliarity with the touchier characteristics of the newer model might have contributed to the disaster. Then again, the autopilot failure may have presaged other electrical or control failures. We will never know."

John Carson

When you become familiar with the story of John Carson, Georgia's last four-letter athlete, it is one worthy of serious review. He was an accomplished athlete, but the folklore of his family would pique the interest of any researcher or historian. There is more to his background than trophies and box scores.

You see, his daddy cavorted with bootleggers and his grandpa was a mountaineer fiddler whose legend will endure for the ages. Fiddlin' John Carson became linked with politicians who sought his mountain music to help attract huge audiences. He would bow and fret his fiddle and one of the state's best-known demagogues, Eugene Talmadge, for example, would subsequently stretch his red suspenders and disclose his promises to eager listeners.

In his early teenage years, John often accompanied his granddaddy on forays across the northern sector of the state. The deal with the politicians was that Fiddlin' John would draw the crowd, and when the hat was passed after his stimulating music, he was allowed to keep what he collected.

"Sometimes there was a lot of money in that hat," John says, "and he would always give it to me. He would tell me that he didn't expect any trouble, but if there was any, he knew I could outrun any hijackers."

Fiddlin' John was one of the best-known fiddlers in the country, and he is credited with some as the performer who actually started country music, which grew out of mountain or hillbilly music. He traveled to New York in 1923 and produced a recording that helps justify the claim that official country music, for sure, had its "record" start with John's granddaddy.

The popular Charlie Daniels tune, "The Devil Went Down to Georgia," is based on the legend of Fiddlin' John Carson, whose ancestors came over from Ireland and settled in North Georgia in the late 1700s.

John Carson, a four letterman

"I learned a lot from my granddaddy," John says. "Coach Butts knew him and really liked him. I was a freshman when he died, and Coach Butts told me to take whatever time I needed at home with the family in the Cabbage Town section of Atlanta. It meant a lot to our family that so many people in the state appreciated his music and his legend."

Much of the family history is well documented in a book by Gene Wiggins, who lived in Dahlonega at the time of his death in 1997. His book, "Fiddlin' Georgia Crazy," was published by the University of

Illinois Press. It is an entertaining and historically informative read. In Wiggins' story, which chronicles the life of Fiddlin' John and his family, you learn not only of the musical talent, but also of the widespread popularity of the family patriarch.

John Carson, the grandson and Bulldog immortal, says that his great-grandfather, Allan Carson, brought Fiddlin' John's famous fiddle to America from Ireland in the 1700s. He told Dan Magill that the fiddle was said to have been made by the son of the late Italian violin maker, Antonio Stradivari.

"I also used to enjoy listening to his daughter, Rosa Lee, sing hillbilly songs," Carson told Magill for his book, "Dan Magill's Bull-Doggerel." Carson noted that Rosa Lee was the Loretta Lynn of her day.

Long John, the name Magill gave the Georgia four-letter star, informed the Bulldog author that his granddaddy would go from town to town with Gene Talmadge when the political campaigning heated up. "He would get up on top of a flat-bottom truck in the courthouse square and play his fiddle for the country folk, an hour or so to get them primed for Gene's speeches. Aunt Rosa Lee, whose stage name was Moonshine Kate, also would sing and buck and wing dance. I remember one of the songs about Gene went like this: 'I've got a Eugene dog, I've got a Eugene cat. I'm a Talmadge man from my shoes to my hat.'"

Fiddlin' John, commonly referred to as "Fiddler," wrote over 150 songs and recorded more than 300. When he died at age 81, he was not a pauper, but Wiggins wrote that the man with the magic touch with the fiddle didn't realize much money from his talent.

A performer with his prolific production today would not only reign as a titan of country music, he could expect side benefits from network TV appearances to stretch limos to entourages akin to royalty status.

With Fiddler's reputation and his influence on country music, a nagging question jumps front and center when you review the story of his life, so thoroughly researched by Wiggins – Fiddler's fiddles photograph and one of his fiddles are displayed in the Country Music Hall of Fame in Nashville; however, he regrettably has never been enshrined. But he has been enshrined in the Georgia Music Hall of Fame. Fiddlin' John's original fiddle belongs to Long John Carson, the grandson.

One thing is certain about the legend of the Fiddler. It is secure as one of those entertainers, who had a profound impact on the development of country music. "Based on my familiarity with the history of country music," Whisperin' Bill Anderson, a Georgia graduate and a long time country music star says, "I'm not sure that anybody can take credit for the start of country music.

"The Grand Ole Opry began in 1925, and the industry evolved from that era. Fiddlin' John was the first to record a country music record, and that is significant. I know that Roy Acuff was the first serious singer at the Opry, but I just don't think that all of a sudden country music burst on the scene. It simply evolved from the hills and mountains of the South and a lot of wonderful performers made a contribution to country music in those early days. Fiddlin' John was certainly one of them."

Carson, both a Georgia and NFL star

Today, John Carson lives on 113 secluded acres in a nature enclave in Greene County. Deep in the woods. He and his wife, the former Betsy Earnest, whose brother, Charlie, was Carson's teammate, are surrounded by tall pines, sturdy oaks and dogwoods. Early mornings, John can sit on his porch with a glass of Ovaltine and relax with the refreshing flora and fauna that envelopes his homestead. He has more deer in his yard than visitors.

How he came in possession of the property is an interesting story itself. The Georgia athletes, primarily the football players, lived at Payne Hall, commonly referred to in Carson's day as, "Milledge Annex."

A janitor named Willie Middlebrooks owned the Greene County property, having had the right to buy the land from the Forestry Service, which wanted buffer farms adjacent to the government lands. John became friends with Willie when he was in school. He didn't know where Willie lived exactly, but from conversations at the dormitory, he suspected that there might be some attractive dove hunting options. Carson went down to the property to hunt a few times.

After signing his pro football contract with the Redskins, he kept in touch with Middlebrooks who told John that he wanted him to own the property. "He wanted me to buy his land," Carson says. "It was one of the best decisions I ever made. I paid him what it was worth, but it turned out to be a bargain because land didn't cost that much at the time."

It was a case of simply being nice to another person. In those days not many people would take up time with a graying black man working as a janitor. The bond between Carson and Middlebrooks, however, was real. When Carson sits on his porch and communes with nature, he often thinks about his friend as he and Betsy enjoy their golden years.

John's mailing address is Farmington. He moves about in an aging Ford pickup truck. The cap he wears displays a Minnesota Viking's logo. The National Football League team he last worked for was the Vikings.

Two highly established quarterbacks in the NFL in recent years caught Carson's eye early on and he recommended them as high draft picks: Rich Gannon who took the Oakland Raiders to the Super Bowl and Brad Johnson who quarterbacked the Tampa Bay Bucs to the Super Bowl title over Gannon's Raiders in 2002. Bud Grant, coach of the Vikings, often came down to Greene County to hunt with John.

There's plenty of porch time, too, to reminisce about Fiddlin' John and Moonshine Kate. Carson is proud that his granddaddy was seven times national fiddling champion and notes that when he lost his title (to Lowe Stokes in 1924) that it was the inspiration for Stephen Vincent Benet's poem, "The Mountain Whippoorwill."

The grandson remembers, as a boy, taking a trip to the State Capitol building, where his granddaddy was given a job as an elevator supervisor.

On one visit to the Capitol, he asked to ride the elevator and was politely brushed off. He became more demanding, raising his voice and causing a noticeable fuss.

Finally his grandaddy pulled him aside and whispered firmly in his ear, "Son, shutup, there ain't no elevator in this whole building." That was the way it was in those times. You could be given a government job like that if you had the right connections, and Fiddlin' John had those connections.

In his delightful book, "Bulldoggerel" Dan Magill had this summary of Carson's spectacular career:

My first observation of Long John Carson was in the late 1940s when he was starring in football, basketball, baseball and golf for old Roosevelt High in Atlanta. I was prep editor for the Atlanta Journal, and I gave him the nickname, "Long John" (apologies to Robert Louis Stevenson and his Long John Silver). I also recommended him for a scholarship to Georgia, and John entered the university as a freshman in the fall of 1949, the same year I came back home as Coach Butts' sports information director.

Long John was Georgia's last four-letter athlete, excelling in football (end), basketball (forward), baseball (first base) and golf (he reached the quarter finals of the NCAA golf tournament in the days when it was match play instead of medal play).

Carson made All-America in football his senior season (1953), setting the school record of 45 catches as the favorite target of All-America quarterback Zeke Bratkowski. This record stood 16 years until Charley Whittemore busted it for 46 catches in 1969, and Carson probably would still hold the record except for the fact he was injured on the opening kickoff in the season's final game against Georgia Tech. Coach Butts utilized Carson's ball-carrying ability by letting him return kickoffs, and on this particular play against Tech, he was about to break into an open field, when he pulled a muscle trying to sidestep the last Yellow Jacket defender. But he still led the SEC as a receiver for the second straight year, and in fact led the nation that year.

Long John Carson played six years for the Washington Redskins, making the pro bowl in 1958. He finished his playing career in 1960, helping Houston win the first AFL title. Then he spent a long time scouting for Philadelphia and Minnesota, frequently coming back to Sanford Stadium on scouting missions.

There's no doubt that Fiddlin' John Carson would have been mighty proud of his namesake.

ART DECARLO

When Art Decarlo – a man for all positions at Georgia – was coaching high school football in Baltimore in 1962, he got a call from his friend, Don Shula, about the possibility of a coaching job.

At the time, the Shulas and the Decarlos had formed a carpool to take their children to school, and Shula knew that Decarlo was deeply serious about a coaching career.

This is the way that long ago conversation went: Shula explained to Decarlo that he had offered an opening on the Baltimore Colt staff to someone else who was not sure that he would take Shula's offer.

"If he doesn't take it," Shula said, "the jobs is yours."

It wasn't a life or death matter with Decarlo, but after thinking it over, he realized that moving from his high school position, which he greatly enjoyed, to the pros would be a positive step for him as a coach – though the coaching salaries and perks, even in the NFL at that time, were far from as enticing as today.

But the other guy took the job. The other guy? Chuck Noll! You know the rest of the story. Shula went on to Super Bowl fame with the Dolphins and Noll experienced that run of four Super Bowl championships with the Steelers in the '70's.

But whatever became of Art Decarlo?

Decarlo got out of coaching and became a sales executive. He has no regrets and looks back on his professional career with this perspective.

'It would have been nice to have gotten into pro coaching," he says in hindsight. "On the other hand, I could say that if I had joined Don's staff, I could have been part of what took place in his career in Baltimore and Miami. But the welfare of our children has always been a priority with us and things have turned out well for them. I'm happy, very happy." Decarlo's principal goal in life was always to train his kids "right and to prepare them to succeed in life."

Their neighbors used to call the Decarlos, "The Waltons," since they were always doing things together. To appreciate this Decarlo objective, you only have to look back on his early life. Both of Art's parents died before he finished high school. He understood the challenge, but somehow or other he was determined to earn a degree. Coming out of high school, he was tall and thin, but agile and quick.

Most major college scouts weren't looking for athletes as light in the pants as Decarlo. But when Quinton Lumpkin offered him a tryout at Georgia, he became intrigued, shunning the bird-in-the-hand in the form of a couple of small college offers and accepted the gamble and challenge of playing at a major university.

At Georgia he played center, linebacker, offensive end and safety. With his versatile style, he could have played quarterback or offensive back if Coach Butts had asked him. About the only position he couldn't have played was guard or tackle, where some heft was necessary.

It is unlikely that the Bulldogs have ever had a greater utility player, which worked in his favor when he was drafted by the Pittsburgh Steelers. The Steelers took notice of the fact that Decarlo was skilled at more than one position. But his career did not take root in Pittsburgh. After one year with the Steelers, he was drafted into the Army for 21 months. It was out of the Army and into the Washington Redskin camp where he made the team for a half year. Released by owner George Preston Marshall, he caught on with Baltimore in 1957.

But there was something odd about how he became a Colt. When the Redskins let him go, an inquiry came from the Chicago Cardinals. Charley Trippi was coaching with the Cardinals and knew about Decarlo from Coach Butts. Trippi convinced the Cardinals to offer Decarlo a job. But Decarlo's wife, Mary, didn't know who Trippi was, and when General Manager Don Kellett of the Colts called with an offer, she told him that Art would take it.

"You can't do that," Art told Mary. "The Cardinals are going to sign me on Monday."

Mary replied, "I don't care. I don't like Chicago."

Mary's intervention turned out positive in that the family has always enjoyed Baltimore, and, besides, Art became a member of a world championship team. He played in the famous "greatest game ever" between the Colts and the New York Giants in Yankee Stadium in 1958, the first sudden death overtime game, when John Unitas directed that heralded winning touchdown drive. That drive gave the televising of professional football perhaps its greatest boost in days when it was on the way to becoming a Sunday passion for America.

Art was a backup defensive back and wide receiver for that NFL title game. He saw action on all the special teams and on defense, more impressed with the fact that he was playing in Yankee Stadium than for a championship. "Back then, you really were impressed when you had a chance to play in Yankee Stadium. That was special to all of us."

In the Eighties I met with Decarlo in Baltimore. I was staying at a downtown hotel and he, an early riser, met me for breakfast. We reminisced about his early life and career in the pros and were getting around to Georgia when he brought up the name of Quinton Lumpkin, his old freshman coach.

Art Decarlo, a man for all positions

Somehow or other he had missed the news of Lumpkin's demise, and when I casually mentioned that Lumpkin's death had saddened a lot of Georgia players, the shock on his face caught me off guard. I was not aware that he didn't know, but there in those several seconds which transpired after the news hit, you could graphically see the sensitivity of special relationships between player and coach. It is a bond that those who are not privileged to experience never understand and often cynically undervalue and pass off as inconsequential.

Art Decarlo's emotion was real. There was pain and hurt to learn that a favorite coach, a friend and confidant at a critical time in his life, had passed on.

"I'm sorry," he said, his eyes becoming glassy for a moment. "He was such a wonderful friend and I just didn't know he had died. Like so many others, I thought he was indestructible. I thought he might live forever." Then he composed himself and began to explain how warmly he felt about Lumpkin and his days at Georgia.

"The only regret I have is that I don't see my old teammates more. That is the problem with living in Baltimore. It is difficult for me to get to Athens very often. My teammates are important to me.

"A team becomes family in football, but with me it went further. I literally had no family and I felt that the players on the team were my brothers. They were my family. I had planned to live in Georgia I loved it so much, but pro football and the Army led to meeting Mary and settling in this area."

Decarlo lettered with the Bulldogs in 1950-52. He was 6-2 and arrived in Athens weighing only 160 pounds. But by the time he left, he had advanced his weight up to 187. He became a solid, reliable performer. They didn't time players for 40 yards, but the pros clocked him at 4.6 seconds for that distance which, at the time, was considered excellent.

Bill Hartman has this recollection of Decarlo at Georgia: "Art is probably one of the best all-around athletes that we've ever had to play football. He was a fine pass receiver. He also played defensive safety and linebacker. He played center too. He was very effective at all those positions because of his tremendous agility and quickness. He was a great competitor who understood the importance of team loyalty. What made him different was that he had such an exceptional attitude. He could make the mental adjustment to play a variety of positions."

There was a poignant rapport involved with Decarlo and Coach Butts. The player looked upon the coach with an enduring and appreciative affection that related to something missing in Decarlo's life. Since his parents had died before he finished high school, Butts' became a father figure along with Lumpkin. Today, you can sense the emotion, you can see his eyes moisten when he is in conversation about his college coaches.

"I looked on Coach Butts as a replacement for my father," Decarlo says. "When I started out in Athens only 18-years-old, I was very lonely and immature. Coach Butts was good to me, and I made it a goal of my college days not to let him down. I worked hard for him, I appreciated him and tried my best to obey his rules. I never wanted to do anything to disappoint him.

"All the time I was at Georgia, I felt that I had a wonderful rapport with the man. He was always offering encouragement, and when he showed me how I could do something better, I listened and set out to follow his teachings. Coach Butts was a remarkable teacher."

Hurley Jones

Hurley Jones played linebacker in 1951-52 for Georgia, a less celebrated position in football, than, say, quarterback or halfback.

You don't expect linebackers to dominate the headlines. They are anchors of the team, however. If they don't succeed, in all probability the team won't. Linebackers motivate and inspire. They are dependable. They are more the blue-collar types. They work hard, they fight hard. They lead by example and, in most instances, they put the team first. Linebackers are always the heart and soul of the defense.

All of that could be said of Hurley D. Jones and more. A Jesup native, who practiced medicine in Brunswick all his professional life, Hurley was, in the simplest terms – a good and decent man.

Unethical conduct never visited his life. He never bent the rules. He never squandered opportunity and he never failed to follow the golden rule in his 72 years on this earth.

After GMC, football under Wallace Butts at the University of Georgia and medical school, Hurley began his medical practice on the Georgia coast, but his second home was Athens. He never took up residence in the Classic City after college, but he considered his beloved University and Athens as much his home as Brunswick and the Golden Isles.

He was not an outspoken man. His emotions never got off track, but he cared. He cared about and loved his alma mater. There was deep and abiding love for his family, his community and his medical practice.

Hurley never wore his altruistic and modest feelings on his sleeves. But he lived life the way it should be lived. Hold malice for no man, goodwill to others and underscore faith, hope and charity. That was not a written creed, but that is the way he lived his life.

His wife, Mary Virginia, recalled, on the day of his death, just how principled a man he was. Many years ago, they were riding to Athens late on a Friday night for a football weekend and saw a Coca Cola machine outside a service station. The operator had closed, but you could buy a Coke if you had the correct change. That was no problem but there was a sign on the machine that said there was a ten cent deposit on all bottles.

Mary Virginia assumed they could put a dime on the top of the machine and drive on. Hurley said, "No. Somebody might take the dime." So they relaxed while she finished the Coke, left the empty bottle and headed to Athens."

Hurley Jones, Wally's ethical center

John Donaldson was one of Hurley's best friends. They talked football constantly they dined on the considerable messes of fish Donaldson caught. "He saved my life," Donaldson says. The old Bulldog coach, an advocate of health and physical fitness if there ever was one, was born with a defective heart valve. Good health habits could not cure that structured defect in his body. He was among the early open heart surgical patients, and Hurley advised him the options available.

When Donaldson went to Emory for the surgery, his friend and doctor went along and stayed with him until Donaldson was released. Know any doctors like that?

Jack Roberts

The early Sixties were a transition time for Georgia football.

The era of Coach Wallace Butts had come to an end and a new regime was in place. Johnny Griffith succeeded Coach Butts, and Ray Graves tried to hire Bulldog assistant Jackie Roberts to head up recruiting at Florida. "But I just didn't want to leave the state of Georgia," Roberts says. Jackie had played for Coach Butts and also played baseball for Big Jim Whatley. His Bulldog pedigree was obvious, and he was well known throughout the state. He didn't like the idea of starting over at another school.

He enjoyed being a member of the Bulldog staff, but it wasn't long before he got out of coaching and wound up taking a job in the lumber business with his uncle, Frank Spain, a long time Bulldog recruiter. Jackie had enjoyed circulating around the state and reminiscing with his former teammates as he sought the outstanding prep athletes to sign for Georgia, but he felt that it was time for him to seek a business opportunity.

"I knew that eventually I'd get fired, and after I spent a year coaching at Thomasville Central, I knew that business was a lot more attractive. I have never regretted my decision."

At the time, Georgia did not have a lot of money for staff and facilities. There were three secretaries in the department. One of them was Mary Ann Kidd who worked in the recruiting office. The other two worked for Coach Butts and Dan Magill.

After he left Georgia, Jack and Mary Ann were married and have remained two of the Bulldogs' staunchest supporters and friends over the years.

They operate a highly successful chain of day care centers in the state and Jack, a "Mr. Fix-It" around the house, finds time to keep his golf game in good order.

Roberts is one of the most versatile athletes to come out of high school athletic circles in the state of Georgia. He is a native of Gainesville and earned four letters in football, basketball, baseball and track. Jack could do it all, but his best sport was baseball. He threw four no-hitters for Gainesville High School. He was state high jump champion in 1949 and was an all-state halfback in 1947-48. He was the leading scorer in the state in 1947. At Georgia he was good enough to earn three letters in football and another three letters in baseball.

Dan Magill, when he was prep editor of the Atlanta Journal Constituiton, saw Jackie play often in high school and recommended him to Coach Butts, Bulldog football coach and athletic director. "He wasn't a big athlete," Magill remembers, "but he had wonderful athletic ability. He was a better baseball player than football and he had a very successful career at Georgia."

Jackie Roberts on the move

Today, he and Mary Ann remain two of the Bulldogs most loyal friends. They have purchased season tickets for years and are usually there for all road games, often in the company of long time friends.

The Roberts even went to Hawaii for Georgia's bowl game against Virginia in 2001. "We have always loved the Bulldogs," Mary Ann says. "Georgia football is a big part of our lives."

If you know Jackie, you know that it was easy for him to go from player to coach to devoted fan.

All it takes is deep and abiding feeling for the University of Georgia.

EARL GUNN

Earl Gunn, the nephew of Georgia immortal, Spud Chandler, was a rugged end who was one in a long line of players who matriculated at the Marist School for Boys and went on to play football at the University of Georgia.

A Marist gridiron alumnus was one who was well schooled in fundamentals. He knew something about sound football principles, and he was familiar with grueling and long practice sessions. Long afternoons of intense scrimmaging were not unfamiliar to players like Earl Gunn.

Earl Gunn, from end to dentistry

From the beginning Gunn set high standards for himself academically. He could withstand the stringent demands on the football field for two very obvious reasons. First, it covered the basic cost of his education, and secondly, it meant that he would gain an advantage in his quest for a dental degree.

An industrious and indefatigable overachiever, he worked hard and succeeded in his goal to become a dentist. He was a good one, too, and was often honored by the Hinman Dental Society of Atlanta.

His dental practice, today, is a buzz of activity. He hasn't slowed down since he was discharged from the Air Force and hung out his shingle in 1959. In his prime, he worked hard and played hard. When he showed up for a round of golf at the Capital City Club on the weekend with his buddies, he might not have had the prettiest swing or the lowest handicap, but his competitive instincts enabled him to hold his own.

Perhaps his greatest contribution to his alma mater came in 1964. He headed up the recruiting activities for Georgia in the Atlanta area. It was Vince Dooley's first year, and the Bulldogs were experiencing something of a rebirth. The youthful coach won six games, including a 7-0 decision over Georgia Tech in Athens. His upstart team defeated Texas Tech by the same score in the Sun Bowl in El Paso.

It would be a good winter. What meant as much to the Georgia faithful as the energizing and uplifting performance on the field was the good recruiting news. The incoming freshmen team would include players like Jake Scott, Bill Stanfill, Billy Payne. Georgia dominated recruiting in Atlanta, and Earl Gunn coordinated the effort, working with Sterling DuPree, John Donaldson and Dooley.

As it was with everything else in his life, Earl applied intense energy and commitment to his volunteer assignment with the Bulldogs. The only time he would take a phone call when he was filling a tooth was when a Bulldog coach phoned.

As serious as he was about his dental practice, when his alma mater called, he responded with alacrity.

SAM MRVOS

When his college days ended, Sam Mrvos signed a contract to play with the Philadelphia Eagles. The Eagles cut him after the first game in 1954, but Mrvos had his degree and decided that he should consider a coaching career. Suddenly, Coach Butts was back in Mrvos' life.

Sam called and told Butts he wanted to locate a coaching job. Butts told him that South Georgia (junior college) was "looking for a coach." He also told Mrvos that there would be an opening in Athens the following year. Sam never forgot this, and anybody who ever offered any criticism of Coach Butts in Sam's presence, had a fight on his hands. Literally.

At South Georgia, Mrvos coached under Bobby Bowden and enjoyed a productive experience. Mrvos was an assistant football coach and also coached baseball. After two years Butts called and invited him to join the staff in Athens as he had promised. Sam was in Athens to stay although he eventually purchased a home in Winder where he now lives.

At Georgia as a player, he lettered as an extra point kicker in 1951, making good on 20 of 26 attempts. In 1952 he was the regular right tackle and a year later he became a regular at guard. In 1953, against Tulane, he kicked a 21-yard field goal which proved to be the margin of victory for the Bulldogs, 16-14.

When he signed with the Eagles, Mrvos was anxious to experience a serious pro career. Philadelphia was a successful NFL team in his home state, and he had a lot of friends throughout Pennsylvania. But he had enjoyed his time in the South and knew that he wanted to return when he began his coaching career. Coach Butts paved the way for him and he has always appreciated his former coach's influence.

When Vince Dooley became the Georgia coach in 1963, he asked Mrvos to coach the B-team and today Sam notes that he coached with two of the most successful coaches in college football, Bowden and Dooley. "Don't forget, I also played for one of the best," Sam smiles, referring to Coach Butts.

BOB WEST

When Bob West finished high school in Marietta, he was chosen to play in an East-West all-star game in Corpus Christi, Texas. That was a big deal in the late Forties. High honor, print headlines, first airplane ride and an exciting brush with a landscape he could only imagine.

It was Texas, but it wasn't the cowboy Texas that he was familiar with from Saturday afternoons at the movies. He had never spent much time away from home, and that trip was his introduction to life-on-your-own. It was not a rude awakening, but what followed that trip certainly became a challenge.

When he landed at the Atlanta Airport from his all-star sojourn, his brother picked him up and drove him to Athens. Football had already begun, and he reported to the practice field immediately.

Within minutes he was out on the field scrimmaging. He didn't even have time to check into his room. That didn't take place until he had spent the afternoon at practice.

He wasn't exactly homesick afterwards, but he had to make an unanticipated adjustment. The first adjustment was to get accustomed to the yelling and screaming on the practice field. Further, he was introduced to a vocabulary with which he was not familiar. At one point, it was just too much. He took off for home, catching his hard working father by surprise.

A conversation ensued which was far from what West expected. "I'm tired of all those coaches yelling,

Bob West: AWOL but nobody knew

screaming and cussin' me," he told his father, expecting a sympathetic ear. He became chagrined when his father, who aspired for his son to return home with a degree when football ended, said. "Those coaches are only trying to help you," his father began. "You went over there for an education, football is paying for it, and you should take advantage of your opportunity. Those coaches are only trying to help you be the best player you can be."

It wasn't long before he was back in his room at Milledge Annex. Nobody ever knew that he had gone AWOL. And from that point on, the practice field vernacular never bothered him.

The extended scrimmage sessions remained a constant. So did the yelling and screaming, but the latter no longer bothered the overachieving West, who was elected captain of the 1952 team.

"When I look back, I remember the hard work, but we all knew that it was standard for the times. You appreciated that you could survive all that scrimmaging. There was never a time in my business life when there was a challenge that I did not think I could manage. When you put it in that perspective, you appreciate the experience.

"I can remember leaving practice and walking to the dorm. There was no bridge at the West End of the stadium back then. We walked that trail down by the south stands of the stadium, through what is now the Science Center. There were times I was so tired, I didn't think I could make it up the steps to the top of the hill on the other side. I remember stopping at the bottom step and taking a rest. Then I would get recharged and climb up to the top and on to Milledge Annex. One thing about all that work on the practice field, you didn't have any trouble sleeping at night."

He is proud of having played with outstanding athletes. "You knew that Zeke Bratkowski, John Carson and Harry Babcock were special. You just knew it. We thought our record should have been better, but I'll always appreciate my teammates and the friendships.

"I always respected Coach Butts. I appreciated him so much I could never say anything against him. He was tough on the field, but if you ever needed a friend, he was there for you."

After Georgia, West signed a contract with the old Chicago Cardinals. Charley Trippi was still with the club, and West was in awe of the man he had heard so much about for so many years. "I couldn't believe I was on the same field with him," West says. "One day in practice I tackled him, and when I got up, I thought to myself, 'I just tackled Charley Trippi. What an honor!'"

A concussion led to his being cut from the squad. The club invited him back the following season, but the draft beckoned and when his military service was finished, he decided to get on with his life. He coached in high school briefly, but entered the business world and became a successful insurance agent, retiring after a 25 year career with Cotton States.

"I keep up with the Dogs," he says. "I am proud that I can say that I am a Bulldog." Always proud, too, of his father's sage advice.

JIMMY CAMPAGNA

Specialization in football has, among other things, eliminated twin receivers on kick returns.

If you followed Georgia football back in the '50's, you remember that the Bulldogs had great success – in 1952 to be specific – putting two men deep in return situations. It allowed for fakes and reverses. It has kept Jimmy Campagna in the Georgia record books all these years.

In 1952, Vanderbilt was coached by Bill Edwards and Georgia by Wallace Butts. Vanderbilt's enrollment was 3,205, Georgia's 5,197. One platoon football was about to return to the college game. A Varsity hot dog cost 10 cents; a ticket to a Bulldog home game cost $5.00. If you followed the Dogs to Nashville and wanted to take in the Grand Old Opry the night before kickoff, chances are that you would have to stand in line at the old Ryman Auditorium longer than it took to play four quarters of football.

A native of Rochester, NY, Jimmy Campagna probably never heard of the Opry when he made his first trip to Music City. But everybody following college football had heard of him by the time the college scores hit the wires for Sunday's editions.

Campagna raced 100 yards down the sidelines with a punt for a touchdown. Campagna remembers that he and the late Conrad Manisera were deep when Vandy punted, and the plan called for a reverse handoff or the faking of a handoff depending on who caught the ball. What the Bulldog coaches were trying to do was take advantage of Campagna's :09.9 speed. If Campagna caught the kick, he was to fake a handoff to Manisera and keep the ball. If the kick came to Manisera, he was to hand to Campagna.

"What happened," Campagna says, "is we wound up standing pretty much side by side in the end zone. You are not supposed to run the ball out from the end zone to begin with, but when Connie caught the ball, he simply handed it to me. They were coming down on him pretty hard and after he gave me the ball, about three players hit him. All of a sudden there was a lane out in front of me, and I took off running and had a clear field most of the way. All I remember is that I just took the ball and ran straight down the sideline."

Campagna believes that Manisera's abrupt "you-take-it-I'm-not-supposed-to-return-it" reaction from the end zone caught the Commodores off guard and set up the return opportunity.

With the return in the '60s to unlimited substitution and the subsequent emphasis on special teams, putting two men deep no longer was practical. "Coverage became so good, you wouldn't have time to set up a handoff," says Bill Hartman.

What he remembers most is that football was a means to an education and ticket out of the cold climate of upstate New York.

"No way," he says, "could my parents have sent me to college. I began to get some attention in high school football, so I made it my objective to work as hard for a scholarship. I wanted a degree and I knew that the best chance was through scholarship assistance. When I came to Athens for the first time, I really liked it and knew that I wanted to live in the South. I had already made up my mind that if I could get away from those cold winters, that is exactly what I would do."

Fred Bilyeu

It was a hot, steamy night in Baton Rouge, Oct. 18, 1952. An LSU All American, Paul Miller, was one tough hombre for the visiting Bulldogs. Those who lined up across from this formidable Tiger could expect anything. He used his hands, legally and illegally. His forearm was swift and deadly. In a pileup, he had no reluctance to resort to dirty tricks.

If you were on your feet, you never relaxed, for he would be intent on taking your feet out from under you. If he could blindside you, the better. You had to know where he was at all times. He seemed to always be lurking nearby, poised to catch you off guard.

This was the game when he kicked Charlie Earnest in the mouth, knocking him out. Additionally, the Bulldog fullback lost two teeth. Miller had also waylaid a couple of offensive lineman.

Georgia was ahead late in the game and Fred Bilyeu, who knew something about hand-to-hand combat, saw Miller clip Art Decarlo on a punt return. He had had enough so he went over and cold cocked Miller.

When he came off the field, with only seconds left in the final quarter, he was met by Coach Butts, who did not chastise him for his retaliatory act. The coach was inclined to deliver a warning, fearing an all out brawl was likely to ensue at game's end. "Son," Coach Butts said, "when this game is over, I want you to sprint off this field and get into the locker room as quickly as you can."

With that, Bilyeu went over to Frank Salerno, a rough and tumble, no holds barred combatant from Chicago, and said. "Frank that is an insult. I'm not going to run off the field with my tail between the legs. I want you to walk off with me." Salerno agreed and they casually strolled to the locker room, ready for action if anybody started anything. Nothing happened. Perhaps, Bilyeu sent a signal to the other Tiger players. If he could take out their biggest, toughest, meanest player, then it was best to call it a night.

Bilyeu was a game player. He didn't believe in proving what he could do in practice. And he, too, was a tough hombre. He could dish it out, and he could take. Once in high school at Cookeville, Tenn., he fractured his right ankle. His team lined up to punt, and the snap was shaded to his left side, so he kicked the ball left footed. For good yardage too.

A versatile athlete, he came to Georgia as a quarterback. His substitute in his freshman year was Zeke Bratkowski. Fred was moved to fullback where there were times he would throw from his backfield position. He threw a touchdown pass in the 1950 game with Maryland. His interception return of 80 yards for a touchdown versus North Carolina in 1951 ranks as the seventh longest for interception yards returned.

At Cookeville, he was coached by Charlie Watson, the grandfather of Mack Brown (Texas) and Watson Brown (Alabama, Birmingham), who reminded Bilyeu of Shug Jordan. "He was always the gentleman," Fred recalls.

Bilyeu liked his gentleman coach, but also appreciated Coach Butts, a different personality on the field. The competitive fire of the Bulldog coach endeared him to Bilyeu. "If you put out for him, he would treat you right," Fred says. "He taught me something about loyalty. I had a good sophomore year and thought about transferring to the University of North Carolina. I had conversations with some of their representatives and was home for the summer. Coach Butts called me to come to Athens, and I will never forget what he said.

"'Son, I don't think you have the loyalty to play for the University of Georgia, but you are not going to play anywhere else.' When fall practice started, he lined up at least a dozen defensive players and made me run at them until I was pretty much beat down. I would run head on into a tackler, get up and there would be a fresh tackler waiting for me. I never thought about transferring again.

"Coach Butts demanded loyalty from all of his players, and he got respect, too. Guys twice his size would walk on the other side of the street so they would not have to face him. He didn't like quitters, and I wasn't going to quit, no matter how tough it was. He always said that a man who quits in football will quit in life."

Bilyeu is French, but Fred doesn't know much about the family heritage. He does know that he descended from French Canadian trappers, those who were hearty and survived life in the toughest of conditions. They could make do; they could take care of themselves, no matter the challenge.

Those genes were obviously passed on.

WILLIAM YOUNG

When William D. Young grew up near Kennesaw, he experienced the hard life. His father died when he was three months old, and life was an ongoing challenge for his mother who had to raise him, a brother and a sister.

She would drop them off at school, go to her job and pick them up after school and take them home. It was a goal of Bill's to someday do something for his mother. "She sacrificed for her kids, and I'll always be grateful," he says. This story had a happy ending. Bill was able to provide for his mother late in her life and football had something to do with it.

A tall, rangy kid, Bill paid more attention to schoolwork than he did football, which was to become his ticket to a college degree. He didn't participate in the sport until his senior year, which happened to be grade eleven.

Then a funny thing happened in the state of Georgia. The twelfth grade was added for all school systems. Suddenly he and all other "seniors" in high school were seniors for one more year.

"It turned out to be the biggest break I could have had," he says. "That meant I played another year of football, and that led to the scholarship at the University of Georgia."

Class and homework never were a drag for him. There were no college graduates in his family, and he knew what a good thing he had in a scholarship. He simply practiced the basics while in Athens. Go to class, pay attention, visit the library, underscore good study habits and develop rapport with instructors and professors.

"I guess you could say I was a better student than I was a football player," he laughs. He played tackle well enough, and he was no academic lightweight.

"I learned a valuable lesson from Coach Butts and football," he says. "If you worked hard you were compensated—you got to play. I found it to be the same way in business. If you want to succeed you better roll up your sleeves and go to work."

That is the way he played for the Bulldogs. Paying attention, working hard, expecting nothing and giving a lot. When his business, General Wholesale, expanded and grew, his sales force included four former teammates: The late Knox Culpepper, Joe O'Malley, Bill Saye and Cleve Clark. "I knew they were familiar with the work ethic. I knew their competitive nature, and their drive," he says. "That is what I wanted for our business. They brought to our company the same qualities they had as players for Coach Butts."

Bill Young benefited from a Wally scholarship

The growth of his company has enabled him to share with his alma mater. If you visit the second floor of the Butts-Mehre Building where the current coaching staff gathers for its daily meeting, you'll find his name on the door—a tribute from the Athletic Association for his family's generous gift to Georgia football.

"I'm very complimented that they put my name on the door. I have a great appreciation for the Georgia tradition and our football program under Mark Richt," he says. "If you appreciate your past, you want to ensure opportunity for the future. I'm happy to support what Coach Richt is doing."

1953

Zeke Bratkowski was a senior. He would lead the nation in passing, punting AND interceptions. This would be the worst performing team Wallace Butts had fielded since he started out in 1939. It only won three games. Bratkowski was a talent; he would distinguish himself in the NFL, but there just weren't enough players to produce enough points to win many games.

The Bulldogs averaged 13.1 points per outing, but the defense was ineffective as well. Every team on the schedule scored 14 points or more. Maryland tallied 40 at College Park and Auburn posted 39 in Columbus. Worst of all, Mississippi Southern shut out the 'Dogs 14-0 in Jackson. That season was Coach Butts' nadir, finishing 3-8.

Only three victories for a Wally Butts coached team! Georgia couldn't stomach such, but unfortunately, there would be two more teams which would claim victory only three times.

Fortunes would improve in 1954, but after that, there would be four straight losing seasons. On top of that, Georgia Tech maintained its consecutive win streak. Oh, how that hurt! Georgia fielding losing teams, accented by an annual defeat at the hands of the arch enemy. Athens was not a happy camp.

Zeke Bratkowski

In 1949 Zeke Bratkowski was driven to Athens from Illinois by his high school coach, Paul Shebby. On the long drive, they talked mile after mile on pre-interstate roads about football and the University of Georgia.

Shebby was familiar with the Bulldog program and Coach Wallace Butts. He had coached Charley Trippi in high school and embraced the fundamental approach to the game that was underpinning of the Butts' system.

Bratkowski was not a player of widespread repute. He played fullback for Shebby, adequately and reliably, but was best known for his punting ability. Zeke would become one of the classic punters in college football, and he would make All-America playing quarterback, where he first lined up at Georgia.

"I never thought about playing any position in the backfield other than fullback or halfback. In high school, I had thrown a few passes out of the backfield, but had never played quarterback," Zeke says.

When his career was over, he could look back with great appreciation for what the move to quarterback meant to him. It meant that he was one of the most highly recognized quarterbacks in college football. He captained his team, and when he had completed degree requirements, the pros rated him among the best. Strong armed and studious, he embarked on a professional career as a player and coach which lasted 40 years.

He played for two of the best known coaches in football, Butts at Georgia and Vince Lombardi with the Green Bay Packers. "Don't forget about George Halas with the Bears," he notes. "He was a smart coach. I learned a lot from Mr. Halas."

A polite, and impeccably well mannered man, Bratkowski is given today to referring to the men for whom he worked all those years as "Mister" or "Coach."

If you talk about his collegiate experience, he constantly refers to "Coach Butts." With the Bears it's "Mr. Halas," and with Green Bay it is always, "Coach Lombardi."

When he arrived in Athens, the first assistant coach he met was Spec Towns. Immediately after he was offered a scholarship, he was informed he would play quarterback, something of a shock. "I was definitely not a passer," Zeke recalls. "I was a thrower."

It was the off season for Charley Trippi who maintained a residence in Athens. He worked out with Zeke, who was eager for the tips from the man many

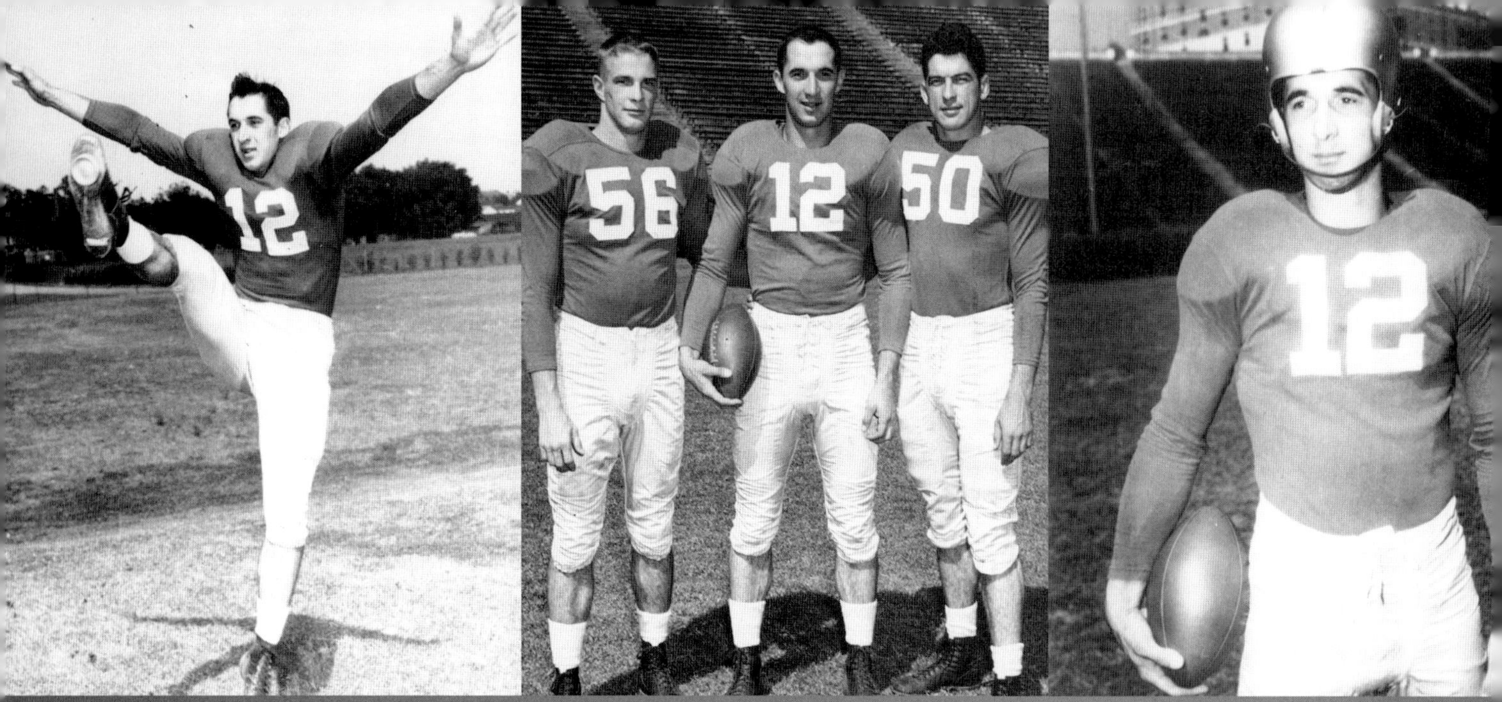

Zeke Bratkowski: From left, as a punter; with Babcock and Carson; with ball on his hip, but ready for action

considered the best all around player ever to play for Butts. Trippi was then in his prime with the Chicago Cardinals and had a reputation as an expert passer from his halfback position at Georgia. With the Cardinals, he had also played quarterback.

Bratkowski was eager to learn. "I was all ears when any coach talked, but it made quite an impression on me to work out with Charley Trippi and have him point out certain fundamental things that I should learn as a quarterback. He was knowledgeable, and he was bright. I learned a lot in that one practice field session."

The first assignment to be mastered for Zeke was taking the snap from center. He became so good at the center-quarterback exchange with Mo McClung that he could take the snap with one hand. "It was a matter of being taught by emphasizing fundamentals and the routine of doing it over and over again. I felt I could take the snap from center in my sleep," Bratkowski says.

If you are going to play quarterback, you must learn fundamentals. Practice was one thing, but pre-practice was just as important, perhaps moreso. "We spent so much time working on such things as footwork, setup, route running, throwing to a spot – it was throw and catch, throw and catch – until it became second nature.

"I was well schooled by the time I got to the NFL. When I signed with the Packers, I had a sensation that I was again working with Coach Butts. Coach Lombardi coached the same way. Get the fundamentals down pat. Get in those reps, do it right, do it over and over again.

"When you are in a game you learn to read the defense, you must have an ability to execute, but if you do enough reps until it becomes second nature, you should be able to complete the pass, to move the team.

"Both Coach Butts and Coach Lombardi demanded perfection. They would not tolerate sloppiness. If they were quiet, you knew you were doing it right. There was never any rave reviews on the practice field. It was like making up your bed growing up. If that was what you were supposed to do, you didn't get any reward. The problem came when you didn't do what you were supposed to do.

"If either Coach Butts or Coach Lombardi got on me in practice, it was because I wasn't doing things right. They never yelled or complained without good reason. I was never up tight about it, and I knew if I did it right I was learning to play the position. In the game I should be able to execute."

The way he was coached in Athens made Bratkowski sometimes conclude the name of the school should be changed to "The University of Fundamentals." The basics were underscored to the extent that he knew he was experiencing something special. Early on, he was not sure where he was going with his degree in business. He knew that he would play in the NFL as long as possible, but after that, he had no plans. He really didn't think about a long career as an assistant.

With his background, however, coaching became a natural extension of his life. Those fundamentals had schooled him for teaching quarterbacks when his playing days were over.

At Georgia, he received special attention from, in addition to Coach Butts, Quinton Lumpkin and Bill Hartman. With Lumpkin, popular with the players throughout Butts' tenure but a no nonsense coach on the practice field, Bratkowski honed his punting skills with the elementary playground game of kick back.

When they started their daily contests before practice, the teacher was considerably more proficient at punting than the pupil. The game, as most of us remember, is that you field a kick and then punt back from where you catch it. Lumpkin had the advantage. He kept backing Zeke up until he was up against a fence between the practice field and Lumpkin street. Eventually, he had to climb over the fence and chase the coach's punts down in the street traffic.

"When you can get to the point that you can make me climb that fence and chase your kicks into Lumpkin street," the Bulldog assistant advised, then you will be ready to punt in the Southeastern Conference." The first time Zeke made his teacher climb over the fence, he knew he had made it as a college punter.

Fundamentals and repetitions prepare a player for games, and Bratkowski says that he started every game at Georgia with confidence that he was the best prepared quarterback in the country.

Coach Butts installed at least 150 pass plays for a game. "Lot for a quarterback to learn and master," says Bill Hartman. "He expected the quarterbacks to learn. He demanded it."

On Friday afternoons, the Bulldog backfield assistant would take Zeke down to Sanford Stadium. They would walk to a point on the field, and the coach would say to the quarterback: "We are on our own 35, give me the 17 series."

After Zeke went through all the passes for that series they would move to: the 29 tear series, the 27 series (which had 50 routes for example), the 35 dip series—until they had gone over every series and every play within the series. The coach would call out a play and asked his quarterback to explain what happens on the play. "What do you do on 28 left end hook? What about 17 pass, rainbow long or 17 pass, ends in front? Fake 37 slant, left end in the middle?" Zeke had to deliver the answers quickly and succinctly. It was expected of him and he expected it of himself.

He arrived early Saturday morning at Sanford Stadium for a casual stroll through the Oconee Hills Cemetery with Hartman, who knew the Bulldog offense as well as Butts.

This stroll, which took place as pre-game excitement of the town peaked, was a mental review. Hartman would call out each series, and Bratkowski would recite the plays in each series. "Zeke had a good memory," Hartman says. "He had to with all the passes Coach Butts put in."

Early in his career, Bratkowski learned the value of taking notes. Much of those notes was committed to memory. The Georgia numbering system was embedded in his brain: The holes between the linemen to the right were numbered 1 to 9; for the left side it was, 0 to 8. Then when he got to the pros, it was exactly the opposite. He has never forgotten the way it was at Georgia and can cite the names and numbers of plays he called in the huddle over a half century ago.

Bratkowski learned his lessons well at Georgia. He made All-America, set records, led the NCAA in passing, punting and interceptions, that last stat reflecting the ongoing hard times that had appeared for Coach Butts, but not entirely, Zeke explains. "I had reached the point to where I had so much confidence in my arm, I felt that I could throw the ball through the eye of a needle. I forced the ball too much, and it was costly," he admits.

After his freshman year – his first collegiate pass went for a touchdown to John Carson against the Auburn frosh – Zeke was redshirted. "That was a real learning experience," he recalls. "I played the role of opposing quarterback every day in scrimmage. On game day, I was on the headset phone from the sideline to the press box. I listened to the plays being called. I listened, I learned and while that was going on, I was watching the game on the field. I could see the defense the opponents were in, and I gained a grasp of how the offensive coaches were attacking that defense."

The Dogs broke even his sophomore year, including losses to Mississippi State, 6-0 in Starkville; to LSU 7-0 in Athens and Alabama 16-14 between the hedges. It was a common refrain throughout those tough times – Georgia lost too many close games. Spread a few points here and there, and the results might have been more favorable, which would have brought momentum, confidence and, more importantly, more capable prospects to campus.

In Zeke's junior year, there was a winning record, 7-4 with Maryland, Florida and Alabama overpowering the Bulldogs and Tech finishing on top 23-9 in Athens. The bottom fell out Zeke's senior year. The Bulldogs won only three games. With victories over Villanova in the opener and Tulane the next week, Georgia would win only one game the rest of the season. Included in the eight losses was a humiliating setback to Mississippi Southern in Jackson, 14-0.

"We had a lot of veterans on our team," Bratkowski remembers. "After World War II, it was no time before the Korean War broke out. All of us faced the draft, and we had a big age difference on our team since a lot of veterans had come back from the military. The older guys had other interests. They had families. They had been shot at, they had jumped out of planes, and I don't think anybody anywhere in college football practiced as hard as we did at Georgia. Times were still hard. Some simply were not up to the regimen. They chose to move on."

Bratkowski, durable and resilient, never missed any playing time. In fact he never missed a practice. When his jaw was broken after he joined the Bears, his mouth was wired shut, he was fitted with a face mask and played the next week. "I was prepared from that foundation that was laid at Georgia," he points out. "I developed mental toughness in Athens."

When he arrived in Green Bay, he was well prepared for the yelling for which Lombardi was famous for. "A chewing out didn't bother me," Bratkowski grins. "It made me a better player. A lot of players took it personally. Many are like turtles, they go into a shell. Coaches, most often, don't remember what they said.

Once Lombardi told him, "I know you are ready to play, but I want to keep the bit in your mouth." Zeke responded, "But coach, my mouth is bleeding on both sides." Lombardi, without cracking a smile, said, "Good."

What makes football work, Bratkowski has often said, is the long hours of work and preparation. Paying attention to every detail. "Coach Lombardi used to preach, 'what good is an audible, if ten guys get it and one doesn't?'"

Even though he was a backup to Bart Starr, who became his best friend, Bratkowski was always ready. When Starr was injured several times, Zeke stepped in and the Packers never missed a beat. Green Bay won three NFL championships, including Super Bowls I and II during his time with Lombardi.

No quarterback has ever had greater moments in relief than Bratkowski, whose most memorable big game with the Packers came in 1965 when Starr was hurt on the first play from scrimmage in a semifinal playoff game with the Colts.

Bratkowski hadn't thrown two dozen passes all year when he went in. He completed 22 of 36 and led the Packers to one of their most important victories.

In three consecutive years of winning championships at Green Bay, Zeke started 12 games and won 10 of them for one of the best starting and winning percentages in Green Bay history.

A Coach offers encouragement to his quarterback

"I always understood my role," Bratkowski says. "Bart and I are extremely close. We still try to spend a lot of time together. We both have lost a son, and we have shared high moments and low moments together."

Zeke Bratkowski played and coached in the NFL non-stop, except for military duty, from 1953 until 1996. The former Bulldog quarterback has one of the longest and most successful careers in NFL history.

He became something of a vagabond for two reasons. The pay was good and he maintained a studious affection for the intricacies of the passing game. It has always been his passion to find ways to make the passing attacks of his teams more effective. Find that seam, that crack, that weakness and exploit it. You do that by spending hours with a projector, until videotape came along, which has made the game more scientific in some respects.

When you watch an NFL game on Sunday afternoon, you probably, like many others, believe that the pro game is stereotyped. That would make a veteran coach like Zeke Bratkowski scoff at such a notion.

What goes into choosing a play at a particular point translates into hours of videotape study during which a coach has scouted not only the opponent of the day, but his own team as well. You seek to know what pattern exists with the competition, but you also expect to conclude how effective your own team is with certain plays in certain situations.

An offensive coach must know the strengths and weaknesses of his team as well as those of the competition although he has but a week during the season to devote to a plan.

The field is dissected and zoned to assist a quarterback in knowing precisely where to attack and how. Execution is the quarterback's job in football, but scouting and play calling are the domain of the coaching staff.

Even though he is a graduate of the less complicated offensive systems of the past – when he either called his own plays or had options to make decisions and adjustments – Bratkowski is not one of those coaches who would allow quarterbacks to call plays.

"You take the coaching staff out of the ball game when you allow the quarterback to make the call," he says. "Why let the quarterback call the plays after all the hard work we've done to devise the game plan? They simply can't spend the amount of time necessary to properly prepare. Plus, when you are up in the press box during the game, you don't have the advantage of knowing what is going on on the field when the quarterback makes the decision. This keeps you from analyzing what you are doing. For example, if we choose a certain play from the press box and it doesn't work, we can begin to get a feel for the reasons a play is breaking down or is successful. It is important as a game moves along to know where you can attack and what you can do best to a certain defense.

"Another thing, when the coaching staff calls the plays, it takes a lot of pressure off the quarterback. Under our plan, you can coach and teach awareness of field position where you are in the game and why certain calls are made."

The challenge of coaching was what attracted Bratkowski to the profession although he was around long enough to retire with considerable benefits from the league both as a player (Bears and Packers) and a coach with Green Bay, Chicago, Indianapolis, the New York Jets, Cleveland and Philadelphia.

"It was great fun to try to build a team," Zeke says. "It was fun to try to outwit the other team on Sunday. It was not the same as playing, but you got a great feeling out of being involved once the whistle blows. There was always the challenge of getting it all together as a team. You get set with the defense, then you have to build the offense. You have to make your Sunday afternoons count."

When Bratkowski finished at Schlarman High School in Danville, IL, his coach encouraged him to consider Georgia because of the coach's friendship with Wallace Butts. This was in the era of tryouts and Bratkowski was given a scholarship based on his high school reputation.

Whenever he threw the ball, it was out of a double wing set. It didn't take the coaches at Georgia long to learn that he had an exceptional arm and by the time he had finished his college career he had produced impressive statistics. The practice field rigors enhanced his future, a fact not lost on the Illinois native.

"That is the thing that made me appreciate Georgia when I got to the pros," Zeke reflected. "We were mentally tough we had practiced things over and over again. With the Packers, the first thing you learned about Coach Lombardi was that he was just like Coach Butts. You would get in those repetitions."

He's heard it before, and he has a quick answer to the question of how Lombardi would fare today – even though in the great coach's time, he kept things simple – a defining contrast to today's complex approach.

"He'd be the same if not better," Bratkowski theorizes. "He would make changes in concepts but in handling people he would be special. He would never change from what worked with him at Green Bay. He was smart. He was intelligent, and he was a motivator. You played and practiced with a certain amount of fear, that fear of making a mistake, and he put you under pressure in practice just like he knew it was going to be in a game. But after practice he forgot all that stuff. He stressed fundamentals and stressed them in your lifestyle.

All the people who played for him and were successful in business will tell you that he made a difference in their lives. They applied that mental toughness to business, and it worked just like it did on the football field."

Bratkowski believes that even though he played for 14 years in the league, that his career would have been much greater if he had started out under Lombardi and if he had not developed bad habits playing service football. ("I'd be embarrassed to show you film of me when I came back from service football.")

He holds a similar reverence for Coach Butts. "He probably made me what I was through hard work. He was very regimented and a taskmaster. He dished out tough criticism on the practice field to make you better, but he forgot all about that when practice was over. Just like Lombardi, Coach Butts employed a lot of concepts similar to what the successful coaches do today. He was ahead of his time, but what made a difference was that repetition and that mental toughness."

Football gave Bratkowski an enjoyable lifestyle and he never found it difficult to get up and go to work. Sometimes the Sunday afternoons were a little long, but not really much of a hardship. If it had ever begun to get to him, all he would think about was the way it was with his parents, who never knew the good life that Bratkowski experienced. He gained strength from the ideals his parents had implanted in his character. Along with his sister, Pat, they were the cornerstone of his life. He regrets that his parents passed away before the real success of his pro career unfolded.

The highlight at Georgia? "The foundation that was laid for me to became a successful NFL quarterback," he answers with deep respect and appreciation. "I always enjoyed being the student, and there is no question that I experienced a long career in professional football because of the fundamentals I learned in Athens. I will always be grateful for the quarterback training I got from Coach Butts."

CHARLIE EARNEST

Charlie Earnest, letterman 1951-52-53, has always delighted in recalling his time at Georgia, especially when the younger set quizzes him about his career.

"Well," he begins with a twinkle in his eye. "We played in the Orange Bowl, the Cotton Bowl, the Sugar Bowl and the Gator Bowl." He even mentions that his teams also played in the Peanut Bowl.

Unless the listener is familiar with Georgia football in the early Fifties, he doesn't catch on until Charlie points out that when the Bulldogs took the field in those venues, it wasn't on New Year's Day.

The teams he played for were the visitors when the Bulldogs competed with Texas A&M in the Cotton Bowl, Florida in the Gator Bowl, Miami in the Orange Bowl and Tulane in the Sugar Bowl. The Peanut Bowl? That was the Georgia-Auburn game in Columbus.

"It was a big deal for us to travel to those places for games. You have to remember that most of us were country boys or boys from small towns, and boarding a train and riding the rails to all those faraway cities made us aware that things were different from what we had experienced growing up in our state.

"That exposure was an education in itself, and I've always appreciated that that experience was a wonderful by product of going to college on scholarship," Earnest says.

On one of those trips to Baton Rouge to play LSU, he endured a forgettable experience in the Bulldogs 27-14 victory. We won the game, but we got beat up. It was a nasty night."

It was October 1952, and with Zeke Bratkowski's penchant and reputation for throwing the football, he began catching the LSU defense off guard by calling the draw play. Needing a first down to keep the ball away from the Tigers, late in the game, Zeke called the draw, handed off to Charlie who fought for the necessary first down yardage. As he hit the ground, he took a peek at the yard marker to see if he had made the first down.

About that time, the lights went out. A lineman, by the name of Paul Miller, whose nickname was "Kayo," because he was not loathe to do as he did to Charlie—kicked him under the chin, knocking him unconscious. "I lost three teeth, too," Charlie recalls. "The big thing is that we won the ball game." Charlie also remembers that Kayo broke teammate Frank Malinowski's nose.

Following Georgia, he spent his professional career coaching and teaching, starting out in Fannin County and finishing up in his hometown of Cedartown. His career spanned 38 years and, in a sense hasn't ended. He still drives a school bus on various outings for his church and school.

Charlie Earnest! A good man committed to his community, staying involved, extending a helping hand in his golden years. It's a life to be respected and appreciated.

DERWENT LANGLEY

One of the most delightful stories of the Wallace Butts years is one about Derwent Langley, a truly nice guy who grew up on a dairy farm in Martinez and became a Bulldog fullback in the Fifties.

If you were a football player back then, you surely know the story. If you were associated with players of that era, you likely are familiar. If you ever heard Coach Butts make one of his witty after-dinner speeches, you may be privy to that practice field incident which cracked up even the Little Round Man when it took place.

If you are among the uninformed, here is what brought about that little bit of levity to an exercise where everything is normally serious and intense – especially under the Bulldog's late taskmaster.

Fullbacks were expected to become as efficient at blocking as gaining yardage in the T-formation days. Missing your assignment was near equal to fumbling a handoff at the goal line. Langley was a dedicated player, one who paid attention in all practice field sessions. He toiled diligently and earnestly, accenting effort and concentration so that he could effectively perform his job. But in one hot and weary practice, he missed a block, which allowed a defensive lineman to pop through and thwart the play.

When Coach Butts, whose practice field wrath was legendary, told the story, he wryly explained that he wanted to find out who busted their assignment so that he could "interview him." Langley beat him to the punch, by running over and saying something like, "Coach, I know it. Ain't I a sonofabitch"

It was one time that practice suddenly was fun, and Langley is remembered as much for that little episode as he was privately for his "walk" to academic achievement. One high school report card revealed that he was late 25 days out of the month, but school officials understood. The work ethic of those times motivated working class folk to manage an assignment on the farm and keep up in school.

In Langley's case, he arose early on the family dairy farm to assist with the milking. After he finished delivering milk, he walked to school at Richmond Academy. Work was mandatory. School work was important too. So was football. Langley managed and managed well.

In the afternoons, he would ride the bus to the county line (Martinez is in Columbia County) and walk four miles home. If the weather was bad, his mother would sometimes pick him up.

Langley actually enjoyed his farm chores, as well as football and track practice at Richmond, never complaining. He believed school was important, he enjoyed sports and understood that it was his responsibility to help out on the farm. To this day, he refuses to sell the family property, one of the reasons being that he remains sentimentally attached to the very acreage which helped shape his attitude and life.

With all-state honors in football and first place in the state meet for three track events – shot put, discus and broad jump – he was highly regarded by Georgia recruiters, although he says today that he was "little more than an average athlete." But that is a reflection of his character. He has never been accused of self-promotion.

Derwent Langley knew when he was wrong

"Something that always was important about Georgia to me when I was in high school," he says, "was that Georgia was one of the best dressed, best looking teams in college. The Bulldogs were a neat team. They were trim. They looked good in those silver britches and those red shirts. That is true of Georgia today."

As a sophomore in 1950, Langley played on what we call special teams today and was a backup linebacker. A ruptured blood vessel in his left thigh kept him out of action in 1951, and he was moved to center for his last two years after being redshirted. He became a starter at center.

After Georgia, he became a career Air Force officer, retiring in 1984 with the rank of colonel. During his military career he was a transport pilot, seeing action in Vietnam. After military retirement, he spent much of his time as a commercial pilot and was a pilot for many of the charters for Georgia athletic department personnel. He gave up flying following an automobile accident which took the life of his wife, Sally, and left him with impaired vision in one eye.

He hasn't given up Bulldog football, however. "I get a warm feeling when I walk into Sanford Stadium. Those hedges are sacred with so many of us even with the passing of time."

BOB REED

There are some great football fans who follow college football. Many have been written about. They have come in contact with the TV cameras, and friends sing their praises wherever they go.

Among these great fans are many who gain celebrity status, shamelessly promoting themselves and their feelings for their favorite team. They are anxious to be seen and heard. There are those whom you can easily identify because of their flash and vocalizing whether in good taste or not. But there also are those real fans who hurt when the team loses, who become misty eyed when they hear, "Hail to Georgia down in Dixie."

It is not often that you find a lot of football lettermen who join the die-hards after graduation. Certainly not recent lettermen graduates.

Most lettermen, those who scrimmaged and fought for four years or more, get away from it all when their careers have ended. They never feel comfortable in the stands. They don't get wrapped up in the program once they leave it behind. Those who once were cheered while they played, often find it difficult to join the cheering section when their eligibility has expired.

Of course, there are exceptions, and one former letterman who has that fervent commitment, emotionally, to the Dogs, and always has, is Bob Reed who lettered as a Bulldog back in 1953.

Those were the days when Georgia struggled. It was in the middle of the drought era when the Bulldogs lost to Georgia Tech eight-straight years. Sparse crowds were the norm in Sanford Stadium.

On the field, the players worked harder than ever, but there weren't a lot of victories. Georgia had little financial wherewithal, and there was great frustration all across the state.

"When you play during a down time, it really is frustrating," says Reed. "But I don't think any of us who played back then ever felt negative about Coach Butts and the program. We actually wanted to win for him because he was such a competitor. So many of us who played under him were affected by his spirit. He never gave up and he never quit fighting."

Bob Reed has never lost his interest in the Bulldogs, and with the passing years, he has devoted his weekends to following the Bulldogs, which was not easy.

Nobody living in another state appreciated televised games more than Reed. But when the Dogs were not on TV and he was not working, he often would rise at 4:00 a.m. and drive to Athens from Nashville for a game between the hedges and back. He also drives to away games from time to time, and his biggest weekend of the year comes when Georgia plays Vanderbilt in the Music City.

At Georgia, Reed received his BA degree in finance in 1954, graduating in the upper one-third of his class. He then spent three years as an officer in the Air Force. His business career began with Genesco in 1957. He joined Texas Boot Company in 1979.

An All-Mid-South fullback at Georgia Military Academy (now Woodward Academy), Reed always wanted to be a Bulldog. His high school playing credentials were outstanding, but when he arrived in Athens, he realized immediately that he had neither the size nor the speed to compete.

"But one thing was certain," he says. "I was going to be there for four years, and I was going to get a degree. "I don't know any college players today and I am seldom around them, but I keep hearing things that make me believe today's players don't have the attachment to the program like we do. That's sad.

"If college football is to be what it has always been, those of us who play for a team need to help carry the banner forward into the future. Lettermen need to support the program more than anybody. If lettermen care about a program, people notice."

Bruce Wimberly

There is something wrong with Bruce Wimberly's assessment of his career at Georgia. He begins by saying, "I wasn't worth a (expletive)," but his teammates say otherwise. Things like an overachieving guard who blocked with tenacity and who was rugged and relentless on defense at linebacker. If overachiever awards had been passed out, he would have been at the head of the class.

In his time, linebackers, and we are talking about good ones, went their entire career without ever intercepting a pass. Bruce got one against North Carolina State in 1952 in a 49-0 Bulldog victory between the hedges. But what does he say about his career? "Oh, I did enjoy offense, but I was the weak link when we lined up on defense."

You might expect that from a self described country bumpkin who enjoyed football (the means) taking him to a degree (the end). That end and his post graduate life is where we could see Bruce Wimberly taking bows, except that is not his style. His teammates, though, know about his starting out with nothing more than a job with the Shell Oil Company. The job became jobber as in a dealer who has made it big in the business world.

Now he owns a number of gas station-convenience stores in South Carolina. All the self-denigrating Wimberly says about his business career is that he "got his degree, went into the Army, was discharged and went to work with Shell and then eventually for myself."

His close friend and roommate, Derwent Langley, laughs when he hears what Wimberly said. "That sounds like Bruce, but don't let him fool you. He was a good football player and he has been very successful in business, much more than he would let on."

A native of Quincy, FL., Wimberly is quick to salute the school of hard football knocks he experienced, playing for Wallace Butts and the Bulldogs. "When the players at Georgia were coming along, they expected football to be tough. Life was tough. We all grew up without much and we thought it was a fair deal to scrimmage like hell with everything paid for. Your room, your meals, your tuition. I might have grumbled like the rest after a long practice, but there was never a time that I lost sight on the fact that football was paying for my education."

The highlight of his career? "The astonishment that I had made the team," he laughs. "I never dreamed that would happen to me. An offensive guard is very unlikely to be involved in any very spectacular goings on in football. For me, however, I never gave that a thought. My football experiences at Georgia were clearly the highlight of my youth. It was more than I could ever even hope for to be a member of the team, to travel with and suit up with the Dogs. And to be called on to be a starter was just beyond beyond. It was the ultimate satisfaction then and continues to give me pleasure even now."

"It was a thrill," he says, "just to ride the train to an away game. When I am with younger players today, they all seem intrigued about train travel. To tell you the truth, it was a big deal for me. Most of us grew up without cars—we weren't far from horse and buggy times—and to get on a train and travel somewhere like Dallas, Texas, was exciting as hell. I know it was for me."

Wimberly played at South Georgia Junior College for Wyatt Posey, who recommended him to Coach Butts. A lightweight guard with an aggressive and indomitable courage – Wimberly, it is worth repeating, was an overachiever if there ever was one in Athens.

Bill Burt

Bill Burt came to Georgia with impressive high school credentials as a quarterback. He would practice earnestly, but he would not play very much. Once when he was in conversation about his career at Georgia, he told a listener he had played for the Bulldogs.

"You played for Georgia?" the listener said. "I never heard of you."

In reply, Bill asked, "Ever hear of Zeke Bratkowski?"

"Why, yes," the listener responded.

"Now, you can understand," Bill grinned, "Why you never heard of me."

Early on, Bill Burt realized the situation he was in. Not everybody will start, not everybody will reap headlines, but there is more to college football than that. A team can't win without headline makers, but often, it is those who toil without glory who become successful in their profession and become devoted alumni who keep the tradition on track. Sometime the best players don't make the best post graduate supporters. Bill Burt is one who has always been a devoted and loyal alumnus.

"I wouldn't take anything for my Georgia experience," he says. "I worked hard, and I played my best games in practice. When I look back on it that education was worth the long practices. I probably can rationalize a lot better now than I could when I was playing. I have no regrets. I am a survivor of the most challenging era of Georgia football. I learned to gut it out, and, most importantly, perseverance. I'll always believe I came out ahead." His practice field training enhanced his business career. He became an executive with C&S Banks.

In high school at Adel, he remembers the starting of football. Everybody in town was excited that there would be a local team. But after losing practically every game, many by large scores, reality set it, and the community realized that patience had to be underscored.

Then a new coach came to town. His name was Knuck McCrary, and he made an immediate impact. His first year, Adel went 8-2, and Friday night celebrations ensued. The town was beside itself the next year when the team beat Newnan for the state championship. From startup to state champs in only three years. Hallelujah!

Burt was the quarterback, who made the team go, and that is what got Georgia's attention.

"My campus experience was rewarding," he says. "If a fellow can't enjoy four years in Athens, he has a problem. I have wonderful memories, and I am always eager to go back."

FRANK MALINOWSKI

With the passing of time, you may not remember the name of the author of a good deed, but you never forget his gesture. That is the way it is with Frank Malinowski who migrated South from Jamaica, New York, to make Georgia his home. Football brought him to the Peach state; he played, and, like many others, he stayed.

His link and his bonding to Athens was a football scholarship. It came about by way of a man whose name he has long forgotten, but left Malinowski with an unswerving appreciation for Coach Butts and Georgia. Malinowski will always be grateful.

The forgotten Georgia alumnus owned a sporting goods store in Manhattan, but his recommendation of Malinowski—from reading area sports pages—resulted in Malinowski's attending Georgia on football scholarship.

There was a detour, however. When Bulldog's line coach, Shug Jordan, following the alumnus' tip, visited Malinowski home on Long Island, Malinowski was interested. However, he was not inclined to commit to playing football so far from home. Instead, he signed with Hofstra. Then, he transferred to the United States Merchant Marine Academy but became unhappy.

"I just decided that I should follow up with Coach Jordan," Frank says. "I called and he sent me a train ticket to see Georgia play in the Presidential Cup. It turned out to be a very smart move on my part. I got to play for Wallace Butts, completed my degree requirements and have made Georgia my home. It didn't take me long to take a liking to Athens, and I feel fortunate to be able to have lived here most of my life."

Malinowski lettered for the Bulldogs 1951-53, playing tackle. He is amused by the fact that he was considered a big man at his weight of 215 pounds. "What gets me," he points out, "is that there are running backs, and I'm talking about good ones with exceptional speed, who weigh more than that now. That is the biggest change I see in college football today—the size and speed of the players."

His era was one when the walking wounded had to play. Times were austere, too. He came south with little more than the few clothes he put in a small suitcase. With room, board and books provided by his scholarship, all he needed was a little spending money. But he, like most of the others, lived by a simple rule. If you don't have it, you don't spend it.

He came to realize, however, that Coach Butts seemed to know which players were experiencing hard times. One day when he was hitchhiking up Lumpkin Street for practice, a car pulled over and offered him a ride. The driver was Coach Butts. After greetings, the coach demanded, "Boy, you got any money?"

"Well, no sir," Malinowski stammered. With that, his coach pulled several dollars out of his pocket and handed them to his astonished player.

That was nice, but when he dressed and lined up for practice, goodwill ceased. He had to endure the intense scrimmaging like everybody else.

Didn't bother Malinowski, who saw the educational benefits in the collegiate grant-in-aid system which became a sermon he would preach to young athletes for over three decades. He coached for 13 years and later became a high school principal, spending a total of 35 years in education.

When he coached—from Thomson to Oglethorpe County to Athens High—he believed, like Coach Butts, in the hard nosed philosophy, but he always reminded his players that those who take advantage of football might, as he did, wind up on scholarship with someone else picking up the tab for his education.

1954

Three shutouts in a 6-3-1 campaign in 1954 were an indication that the lack of offensive production continued to trouble the Bulldogs. Two of those shutouts were games which could have gone Georgia's way. Texas A&M won 6-0 in Athens, and against Alabama in Birmingham, the two teams fought to a 0-0 tie. It is easy to surmise what a couple of touchdowns would have meant to Coach Butts that season. Surely a bowl bid would have been there with two more victories. Except for a blowout by Auburn 35-0, Georgia gave up only 54 points for the other nine games, a per game average of only six points.

A seven win season looked promising after a half against Tech in the rain and mud in Athens. Georgia completely dominated the first 30 minutes and led 3-0.

The Bulldogs took the second half kickoff, fumbled in the first series and Tech immediately threw a touchdown pass to claim a heartbreaker 7-3.

Today, the players from that team talk about how they believe the gods of fate had an evil focus on the Bulldogs. "Except for one lousy play, we stopped the drought," remarked Captain Joe OMalley.

Joe O'Malley

One look at Joe O'Malley in his prime, and it was easy to likely conclude, without hesitation, "that's a rugged man."

His chiseled features, his rippled muscles, his compact build, his physical makeup, gave him the perfect football image. He was indeed rugged and unyielding in matchups on the field. He could dish it out, and he could take it. He asked no quarter and gave none.

Not only was he willing to pay the price to become a successful football player, he made ball carriers who tried to turn his end pay the price when contact was joined.

Joe O'Malley is one of those former Georgia players I have always respected for many reasons, not just his reputation as a rugged football player.

He came South in 1951 from Scranton, Pa. (a story to be dealt with later). When he settled in on campus, he identified with the environment, the rolling hills, the freshness of the tree shaded campus and the emotionally uplifting spirit of the college experience. That influenced him, in part, to make Georgia his adopted state.

Football was a challenge. It had to be to survive the practice field regimen of Wallace Butts. O'Malley did experience one moment of second guessing his commitment. He, like others, wondered if he had had enough. During a week of extended head knocking sessions, he called his dad and informed the father that he was coming home.

Fortunately, Joe did not receive a sympathetic ear. "You stay there," his father, a steam fitter, commanded. "You better not think about coming home."

The father knew the importance of an education. He appreciated the fact that football would pay for Joe's degree. While the senior O'Malley never played the game himself, he couldn't imagine the demands on the practice field warranting a yielding in the face of exceptional opportunity.

"It was the best advice I ever got," Joe says today. Then he pauses and notes it really wasn't advice, it was an order. "I'm glad he gave me a challenge and motivation when I was at a down time emotionally."

Not only did Joe stay and succeed at football, he concluded that Georgia would always be on his mind. The Peach State would become home.

O'Malley became one of those players who remained intensely loyal to his alma mater, buying season tickets and spending his fall Saturdays in Athens. Throughout the regime changes and the stadium expansions which make the game and venue far different from his time in the mid-fifties, he, nonetheless has enjoyed a lifetime affiliation with Bulldog football. "When the Dogs kick off between the hedges, I expect to be there," Joe says, with a warm smile of commitment.

He watches Mark Richt coach the Bulldogs with special affection. "I like his offense," O'Malley says. "He coaches a lot like Coach Butts, sending out as many receivers as the rules allow. Coach Butts would enjoy watching Mark's teams play."

There's one difference, however. Didn't matter about your offensive philosophy in Joe's time – when the other team got the ball, you stayed in the game to play defense.

Coach Butts speaks to Joe O'Mally (on right); former end Joe Tereshinski looks on

The rules, beginning in 1953, required what was commonly called one platoon football. It lasted for over a decade until free substitution returned in the mid sixties.

Joe could play both ways with aplomb. And not insignificantly, with reckless abandon. He was an efficient blocker and receiver on offense, and that rugged build made him as hard nosed as you could want when it came time to line up on defense. But he agrees with any critic of one platoon in terms of putting the best team on the field. "Can you imagine what it was like for us when Zeke (Bratkowski) had to play defense?" he chuckles.

In Zeke's senior year, 1953, (when Joe was a junior) the Bulldogs averaged 14 points per game on offense, but gave up an average of over 23 points each Saturday.

The low came when Georgia could not score a point on Mississippi Southern. Southern, a talented and capable team but without a big time reputation, defeated the Bulldogs 14-0 in Jackson.

One platoon football contributed to that depressing 3-8 season. It would be better the following fall, Joe O'Malley's final season, when he captained a team that posted a 6-3-1 record, but after that Georgia would experience 4-6, 3-6-1, 3-7 and 4-6 records bringing gloom and depression throughout the state.

When things turned around in 1959, Georgia winning the Southeastern Conference championship, Joe had become a football assistant and head basketball coach at Brown High in Atlanta.

He took his boy's basketball team to the state title, achieving a championship in the year in which his old football coach would finally claim another SEC title after a long drought of eleven years.

"Even after you leave, you follow what is going on where you played," O'Malley says. I respected Coach Butts. He was good to me and I was happy when he made that comeback to win the conference title in 1959. My coaching responsibilities had me preoccupied but not to the extent that I didn't keep up with what was going on in Athens. I was really happy for him."

Growing up in Scranton, a textile and coal region, west of Lake Wallenpaupack in Northeast Pennsylvania, O'Malley was an athlete who excelled in football, basketball and track. He could have made it to college on basketball scholarship—he once scored 40 points in a high school game—but chose to enroll at Georgia when an assistant coach, Harry Wright, coaxed him into coming to Athens with a friend, Spike Svadeba, who was more highly recruited.

Apparently, when Svadeba called his family and told them he had had enough of football and was coming home, he was welcomed back. Conversely, O'Malley is pleased that he got no such acquiescence.

"I enjoyed my career at Georgia," Joe recalls. "The only thing that was hard was that we lost a lot of games we always felt we should have won."

His senior season is a good example of the frustration that Coach Butts had to endure. Three games that were particularly agonizing were losing to Texas A&M, 6-0 in Athens, a scoreless tie with Alabama in Birmingham and a defeat at home by Georgia Tech in the rain and mud, 7-3. By winning those three games, the record would have been a sparking 9-1. Unfortunately, you can't replay games. Even with lengthy post mortems, you realize the scoreboard never changes. History will always reveal that those three games will never be posted in the win column. Nonetheless, O'Malley and his teammates are troubled today about past results because they have enduring pride in their school and their coach.

Joe and his teammates don't harp on their misfortune but who could blame them if they felt some force – the gods of fate – were against them between the hedges Saturday after Thanksgiving in November '54.

"There was no reason for us to lose that game to Tech," Joe painfully remembers. "Just look at the statistics. Tech only gained a total of 73 yards. We led in first downs 12 to 3. The field, muddy from heavy rains was a mess, you really couldn't throw the ball, but Tech completed one pass which was for a touchdown and we got beat."

Later on Joe coached an outstanding quarterback, the late Kim King, who chose to play at Tech. King, who died in 2004, never beat the Bulldogs. Joe never spoke with his former quarterback about their experience in the big rivalry, but he knows how King must have felt.

After 12 years of high school coaching, O'Malley chose to enter sales with a former teammate, Bill Young, of General Wholesale Co. where he stayed until retirement after 27 years.

ROBERT "FOOTS" CLEMENS

In 1950 in the little town of Scottsboro, AL there was a big ol' country boy playing in the backfield, and he was causing problems for opposing teams.

When you find a high school running back who weighs 205 pounds and is blessed with good speed, you conclude he is a special talent. Especially back then. Georgia alumnus, Bill Cloud, who was a long time recruiter for the Bulldogs, took notice of Robert "Foots" Clemens early on, and not because he wore a size 14 shoe which spawned his nickname. Cloud knew that Clemens would look good in silver britches and that with his size and speed he ought to provide Wallace Butts' Bulldogs a big offensive assist. He went to work early, selling Clemens on enrolling in Athens.

"Actually, it wasn't very hard," Clemens says today. "I had enjoyed my trips over to Athens with Bill and felt very comfortable with him. He was an honest person who really loved his school, and I could see that back then. But there was just something about Athens and the University of Georgia. It was such a pretty place. I really liked the rolling hills and the campus. I was impressed with the football program and Coach Butts' reputation. The man who meant so much to so many players over the years, Coach Quinton Lumpkin, really was nice to me, and I knew all along that The University of Georgia was the place I wanted to be."

In the end, it was tough to say "no," however, to Auburn, a school whose representatives literally camped out at his door when it came time to sign. Finally, Clemens told everybody it was going to be Georgia. He called Lumpkin, who drove all night to get to Scottsboro for Clemens' signature.

There were other factors in his decision, like the commitment Georgia made to him that he could play in the backfield. Most college scouts drooled at his size and speed, but felt that he would be better suited in the line. They could see a pulling guard with such speed that they could build a great rushing attack with him leading interference. "My speed was pretty much straight ahead," Clemens says today, "but I felt that I could play in the backfield and will always appreciate Georgia giving me that opportunity."

But a funny thing happened on the way to running the football for the Bulldogs. The one-platoon game came back in 1953, when he was a sophomore, which meant he had to learn to play linebacker. Everything had been a learning experience for him anyway, even though he was raw talent with great promise. "When I got to Georgia," he says, "I saw that the players who had come out of the better high schools had more fundamental training and were ahead of me. I got discouraged my freshman year, but that is one of the things I appreciate about my college experience and that is why I stuck it out."

He had enrolled in Athens with plans to obtain an economics degree, which he did, and return home and become a farmer like his father. But when he made a choice between the Army and Air Force mandatory two-year ROTC program, his life would be changed forever. He became a career military officer, retiring after 21 years as a pilot.

"We didn't have great years when I played at

Georgia," Clemens says. "My situation was complicated with knee surgery in the spring of my junior year, but the experience is one which I will always appreciate. I learned how to take the hard knocks of the football experience, how to stick it out when things were tough, how to make the best of a tough situation and how to cope with challenge and adversity. A farm boy looks at it as the making of the man experience and you come away with a positive appreciation."

Clemens was one who always took advantage of every opportunity and always looked for self-improvement projects. He always took on odd jobs in high school for spending money, and when he got to Payne Hall, the athletic dormitory, he immediately landed a dry cleaning route. Athletes were not forbidden to take part-time jobs in those days. Clemens had a flourishing dry cleaning pickup and delivery service in Payne Hall. "There were a couple of freshman who worked for me and they did the collecting – of both the dry cleaning and the money – which gave my business a big boost."

Even while in the military h e had a few side jobs and his entrepreneurial bent led him to his post military occupation, head of Automobile Consumer Services Corporation in Huntsville, AL. "Business is a lot of fun," he says. "It is just like football, a great challenge," he says.

After Georgia, while waiting for his military obligation to begin, he played a year with the Green Bay Packers. In training camp Lauren Hargrove was there, and it always puzzled Clemens as to why the NFL team released his former Georgia teammate. "He could outrun everybody, and I thought he would make it," Clemens says. It was the case of two Bulldog backs with different missions. Hargrove ran around them, and Foots Clemens ran over them.

JOHN BELL

Georgia had faith that Bill Godwin could play college football, and he never forgot it. When he had an opportunity to influence his alma mater to offer a scholarship to John Bell, he put his efforts in overdrive. He wanted to repay his alma mater.

Godwin saw a diamond in the rough when he watched Bell play one year of high school football at Jordan High in Columbus. He called Bill Hartman and gave the highest recommendation for his young friend. It reminded Hartman of the time he took a chance on Godwin, a small town Arkansas boy, who, too, was not a polished young athlete.

"I don't think Georgia would have taken a second look at me, if it hadn't been for Bill Godwin," Bell says. "He drove me to Athens, and I worked out with Coach Quinton Lumpkin. Nothing was said, but when Bill drove me back to Columbus, he remarked, 'If you want to enroll at Georgia, they will take you.'

"You can't imagine the surprise. I was flabbergasted. I didn't think there was any way I could play college football on scholarship. You can understand why I have always been grateful for a former Georgia player taking an interest in me and driving me up for a tryout. Interestingly, Coach Godwin never saw me play in high school. Nobody at Georgia saw me play either."

Godwin had something to go on, however. He was hired as track coach at Jordan the spring of Bell's senior year. He knew Bell had college football speed, and that was the basis for his recommendation to the Bulldogs.

Bell once ran the hundred yard dash in :09.9 seconds and beat Tennessee's Johnny Majors in both the 100 and 220 in an SEC track competition.

Lettering in football in 1953-55, Bell's most memorable game was in Columbus where the Georgia-Auburn game was played every year. It was at Memorial Stadium where he had played high school games. "Imagine me as a sophomore at Georgia walking on the same field where I played high school football as a sub and starting against Auburn and playing both ways. I was really excited and proud. Moreover, in that game Jimmy Harper, subbing for Zeke (Bratkowski), threw me a pass, and I scored on the play. After the game Coach Godwin and some of the guys I played with at Jordan came up to me afterwards and told me how proud they were. After all that I knew I would need a bigger helmet."

Following graduation, Bell went to work for Southern Bell, later to become Bell South. He became involved with the Gator Bowl Association as a volunteer and was head of a search committee which hired Donnie Duncan, who now is on the administrative staff of the Big Twelve Conference.

Then a funny thing happened on the way to retirement from Southern Bell. Here's Bell's story of his second career.

When Donnie Duncan left us after only a few months as our executive director to take the Oklahoma AD job, he convinced the Search Committee to hire me. I had worked for Southern Bell for 30 years, and had planned to only work for another five to seven years as I wanted to retire no later than age 60. I agreed to become the executive director for five years. ABC did not renew our contract, and we only had a one year contract with CBS that paid us only 25% of what ABC did. We did not have and never did have a corporate sponsor or sponsors as some of the other bowls did.

In the first year we acquired a corporate sponsor, Mazda Motors of America. In subsequent years we acquired Outback Steakhouse as our sponsor and negotiated a very good TV contract with ESPN. In my final two years we negotiated an even better TV contract with TBS and acquired Toyota, along with Outback, as sponsors. Toyota has subsequently become the sole game sponsor. During those five years our per team payout increased from $600,000 to $1,000,000.

In my fifth and final year we submitted an application to the IRS to become a Non-Profit Association, which meant we would not have to pay state sales tax on the purchase of our tickets or anything the Bowl purchased.

We were granted that application, saving the Gator Bowl more than $150,000 per year. At the end of my fifth year I advised the Trustees of the Gator Bowl Association that I did not wish to continue as the Executive Director. They asked me to stay on for another year to give them time to find a replacement. I agreed. After one year the Trustees advised that they could not agree on a replacement for me and would I stay one more year. I agreed but told them I would stay only as long as they found a replacement who I could train during my 7th year. They agreed.

During my 5th year at the Gator Bowl, 1992, I was elected Chairman of the College Football Bowl Association and re-elected for a second term in 1993. I retired from the Gator Bowl in 1994.

Bill Godwin knew John Bell had talent, and the Bulldog halfback-sprinter proved that Godwin's instincts were on target.

CHARLIE MADISON

When Charlie Madison recalls his time in Athens, he underscores three memories: one, the fact that he was intensely proud to be a Bulldog, two, that he played for Wallace Butts, and three, that he survived. It is difficult for him to review his career without emphasizing that survival was the most definitive point of his career and, subsequently, life. He passionately enjoyed his life at Georgia; he clings fondly to the memories of the times he spent with his teammates, and it is a point of lasting pride that he has always looked ahead and made the best of things.

This is a man who had to learn to control himself emotionally. There were a lot of times when he admits he should have walked away from trouble, but it wasn't his nature. If he were challenged, he would respond accordingly, even if it meant duking it out. He would take on all comers, too. He wasn't given to sucker punching; he simply accepted any invitation to square off. There was more than one occasion when he issued the invitation himself.

Once, he even challenged a teammate, Joe O'Malley, who was bigger, stronger and just as swift with the right cross. Madison suffered a broken jaw, but laughs about it today and counts O'Malley as one of his friends. "I survived that," Madison laughs.

He survived the third floor residency where he was the only rebel with a billet. "Had to," he laughs. "Those Yankee boys were so far from home, they had to remain in the dorm when holidays like Easter came around. It was the same with me since I was from Atmore, a little town in Alabama which is about halfway between Mobile and Pensacola."

His roommate, for a spell, was Angelo Monti from Tarrytown, N.Y. One St. Patrick's Day, he went home with Angelo. They took in the world's largest St. Patrick's parade in downtown New York. There was plenty of beer which was colored green. Madison couldn't get enough, and late in the evening he questioned the prospects of his survival when he went to the bathroom and was shocked to see what he discharged into the urinal was as green as what he had been consuming at the bar. Following the sobering shock came uproarious laughter. "You just don't suspect things like that when you are from Atmore, Alabama," he laughs.

Surviving on the practice field was not as much challenge for Madison as it was for many. He was, as they said of survivors like him from back home, tough as a "litard knot." Madison enjoyed the physical requirements of football even when the guy lined up across from him was bigger and stronger.

Madison was as tough as they came, but admits he would have benefited from a little more speed. "I thought I was fast," he says, "but when I got to Georgia, somebody said I was the slowest halfback in the SEC." He never backed away from anybody, however. "Let me tell you, I believed in contact, which is one of the reasons Coach Butts and I got along so well. When you are out on the field, you are supposed to hit people, aren't you," he questions in the form of a statement. Madison lettered 52-53-54 and played in the Senior Bowl, taking great delight in playing his final game in what he considered his hometown.

Often he reflects back on his career, and his survival, recalling that he would hitchhike to Athens and back. He found out right away his suitcase with the "G" on the side attracted a lot of friendly drivers who were always accommodating a young college student. He pocketed the money from the bus ticket whenever Georgia sent him one.

When he wasn't enjoying contact on the football field, Madison could always be found pursuing his hunting and fishing interests. "My shotgun and my rod and reel," he says, "have given me a lot of pleasure in life."

Not even personal tragedy could keep Madison down. His wife, and his five year old daughter were killed in a car wreck early in his marriage. But that marriage also produced a son, Scottie, who played football and baseball for Vandy. Baseball was his better sport, and he spent five years in the Detroit Tiger infield when Sparky Anderson was the manager.

"I was his first coach," Charlie says proudly. "I taught Scottie to switch hit, and he became an outstanding athlete. For a while, we worked with him throwing with both hands. I could envision him as a quarterback who would roll to his left and throw downfield with his left hand. That would have been something, wouldn't it?" he says.

Scottie's success became a reminder that when tragedy brushes your life, you just have to do the best you can and move on. Charlie, the survivor, remarried and moved on with his life. "You don't give up," he says.

In recent years, Charlie spent much of his time, in Good Samaritan fashion, assisting, as best he could, a former teammate, Dick Young who died in late 2004. Bed ridden with multiple sclerosis, Young could expect his friend Charlie to show up weekly to check on him.

"We all enjoyed Dick when he played, and he was a good quarterback," Madison says. "It was sad. Dick lay there for two years, but he never complained. Some of his old teammates came to see him, and he knew who they were when they came in the door."

There is a pang of regret in his voice, when Madison speaks of Young. Perhaps, he thinks about the fact that his former teammate is one who was not a survivor.

GEORGE MITCHELL

George Mitchell got attached to Georgia football listening to the radio in the forties. He would lie on the floor in his home in Dalton and listen to the announcer talk about John Rauch and Charley Trippi and their exploits on offense.

It was not lost on him, however, that somebody in the line had to be making a significant contribution. He became fascinated by the play of Herb St. John, who was to make All-America for the Bulldogs.

"I always thought Herb was something special," Mitchell recalls. "I thought he must have been the strongest, toughest lineman in the country. It made me want to try to play like he did—all out."

Mitchell spent three years with the Bulldogs, making friends, enjoying the college scene and wishing things were better on the field for Coach Butts.

In all the down times of his varsity years—1955-56—he concluded that the Bulldogs played hard, should have won more games because of the work ethic, but just came up short too many times.

"Tech had it going pretty good, but my favorite memory came against Tech one year in Athens. We didn't win the game, but the halftime show was the most memorable time of my life. At the game there was an older fellow, Howard Moss, who loved Coach Butts and hated Tech.

"When the Tech students brought their model airplane out at the half to do their act, Howard stood on the sideline with his temperature boiling. After the model airplane did a number of acrobatics, buzzing about the field, it landed to great applause from the Tech cheering section.

"With that, Howard sprinted out to where the plane had landed and stomped it to pieces. He did a number on that plane before you knew it, and then he raced away and hid from the Tech students who were chasing him. It was one of the greatest performances I ever saw between the hedges."

Mitchell returned to Dalton and became a successful contractor, operating Dalton Paving and Construction, which is now operated by his son Billy, who lettered in football for Georgia '82-'85 at linebacker.

1955

Offensive inconsistency in close games kept the Bulldogs from posting a winning season. There were four victories, but it was another losing year, 4-6. For so long, in the forties, the expectations in Athens, preseason, were about which bowl might invite Georgia for the holidays. Now, there was eternal fretting about when would there be a winning season, and when would the dastardly losing streak to Georgia Tech come to an end?

It was getting to everybody, most of all the combative and feisty head coach. He needed more players; he needed a little luck, and he now realized who his real friends were. There were few high times to be enjoyed in Athens. The worst was yet to come.

Jimmy Harper

With a business degree and his Air Force military obligation behind him, James K. Harper had plans to return to Athens to study for his Masters and coach the Bulldog football freshmen.

Coach Wallace Butts had already promised him the frosh job, and all he had to do was secure his discharge and process his Masters application for admission.

He had also applied for a pilot's job with Eastern Air Lines, but his commitment was to Butts and Georgia. As it turned out, if Eastern had hired him, it would have been a bad move. It wasn't long before the airline was embroiled into a prolonged strike and eventually went out of business. "I look back and see that Eastern would have been a disaster," Harper says today.

Coaching was what he preferred all along. But before he had an opportunity to settle in Athens, Pete Ferris, who had played at Georgia Tech, informed him about an opportunity at Merrill Lynch.

"I felt like it wouldn't hurt to interview," Harper says today, "and they offered me a job paying $400.00 a month. That was very attractive, so I took the offer and never left the company."

Harper was well known throughout the state of Georgia, having always played quarterback for teams identified with Bulldogs. His father, Doc Harper, a long time coach in Thomasville, was Jimmy's first coach. Harper's Bulldog affiliations, among others, put him in position to start out with a significant prospect list when he entered the business world.

Many of his former teammates became clients and a great number of them referred their friends to the easy going Harper who parlayed his contacts into a productive business relationships.

About the time he was starting out with Merrill Lynch he bumped into Joe Delany on the street one day. Delany, another former Tech player, asked Harper if he had thought about officiating high school games in the Atlanta area?

As a matter of fact Harper was since he had officiated touch games on the base during his Air Force time in New Mexico. He also had worked high school games while he was on active military duty.

At the time of his conversation with Delany, Harper didn't think much about the value of officiating for his business. Former players, who don't go on to the National Football League, in general, usually have a desire to remain close to the game, and one of the ways to do that is to move into the officiating ranks.

Good for business, too, although that was not an objective when Harper was starting out. But when he became the top rated referee in the Southeastern Conference and television came about, his name got widespread attention on fall Saturday's. When technology brought about the live microphone, everybody soon knew who referee Jimmy Harper was. His distinct drawl made him one of the best-recognized officials in college football.

This, too, was good for business. Here again, that wasn't his objective at the outset. Although rules denied him an opportunity to work games in Athens, he was heavily immersed into college football. He would spend time on other campuses, observe the color and pageantry of a game he has loved since grade school. He would be part of that great scene.

And now he sees lasting fulfillment in his professional career. In officiating, he maintained an interest in college football which was important to him. Furthermore, prized and enviable assignments came his way. He worked three national championship games including the Rose Bowl. It doesn't get much better than Harper's experience.

Harper as Wally quarterback

In December 2002, he was inducted into the College Football Hall of Fame official's wing, the highest honor he has ever received. "I was quite overwhelmed when I heard the news," he says. "Those kinds of honors are really nice, and I am grateful. But what I appreciated most of all is what it means to my family. It makes all those weekends when I had to be away worthwhile.

"This is a wonderful honor," said Harper, a four-time letter winner in football and twice a letterman in baseball at Georgia. "As I am recognized, I think of all my teammates and friends, the University of Georgia and especially my coach, Wallace Butts. They certainly contributed significantly to my achievement. I thank all of my friends and the University. I would never have achieved anything in life without the University of Georgia."

At Georgia, Harper lettered as a freshman in 1952. He would letter four years, but all of college football was thrown into a tailspin when, in 1953, the rules changed. Drastically. One platoon football became the order of the day. Players were required to perform on both sides of the ball. This meant that you would not only line up on defense when the ball went over, you also played on all the kicking teams.

If you entered the game in any particular quarter and came out, for any reason, you could not return until a new quarter began. Harper believes one platoon football contributed significantly to Coach Butts' problems in the Fifties.

"We had a lot of players who simply could not play both ways. We lined up almost every game facing better players across the line of scrimmage. I think one platoon set college football back tremendously. It also gave pro football an advantage as the fifties came to a conclusion. Think about it. The pro game was just getting established, and at the same time television became entrenched, which gave the pro game even more of a boost. NFL games were lively and specialized. They scored a lot of touchdowns while we were playing with our tongues hanging out in the fourth quarter.

"The pros were winning big games in the closing minutes and we were dog tired, too whipped to create much excitement. At least that was the way it was with teams which had lesser players which was the case for us at Georgia.

"I remember one game in 1954 when it was hot and we were tired as hell. Joe O'Malley had gone downfield for a pass, and when he got back to the huddle, he looked at me and snapped, 'Don't you throw that damn ball again. I'm too tired to run downfield.' One platoon football put Coach Butts at a disadvantage.

"In a conversation with Coach Bill Hartman he told me that between the Miami game in 1952, our last game of the season, and our opening game in 1953, we lost 32 lettermen. Most of them quit. They just couldn't last through our spring practice, playing both sides of the ball and then scrimmaging tough every day in the fall before playing on Saturday. Naturally, football was tough, but I will always believe it was tougher in Athens than anywhere else."

Now that he is retired from officiating, Saturday afternoons in Sanford Stadium have returned for him. "I still go to games on other campuses as an officiating observer, but I am in Athens as often as possible. Being away so many years makes me really appreciate the sheer beauty of Sanford Stadium and the Georgia campus."

BOBBY GARRARD

It has been more than fifty years since Bobby Garrard got a summons to Coach Butts' office.

A player who identified with the work ethic and was always motivated to improve – never a slacker – Garrard, nonetheless, wondered aloud: "What have I done now?"

Often such a directive left players with emotional dread, but Garrard should have known better. If the Little Round Man was upset with you, he usually let you know about it on the practice field. Away from it, he was forever extending a helping hand. His office generally was an enclave of goodwill.

That's how Garrard found it in 1953.

In the spring of the year in which this book was being produced, Bobby Garrard came by my house while on a trip to Athens to see his former teammate, Walter White.

We were sitting on my porch in late afternoon. It was overcast, but Garrard's disposition was as cheerful and sunny as if it were Florida in February. He was only exposing his natural disposition.

He recalled the details of his visit to Coach Butts' Stegeman Hall office with intermittent stops to wipe his eyes. A half century later, he could not hold back the tears.

"It was after my father's funeral, and I had returned to school when he sent word for me to come to his office," Garrard says. "He told me that he couldn't replace my father but that if I ever needed anything to call him. He said, and I'll never forget, 'Whatever you need you come see me and I'll get it.'" As he collected himself, Garrard said affectionately, "I loved the man."

That was the side that many who played for Wallace Butts were familiar with. Some only experienced his practice field personality, which could be raw and biting. It was a function of the way Butts was raised. Depression alumni came from the school of hard knocks and passed it on, especially if they were members of the coaching profession. It was their belief that no-holds-barred-scrimmaging best produced one who could manage the vicissitudes and challenges of life.

Garrard valued his scholarship and educational opportunity so unswervingly that he didn't worry about long and physically demanding workouts. The trade off would be that he would hang a sheepskin on his wall. "That was very important to me," the former fullback says.

It almost didn't happen, however, that thing called a grant-in-aid. After playing at O'Keefe High in Atlanta, he decided to walk on at Auburn. "No scout, to

Bobby Garrard loved Wally like no other

my knowledge, ever took at look at me. I am not sure why I went down to Auburn except that I was born in Birmingham and I guess my Alabama background influenced me," Garrard says.

If nobody wanted him following high school, it was a case of him feeling totally unwelcomed and uncomfortable at Auburn even in the day and age when everybody could try out—the walk on term of that era.

"After three days of going to see the equipment manager and not being issued a uniform, I said, 'to hell with it,' and went back to Atlanta."

He was hired by Davison-Paxon company, unhappy not to be furthering his education, but not really knowing what to do. One summer day, hot and sweaty, from working as a stock room attendant, he said aloud, "I'm not going to do this the rest of my life. I'm going to find a way to go to college."

In the back of his mind, he still felt he could make it as a college football player. He enrolled at Georgia Military Academy in College Park. Guess what happened? Good team, good year and the scouts come calling.

Auburn sent a representative to his home. Bobby couldn't help it. "I was downright rude even though I had no other offers on the table. I told the man that I had been to Auburn. 'I'm not about to go back,' I told him. 'If you want to recruit my mamma and my daddy, go head, but I'm leaving. I don't know where I'm going but it won't be Auburn.'" He got up and walked out of the house.

A couple of days later a big car pulled up front and what seemed like an even bigger man got out and came to the door. It was Georgia assistant, Quinton Lumpkin. A life long friendship began. "It was the way he handled the conversation that sold me," Garrard remembers.

Lumpkin said Georgia wanted to sign him to a scholarship. After his experience with Auburn, Garrard looked Lumpkin in the eye and said, "Do you really want me?"

"We'll shake on it," Lumpkin said. The deal was sealed and Garrard from that moment on tried to emulate Lumpkin. If he gave somebody his word, he expected to keep it.

He enrolled at Georgia in 1952, lettering as a freshmen, playing safety primarily. Later his ability as a fullback was enhanced by his affection for the work ethic. Soon his pure enjoyment of college life was exhilarating.

"We worked hard, practice was long and taxing, but being on a college campus was so much fun. I developed friendships that have been a source of constant encouragement. Today, the most uplifting time of the year is when I get together with my former teammates, my Payne Hall buddies.

"We laugh, we joke, we reminisce and we would literally die for one another. You can't put a value on the friendships that I have with those guys."

In looking back over his career, Garrard, who was captain of the '55 Dogs, considers his best games were against Alabama and North Carolina in '54.

As a senior, he returned an interception for a touchdown (51 yards on tipped pass by Roy Willkins), rushed for 538 yards (5.0 average) and punted for an average of 37.6. Garrard was one of the most versatile players on the team. Because of his work habits and attitude, he was a favorite of his coach.

One of the last conversations he had with Coach Butts came prior to the Saturday Evening Post trial in Atlanta. Bobby was in Athens and Coach Butts invited him to the Elks Club for a drink.

"I can remember it like it was yesterday," Garrard says. "It showed you what kind of fight the man had – which is why so many of us admired and loved him – when he said about the lawsuit: 'Those s.o.b.'s have got me down, but they ain't gonna whip me.'"

DON SHEA

Don Shea grew up in the West Philadelphia suburb of Collingdale. He was the eighth in a family of thirteen kids. His father had a good job as a supervisor at the DuPont plant, but austerity prevailed at 210 Lincoln Avenue.

There was one bathroom in the house, which is where he first learned something about organization. "We each had a turn, and when it was your turn, you didn't linger," he laughs. "My mother—what a saint. She kept order. We were all expected to help out with chores around the house, and the most important thing, stay out of trouble."

From that experience, he learned important lessons in humility. Don't forget where you came from, don't take anything for granted and appreciate what you have. It made him aspire, however, to achieve enough success to where he could have his own bathroom.

A childhood and teenage memory that has remained indelible throughout the years was the bitter cold in winter. Long before he could find Athens, Ga., on a map, he reflected on the long, cold, dark days from Thanksgiving until spring. "I recall going to school when it was dark, and when you got home from school, it soon was dark again," he says.

At that point in his life, he didn't think about locating in the South, but when he arrived in Athens on a recruiting visit, he said aloud, "This is the place for me."

He was proficient in football in high school and received a congressional appointment to the United States Naval Academy at Annapolis. The weather was not a whole lot better in Annapolis, and before long, he concluded he wasn't cut out to be a midshipman.

"I didn't mind the regimentation and the discipline, but I was not interested in a career in the Navy. I got to thinking about those cramped quarters on those big ships, and I began to wrestle with a decision. I knew I wanted a college education, but I decided that it was best that I go somewhere else."

Bud Dudley, the promoter who originated the Liberty Bowl, had ties with Frank Leahy at Notre

Don Shea captivated by the Georgia weather

Dame, Wallace Butts' good friend. Bud called the Irish coach, who advised that the school had a policy that it would not sign players who had been previously signed by another school. Dead end at South Bend, but not to worry.

A call went out to Coach Wallace Butts, who sent assistant Harry Wright to see Shea and immediately invited him to Athens. Since that recruiting visit, Shea, who was alternate captain of the 1955 team, has had a Georgia address.

"I came down when it was snowing back home. It was nice and pretty in Athens. People were in short sleeves, and there was no snow nor slush on the ground. I knew I had found a home. I knew where I wanted to be."

With his background, Shea was nothing if he wasn't grateful. "A scholarship meant something back then," he notes. He made a pact with himself—he would never gripe and bitch about practice.

His respect for Coach Butts was like a disease. It was chronic, and he never was at odds with the man who brought him south. "Maybe there was a little fear involved, but I know one thing. I was never going to cross him." Not even when he was hit so hard in the Florida game that his eyes crossed to where he couldn't see.

It happened on the Georgia sideline. He was blindsided and his eyes literally crossed from the lick. He got up on one knee and tried to gain control of his senses. Suddenly, he realized that he never wanted to come out of the lineup. "Coach Butts might not put me back in, and I didn't want that. He might take my scholarship," Shea laughs, but certainly not in jest.

Shea staggered back on the field, still in a daze and headed to the Florida huddle. Finally he righted himself but played a couple of snaps before his eyes uncrossed and his vision and self control retuned to normal.

"That's a funny thing when I watch football today with all the specialization. Not only did we play both ways, we were in there on kickoffs, kick returns, punts, punt returns—when the game was over, I was always ready for bed."

Life after football for the all-SEC lineman led him into basketball officiating. While working in sales with Nationwide Paper Company, he became one of the top rated basketball officials in the country. He had played briefly with the Washington Redskins (waived after being sidelined for a year with three broken bones in his foot) and was a high school coach, starting out in Covington.

He officiated SEC basketball for 27 years, retiring in 1993, but today is an official observer for SEC and NBA games, which keeps him constantly on the move. "I spend a lot of time in airports, but the work is stimulating." Speaking like a good Irishman, he further notes, "I'm never hurtin' for spending money."

Joe Comfort

Joe Comfort, quarterback from Washington, Pa., 25 miles south of Pittsburgh, has often thought about the hard times of the Fifties when he was at Georgia.

Like many of his teammates, he remembers the long scrimmages session but makes an interesting point of why it was difficult to win games. "If you check the record, we played Alabama, Florida, Auburn and Tech in a row to end the season. Not many teams could face that lineup and not get worn down.

"Those were heavyweight teams. We worked hard, scrimmaged often during the week, and Saturday was an extension of what we had gone through in practice. I can remember playing those teams, realizing they had more depth than we did and wonder how we ever won any games with that schedule.

"None of that mattered to Coach Butts. He didn't shy away from tough games. It strengthened his resolve, and he wanted his teams to accept the challenge. It was tough Saturday after Saturday, but that was the way it was supposed to be. That is how I always felt Coach Butts looked at it."

Joe came to Georgia as a fullback, enrolling in the fall of 1954. This meant his last game was on Grant Field versus Georgia Tech in 1957.

"What a way to go out," he says. "If you win that last game and it was the biggest victory of my time at Georgia, then you always reflect back on your college years with special appreciation. I know that is the way I have always thought about it. We broke the drought. The seniors finished their careers on a high note. It made it all worthwhile."

BUTCH MULHERIN

Butch Mulherin is a Wally's Boy who has a distinguished resume in sports medicine, but how he became a doctor and eventually the first orthopedic specialist in Athens is certainly out of the ordinary.

To begin with, he never played football growing up. That would come later. Tennis and golf were the sports he preferred. Before football he took up basketball, having to do with the fact that he stood 6-4. His height made him the tallest center in the state at that time. His football coach, Frank Inman, took him out of chemistry class one day and began teaching him how to play under the basket, home for a center.

Didn't matter about him missing a class or two in chemistry – he had no plans to study medicine. As a matter of fact, he had no interest in studying period. School was a place to occupy his time. All he wanted was to get by. The future? "I had no clue as what I wanted to do, but one thing for sure—I had no thoughts about becoming a doctor," Mulherin says.

He had even less interest in football, but decided to play his senior year. Then he stayed for an extra year of high school, and Georgia offered him a scholarship which greatly excited his dad, Phillip. "He loved football," Butch says. "He was happier about that scholarship than I was."

Bear in mind that Butch was like a ship floating aimlessly about without a rudder. He had no plans and made none—he was simply college boy without a serious commitment, one who enjoyed the social scene and found the physical exercise of football stimulating.

"To be honest," he says, "I really didn't know much

Butch Mulherin receives award from Coach Vince Dooley

about football when I got to Athens. I had to go through what I suspect all players experience and that was whether or not I wanted to continue. Got disenchanted my sophomore year and actually quit.

"One of the things I enjoyed was going out early and practicing with Zeke Bratkowski. He threw a lot of balls, and I enjoyed being his receiver. Although I played in a lot of games, I reached a point where I became serious about school and had too many labs in my senior year to be able to continue football. I consider my experience a good one, but I was to learn that you have to be fully committed to succeed in a sport like football.

"Years later when I was working with the Georgia

team, I was amazed at the effort of Mixon Robinson, who joined me as a partner after medical school, giving 100% all the time. He and Chuck Heard, who also became a doctor, were physically spent when practice and games ended. I always held a little something back. If I had treated football like they did, I might have accomplished more. Georgia football was big in the state at that time, and I enjoyed being a member of the team. My memories are good, but the best thing was finally discovering what I wanted to do.

"Fortunately, although I fooled around for so long, I was able to become a serious student and to get myself properly directed. In football you learn that there is a game plan and that you have to execute. I think that helps a lot of young men develop a plan for their life. I know it did for me, but only after my wife-to-be, Ann, motivated me to realize that I had to also make a commitment in the classroom."

His father and grandfather were pediatricians, and Butch was certain he would never follow in their footsteps. When he finished medical school, however, there were seven Dr. Mulherins in practice in Augusta. Still, he enrolled at Georgia with no plans to become the eighth.

Following a turn around in his life, he became one of the first orthopedic specialists in the SEC to travel with a team and take a position in the locker room and on the sideline for every game. When he became established, he dropped by the training room after practice each day. He was not the first orthopedist in the SEC, but he was one of the first to make daily calls after practice and take road trips as a member of the medical staff.

He started examining Bulldog athletes in 1966, and the basis for his practice was his affiliation with Georgia. Being new in town, doctors who performed routine surgery for orthopedic related injuries, were, initially, reluctant to accept an orthopedic specialist. Dr. Marion Hubert, long time team physician, took him under wing and helped him get established. It wasn't long before patients were flocking to his door. He had to expand almost overnight. His clinic has grown today to a staff of seven doctors.

One of his associates, Mixon Robinson, was an athlete who planned to study medicine. Robinson was so impressed with Mulherin's work, that it influenced the Bulldog defensive end to study orthopedics and later join Mulherin's practice. The Mulherin founded clinic continues in its orthopedic role with Georgia athletes.

To fully appreciate where Mulherin was and what he became, you must go back to two developments in his life. First, he started dating Ann Collins, who became his wife. She is the one who influenced him to develop a serious interest in his class work. When they went out on dates, it was usually to the library.

"She truly turned my life around," Butch says. "She made me think about medical school, and it was hard because I had wasted so much time for so long. I made it in medical school by sheer hard work. I paid for the time when I was not serious about class. If I were coming along now with the attitude I had when I enrolled at Georgia, I would not have a chance to enroll at any medical college."

It wasn't until residency that he made a decision about his specialty. He had always enjoyed carpentry and woodworking. He was good with his hands. During residency he had an opportunity to "fix" broken bones constantly. He found that he enjoyed repairing breaks and that it came easy for him. That ability with his hands led to him becoming an orthopedist.

Since Mulherin established his practice in Athens, UGA athletes have been in good hands, but it is doubtful any of them are aware that they should thank Ann.

BILL SAYE

It's November 1954, and a linebacker intercepts three balls in a big game. Who could believe that? In those one platoon days they didn't throw the ball all that much. Furthermore, you might expect a defensive back to have that kind of day, but not a linebacker. However, that is what happened in the Florida game that year.

Bill Saye, the Bulldogs center and linebacker, had the biggest game of his career in Georgia's 14-13 upset of the Gators. In addition to the interceptions, he was credited with a fumble recovery late in the game with Florida driving for what could have been the winning field goal. He and end Roy Wilkins blocked the extra point that turned out to be the difference in the game.

Of the interceptions, he says, "I was in the right place at the right time. One of them didn't actually count. I was credited for two since their quarterback threw as he crossed the sideline while rolling out. The officials said he stepped on the boundary before he threw. Didn't matter about all that anyway. What was important was that we won the game.

"Things weren't all that good for us at that time.

We had been told the week before the Alabama game that Coach Butts was going to be fired if we lost the game. We tied them. The same kind of rumors started up again for the Florida game and we beat them. We then lost by a big score to Auburn (35-0) and lost a heart breaker 7-3 in the last game with Tech. Coach Butts was still with us and lasted six more years."

That rainy, muddy day in Sanford Stadium, Georgia dominated Tech. The Bulldogs moved the ball up and down the field but never scored a touchdown.

Bill remembers the upbeat mood in the Georgia locker room at the half. "Coach Butts wanted to kick to start the second half. The players, confident we could move the ball, lobbied to receive. We fumbled the hand-off the first play from scrimmage. Tech recovered at the Georgia 19, then threw a touchdown pass to beat us 7-3.

Bill Saye played on and under Sanford Stadium's turf

"We couldn't believe we lost that game. That's one where I felt the gods of fate were against us. We finished 6-3-1 in 1954 but we were an erratic team. We played over our heads at times, but we didn't finish that strong except for Florida. When I got into coaching after Georgia, I realized early that whatever you do in football, it is best to finish strong – if you can, but it is easier said than done."

Growing up in Athens, Saye was always focused on the Bulldogs. He attended Barrow Street School, across from where the Butts-Mehre Building is today. Each afternoon when the final bell rang, he would dash over to the practice field and watch the Bulldogs scrimmage. Coach Butts allowed him to work with the team as a manager, and it was his lifelong dream to play for the Bulldogs.

Saye chuckles when he recalls his senior year at Athens High. He and his close friend Willie Fowler had signed to play for Georgia and participated in spring practice with the college boys. "I don't think that was exactly legal since we weren't enrolled in school, but back then rules were different. I know one thing, Willie and I had a terrific advantage over all those other freshmen when they reported in September. We had already been exposed to head knocking, Wally Butts style."

He and Fowler practiced in white jerseys. They were eager and highly motivated. When they bested a varsity player in any drill, Coach Butts was quick to chime out, "Look, you let those little old high school players beat you."

It was an elevated circumstance emotionally for the two of them. When school let out at Athens High, they headed over to Ag Hill to practice with the Bulldogs. "We thought that was a big deal," Saye says.

After earning his degree, Saye spent three years in the Marines and began a ten-year high school coaching career (one year at Sylvester and nine at Hartwell). He then joined his old teammate, Bill Young in sales, at General Wholesale in Atlanta, where he has worked since.

He has purchased season tickets for Georgia games since graduation, and he and his wife, Margaret, never miss a home game. Often when he is sitting in the stands, he thinks about the fact that he played on Sanford Stadium's field and under it.

"When I was a kid, we often played in the culvert which goes underneath the stadium. It runs the length of the field, and we spent a lot of time, as boys, underneath Sanford Stadium."

WALTER WHITE

In the Seventies, preparing for a trip to New Orleans, Earl Gunn suggested that I call Walter White, who lettered at tackle for the Bulldogs 1953-55. While

I was familiar with this native of Toccoa and his time on campus, we had never actually met. It was the first of several meetings, some in far flung places.

Following his time in Athens, White began a soft drink career which found him all over the map—first in the U.S. and later in Europe, Asia and Russia.

At one point, when he was based in Istanbul, he lived in Asia, but worked in Europe. He got up every morning, awakening to the thundering voice of Pavarotti on tape, dressed on the East side of the Bosporus, crossed a bridge over the straits, and arrived at his office on the continent of Europe.

I found that simply stunning. Istanbul was one of several places my wife, Myrna, and I visited Walter and his wife, Charlotte, but our friendship began on that meeting in New Orleans. He chose Pascal's Manale, the Big Easy restaurant, famous for its barbecued shrimp. Vince Dooley was with me, and Walter was eager to reminisce about his days at Georgia and express his deep and sincere feelings for the Bulldogs.

Growing up in a middle class family, he was the son of a foreman at the biggest industry in Toccoa—LeTourneau-Westinghouse—and a school teacher, who was a rabid Georgia fan, attending games in Sanford Stadium until she was physically unable.

Walter always "knew" he would enroll in Athens. "That was just the way it was," he said later in life after he had retired from all those stops abroad with the Coca Cola Company. "I was a product of the Butts' system. My high school coach, Red Boyd, had played for Coach Butts, and I had grown up with strong emotional feelings for the Bulldogs. I could have gone somewhere else, and Tech recruited me pretty hard. That would have been a good deal. Tech paid off its players with tickets, and their games were always sold out. That appealed to many young high school players, but I just wanted to play for Coach Butts and Georgia."

Red Boyd, who blocked a punt in the '43 Rose Bowl which was a significant contribution to a 9-0 victory by the Bulldogs, often took Walter to games in Sanford Stadium. It was an easy drive down from the mountains. "I never heard anything but Georgia," Walter says of his relationship with his high school coach. "I always admired that kind of loyalty."

Signed by Coach Jim Whatley, White appraises his ability as "Not very good, but I always tried hard. I didn't mind all that work. Back then that was what you were supposed to do. Working hard in football helped me in business. Sometimes it is not the smartest guy who succeeds in business, but the one who works the hardest."

People in business, as The Coca Cola Company learned, come to appreciate such philosophy from a lineman with an enduring blue collar work ethic.

It was a matter of survival at Georgia. There were 12 seniors on the team, but he notes that, "seven received degrees." Playing football between the hedges was not the only objective White had when he signed his grant-in-aid; he was determined to leave college with a degree, which, in large part, was due to the influence of his schoolteacher mother. He retired in 2002 from Coke, and settled in Athens.

Walter White, Wally's well traveled post graduate

Walter is a big man with a robust personality, but a few years ago, we were having breakfast at my house, and I invited his friend and coach, the late Jim Whatley to join us. There was a lot of laughter and reminiscing. At one point, Walter began to tell his old coach how much he appreciated his influence. But it was difficult as his eyes clouded up and his voice began to crack.

There is nothing more touching than a player who proudly displays emotion for his old coach.

ROY WILKINS

When he played for Georgia, the late Roy Wilkins looked the part of a devastating end who could dominate a game. And, unquestionably, he could when he was turned on. At the time, he was an imposing 6-3, 225-pounder with remarkable strength, agility and recklessness. Nobody to fool with when he was revved up and turned on.

Wilkins' best game came against North Carolina in 1955. He was a defensive terror that day. Wilkins deflected a pass from UNC quarterback Buddy Sasser into the hands of Bobby Garrard, and the team captain ran 51 yards for a touchdown.

Wilkins' sacks contributed to the heavy loss of yardage sustained by UNC quarterback Dave Reed. Reed ended the afternoon with minus 72 yards.

On one play Wilkins tackled Reed, who fumbled the ball to guard Alex MacDonald. Wilkins then caught a screen pass and ran for 42 yards.

Headlines in the newspapers after the game said, "Wilkins beats North Carolina." The Tar Heels were held to minus yardage rushing as a team.

At Georgia he lettered four years in a row for the Bulldogs during a time in which the Bulldogs were not a championship contender. But Wilkins gained great respect for his physical ability and competency at end.

The pros certainly took note of his playing ability. The Los Angeles Rams drafted him as a future prospect in the sixth round when he was still in the Army, following his Georgia career. He played two years for the Rams (1958-59) and two with the Washington Redskins (1960-61) before giving up football due to a back injury.

"I would really have liked to play longer," he said late in life, "but when you have a back problem, you have to listen to your body. I didn't want to give up pro football because I wanted to keep on playing. I really enjoyed the game, but I knew that it was time to get out."

Following his retirement from pro football, he joined General Motors in 1966 and spent the rest of his professional life with GM until retiring.

When asked what he enjoyed most about football, he never hesitated. "The contact," he said.

And when Roy Wilkins made contact on the field, you knew the meaning of the word. Literally.

JIMMY WILLIAMS

Jimmy Williams' story is one you might expect of an Athens boy who grew up with an intense desire to play football between the hedges for Wallace Butts.

He, like many others, began competition at the YMCA and followed that with four years of high school football at Athens High. While he never presumed that he would be offered a scholarship, he always held out hope. When it came about, he was overcome with good feelings. It was what he always wanted.

Not only did he play on the plush Bermuda grass carpet at Sanford Stadium as a Bulldog halfback, he played underneath it. A culvert runs under the stadium, as many are aware. Tanyard Creek, where gold was once panned in the old days, runs through that culvert, but its waters are hardly ankle deep at the deepest point.

It was a good hideaway for young boys, curious about was going on in the black hole. It is where Jimmy learned to catch snakes, a habit repugnant for most of us, but he was compatible with the ways of a herpetologist.

There were times when he would catch small snakes and slide them under the door of freshmen football players. Talk about all hell breaking loose. By the time they had thrashed around the room, trying to avoid the wriggling reptile and finally escaped into the hall, Williams had moved on with a stealth that often characterized his moves on the football field.

"I never let on that I was the culprit," Williams laughs as he recalled his days on campus. "Some of those boys were pretty big, and they would have gotten even somehow or other. It was best that I never allowed myself to be identified, but it was fun to hear them yelling and knocking over furniture to get out of the room."

On the football field, quickness belonged to his feet. An accomplished runner with the football, it was defense where Williams excelled. Bony and lean, Williams was efficient at running through a ball carrier or a receiver. His tackles were crisp and deadly. Coaches speak of players who have a knack for a certain responsibility. With Williams, he somehow or other seemed always in a position to react on the ball to where he gained the advantage when the confluence of receiver, ball and defender came about. Usually, the receiver went one way and the ball went the other.

If the receiver maintained possession of the ball, he would be looking over his shoulder the next time he entered Williams' quarter of the field. For sure, he would, on Sunday morning, remember meeting the Georgia defensive back the previous day. Needless to say, the introduction wasn't from a warm and friendly handshake.

In high school, Williams scored touchdowns in bunches, many of them at Sanford Stadium where the Athens High Trojans played their Friday night games.

"Anytime I had a good game, I always thought what it would be like to have similar success on Saturday, wearing silver britches at Sanford Stadium," he says.

Following the Georgia high school all-star game in 1952, Coach Butts met him after the game and advised him to report with the Varsity in late summer. Two platoon football was in place at the start of Williams' career which meant that he could concentrate on defense. He started as a freshman.

Lean and lithe Jimmy Williams

In football you never know when bad news might follow good news, and that was the case with Williams in his junior year. Vanderbilt came to town in the fifth game. Georgia forced a fumble early, and on the next offensive play, Williams took a handoff and slipped past the line of scrimmage. When he planted his right foot to make a cut, he was hit on his knee right at that precise juncture. That doesn't happen all that often, but when it does, the planted foot causes the knee to give way.

His knee cap was forced out in an ugly position. Jimmy knew it was bad as the trainer and the doctors worked to get his bones realigned. With tears streaming down his face—not because of the pain, but the reality he would play no more that season, maybe ever—Williams was carried off the field on a stretcher.

The next spring, he had a decision to make. His heart belonged to football competition, but he knew he wasn't his old self physically. A compassionate Butts advised him he could coach the incoming freshmen as an assistant to Quinton Lumpkin.

Following considerable thought, his heart won out, and Jimmy played football, but the injury took something away. He was never the same. Many of his teammates felt he could have played professionally, had he not been injured.

CLEVE CLARK

In his time, Cleve Clark at 6-5, 220 was the incredible football hulk, but things have changed considerably since 1952 when he enrolled to play end for the Bulldogs.

Today, a lineman of that size probably wouldn't be big enough to make the team, but back then, Cleve was an impressive football player, physically, to say the least. Emotionally he was not bad, either, since he was blessed with limitless passion to play the game. He identified with the practice field rigors of his time, and he understood when the coaches preached, that you should expend yourself to the extent that you had nothing left when the game was over.

"When I played high school football for Bernie Reid at Albany," Cleve says, "I learned that you work hard ever day, you practice hard and you play hard. I guess one of the greatest compliments I ever got in football was that Bernie told me after my first year in Athens that Coach Butts told him I was the hardest working freshman that he had ever had at Georgia. If you knew Coach Butts, you know that he didn't throw compliments around loosely. You had to prove yourself to him, and for him to say something like that was special. Years later, when I think about that comment, it makes me feel proud."

When he reported for pre-season practice in Athens in late summer 1952, Clark weighed 207 pounds, and he was trim and sleek, without an ounce of body fat. He had worked himself into shape for the summer high school all-star game and was eager and anxious for his college career to begin.

As hard as his old coach Bernie Reid had worked and trained him, he discovered that he didn't know what work was when it came to football Wallace Butts style. By the Bulldogs' opening game, he tipped the scales at 183.

"To tell you the truth," Cleve laughs, "I don't know how I lost that much weight. I was in shape when I got there, but all I know is that when we opened the season I weighed 24 pounds less."

Cleve Clark, tall and tough for Wally

When he arrived in Athens, he was expected to provide backup help for the offensive ends, who happened to be Harry Babcock, John Carson and Gene White.

Babcock and Carson were highly regarded nationally, and White was an outstanding player who never got the recognition he deserved because of Babcock and Carson. "I'll tell you how easy it was to recognize Babcock's greatness," Clark says. "He was hurt in a car wreck before reporting for practice. As I recall, his sternum was smashed up pretty bad and he could not practice, but for the games; they would put padding over his injury and he would play anyway. In my book, he was an All American if there ever was one."

When he was being recruited in high school, Clark never thought about all the talent in Athens, nor was he attracted to the Bulldogs' reputation as a passing team.

"I had always been a Georgia fan. Growing up I listened to the radio and loved the style of announcer Ed Thilenius. He made the games sound so interesting, and then I was familiar with Charley Trippi and Frank Sinkwich and the Silver Britches. I thought it would be a great honor just to play between the hedges, and years later, after all this time has passed by, I still feel the same way. It *IS* an honor to play between those hedges. They are sacred with a lot of us."

WILLIE FOWLER

Saturday's heroes come and go, often forgotten with the passing of time. With the truly great ones, however, memories of their past achievements, especially the offensive playmakers, live on.

What about those salt-of-the-earth types, who gave as much effort as the brilliant stars, but never gained a headline? Those whose pure love for the school never wanes? Those who toiled in the background with few moments of glory or stops before the camera? Those who knew there would be no professional celebrity or enrichment? Those who loved the game, loved their school and headed into a life of good citizenship, raising a family and never forgetting nor ceasing their deep and abiding affection for the Bulldogs?

Like Willie Fowler.

I have always thought of Willie as special. He didn't win any awards, he didn't make headlines, but his heart has always belonged to Georgia. That was the case both as a player and an alumnus.

His was not a career of storybook, headline-grabbing afternoons. His file in the sports information office is bare of newspaper clippings and action photos. All there is, is one aging file photo of him in his three-point stance. He doesn't have voluminous scrapbooks of his on-the-field exploits. But his heart is filled with the love and devotion to his alma mater.

He lettered twice and distinguished himself in a couple of games, particularly against Alabama in 1954 and Auburn in 1955. There was a critical fumble recovery against Vanderbilt, but he never earned a banner headline or stimulated the attention of a sports columnist.

Today, he has settled down considerably, but for years he was a wreck during a game with his energized cheering, beating of his game program and wringing of hands when Georgia lost a ball game, or when victory was in doubt.

In a confined group, he is demonstrative with his fretting, his emotions often getting the best of him if things aren't going well, but he is the last man to seek attention or to show-off. He complains when Georgia loses, but his complaining is one of regret that his favorite team lost. He has no epithets for the coaches or players. He dials no call-in shows to let off steam; he writes no letters to editors, and he joins no group (or table) with venom-for-those-in-charge on their agenda.

Willie Fowler, stout-hearted for the Dogs

There has never been a more genuine friend of the Bulldogs. There is no greater good citizen alumnus. He is a man of good will toward his school. His smile widens with the best of them when the Red and Black waves victoriously, his hurt deepens to the bone when the Bulldogs lose.

"To me, Georgia means so much that when the Bulldogs fail, it is like your family failing," he says.

LEN SPADAFINO

Doctors and lawyers – among Wally's Boy's alumni – there are many, but a PhD? At least one Wally's boy gained that distinction—Len Spadafino.

Playing football as a kid in Jersey City, N.J., the son of Italian immigrants, Spadafino saw educational opportunity when a man, whose first name he has long forgotten, encouraged him to play football in a town he knew nothing about. He had heard of Athens, Greece, but not Athens, Georgia.

"I just remember his last name, McCaign," Spadafino says, chuckling when it is suggested that such a memory lapse brings comfort to his teammates. If a man with a PhD forgets a name, it signals that the rest of them can be only normal as a half century of time has elapsed since their days on campus.

The first objective for Spadafino when he arrived in Athens was to embrace academic responsibility. When he took an organic chemistry class, he was emotionally overwhelmed. Excellence in chemistry class was just as important to him as making the football team.

He lettered in football in 1954-55 and wound up throwing the javelin in track, but his greatest accomplishment was moving from an undergraduate degree into the doctoral program. His big challenge was figuring out how to support himself while he burned the midnight oil on the way to that doctorate.

"Coach Butts took care of that," Spadafino in grateful appreciation. "He told me I could stay on scholarship and participate in track." Spadafino became successful in the javelin event, teaming with Bill Duckworth, one of the best in the country. Georgia dominated the javelin competition in dual and invitation meets all over the map. The Bulldog duo often finished first and second, and Spadafino sums up the relationship without acrimony: "I happened along when Bill was one of the very best javelin throwers in the nation. I learned a lot from him and was pleased to be his teammate. I'll always be grateful to Coach Butts for the opportunity in track."

Finishing runnerup in the javelin event meant that it allowed Spadafino an opportunity to end up first in the classroom. He earned that PhD and spent his professional life working as a chemist for The Eastman Company in Kingsport, TN.

Following are his thoughts on how an athlete should view his academic responsibility.

Being the third eldest of a family of ten children. there was not much thought of academics, college, or varsity sports. We three older boys in the family held part-time jobs at a very early age. When I was 12 years old, I delivered milk eight hours a night, seven days a week for two years. I believe all that running developed my legs. At 14, I worked in a supermarket after school.

When I entered high school in Jersey City, New Jersey, my advisor said that I should pursue an industrial course of study because I would never be able to afford to attend college due to the size of my family. I agreed. For example, my older brother, George, quit school in the tenth grade to work full-time.

Following graduation, I received several football scholarship offers and selected nearby Columbia University. The Columbia freshman coach said that I did not meet their language and science requirements. He then arranged for me to attend Riverdale Preparatory School in Westchester, NY. After my father and I talked to the Chancellor about the school, he said that he would like to have me attend Riverdale. However, he advised me to go to one of the colleges that had made me offers, or I would be drafted into the Army. The Korean War had begun. When my father and I arrived home, I received a telephone call from the University of Georgia scout asking why I had not used the train ticket he had given me to visit UGA. It was September, and football practice had started in Athens. It seemed like an omen to me, and I told my father that I might as well go down to Georgia and see the "palm trees."

At 6:30 A.M., I arrived in Athens and was met by Coach Lumpkin. He asked me what I weighed as he squeezed my shoulders. My answer didn't seem to bother him when I told him my weight, 185 pounds. "Don't forget Bobby Ward (of Maryland) made All American guard at 185 lbs. last year," he said with a smile. There weren't any palm trees, but I liked what I saw as we drove through the campus.

On Ag Hill about an hour later, Coach Butts "eyed" me from head to toe and asked, "You did make all state, didn't you?" I'll be back on the train in a day or two, I thought. That afternoon the varsity was running pass patterns versus the freshman team behind the "Iron Curtain." After a short time, I was put in at nose guard. The center and guards were not prepared for my quickness. I spent about 20 minutes in the offensive backfield chasing the quarterback. I was not blocked once during that time. Coach Butts threw his hat down and danced about like Rumplestiltskin. "You piss ants are allowing a man to run ten yard sprints into the backfield," he shouted. He spit in his hands and rubbed them together, and shouted, "huddle up!" I knew he would run a draw play because I had been running around the blocks. I made the tackle on the line of scrimmage. Coach Butts said, "Get him out of there so we can get something done." Coach Lumpkin laughed out loud and said, "You can go out now, Bobby Ward." I knew at that moment I would not be going home.

I had made up my mind in high school to always give a 100% effort in football practice as well as in the games. As a sophomore at Georgia, some players would remind me that it was practice and we were all on the same team, After each practice in preseason, Coach Harry Wright would grade each guard's effort that day. He rated most of the veteran guards from 75% to 85%. When it was my turn for a grade, he would stick out his hand and say," Leonard, you gave 100% today." It was his way of motivating and pushing veteran guards. We all laughed as some of the guys would drawl out my name longer and longer as they teased me by mimicking the coach.

The day of the first game against George Washington University, the newspaper and program printed the probable starters. I was not listed. Just before we took the field for the kickoff, Coach Butts read out the starting lineup. When he called out," Spadafino - offensive left guard," my mouth must have dropped open. Coach Wright said, "I can put you in later if you are too nervous to start."

"Are you kidding?" I said. Wouldn't you know the ball on the kickoff came to me. I was determined to take the ball in for a touchdown. Tacklers grabbed me but could not bring me down. I realized they would knock the ball out of my arms if I didn't go down. I dropped to my knees. That was my initiation to varsity football.

Regrettably, I quit the team and left school before the end of that 1951 season — due to injury, homesickness and immaturity. Although I had given a 100% effort on the football field, my effort in academics was not efficient and lacked direction. I was an art major at that time.

It was not long before I was drafted into the Army. The Army has a way of getting your head straightened out, especially during times of war. I made a commitment to put the same effort into academics that I had put forth on the football field when I returned to Georgia. If an 185 pound guard could win a starting position as a sophomore, why couldn't he obtain a degree in chemistry? I returned to Athens on September 1, 1954 and got even stranger glances when I said I was going to major in chemistry than I got when first enrolling as an art major. Because of transferring from art to chemistry, I needed an extra year to complete my degree. Coach Butts agreed to give me that extra year. I think he was proud of my academic effort while majoring in chemistry. "We'll call it a track scholarship," he said, since I was throwing the javelin on the track team. I was rewarded for my 100% efforts in academics by making the All-SEC Scholastic football teams of 1954 and 1955.

Approaching graduation, I decided to apply an all out effort to what appeared to be the unreachable goal of earning a Ph.D. in chemistry. When I successfully defended my dissertation and was congratulated by the faculty committee, I thought to myself, "Leonard, you gave 100%", imitating Coach Wright in my mind.

In 1997, I retired from Tennessee Eastman, in Kingsport, Tennessee as a Principal Development chemist. Football gave me exceptional opportunity in my chosen profession. I'll always be grateful.

I recall the last time I saw Coach Butts. I was on a recruiting trip to the University of Georgia for Eastman. Coach Butts was retired and was buying a newspaper at a downtown newsstand. After telling him where I lived and worked, I thanked him for his support and for helping me achieve my goals by toughening me up on the practice field. He smiled and said, "Football is a good teacher."

Angelo Monti

Angelo Monti's high school coach, Dave Millman, recommended him to Georgia. The coach told him, "Son, they have a coach, Wally Butts, and he likes to throw the ball."

Angelo's ears perked up with could run, sprinter's speed, and he could catch the ball. Only one problem – his size, but the size of his heart was not lacking. He only stood 5-9, but he never met a scrimmage he didn't like, which, in turn, made him a favorite of Coach Butts.

His high school coach had a talent scouting relationship with Coach Butts and recommended players from the Tarrytown, New York area to Georgia. Angelo considers himself fortunate to have played for Millman and is grateful that his coach sent him to Athens where he found a home. Some of the players from Tarrytown came but didn't take to the Southern lifestyle and the hard nosed coaching style of the Little Round Man. They left.

Angelo was one who found Athens and Wallace Butts football appealing. He was compatible with both. He stayed but has one regret. "One platoon football," he explains. "I was not big enough to play both ways. I always felt things would have been better for me if it hadn't been for one platoon football," Angelo says. "Nonetheless, I enjoyed my time at Georgia. It was the greatest experience of my life. I was one who appreciated Coach Butts. I never thought of leaving."

It was tough, he admits. When he saw the movie, "Junction Boys," the story of the first pre-season camp under Bear Bryant at Texas A&M, he thought to himself, "That's the way it was with us." Then he adds: "Coach Butts made a man out of me, and I have no regrets except for the rules change requiring us to play both ways. I realize there are some who found fault with Coach Butts' practice field requirements, but I think if you analyze it, he was trying to make men out of all of us. Anybody who stuck it out has nothing to complain about. I know that is the way I feel."

The summer before his senior year, he was married, and he and his wife, Mary, both had summer jobs in Tarrytown. He had to leave early to report for football practice. When his wife finished her summer job, she joined him in Athens. She drove up to Payne Hall, where the athletes lived, and didn't recognize him. "I was sitting between two of my teammates on a bench outside the dorm, and I had lost so much weight—she asked one of the guys where she could find me. We all got a big laugh as they pointed to me."

He came as a running back, but switched to end, lettering in 1955-56. After a 25 year career, coaching and teaching, he retired. He remains a substitute teacher, however, living in Monroe, only 30 minutes from Athens where he spends most fall Saturdays. He identifies with the emphasis on the passing game that is prevalent in college football today, especially what he sees in Mark Richt's teams.

As he watches the Bulldogs play, he is acutely aware of how he might fit in today. A receiver with exceptional speed who could rest when the defense took over has golden opportunity in today's style of football. Angelo Monti—the shortest end in the SEC a half decade ago – would have been a perfect fit.

1956

There was controversy galore in the state, and whatever doom and gloom had settled over Athens reached its highest point in 1956.

Coach Butts' famous banquet story poignantly characterized his team that season. You remember, the one about accidentally bumping into the lady in a hotel lobby after a game, and politely saying, "Excuse me, ma'm, no offense." She replied, "Hell no, and no defense either."

Even Coach Butts would have agreed with the lady after 1956. Shutout four times—the opener with Vandy and the last three against Florida, Auburn and Tech—the Bulldogs scored only 66 points the entire year, an average of 6.6 points per outing. (Take away the 26 points versus North Carolina and that average dropped to four points per game.) The point total for the season would have been about two games worth in 1942. Georgia defeated FSU, 3-0, in Athens, North Carolina 26-12 in Chapel Hill and Alabama 16-13 in Birmingham.

The defense allowed 162 points, not bad, but too much to aid a maladroit offense. The worst year of Wallace Butts coaching career? No doubt. Times were hard, but a silver lining lay ahead.

Knox On Knox

Knox Culpepper, Jr., a Bulldog letterman, 1981-84, was captain of his team, his senior year. He learned football toughness under his father, who passed away when Knox was fifteen-years-old. By that time his dad had instilled in him the Wallace Butts' principle that to succeed in the game, "you must pay the price." While his dad cared for him, he instilled in young Knox the realization that mental toughness was important. Following are his other recollections:

He played without a face mask and once told me

The Bulldog seniors of 1956

that it was not unusual for somebody to get hit in the face, lose a couple of teeth and keep playing. They would go to the water bucket, wash out their mouth and go back into the game. My mother said his faced was always scraped and that his nose took a beating. One of the things he told me he enjoyed about defense

Knox Culpepper and his teammates stood up for Wally

was that it felt a lot more satisfying to deliver a lick than to take one. I tried to remember that throughout my career at Georgia.

My dad Walter Knox Culpepper Jr. was captain of the 1956 Bulldogs. He had very little to say about his coach, Wally Butts, but what little I did learn about him, Coach Butts obviously had a huge impact on his life. For dad, you either loved him or hated him. My dad happened to be one of these individuals who adored coach Butts.

Following are some comments I remember from my father: Despite his somewhat squat frame, he was an incredible athlete. His players both feared him and respected him.

Coach Butts had intense desire to win; so intense, that in some instances, he was so hard on his players in practice, they were too 'beat up" to perform in games.

Not only were players were not allowed to drink water during practice, but they were instructed to not drink water until after they finished their showers.

If coach Butts ever closed the "Iron Curtain" that surrounded the practice field, there would be "hell to pay".

His knowledge of the game was way ahead of his time. UGA had a devastating passing game during coach Butts rein.

Coach Butts was unfairly accused of giving an opponent inside information on Georgia's team. My dad wrote a letter posting signatures of former players and coaches in order to rally support, and to denounce the accusations as absurd.

My mother, formerly Judy Jenkins, was a cheerleader at UGA, and offers a different perspective on Coach Butts. Coach Butts had three daughters, Faye, Jean, and Nancy, all of whom attended and graduated from the University of Georgia. She also remembers that Coach Butts would do anything to help out a current or former player. He treated his players like family. He cared deeply for his players and went "way beyond the call of duty" in times of need with his time, with his considerable political clout and with his personal finances.

In reference to Jimmy Harper....Once while at the Butts household my mother over heard Wally shouting to his wife Winifred " I understand that my daughter may want to date my players, but please keep them away from my quarterbacks!"

Pud Mosteller

There are players with special talent, usually the backs who command more attention — even when they misstep. It is only natural that we focus on those who reside in the backfield. We follow the ball, and the ball never goes to a lineman unless it is a trick play by some ingenious offensive coordinator.

One way or other, the headlines reflect how the backs perform, and with the advent of the passing game in college football today, we pay attention to the wide receivers, who get more balls in a season today than many got in a career yesteryear.

Even when the ball is thrown with consistency, as in the Wallace Butts era, there was not much Sunday newsprint devoted to linemen.

Often, the linemen are the ones with heart, however. Anonymity accompanies them throughout their career. If you ever played in the line, you understand. It's like the song about loading sixteen tons: "Whaddayouget? Another day older and deeper in debt."

When I called Pud Mosteller about Wally's Boys, you could sense the humility, the pure affection in his voice. Pud didn't care that the practices were long. He wasn't bothered by the scrimmaging and the hours required to sustain his scholarship.

He didn't gripe and carp about the time on the practice field. What he took from his time on campus was the appreciation that he could compete on the college level and not, coincidentally, earn a degree.

Pud Mosteller, always in the thick of the action

The campus experience was one of enduring appreciation. For Pud Mosteller, it was special to play college football, and if a man didn't see the good in the game, there wasn't much to him. When it was over, there wasn't a professional option for him, but he wanted to remain close to the game. So he became an official, not the referee who got to tell national television audiences what had just taken place when a yellow flag had dropped on a play—but the most obscure official on the field—the umpire.

Just like in football, it's the unheralded umpire who often counts the most, the guy who stands in the middle of the field about three yards behind the line of scrimmage on the defensive side. Pud was in the thick of the action as a player It was the same for him all those years he officiated in the Southeastern Conference.

When he played for Wallace Butts, he always gave it his best, and the inspiration he gained from the former Bulldog head coach influenced his philosophy as an official.

"You always try to make sure that you make every game the best one you have ever officiated," he says. "Coaches expect their players to do their best, and we, as officials, should demand the best of ourselves." When Pud reached the mandatory retirement age for SEC officials, he looked back on his career with the same perspective he had as a player. He deeply appreciated the experience.

He kept himself in good shape over the years and felt young enough and healthy enough to continue. However, he did not disagree with the SEC rule in that the mandatory retirement age was reasonable and fair.

"But I hated to give it up," he says. "It was so much fun. I enjoyed it so much. But there is one good thing about retiring – I could see the Bulldogs play and that is very important to me. That is the only bad thing about being an official in the league. You can't officiate games in which your team plays. I certainly agree with the rule. If you enjoy a long term officiating career, you can't see your own team play."

His last year as an official, he did work a game in Sanford Stadium, however. For a game with Kentucky he was asked to work as the TV coordinator/clock operator, which the rules permit.

He has worked in other big game stadiums like Tiger Stadium in Baton Rouge and Tennessee's massive Neyland Stadium in Knoxville, which is one of the aspects he enjoyed most about officiating through the years.

"By being an official, I was able to remain active in football," Mosteller says. "I have been fortunate to work a lot of big SEC intersectional games. I've been able to see a lot of great players play, and I consider that something to really appreciate. I know that I will enjoy looking back on big games I've worked. You appreciate the coaches and players and the work they put into being successful. It was fun to watch them perform."

His most memorable game was Alabama and Auburn in 1981 when Bear Bryant set the record for victories with a Division I school. "Working a game like that made you feel that you were a part of history," Mosteller says.

A native of Conover, NC, Mosteller was a highly recruited high school lineman and was brought to Athens by coach Jim Whatley for a visit. Mosteller made an instant decision to enroll at Georgia.

"First of all, I wanted to play in the SEC," Mosteller said, "I thought it was a strong conference, and I preferred the SEC to the ACC schools which were recruiting me. But there was just something about the campus and the setting in Athens. I thought it was special, and it turned out that I was right. Then there were the feelings I had for Coach Butts. He was like a second father. I always loved him and wanted to play for him from the time I first met him."

When he came to Athens in the fall of 1953, freshmen were eligible to compete, and Pud lettered as a lineman behind Jerry Griffin and Frank Malinowski. By the second game of his sophomore season, he became a starter and remained one throughout his career except for an injury in his junior year. Many times during his career he played 60 minutes.

"That is about the only thing I would say about today's athletes compared to my time," he says. "I don't think many of them could go 60 minutes, but they are bigger, stronger and faster. The game has really changed since I played. It has been amazing to see the changes with players and rules. It is really a game for the fans now. The fans like that offense."

In addition to following the Bulldogs, he still serves as an observer for the SEC officials' office.

TONY CUSHENBERRY

Even today there are lot of Tony Cushenberry's old friends and teammates who don't really know about his harrowing experiences as a pilot in Vietnam.

Mainly because he doesn't volunteer information about his tours of duty as a fighter pilot. He was committed to the military and it was his duty. He was simply doing his job.

During his assignment in Vietnam, he flew 125 missions. A total of 100 missions to the Hanoi area would have you sent home, but missions over Laos and South Vietnam didn't count toward the total to exit a pilot from combat. Not that he gave that great emphasis.

On one of his forays over Laos, the engine of his 50,000 pound F-105 Thunderchief went out. It could have been the result of a single enemy bullet, but there was no explosion, however. He believes today that the engine probably imploded.

Didn't matter, a plane of that weight can glide only so far, and he wanted to eject as close to Thailand as possible. At 3,000 feet he bailed out. When he hit the ground, he set off a smoke flair, which started a fire, which he had to stomp out. By that time he saw that he had drawn a crowd of about 150 farmers. He pulled his pistol but soon realized they were there to help. He

Tony Cushenberry, distinguished pilot out of uniform

motioned to them to keep his parachute, put his firearm away and waited patiently for an hour to be rescued.

It could have been much worse. Pilots shot down after dark risked being taken prisoner by forces friendly to the Viet Cong who traversed the nearby Ho Chi Minh trail.

Was he afraid? "Certainly apprehensive at first," he laughs, "but when I realized those on the ground were friendly, I felt pretty good. I knew that my squadron commander had radioed my position so I felt good about being picked up."

Today, he is grateful for his experience, lamenting

in thoughtful and appreciative vernacular the fact that he knows he is a fortunate man. "I had a lot of buddies who flew the same missions I flew and never came home. When you think about it, a knot forms in your stomach. The only good thing about war is survival."

In his tour of duty, he often returned with small holes in his craft, but never really got hit hard. He learned early on that a fighter pilot's ability to survive anti aircraft flak is to keep the gunners on the ground from getting a "tracking on you." On one of his very first missions, he came out of a bombing run at Haiphong and made an abrupt turn to head home and saw an explosion to his rear. He knew some gunner had anticipated where his plane would be, but he had changed his course at a critical time. From then on, he instinctively made abrupt turns and maneuvers to ensure his survival.

Football at Georgia contributed to his survival in Vietnam. "It is a team sport obviously, but you have to fight for a position and playing time. That becomes an individual thing. I had to prove myself in football and knew that I had to use some of the same techniques and develop mental toughness to survive in combat," Cushenberry says.

Another influence in his training came from shooting doves. "You never know when those suckers will suddenly change altitudes and direction. I learned from the dove field that when you are in combat, you can't be predictable," he says.

His career path ultimately brought him to the University of Georgia where he was the Air Force ROTC commander until he retired from the military after 29 years. While he was in the Air Force, he received a master's degree in sociology from the University of Northern Colorado in 1972. Following Air Force retirement, he was hired as Assistant Athletic Director for Facilities at Georgia, which placed him in an office which overlooked the Bermuda grass fields where he toiled long hours, scrimmaging with the Georgia football team, 1953-56.

Tony played in the mid-Fifties on teams that didn't win a lot of games, but he learned from the experience that perseverance can enable you to extend yourself and to achieve, even when the rewards seem futile. There is something to be said for survival, and a lot of what he learned on the Georgia practice field, enhanced his survival skills in war.

Tony Cushenberry was awarded the Distinguished Flying Cross for his aerial skills and devotion to duty during combat as a flight leader. While assigned to a base in Spangdahlem, Germany, he was the "Top Gun" in the F-100 and the F-105. In 1966, at Seymour Johnson Air Force Base, North Carolina, he transitioned to the F-4 Phantom and was again named "Top Gun."

BILLY HEARN

Billy Hearn was very much like his daddy, Tiny Hearn, except for one thing: in his choice of college.

Like father, like son was evident in that Billy, as a young athlete, could play any sport fluidly and competently, just like his father, who had excelled in baseball, basketball and football at Eatonton High School and lettered in basketball at Georgia Tech. Tiny Hearn also played pro baseball and basketball.

Tiny assumed Billy, who was also an accomplished prep performer in baseball, basketball and football, would follow in his footsteps at Tech and prepared his son for that eventuality. He believed that Billy could succeed as a multi-sport athlete and that his study habits and discipline meant that he would never become an academic liability, regardless of his choice of college.

There was one problem, however Billy, like his father, played for Class B Eatonton in Putnam County, and Tech had gone on record with Tiny that the lower class competition often meant athletes from that level would have difficulty making it. Tech could be wasting a scholarship.

"That was not troublesome for me," Hearn says. "I didn't want to go to Tech anyway. I liked it in Athens and enjoyed my career as a Bulldog." At Georgia Billy earned three letters in football, three in baseball and one in basketball.

While he performed efficiently at quarterback and was adequate on the basketball court, where he was best was on the mound, pitching for Jim Whatley's baseball Bulldogs. He was so proficient, that in the summer of 1956, Billy says, a baseball scout told Tiny the Phillies would offer him a $50,000 signing bonus.

"The rule, as I recall," Billy notes, "didn't allow a scout to talk directly to a player. When they told my daddy what they had in mind, he didn't tell me. He never finished college and wanted me to stay in school."

Billy's high 90 m.p.h. fastball had scouts drooling, but he never had an opportunity to try pro baseball. He holds some bitterness today, and it is reserved for Auburn.

"We were playing in Columbus in 1956, and I ran out of bounds on a play, and an Auburn linebacker hit me out of bounds, separating my shoulder. Auburn got penalized 15 yards, but it ruined any opportunity I had for major league baseball. The separation left me with an inability to snap off that fastball in my throwing motion. I was never the same after that."

Football at Georgia left him with good memories, however. He developed a strong appreciation for Coach Butts' quarterback teachings, and he gained confidence as a passer when Jimmy Orr was in the lineup as well as when he began his professional life, which included a long career on the side as a high school football and basketball official. He left campus with a degree. "Georgia paid for my education, and I will always be appreciative of that," he says.

In the 7-7 "upset" of Miami in the Orange Bowl in 1956, Billy played 58 minutes. "Late in the game they drove down to the one yard line. It took them four downs to get it into the end zone. We didn't tie them; they tied us, but they should have never scored. I missed a tackle earlier in the drive which helped them, but I don't think I have ever been associated with a team that played its heart out more than ours did that night."

With a degree in business, Hearn spent his professional career in textiles. Those 33 years of officiating left him with hip problems, enduring hip replacement surgery four times. He has also experienced surgery for his back and has successfully fought prostate cancer.

"You learn to pull through medical problems like that when you play football for Wally Butts," he laughs. "You learn to tough things out, whatever comes your way."

"BUCK" WILSON

Gene E. "Buck" Wilson, letterman in 1956-57, remembers that the G-Club initiation was something which caused a lot of apprehension for the initiates. They were quite worried as the initiation date approached, forewarned that new lettermen could expect the worst.

"The initiation started in the evening at the practice field house," Buck recalls. This was known as the Alumni House and is now the Rankin Smith Academic Center. Eligible candidates were issued sweat clothes and canvas shoes and told to form a line. Blindfolds were put in place and molasses and sawdust chips poured into the sweats. A rope was then tied around each man's waist and initiates were marched around to perform initiation rites. Performance was enhanced by use of an electric cattle mover. You could hear the ZAP moving up and down the line. The group was then split up in threes. In my group were Travis Vinsestt and Jimmy Orr. We were driven out of town and were dumped near a creek bank. The auto drove off. Our hands and feet were tied and we were still blindfolded. I was first to get free and untied my comrades. We washed up as best we could in the creek and returned to the hard road. After walking approximately fifteen minutes, a state trooper picked us up and took us back to the dorm." If you talk to lettermen about the initiation, they'll probably tell you that the hot shower back at the dorm to remove that sawdust and molasses was the highlight of their weekend.

Buck even kept his sheet of instructions for the G-Club initiation of 1957: Two four leaf clovers, Ten University parking tickets, Two dirty diapers, Double yolk egg, Live black cat, One exact foot of railroad tie, Coach Posey's signature and two of his cigars, Signature and picture of the queen of the Military ball, One Tech rat cap, Two wrappers from Clark candy bar, Signature from the Fire Chief of Athens, Signature from all personnel at the Varsity.

Other memories of Buck's days on campus include: During early pre season practice, (two-a-days), at night after bed check you could hear a loud bumping coming from the hallway steps. This was the telltale sound of bouncing footlockers as players quitting had gathered and packed their belongings and were headed home.

There were no lights on the practice field, and if Coach Butts was displeased, white tape would be placed on the balls and we would continue as darkness fell.

A likeable guy, whom we called Smitty, was the "in charge guy and cook" at the Payne Hall dining facility which was located in the basement of the dorm. The food was generally so bad that after practice, players would go by the Jenny Belle at the North end of North Myers dorm, get free sandwiches, milkshakes etc., play the jukebox and mingle with the coeds.

During the late 50's and early 60's the coaches didn't recommend weight training for players. We were told it would tighten you up and you couldn't run, catch the ball, etc. However, there were weights in Stegeman Hall and some of us used them. That is one of the many changes in football. All players are expected to lift weights today.

24

PART IX

LATE FIFTIES

Good Times Return

1957

This team, like the '56 Bulldogs would post only three victories, but the drought against Georgia Tech finally ended with a 7-0 victory on Grant Field. Thunderin' Theron Sapp brought relief to all Bulldogland with his touchdown smash late in the game on a harshly cold afternoon that warmed Georgia hearts all across the state.

The Bulldogs were shut out thrice, they lost seven times, but that was not the story line of the season. Tech had been vanquished, and nothing else mattered. Nobody talked about the 3-7 record. Everybody forgot prior failures; they were too busy singing Sapps' praises.

Theron Sapp

In all likelihood, there has never been a player who wanted to play college football more than Theron Sapp, who overcame a broken neck to play for the Bulldogs. Life-after-Athens, for him, included eight years in the National Football League.

Consider the circumstance and reflect on the medical reaction today of a player continuing football after cracking two vertebrae at the base of his skull. Unquestionably, his playing career would be over. But not for Sapp, who was determined to line up between the hedges for Wallace Butts and the Georgia Bulldogs.

He did play—four years in the Southeastern Conference and eight in the NFL. "I never really thought about not playing," Sapp says in recalling his career. "My neck healed and never bothered me. I broke everything else after that, but my neck was okay. I broke my pelvis the year the Eagles won the NFL title. I broke a leg after being traded to Pittsburgh. I dislocated a shoulder and broke both hands and a few fingers, but that is all part of football."

Today, it would not be medical opinion alone that would send him to the sidelines, no school or team would assume the legal risk. A blow to the same spot at the right time could result in paralysis. Even death.

Most Theron Sapp stories begin with either an account of his broken neck or the touchdown he scored on Grant Field to break the drought. He remembers the drive against Tech in 1957 like it happened yesterday:

"We recovered a fumble late in the fourth quarter. I was fortunate to recover the ball which gave us a chance to drive for a touchdown and win the game. All during the drive, I kept asking for the ball. I felt like I was on a roll and a lot of the linemen were telling Charlie Britt, 'Give it to Sapp,' which encouraged me. When we got down to the goal line, the Tech defense really stiffened. On third down, Britt sneaked for no gain. In the huddle, somebody said, 'Give the ball to Sapp.' I wanted the ball because I felt like I could score. On the right side of our line, Billy Roland, Nat Dye and Jimmy Orr blocked well, and I've never been more determined. I ran over one guy and didn't look up until I had blasted almost through the end zone. We were not going to be denied.

"After the game, people came down on the field and literally mobbed us. We were all happy for Coach Butts. He deserved that one. We were aware of the criticism he had experienced. We knew what it meant for us to win and make things better for our coach.

"It took forever to get off the field, and I remember the team spent the night at the Biltmore Hotel. Several of us went to a fraternity party on the Tech campus. They were all very nice. Another thing I remember was how cold it was. It wasn't cold when we left Athens Saturday morning bussing over for the game, but by kickoff the temperatures really dropped. It didn't bother us; we were really ready to play. We were so fired up, we could have played in our underwear and the weather wouldn't have been a problem."

When he retired from pro football, he purchased

several Maryland Fried Chicken franchises in Augusta and became successful in business. He was one who worked hard, often seven days a week. He opened up, he ordered his supplies and foodstuffs, he worked in the kitchen and he was there at quitting time. "That's what it takes to make it in business. You don't have to go to school to learn about hard work, which I think is the most important thing for success."

Even when he became established, he remained a "hands-on" operator. He never propped his feet up and deferred to staff. In recent years, his work routine evolved into semi retirement. He had earlier purchased 12 acres of land in Evans, outside Augusta. His pretty wife, Kay, a finalist in a Doris Day look-alike-contest in Hollywood, enjoys horses. Her equine interest has given way to a latent appreciation for art. There are a number of paintings around of No. 40 crossing the goal line.

Another memorable moment in Sapp's Bulldog football career took place against The Citadel in Athens in 1958. Georgia won by the whopping score of 76-0. Coach Butts was trying to hold down the score, but Sapp wanted the ball. He needed 60 yards to catch Billy Cannon of LSU as the rushing leader in the Southeastern Conference. In the third quarter, he sent himself into the game and announced to Charlie Britt in the huddle, "Coach Butts said run 37 slant." He took the handoff and gained about 20 yards.

On the sideline, Coach Butts was appalled. He sent in a substitute, upbraided Sapp for his insulting act and sent him to the bench. "He gave me hell for putting myself in the game," Sapp chuckles. "A friend of mine, Ansel Quattlebaum, was in the student section, and he got a chant going, 'We want Sapp,' 'We want Sapp.'

"Ansel ran down to the hedge and shouted, 'Coach Butts if you don't put Sapp in, we are going to run you out of town.' Coach Butts wheeled and ran over to the hedge and kept asking, 'Who said that?' By that time, Ansel had sneaked off. There is one thing we all knew about Coach Butts. If you challenged him, you would have a fight on your hands. His attitude was that if someone didn't like what he was doing, he could come over the hedge and fight it out, right there on the spot. All of the players admired that about him. He was a fighter. He would take on anybody."

More about the story of Sapp's neck injury: practicing for the South team for the annual Georgia high school all-star game. He broke his neck in a pileup, but didn't know it at that time.

In fact he walked around for about three days unaware of the seriousness of the injury. "It was hurting me pretty much although the doctor told me he thought I'd be okay," Sapp recalls. What happened is very interesting. The doctor had actually read the X-Rays when they were wet and didn't see the break in the two vertebrae. A couple of days later the negatives were still on his desk and he was about to file them away when he noticed the fracture.

By this time, Sapp had left the all-star camp and was spending a couple of days with a sister when game officials frantically got in touch with him. He was sent to the

Theron Sapp smiling (left) and Breaking the Drought against Tech

hospital post haste for treatment and rehabilitation.

All of his freshman year was spent in a cast, but Sapp was on hand for the opening of September drills at Georgia in 1955. He ran laps around the field for a couple of days and had no fears about scrimmaging when Coach Wallace Butts gave the signal, but trainer Sam Richwine stopped him on the third day and informed him that he couldn't continue to practice without a doctor's approval.

Sapp's disappointment was great, but not as great as his determination – the one factor which characterized his play from the time he started football in the fifth grade at Cynthia Weir Grammar School in Macon until his retirement from pro football in mid-1967.

"I went back to Macon to see my doctor, Dr. John I. Hall, and asked him to okay my playing for Georgia, but he wouldn't. He told me that I might be all right and that I might not, but that if I were his son I definitely wouldn't play." Sapp was polite but firm. He told the doctor: "I'm glad I'm not your son, because I am going to play."

That didn't stop the Macon Mauler, who was destined to become one of the best known and best loved football players in Georgia history.

"I was determined to play football. It was in my blood, and I didn't worry about the neck. Football was something I wanted more than anything else, and finally they had to let me make the decision, which took about a half second.

"While I was in the hospital in 1954, Coach Butts and Coach Quinton Lumpkin came to my room and told me that Georgia would honor my grant-in-aid whether I played football or not.

"That really was something which I appreciated and I'll never forget it, but one of the reasons that I wanted to get back in uniform was that all my life I had wanted to play for the University of Georgia Bulldogs."

Soon after he rejoined the team as a B-teamer, he got the coaches' attention right away with his power running, which caused Coach Butts to offer him an opportunity to move up to the varsity.

Sapp shocked the tough Bulldog coach (but must have pleased him as well) by turning him down because he felt he needed the experience of playing longer with the B-team.

"It had been over a year since I played any football, and I knew I needed the work," Sapp explains. "Even if I had gone up with the varsity had gotten into any games, it would have been a year of eligibility wasted."

He was accurate in his appraisal, for in 1956 he was a third string fullback even though he continued to catch the eye of varsity coaches by knocking down would-be tacklers in scrimmages when he backed up the line.

It was different in 1957, following a great spring practice. He started at fullback in the opening game against Texas and was the starter the rest of his college career, 20 straight games.

He made all-conference and was team captain, his senior year, but it was as a junior that he won the hearts of Bulldog fans everywhere. As all loyal Bulldogs know, Sapp scored the touchdown against Georgia Tech, in Atlanta, for a 7-0 victory which broke an eight year losing streak to the Yellow Jackets. Georgia fans still thrill to the accounts of that win, and, today he is known as the "Drought Breaker" and continues to be praised wherever he goes. He was mobbed after the game and one of the wonders of his career is how he escaped injury that particular day. It is doubtful that a single Georgia fan failed to clinch his hand or pound his back. Pretty ladies he had never seen before hugged and kissed him and some alumni, tears streaming down their faces, reached out and touched their gladiator who had just felled the giant.

He starred again in Georgia's 17-3 victory over Tech in 1958, which prompted a move to have his jersey 40 retired – one of the remarkable events in his career. Only three other Georgia players, immortals Frank Sinkwich (21), Charley Trippi (62), and Herschel Walker (34), have had their numbers put away permanently.

His pro career began similarly to his college career – injury bad luck. In the Eagles' second pre-season game at Los Angeles in 1960, he was running off-tackle for a good gain against the Rams when a tackler knocked him off his feet. As he was falling to the ground, all 295 pounds of big John Baker crashed on top of him and broke his pelvis.

The doctors were amazed by Sapp again. He got out of bed and was back into his uniform with three games left, playing with the suicide teams.

The Eagles won the NFL championship over the up-and-coming Green Bay Packers of Vince Lombardi, and Sapp was in the lineup for that great victory.

"I wanted to get back for the championship game because it meant a lot to me. I wanted to be a part of the team. When it looked like we would win the division title, I got back to work because I didn't want them to leave me out when they passed out those winning paychecks," he chuckles.

Traded to Pittsburgh during the season, he had his greatest year in 1963. He gained over 500 yards in nine games and scored the winning touchdown against Dallas in the last game of the season on a 25-yard run in the last minute, enabling Pittsburgh to tie New York for the Eastern Division championship.

In 1964, he was off to a good start but broke his left hand in a pre-season game; nevertheless, he was ready to go by the third game when he got stepped on in a pileup and broke his right hand.

Then, in 1966, he went down for good in a training camp scrimmage when a former roommate, Clendon Thomas, crashed into his left leg, breaking it just below the knee.

"That was the only time that I've ever been hit when I couldn't get up and walk off the field on my own," he points out. "With both the neck and pelvis, I got up and walked away, but when the leg was broken, I knew I had a bad one when I couldn't get up."

These are only the major injuries. Others include the loss of teeth and a broken nose at Georgia and a dislocated shoulder, severely sprained ankle and knee operation with the pros. Even today, he appreciates football with deep affection and has no regrets.

"Football was good to me, and I'd do it over again. The only disappointment I had was that I didn't get to play more than I did – that was the thing that hurt. Your pride hurts more than the actual physical pain of an injury.

"If it hadn't been for football, I would never have gotten an education and I'll always be grateful for that. Looking back, football taught me the value of team play and that is something you have to stress in business with your employees.

"Another thing about football that I appreciate now is that you have to be organized. You have to know where you are going and what you are going to do, and that is one of the important things in business.

"Now that I am the owner and operator of my own business, I see things somewhat like a coach did. I have to give orders rather than take them, and I know how tough it must have been for some of the coaches to make some of those decisions I didn't like."

KEN COOPER

Ken Cooper lives quietly and virtually unrecognized among the moss draped oaks of tourist-favored Savannah where it is unlikely that any resident—not even Uga—would remember his place-kicking feat that will likely endure for the ages.

Talk to Bulldog fans about the abundance of all-star kickers who have passed through Athens, and, no doubt, they are aware of the remarkable and sparkling place-kicking success of the past.

Ken Cooper, last of the drop-kickers

Most are also familiar with accomplished kickers like Kevin Butler, who is the first pure specialist to be elected to the College Football Hall of Fame.

They probably can tell you about the many others who wore the Red and Black with distinction, but the guess here is that none of them could tell you what Ken Cooper did that no modern Bulldog placekicker ever even attempted let alone succeeded — scoring via the drop kick. You heard right! Cooper dropkicked the ball through the uprights against Texas in Atlanta in 1956. Following a Bulldog touchdown, Cooper fielded a bad snap, ran to his right a few paces, avoiding the rush and drop kicked it through.

Dropkicking went by the wayside about 1932, and

it had to do with the advent of the passing game. The shape of the ball was changed from a more round ball to the oblong shape similar to what the game is played with today. An oblong ball enhanced passing.

"The old ball gave you a true bounce," says Bill Hartman. The new ball was better for passing but it pretty much ended the drop kick."

It was not so amazing that Cooper was able to pull off his successful drop kick. As a boy growing up on a farm in Tift County, he fashioned goal posts together in his back yard and practiced drop kicking every day and became unusually proficient.

He was his team's place-kicker in high school and was never called on to attempt a drop kick, which was the way he expected it to be at Georgia. When he made his point after against Texas, Cooper was, as the result of that bad snap, put in a situation with which he was familiar. Albeit a latent circumstance, he executed to perfection.

Cooper was a shy and handsome collegiate end who was withdrawn, never comfortable in the spotlight, even when he became the head coach at Ole Miss.

Retired from Bell South, even today he prefers life in the background. He seldom attends reunions and public events, spending much of his time watching his son compete in tennis. He enjoys tennis, occasional golf and fishing outings, and has only returned to Oxford a couple of times since his coaching career ended in 1977.

I'll always remember him for something he said and something that was said about him: One summer I went home and returned to Athens with fresh butterbeans from my parent's garden. He was then a Bulldog assistant coach, and I gave him a package, which he cooked for supper that evening.

The next day at the office, Ken, who had grown up with vegetables on the kitchen table every meal except breakfast said, "Those butterbeans were so good, they tasted like M and M's."

Though Ken's head coaching tenure was brief, I recall what Johnny Vaught, the legendary Ole Miss coach, once told me: "Ken Cooper is one of the brightest coaches I've ever been around."

It is a shame that Cooper didn't enjoy enough recruiting success during an unsettled time at Ole Miss to extend his career, but he did have his day in the sun.

That is all in the past, however. Now he'd rather talk about a new lure for spring fishing.

Jimmy Orr

It didn't happen in Athens, but it is a story that will be handed down, especially when the history and lore of the Johnny Unitas' Colts are recalled.

Jimmy Orr, Georgia's cagey receiver and punter, surprised the National Football League with his remarkable pass catching ability in 1958 to become "rookie-of-the-year." He was so proficient at his wideout position that he became a legend in Baltimore after starting out in Pittsburgh.

One corner of old Memorial Stadium end zone became known as "Orrsville" because that is where Orr wound up after catching countless passes from Unitas. Injured one Sunday afternoon, Orr left the game with what turned out to be a slight shoulder separation. The adoring Colt fans groaned dejectedly when they saw him head for the locker room, naturally assuming his injury might have been far worse than it turned out to be.

The trainers subsequently drove him to a hospital about four blocks away. He remembers being seventeenth in line for x-rays. Everybody recognized Orr and knew the Colt game was in progress. The radio broadcast was being played over the hospital house speaker system. The trainers asked those in line if Orr could move up. Nobody disagreed. The x-rays revealed no serious damage, and he returned to the locker room before considerable game time had elapsed.

Prior to the trip to the hospital, he had undressed and had removed the tape from his ankles. He quickly redressed and returned to the field. The Colts had the ball, and as Orr jogged on the field the head coach, Don Shula, pointed to the huddle. Orr trotted into the huddle as the crowd went wild.

Unitas welcomed him back. Orr said, "Hit me in the corner." The quarterback grinned, nodded and was on target. Orr plucked the ball out of the air for a TD, untapped ankles and slight shoulder separation notwithstanding.

It was Nov. 21, 1965, with less than five minutes to play when Orr returned to the action. The Colts were leading the Eagles, 27-24. Orr's catch iced the game, 34-24.

Orrsville was next to the third base dugout in the stadium shared with the baseball Orioles. "It was very tight down there," Orr remembers, "but we had a lot of fun. We scored a lot of touchdowns." Notice he said, "we" scored a lot of touchdowns, a reflection of his

Jimmy Orr could run and catch with the best

modest and team oriented personality.

Orr was not a player with impressive top speed, but he was remarkable at getting open. He played flanker and Raymond Berry, who was slower than Orr, was the split end. The two of them and their success prove that a lack of speed doesn't mean you can't make it big in the NFL.

They made up clever names for the routes they ran and reviewed them with Unitas. "It was a rewarding experience playing with John Unitas," Orr says. "He would ask us what patterns we wanted to run, what we thought would work. He was concerned with the protection and let us call the routes."

When his celebrated days ended in Baltimore, Orr affiliated with a number of ventures from radio to a stint as an assistant coach with the Falcons to casino public relations assignments in Atlantic City and Mississippi.

Throughout his career, Orr constantly fooled NFL defensive backs with his ability to get open. "First of all," he says, "I spent time studying film. I paid attention to what the opposing team was doing. I had a good feel for what would work and what wouldn't by the time we were ready to line up on Sunday."

This didn't mean he would stay up all night watching film. He had such a good feel for the game that he made his assessment after a few sessions with the projector. He caught on quickly to habits and tendencies of opposing defenses.

One day Shula caught him asleep in a meeting and predictably chastised him in front of his teammates. Didn't bother Orr. He knew how the Chicago Bears' backs were going to play him. He knew he would face a bump and run scheme. He was ready for the game, early in the week. He scored twice, and reminded Shula that a little nap rested him for the competition.

In recalling his career, Orr says that footwork was the key to becoming open. A receiver headed for the right corner of the end zone is taught to pivot off his left foot. Orr made his cut off his right foot, an unorthodox move, which often brought defensive backs to their knees, out of position to make the play on the pesky receiver.

He would change his routine, knowing he was scouted on film. He would change up his step combination, he would flatten his routes, he would stop and go, add a new counter or stutter step from week to week. "The key," he says, "is to get underneath."

Orr was not one to talk back, but he could apply the needle with poignancy and alacrity. Once, Shula remarked at the halftime of a game that since Orr's uniform was clean and unmarked that Orr "must not be doing any blocking." To which Orr replied, "You don't send a thoroughbred out to do a mule's job."

In his NFL prime, Orr was as good as you could find at wide receiver. When you saw him in his shoe leather, he certainly was not an imposing athlete to say the least – 6-0, 180. His physical dimensions were far from impressive, and when it came to foot speed more than half the wideouts in the league were swifter. But few were as adroit when it came to effectively running patterns and getting open. He lulled the best of the defensive backs to sleep, threw a convincing fake at them and, presto, he was open for a touchdown pass.

If you are a receiver, it doesn't matter how you look, however; what matters is whether or not you can produce and this means that the primary responsibility for a receiver is to, first of all, get open. Then catch the ball.

Orr could pull off his maneuvers with the best. That was because he did not appear to be that much of a challenge when he ran his routes. Of course, he will freely suggest that it certainly didn't hurt his career any to have the great John Unitas throwing the ball his way.

"John," he says, "was simply the best, the best of his time. Also, we had a lot of good players and that certainly helped. In addition, we had great harmony on our team. If you didn't fit in, they traded you. A good situation like that enables you to play longer."

Like so many pros of his era, Orr often wonders if today's players have as much fun as those in his day. "They certainly make more money," Orr says, "but I'm not sure they truly enjoy it like we did." The selfishness and greed he sees and hears about is the basis for his view.

After being drafted by the Los Angeles Rams following his senior year at Georgia in 1957, Orr was traded to Pittsburgh, where the late Bobby Layne took him under wing and taught him the nuances of the passing game. Even later when things soured with Layne and the Steelers, Orr still credits the late quarterback with a substantial impact on his playing career. "I learned a lot from Bobby," he says, "and I'm grateful." Layne had savvy, crass, con, heart, flexibility, inventiveness and a winning competitiveness. It was Lane who said he never lost a game but that time ran out on him a few times. Orr identified with all that in a quarterback and when he claimed NFL rookie of the year honors in 1958, he was quick to note that playing with a quarterback like Layne was to his advatage.

One thing he learned from Layne was that staying out late the night before a game and partying didn't necessarily mean you might render a weak performance on Sunday afternoon.

Orr could quaff down a few beers the night prior and then gather in touchdown passes Sunday as easily as ordering another round.

A native of Seneca, S.C., Orr, the son of a doctor, Orr didn't enjoy football at the close of his high school career. After surviving two broken collarbones, he felt it would be better to walk on and play basketball at Clemson.

Funny thing, Orr had turned down Frank Howard's offer to play football at Clemson, because he felt he was better at basketball. But he became uncomfortable when he settled in at Clemson. "Too close to home. Too much military. No girls," he laughs.

He transferred to Wake Forest, where he discovered quickly that if he stuck to basketball, he would get in a lot of scrimmage time, but when games were played, he would be up in the stands with the fraternity boys.

He transferred to Athens with quarterback on his mind, and while Georgia was experiencing hard times, he discovered right away he was not going to crack the lineup at that position. The competition was too tough. Backfield coach Sterling DuPree advised him to move to receiver. He wasn't big, and he wasn't fast. But he was quick, and his soft hands were like glue when they came in contact with a forward pass. Furthermore he developed an easy rapport with DuPree, who taught him advanced receiving techniques which would later give him significant advantage in the National Football League, which, at the time, never crossed his mind. He would lead the SEC in receiving, even with Bulldog teams which won only 10 games during his three varsity years.

While at Georgia, the breaking of the drought against Georgia Tech in Atlanta in 1957 took some of the sting out of the losing seasons. And, too, while individual accomplishment was never an objective of his, he realized that his training at Georgia enabled him to make it as a receiver with the pros. When he recalls the 1957 game with Tech in Atlanta, like everybody else, he remembers the bitter cold and the stinging wind. But none of that mattered. He and his teammates defeated Tech 7-0 to take the bitterness out of an eight-year losing streak. "The thing that I appreciate is that it started a four-year win streak over Tech," Orr says. Sapp's touchdown is well documented, but Orr caught a third and 12 pass to keep the drive alive.

To this day, when he reminisces about his playing career, he never fails to think of Wallace Butts and Unitas. "Coach Butts was just smarter than everybody else when it came to the passing game, and I benefited from that. It gave me a tremendous advantage."

Unitas quietly set an example that permeated the entire Colt roster. Every team in the NFL knew that if it had a chance to beat the Colts, the defense had to get to the Colt quarterback. Orr, like the rest of his teammates, watched Unitas take pounding after pounding, including cheap shots, and not once did the quarterback fold or display any reluctance to come back for more.

"It made you play better," Orr says. "We didn't drop balls. No coach got on us. Nobody made us run laps. Nobody fined us. You just saw that man do his job at quarterback and you simply concentrated on doing yours."

Today, Orr lives at St. Simons with his wife, Gloria. There's seldom a day, unless there is constraining weather, that you won't find him on the golf course. All this means is that Jimmy Orr, a natural born competitor, is still competing.

TRAVIS VINSETT

When Georgia broke the drought against Tech in 1957, Travis Vinsett, alternate captain, remembers two things: One, how eager Theron Sapp was to run the ball. Sapp was confident he could make yards no matter the defense. "He kept coming in the huddle," Vinsett says, "and saying, 'gimme the ball, 'gimme the ball.'"

The other long standing memory was a tackle Vinsett failed to make.

"I thought I had the Tech runner cornered, but let him get away right in front of the Georgia bench," Vinsett recalls. "I rolled over and saw Coach Butts slam his baseball cap on the ground and jump up and down on it. He stomped that hat like he was killing a snake."

Travis knew what was coming next. "I looked up and somebody was coming in for me," he laughs today. "I've never known a competitor like Coach Butts."

Vinsett left college early to take a coaching job in Baxley with his high school coach, but returned to Athens each summer until he completed degree requirements.

"When I told my major professor my plan, he said: 'Too bad, you'll never get your degree. You'll go down there and never take the time to finish.'" Travis looked him in the eye and said, "Yessir, I will."

He knew he wanted to coach long term, and without a diploma, he would never have that opportunity. After 15 years of coaching (five in Baxley and ten in his hometown of Gaffney, S. C.), he joined Spartan Foods for 23 years, retiring recently. Now, he works part time to remain active.

"When I look back on my career, the thing I appreciate the most is my teammates. We didn't win a lot of games, but we had some good boys. I enjoyed living in Payne Hall and making friends. For teams that didn't win championships and go to bowls, we were very close."

J.B. DAVIS

You won't hear a more touching football story than that of J.B. Davis, perhaps the most lightweight captain in the history of Bulldog football. Davis finished his career at 154 pounds.

Little guys who succeed make interesting copy but

Wally with '57 captains, J. B. Davis (left) and Travis Vinesett; J. B. high stepping for the camera

you'd probably have to go back to the days of the Notre Dame box to find a captain who weighed less than J.B.

In my estimation, there has never been a Georgia player who has exhibited a more humble appreciation for his alma mater than this one-time Guntersville, AL, star halfback and baseball pitcher.

Then, for added measure, there is the subject of his name, which started out far from what it became. In the beginning he was simply Baby Davis. That was the way it was listed on his birth certificate. After that he became J.B. with the initials standing for nothing. Then he was Jefferson Beauregard, a handle applied by the creative and imaginative Dan Magill. Finally, he made it official: Jefferson Bradley, which it became only after college graduation and the assumption of his first job.

An amusing name in the Fifties era, as any old scrapbook will reveal, can bring an athlete an abundance of publicity. But it is doubly effective if a lightweight has an attention-getting name. Magill was the man for creative nicknames. J.B. became the grateful beneficiary.

J.B. was a pint-size David frequently knocking off Goliaths on the football field, which endeared him to Coach Butts, who was also a little man. The coach's heart was warmed by the diminutive back packing a powerful punch.

But the most interesting thing about J.B. Davis, captain of the Bulldog team which broke the drought with that memorable 7-0 victory over Tech at Grant Field, is the way he got to Georgia and how he feels years later.

His high school coach had played for Alabama and preferred that J.B. enroll at Tuscaloosa. Auburn also recruited him and so did Vanderbilt. He had visited those schools, but there was always Bill Cloud, a Georgia alumnus who lived in the area, talking about playing between the hedges. Cloud, one of the truly nice guys with a deep and abiding loyalty to his University that few, if any, could match, kept reminding J.B. of the "great school in Athens." Bill told J.B. he would fit in well with Coach Wallace Butts' offensive style and took him to games in Sanford Stadium. J.B. was impressed and interested, but Alabama was home. Sentiment for one of the home state schools was understandably strong.

However, he had made no decision when, on a late spring Saturday, he was sleeping in. The biggest man he had ever seen in his life walked into his room, pulled the covers off and said, "Get up, let's go eat a steak and go to Georgia." It was Jim Whatley, the baseball coach, who was also a football recruiter. Whatley's orders sounded fine to J.B. For a kid who never had much, eating a steak was a big-time adventure. Besides, Whatley was a giant of a man whom J.B. had no intentions of crossing. As soon as he and Big Jim had finished off a couple of steaks at Ray's Barbecue Restaurant on Sand Mountain, the coach and prospect were soon to be on their way to Athens. First, J.B. told Whatley he needed to go by the local cotton mill and inform his mother.

It was a hard life in the mill villages in those days, and J.B. wanted to escape. Georgia would provide that opportunity. Even though he was a Tom Thumb in Big Jim Whatley's presence, he was charmed, not intimidated. He knew it was time to make a decision and soon concluded that his preference was to settle in at Athens and line up for the Bulldogs.

They went down to the cotton mill where his mother labored daily as a spinner, even for a half-day on Saturday. They rang the bell at the outside fence which encircled the mill.

A guard sent for his mother. She talked to J.B. and Whatley through the fence, the son breaking the news

J. B. Davis takes a handoff from Jimmy Orr and streaks down the sideline

to his mother that his decision was to enroll at the University of Georgia and play football and baseball on scholarship.

His mother supported the decision, and J.B. was happily chauffeured to Athens. His affection for Georgia increased significantly over the years, yet he supports the Bulldogs in a quiet way. No former letterman, however, is more sincere. He received his degree in education in the spring of 1958, but before leaving town to embark on a teaching and coaching career in DeKalb County, he stopped by the business office in Stegeman Hall and ordered two season tickets from ticket manager, Virginia Whitehead. He has purchased those same tickets every year and has missed home games only when ill or when there has been a personal emergency.

During his era, Georgia's football program had fallen on hard times. The Bulldogs won but 10 games his varsity years (1955-57). One of those victories came against Alabama in Birmingham (1956) and all of Guntersville was in the stands, pulling for the Tide.

"They told me that I wouldn't last three days under Wallace Butts," he says. But not only did J.B. last, he lettered three years, captained the 1957 team, and against Alabama that hot afternoon at Legion Field, J.B. returned a punt for a touchdown, which won the game for Georgia 16-13.

"I remember it well – it was the greatest thrill of my life. They kicked out of bounds, but were offsides. I had watched the coverage on the play and saw them cover sharply to the ball, so I went over to the sidelines and told Coach Butts to take the penalty. I told him I thought we might be able to make a big return because of their coverage. He agreed, and I was able to take it all the way by getting outside. You can't imagine how happy that made me there with all my friends and folks from home in the stands."

Today J.B. is not much bigger than he was in his playing days except in heart. His feelings for Georgia have quietly grown over the years to where he is, on that count, as big as his close friend Jim Whatley.

CICERO LUCAS

He's as Southern as they come, from down home vernacular and lifestyle to an unending love of hunting and fishing, to meals of cornbread, collards, fried chicken and black-eyed peas, all of which he daily craves.

But you wouldn't recognize his affinity for the outdoors and down home living by his name. The woods are full of Billy Joes, Robert Earls, John Henrys and a host of other double-named characters and good ol' boys who like country music, huntin' and fishin', but you would have to look long and hard to find one named Cicero, even in Washington, GA. His family, however, is an exception.

In all likelihood, he was the only Cicero who ever lived in Snellville, which made the Capitol, where he worked until retirement, more accessible. A letterman in 1955, '56 and '57, Cicero Lucas is a country boy through and through, regardless of address and by whatever name he answers to.

He grew up in Washington, the son of a jeweler-professional boxer-pilot-ham radio operator – everything but a fiddler – and the grandson of a pharmacist. Both father and grandfather were named Cicero, and he became Cicero Lucas, III. He named his son Cicero, IV.

While his father did not have that much interest in sports, he was pleased when his son was offered a Georgia football scholarship in late 1954. Young Cicero didn't pursue any of his father's interests except that he became a pilot.

Cicero enjoyed football and his time with the Bulldogs. He remains one of Georgia's staunchest fans, but his greatest passion has always been the outdoors. Nothing gives him more pleasure than to find himself casting for bass at daylight on a quiet pond or sitting motionless in a blind, waiting for a turkey gobbler or a multi-antlered buck to come his way.

Throughout his professional life, he tended to a variety of duties in the Secretary of State's office at the Capitol, and afterwards as assistant clerk of the house when the legislature was in session, with that eager anticipation of finishing the week and having the weekend all to himself with either his shotgun or his tackle box.

His family homestead in Washington was actually a 65-acre plot within the city limits, but it did not offer him the outdoor options that gave him the greatest satisfaction in life. He located a few wooded acres which were just right for constructing a cabin and creating a fish pond. Life doesn't get any better for a man whose outdoor passions run as deep as Cicero's.

Ducks, geese, turkey and deer are there for him each hunting season. Each year he stocks his freezer with fish, fowl and venison from his few acres of heaven. To experience the thrill of bagging his own game and then to enjoy a meal from his outdoor pursuits is one of life's grand rewards.

After a highly regarded high school career with Washington-Wilkes, Cicero had offers from several schools, including Tennessee and Alabama. But he always had affection for the Bulldogs and especially appreciated the hard-nosed philosophy of Wallace Butts. Athens was close to home, which meant that he would never be far from his happy hunting grounds. He proudly and eagerly became a Bulldog.

After his freshman year in 1955, when he was a hard-running fullback, the Georgia coaches moved him to guard. He played behind Tony Cushenberry in 1956 and became a starter in 1957. His senior year, he was moved back to fullback, sharing the position with Theron Sapp.

This was the one platoon era, and while he established early in his career that he could block proficiently, he was at his best when he was backing up the line. It was fun crashing into all those offensive players, shedding blockers and running down a back behind the line of scrimmage. He especially did a lot of that in the 1957 game in which Georgia broke the drought against Tech at Grant Field.

"I always regretted that I didn't have another year when it was all over in 1958. That championship season followed in 1959, and I would have liked to have been a part of that. I always felt that things were going to get better by the time I graduated. I enjoyed playing with Fran Tarkenton and his group. Those were some good young players. You knew they were going to win games."

Cicero received an offer from the San Francisco 49ers, but was not interested. The pay was not that attractive, and he felt a full time offer with Secretary of State Ben Fortson was an opportunity he would be ill advised to pass up.

JOHN LUCK

John Luck lettered at tackle, 1954-56, finished his degree in education and returned to Pittsburgh, which has always been home since he grew up in nearby Cuddy, Pa. He coached and taught for over 38 years.

He has never made it back to Athens although he has trekked down to the Atlanta International Raceway a couple of times. "I couldn't go back during the fall because I was always coaching," he says, "and it just never worked out when I was following the NASCAR circuit."

When he spoke, he sounded wistful at the thought of returning to a place for which he has fond memories. "I gotta go back," he said. "Athens will always be special for me."

As he talked, he looked up to the wall in his game room where prominently hangs a picture of Coach Butts. He recalled a letter from his coach that helped him though a difficult time in life. It was after his 28-year-old daughter, Barbara Ann, died from cancer. "In football you teach people never to give up, you teach them to keep fighting back, but I'll tell you my daughter's death was so difficult, I didn't think I would be able to get over it. When I was the most depressed, when I was at my lowest, Coach Butts sent me a letter of encouragement. It gave me a lift. I rallied and moved on, but I don't think I would have been able to get myself back on track if he had not sent me that letter.

"I always admired and appreciated him after playing for him. He was a little guy, but he demanded respect. I will always remember his fighting spirit. It motivated me. I never wanted to let him down."

Luck came to Athens in 1953 when Zeke Bratkowski was a senior. He was recruited by Harry Wright and developed a fondness, among other things, for Poss' barbecue. A regrettable memory, one which he can laugh about now, had to do with taking a spring break in Savannah, where he partied a little too much one night and slept through the next day—but on the beach. The sunburn was thorough and so painful he could not put on his pads when he returned home. He got no sympathy, however. "We got back to Athens on Sunday, and spring practice started the next day," Luck remembers. "It took me a week to heal from the sunburn. Think about how tough practices were under Coach Butts and then think about participating in those practices when you were sunburned. That was agony prolonged, and it was 24 hours of pure agony until I healed."

Winston Cup racing became big in Luck's life after he settled in as a coach and teacher in the inner city school system in Pittsburgh. His favorite NASCAR stop is Taladega and seldom misses the big race there. "I love those Southern stock car tracks," he says. "For an anniversary present in '04, my daughter gave us a trip to the last race at Darlington. That was about as nice of a present as I have ever received."

His favorite driver is Bill Elliott, "Awesome Bill from Dawsonville." His friends told him he only pulled for Elliott because the NASCAR champion was from Georgia. "Yep, you're right," Luck would remark. "Georgia means a lot to me."

1958

The best team in the country to post a losing record? Many concluded that apropos for the 1958 Georgia team. Losing close games plagued the Wally Butts' Dogs, his 20th team, but the new faces in the lineup belonged to heralded sophomores, like Fran Tarkenton, Fred Brown and Pat Dye.

Georgia lost its first three games—all by close scores, won two and then saw its offensive firepower flame out, dropping games to Alabama, 0-12, Florida, 6-7 and Auburn 6-21. But all is well that ends well, right? After destroying The Citadel 76-0, it was time for the finale with Georgia Tech. The worm had turned. The Dogs were into a streak. They whipped Tech 16-3. Hallelujah! It wasn't by a big margin, but Tech never was in the game.

Dye Brothers

For eight straight years in the decade of the Fifties, there was a Dye playing football and lettering for the Bulldogs. First, it was Wayne, a lightweight guard with a feisty and combative makeup, then Nat, the biggest of the three, a tackle who probably was the best athlete in the family and finally Pat, who achieved the most honor.

Pat made All-America for the Bulldogs and later was to become the head coach and athletic director at Auburn, where he still works as a fund raiser for his adopted school. His case is similar to that of Vince Dooley, an Auburn quarterback, who settled in at Athens and became a Bulldog.

"I'm not working against Georgia," Dye says. "I'm working for Auburn. I have always maintained a great feeling for my alma mater and I certainly have a great regard for the people in Athens. "When Georgia and Auburn play, I am for Auburn, just like Vince is for Georgia."

Then his voice trails off briefly, and he notes. "It is a little strange that in 1959, in a game which enabled Coach Butts to win his fourth conference title, we whipped Auburn in Sanford Stadium 14-13. All my Georgia friends talk about that game, which I suppose is one of the greatest games in Bulldog football history. At least it was for those who wear red and black. I never thought that I might some day return to Sanford Stadium, head coaching the team we beat for the conference championship. You never think about things like that when you are playing."

The Dye brothers grew up on a farm near Blythe. It was hard work, sunup to sundown. Farming was not very mechanized in their day, except for tractors. Work was pretty much done by hand. Their father, Wayne Sr., expected his boys to pitch in and do their part to help run the farm on a daily basis. He was never reluctant to apply the belt when chores were not done or if discipline demanded such.

They chopped cotton, they picked cotton, they baled hay, they cut firewood, and today are grateful that playing football offered an athletic scholarship opportunity at their state university which led to a degree and a life away from the rigors of farm labor.

"Football was easy for us," Pat says. "We never considered it work, and for me, personally, when I left the farm in Blythe my life has been downhill ever since. I wouldn't take anything for having experienced hard work on a farm, but I don't think any of us would want to go back."

In truth, the youngest Dye has never lost his affection for the farm environment, in that he currently lives on wooded acreage with a pond in Notasulga, AL. He could not enjoy life without a place to run and train his birddogs, shoot a turkey or walk up a covey of quail.

That was the plus side of a farm background for all the Dyes. In down times, they could fish and hunt, which they still do with great indulgence. Nat took up golf and spends more time on the golf course nowadays, but one of his big excursions each year is to travel to Blakely and spend a long outdoor weekend with his former teammate, Jimmy Sealy.

For those who know them, something would be out of focus if the Dye brothers were not affiliated with football in some way and were not keen on heading to the fields with a shotgun or to some body of water with a rod and reel.

"I guess it is in our blood," Wayne says. "That is how we grew up, and being on the winning team in football and spending time outdoors has always been a way of life for us. We can't play football anymore, but we can watch it, and we can still find a covey of quail or a bass somewhere."

Their mother, Nell Slaughter, was a native of Athens, and the Dyes spent many holidays and summer stays in her hometown with the Fain Slaughter family. Their cousins, Fain Jr., and Billy, competed against them in sports, the Slaughters at Athens High and the Dyes at Augusta's Richmond Academy.

Georgia was always on their mind. They listened to the Bulldogs on radio, dating back to when George Theringer was the play-by-play announcer. When they played, their parents, if they didn't make it to some distant road game, listened to Ed Thilenius talk about their sons on the Bulldog football radio network. They remember their parents going to games in the Forties, big ones like the matchups between Georgia's Charley Trippi and Harry Gilmer of Alabama and Charlie Choo Choo Justice of North Carolina.

The family affiliation with the Bulldogs made it easy for Wayne and Nat to decide where they were going to school. "I never thought about going anywhere else," Wayne says. For Nat, who received multiple scholarship offers, he, too, never considered another school.

With Pat it was different. Each of the Dye boys could run, that was their hallmark, but the youngest had a little something special. He had exceptional quickness, which prompted scholarship offers to come from dozens of schools.

Although he had grown up with an overwhelming Bulldog influence in his life, Pat was frustrated by the fact that the Bulldog program was down when it was time for him to make a decision. "They just weren't winning, and that did worry me," Pat says. But it tugged at his emotions as he realized that if he enrolled in Athens, he would be able to join Nat as a teammate and that Wayne would be an assistant freshman coach.

Still, he was attracted to the small guard opportunity he saw at Tennessee and Georgia Tech. He didn't like the fact that his early preference, Tennessee, was

Brothers and Dogs, Nat Dye (left) and Pat

just too far away, especially for his family to follow the team. Tech had a small guard, Franklin Brooks, who made All America and that persuaded him to strongly consider Bobby Dodd's team. He was ambitious, and making All America was one of his goals. Such honor has always been enhanced with winning.

However, he was troubled that a Tech staff member suggested to him that he would not play for a winner at Georgia and told Wayne that he "knew" Pat would sign with Tech.

Today, with a grin, he says, "I don't know whether he told Wayne that or not. Wayne said he did, and my brother made sure I knew about the comment. I got a little miffed about that."

When Pat told Tech he was going to sign with Georgia, the Yellow Jackets were in the midst of an eight year winning streak. One coach told him that he would never beat Tech while he was at Georgia.

"You think that didn't get me revved up when we played Tech every year?" Pat says. Then he notes, "I've got a lot of good Tech friends, but they never beat me as a player at Georgia. As a matter of fact, I am 12-0 against them as a player and coach."

As a freshman, he and his Bullpup teammates defeated Tech in the Thanksgiving Day Scottish Rite Classic on Grant Field. They stayed over for the varsity game and saw a thriller, Georgia breaking the drought, 7-0, with Theron Sapp scoring the only touchdown of the day. Pat was particularly pleased that Sapp scored behind dominating blocks by Nat and the offensive line.

Good days were ahead. Georgia in 1958, won in Athens, 16-3, and in 1959 triumphed 21-14, having clinched the SEC championship two weeks prior against Auburn in Sanford Stadium. In 1960 Georgia won its fourth in a row over Tech, 7-6, with Pat blocking an extra point attempt and a field goal attempt, the margin of victory.

After a brief coaching career, Wayne returned to the Augusta area and worked in the lumber business. Nat enjoyed a productive career in the Canadian Football League, playing five years with Edmonton and two with Saskatchewan.

At Edmonton, he was a teammate of Jackie Parker (quarterback from Mississippi State), who is one of the most beloved stars in CFL history. Nat named his son Fain Parker Dye, and his grandson, Parker Dye, enrolled at Georgia.

Pat joined Nat at Edmonton for a couple of years. Nat lined up at end on defense and Pat right behind him at linebacker. Nat chuckles at having to tell his younger brother what to do. "Pat never was one," he laughs, "to worry too much about his responsibility. He wanted to find the football, and he was pretty good at that. I used to kid him that if I hadn't showed him what to do at Edmonton, he would never have been a successful head coach.

"It didn't matter. Pat was a fast learner and nobody has ever been more dedicated to football. He was a winner. He played hard and nobody was a greater competitor."

Wayne, in recent years, enjoyed success in the restaurant and convenience store business. Nat retired from sales from Georgia Crown Distributing Co., owned by his former teammate, Don Leebern, and dabbles in real estate.

Everybody is more familiar with the professional life of the youngest brother. After spending time as an assistant coach at Alabama, Pat moved to East Carolina as head coach and held the same position at the University of Wyoming for a year.

In late 1980, the Auburn job opened up, and, for a time, it appeared that Georgia's head coaching position might be vacant, too. Auburn asked Dooley to interview for the head coaching and athletic director positions. Pat informed Auburn representatives he would be interested in the job. If Vince took the Auburn job, he naturally wanted to return to Athens.

"I knew, however, that I probably would not be hired at Georgia. I felt if Vince had left, Erk Russell would have been hired, and he should have been."

When Vince decided to remain in Athens, Pat redoubled his efforts with Auburn. "Frankly, I told them that I knew more about the job and the two states where Auburn had to recruit, Alabama and Georgia. I was their best candidate."

When it appeared that Auburn was warming up to Pat as their coach, he had a conversation with the late Bear Bryant at Alabama for whom he had coached. Bryant challenged, "You're not going to Auburn!"

Pat replied, "Coach, I am if they will hire me."

"You're gonna get this job," the Bear countered.

With that, Pat gave him a brief dissertation which made Bear Bryant realize the competition for Alabama with the Tide's in-state rival was really going to heat up.

"Let me tell you, coach," Pat remembers saying. "I don't want that job and you know why? First of all, when you get out, an Alabama man is going to be hired.

Nat lines up (left) and conferences with Pat

I don't want it because if I took it, it would only be a maintenance job. I would have to maintain what you have done and I don't want that. I want to start fresh somewhere and build my own program."

When Dye took over at Auburn, the school had captured only one Southeastern Conference championship, in 1957, when it also won the national championship while on probation.

Pat coached the Tigers to four SEC titles and led Auburn to its greatest era. He is revered by the Auburn alumni who have identified with his down home personality, his love of the outdoors and rural haunts.

A man who spends time with birddogs, drives a pickup truck and is prone to stuff tobacco in his jaw while hunting quail or fishing for a bass wears well with most of the Auburn alumni.

He is proud – like his brothers – that he trained and learned football under Wallace Butts.

George Hansen

During his coaching tenure Wallace Butts recruited players from far away places, but his most unlikely recruit had to be a Canadian, George Hansen, who lettered for the Bulldogs in 1957-58. Hansen didn't arrive in Athens directly from his hometown of Calgary in the province of Alberta, but he was, nonetheless, excited about completing degree requirements and playing football in the Southeastern Conference.

How he landed in Athens is an unlikely story. After finishing high school in Calgary, he wound up at Sunflower Junior College, Morehead, Miss. He played in a junior college all-America game in 1956, and Wyatt Posey, Bulldog assistant, brought him to Athens in the fall for an official visit.

"Coach Butts told me I could play immediately, and I came early so I could enroll in school and participate in spring practice. He had never seen me play, but he volunteered as soon as I met him that, 'we can use someone like you.' That was great for my confidence, and I have always appreciated my experience in Athens."

In the spring of '55, he spent time at Mississippi State in Starkville, and actually scrimmaged with the team during spring practice. "Things were a little different back then," he laughs. "What I learned from that experience was that I could play in the Southeastern Conference."

State coach, Darrell Royal, advised him to enroll at Sunflower, and George did with plans to eventually return to Starkville. The next season, Royal moved on to the University of Washington for a year, and the Maroons, which Mississippi State was commonly referred to in those days, seem to lose interest. Fortunately, Wyatt Posey took serious note of Hansen's ability. "I've always appreciated Coach Posey," Hansen says. "He told me from the beginning I would be a starter at Georgia."

An interesting development took place in his first game as a Bulldog. Georgia opened the season against Texas as part of a doubleheader on Grant Field, and Darrell Royal, by that time, had become coach of the Longhorns.

"He walked out on the field, pre-game and looked me up," Hansen remembers. "He wished me well at Georgia. That always meant a lot to me that he had the class to do that. I've always had a lot of respect for Darrell Royal.

"I'll tell you something else. I knew about Georgia's losing streak to Tech. We played two games on Grant Field that year; against Texas, lost to them, but when we played our final game back at the same place, we broke the drought. I was very happy for Coach Butts.

"Here again, things were different, but there was a side to Coach Butts that I will always appreciate. When my mother came down to Mississippi, I wanted her to travel over to Athens to see the University. Coach Butts let me use his car to drive to Mississippi and bring her to our campus. He arranged for her to stay at the Georgia Center, which was such an attractive place. He expected you to be physically tough on the practice field, but he couldn't do enough for you off the field."

After Georgia, Hansen played for eight years in the Canadian Football League and later became personnel director with his hometown Stampeders for nine years. Later he spent seven years in Dubai working with an energy business and now is retired, living in his hometown.

"I keep up with Georgia," he says. "I still visit Augusta, where I lived for a couple of years at one point. When I go back there, I try to look up former teammates like Theron Sapp, Charlie Britt and Nat Dye. The friendships I made in Athens are very special. I have fond memories of Payne Hall. There was a special bond, and genuine brotherhood, and that is, perhaps, my favorite memory of my college football career."

In Calgary he is president of the Stampeder Alumni Association and volunteers for local organizations. He is known around town as "Bulldog," which is appropriate. Not only did he play for the Bulldogs, he has a collection of over 200 bulldogs. "Not many duplicates," he says, noting that he collects mostly originals.

Hansen remains something of an original himself. He is the only Canadian born member of the Wally's Boys fraternity.

TOMMY PARIS

While on a business trip out of state, Tommy Paris, Georgia halfback and punter, 1958-60, got into conversation with a stranger who learned that Tommy had played football in Athens. In the course of the conversation, the stranger asked if Tommy kept up with his former teammates. When he replied affirmatively, "I try to keep up best I can," the stranger said: "The next time you see Scrap Iron, tell him I said hello."

The stranger was referring to one of Paris' teammates, Roger Dansby from Columbus. Dansby wasn't big, but he was tough. He was nicknamed appropriately because of his indominatible fight. The coaches loved Scrap Iron's remarkable heart and courage. They just wished he weighed a little more.

It meant a lot to Tommy Paris to bump into a stranger who, too, admired and remembered Dansby, who never advanced far beyond the daily scrimmages. Roger dressed out a few times for games between the hedges, but he seldom played. His teammates, however, will always remember his remarkable toughness and his nickname. So did his friends.

Tommy, a successful businessman, has had a wide exposure in his career. There have been other introductions to strangers who know about his teammates who were successful both at Georgia and afterwards. Conversations about his old teammates are a rich reward in life in Paris' opinion.

"I think a bond develops when you play on a college team," he says. "You never forget your teammates, and your friends. When you don't see them all that much, you run into somebody who either keeps in touch with a certain player or knows what he is up to. I get a warm feeling when I bump into somebody who asks about a former teammate like with Scrap Iron."

Paris would probably have been the regular punter during his time at Georgia had it not been for the fact that he matriculated at the same time as Bobby Walden. The Big Toe from Cairo was a long distance, power punter. Paris was more of a finesse type, and was often called on in short yardage kicking situations. If the situation called for kicking out of bounds, the coffin corner objective, Paris had the right touch. Against Texas in 1958, in Austin, he punted dead to the one yard line in a crucial situation.

His father, Thomas H. Paris Sr., lettered at Georgia in 1929, the year Sanford Stadium was dedicated. He became a member of the Georgia athletic board, but told Tommy he could sign with any school he preferred. Tennessee recruited him seriously, but he was never as comfortable on another campus as he was in Athens.

"Athens was close to home, and that was important," Tommy says. "I had a lot of friends who were going to Georgia, and I just felt comfortable there. I knew I would work in my father's business after graduation. It was not lost on me that if you planed to live in the state, it helps you in business to enroll at your state university. I think that has certainly enhanced business opportunity for me."

JIMMY SEALEY

When Jimmy Sealey is out and about the woods and fields of his farm near Blakely in deep Southwest Georgia, he often pauses and pays silent tribute to Jim Whatley, the late Bulldog coach and recruiter who influenced his life. There was a certain circumstance which became the focal point of the relationship of the two men which brought about a warm and enduring friendship that ensued right up until Whatley's death.

"When I grew up, young people had respect for those they were responsible to in life," Sealey says. "Your father, your coach, your teachers—we were expected to do what they told us to do. Those of us who paid them the proper respect, gained an advantage in life, in my opinion, and nobody meant more to me while I was at Georgia than Coach Whatley."

An uninterrupted bond of friendship began when the coach befriended the player who was going through one of those down times emotionally. Sealey was hurt in practice one day, resulting in a nagging injury which lingered on indefinitely. Sealey admits today several things depressed him to the extent that he began to feel sorry for himself.

That is when Whatley's influence became consequential in Sealey's life. That much needed counsel and advice only resulted after the player set out for home. He thought he had had enough. He was going to hitchhike to his hometown of Dothan, Al. when Whatley discovered him on the side of the road with his thumb poised for an opportunity for a seat in the first available car headed south.

Sealey will never forget the scene. He was standing on the shoulder of the road of U.S. 441 on the south edge of town when Big Jim drove up and stopped. He told Sealey to climb in and began talking in that slow, comforting vernacular which characterized the likeable Whatley, who could also be salty and cynical in conversation with his friends and neighbors.

Whatley knew, however, how to console a depressed football player. Before you knew it, the coach had allayed the player's concern about being injured and seeing no future with the team.

Before Whatley had used up a gallon of gas riding Sealey around town, they were at the coach's homestead on Hampton Court, where they sat down for a home cooked meal and rambling conversation about bird hunting, the way of life in South Georgia, the outdoors, and how Sealey would be able to fit in with the team.

It was not lost on Sealey that he aspired to complete degree requirements, and if he stayed and managed properly, he would achieve that objective. Quitting the team would kill that opportunity. Jimmy slept on it—at Whatley's house. The next morning, Whatley cooked breakfast for Sealey, and returned him to Payne Hall where his AWOL considerations ended.

"After that," Sealey says, "I never thought about leaving again. Things got better, but what I'll always appreciate is that he took the time and interest in me when I was in a fragile emotional state. He gave me confidence that I would be able make a contribution to the team and get my degree in business, which is one of the things I am most proud of today."

The on-the-field highlights for Sealey were the 7-7 tie at Miami in 1956 when the Bulldogs played a nationally ranked Hurricane team off its feet, and, of course, the drought breaker game on Grant Field in '57.

"I was like most of the players in those days. We were tired of losing to Tech, and while we wanted to win for ourselves, we wanted to win for Coach Butts. We felt that he had become a victim, that he deserved better, and while we may not have had the greatest players, we worked hard and we fought hard. It was such a thrill for all of us to see the Georgia fans swarm down on the field and put Coach Butts on their shoulders and parade him around. It brought tears to my eyes."

Sealey went from Georgia to the Air Force and began his business life in construction with a general contractor. He spent 18 months in St. Croix before coming home and taking over his father's farm. Later, he combined a business career with volunteer coaching at the Southwest Georgia Academy.

He coached football for 19 years and won the state

AA championship at private schools three times. He tried to emulate both Coach Butts and Coach Whatley. Sealey, as the former taught him, coached his teams tough. With the latter, when he saw a kid emotionally down, he would remember Whatley rescuing him on the highway south of Athens in the late fifties and would offer sage counsel to his player just like Whatley had done for him.

George Whitton

While playing halfback at Georgia, lettering in 1956-58, George Whitton expanded on his keen interest in the outdoors. He was one of those Payne Hall residents who took to the fields and woods at every opportunity.

His affection for wildlife and nature actually began in high school in Columbus and continued through his days with the Bulldogs and in the Army with which he served, either active duty or the reserves, for 26 years. Success in the sale of mutual funds, and by carefully weighing his options, enabled Whitton to purchase 200 acres of land with a 14 acre lake near Tignall in Wilkes County, where he has long hung out with his former teammates, Fred Brown and Cicero Lucas.

Taking a shotgun and a rod and reel to the fields and streams has become the most important thing in Whitton's life. Now he is serious about conservation projects. He often attends seminars having to do with wildlife conservation, seeking to learn and to apply recommended practices on his own property.

"Nature is a wonderful thing," he says. "It is something to be treasured. We should do all we can to preserve nature and the outdoors for future generations."

Outdoor art has become a hobby for Whitton, who has experienced success with his water color paintings. When he was stationed at Ft. Benning, he was invited by the manager to a hunt on the Richard King Mellon Plantation, near Columbus. He gave one of his paintings to the manger, who showed it to the wife of the owner, Constance Mellon, who was impressed and bought several for the main dwelling on the plantation.

Whitton continues to paint outdoor scenes but has never gotten into producing them as a business venture perhaps that may yet come about. "When I get to the point that I don't enjoy getting out in the fields and woods as much, now that I'm getting older, perhaps I'll spend more time with my paintbrush," he says. "It's certainly an option that I have."

Whitton lettered three years with the Bulldogs, fondly recalling his junior year when the Dogs broke the drought in Atlanta. He remembers, too, playing and scoring in a game against North Carolina at Chapel Hill.

"We played up there when the leaves had turned, and I was so impressed with the sheer beauty of the campus which reminded me of Athens. Their stadium sits in a little hollow with a lot of trees surrounding it, and I had an inspirational feeling when we took the field."

He had listened to the Sugar Bowl broadcast Jan. 1, 1947, when Georgia defeated North Carolina, 21-10. The Tar Heels were led by their great back, Charlie "Choo Choo" Justice, who wore No. 22. That was Whitton's number.

"When I walked on the field, I remembered that Sugar Bowl broadcast and remembered Choo Choo's legend. I couldn't help but be affected sentimentally to be playing on the same field he played on and to be wearing his number."

You would expect thoughts like that from a man who appreciates nature and gets high marks when there is an outdoor scene to appreciate—even in a football setting.

Jim Roberts

James McMullan Roberts Jr., lettered for the Bulldogs in 1958. His father lettered as a manager in 1927 and his brother Billy lettered in 1963, signing with Georgia as a freshman in 1960, Coach Butts last season.

Jim and Billy's brother, Roy, was a basketball star under Adolph Rupp at Kentucky. The Roberts family has been loyal friends of Coach Butts, and Jim got to know the Bulldog's head coach before he enrolled and played in the line.

The family farm, near Monroe, offered many hunting options, and Jim remembers the only time he ever got out of practice was when Coach Quinton Lumpkin, an outdoor advocate, told him one day. "If you'll invite me to your dove hunt, I'll take you and you won't have to practice." Jim could hardly believe his ears.

After practice one day, he could hardly believe his eyes. "He would talk to us after we finished scrimmaging," Jim says. "We would take a knee and look straight at him, right into his eyes. One day, Bobby Walden let his eyes wander, and Coach Butts went over and forearmed him over backwards. He got our attention right quick."

TWENTY SIXTH ANNUAL
Orange Bowl Classic
SOUVENIR PROGRAM
50c TAX INCL.
1960 GAME
GEORGIA
VS.
MISSOURI

PART X

HAPPY DAYS

The Championship Again

1959

The season started with Coach Butts' fretting about losing a rock of a center-linebacker, David Lloyd, to the pros. He had been drafted as a future by the Cleveland Browns, but two important influences would make a difference in helping Coach Butts win his fourth conference championship and send him to the Orange Bowl for a third time. First of all, J. B. Whitworth, who had been his line coach in the glory days of the Forties, came back to Athens, and those capable sophomores, now juniors, would provide inspiration and production that would enable Georgia to surprise the SEC.

Only a "misery loves company" afternoon in Columbia, when nothing went right and South Carolina defeated the Bulldogs, 30-14, was there a blemish on the schedule.

Georgia now won the close games, which a championship team must do. There were five tough conference games in which Georgia prevailed that propelled the Bulldogs to the championship: wins over Kentucky 14-7 at Lexington; Florida 21-10 in Jacksonville; Auburn 14-13 at home and Tech 21-14 in Atlanta.

The season highlight was coming from behind—the famous touchdown pass from Fran Tarkenton to Bill Herron against Auburn—between the hedges which clinched the conference championship. Two weeks later on Grant Field, Georgia, scoring three touchdowns for a 21-0 halftime lead, held off a second half Tech rally, and the Dogs were Orange Bowl bound.

Those hard times earlier in the decade had been replaced with one of the greatest years of Wallace Butts career. The Little Round Man was, again, on top.

Nobody like Magill To Sing Dog's Praises in '59

Dan Magill, the greatest of Dogs, thrilled to every Georgia accomplishment with the highest praise. He also agonized more deeply than any loyalist in down times. He was at his all time best promoting and celebrating the SEC Championship in 1959. here's his synopsis for the '60 media guide:

The Georgia Bulldogs looked every inch the part of SEC champions against Auburn on November 14 before the largest crowd in the history of Sanford Stadium – an overflow of 54,000.

They won the greatest, most thrilling game any of them had ever seen. The final score was 14-13. Perhaps it should have been, 7-6, because both teams were fortunate to get breaks to cash in for their fourth quarter scores. But the Bulldogs deserved to win, no matter the score.

The tough Tigers took advantage of a 15-yard penalty to kick a first quarter field goal of 43 yards by Dyas. They capitalized on a fumble in the second quarter, and Dyas came through again with a 40-yarder to put Auburn out front, 6-0, at halftime.

The second half was all Georgia's except for one play. Walden kept the Tigers bottled up in the third quarter with booming kicks and finally he set up a score with a 45-yarder out at the Tiger 2. Britt returned the punt 39 yards for a TD, zig zagging his way through the No. 1 Auburn unit, which included three All-Americans, Smith, Burkett and Rice. Pennington converted to make it 7-6.

Twelve plays later, however, Walden lined up short for a punt and kicked into his blocker, Britt. Auburn recovered at the Georgia 1 and went ahead 13-7.

But Bill Herron, with less than three minutes left, tackled Harvard for a loss, causing a fumble that Dye recovered at the Auburn 35. Immediately Tarkenton unleashed an air raid. He hit Soberdash for 16, Soberdash for 9 and Herron, on fourth down with 30 seconds left, for 13 yards and the TD. Pennington converted to win the SEC championship, 14-13.

It was the earliest the SEC crown had ever been clinched.

FRAN TARKENTON

The evolution of playing quarterback for Francis Asbury Tarkenton had its origins in the alleys of the neighborhood where he lived in Washington, D.C.

Even when the competition was only his brother, it was poignantly significant. Perpetual motion, hours on end was his way of life. He moved, he ran, he dodged, he ducked, he jumped, he cut, he danced, he kicked, he twisted, he sidestepped, he skipped — he became the master of movement. His feet became remarkably deft and swift – as fluid and as efficiently abrupt as Bojangles.

A quarterback's worth is often measured by his arm, however. But with Number 10, it was as much his feet and his head that brought greatness to his long and accomplished career.

The whole time he played, he was thinking. Cogitating, inventing, figuring angles, possibilities— jerry rigging. Improvise, scheme and create. Who says you have to do it this way? Or that? Simply find a way — that was his everlasting goal. As a kid every waking hour was for honing his athletic skills. He had an insatiable appetite for sports. Squeeze in 15 minutes of action before school. Holidays, weekends and vacation days were for games, sun up to sun down. He paid attention in class, ultimately becoming Georgia's first All-America academic honoree, but he yearned in his formative years for the recess bell, the end of the school day so he could get on with his passion to develop his athletic skills.

When darkness forced him indoors, there was time to organize his baseball cards, read about sports heroes, and, in later years, diagram plays and keep book on what he had learned.

"I was a diseased nut," he says. "I absolutely knew I was going to be successful. There was never a day when I was not obsessed with learning, competing and trying to be creative toward being the best. As a kid, I actually thought that I would play all three of the big professional sports: football, basketball and baseball. I actually believed that."

When he became a Saturday star, he wasn't a physical quarterback, certainly not the prototype NFL signal caller. That perennial negative — lack of pure arm strength — was not an accurate appraisal of his abilities however. "I had athleticism," he says emphatically. "I was not one dimensional. I wasn't the fastest player on any of the teams on which I played, but nobody was quicker. And, let me tell you, that counts for a lot."

Over the years, I have often noted to him on the abilities of Georgia quarterbacks or those lining up against the Bulldogs, suggesting that the player in question, "is a hell of an athlete."

"There you go again," he would laugh. "I keep telling you that the greatest athletes don't make the greatest quarterbacks." However, he has often said privately, not lamenting, nor regretting — "If I had his arm, no telling how many games I could have won." He might be talking about John Elway, for example.

Coach Butts with Fran Tarkenton (No. 10) and Pat Dye

The fact remains, this overachiever, however you rate his arm strength, still won big, lasted long and never lost a game because he wasn't prepared or because he failed to give it his dead leveled best. He was consumed by the game he loved, and he was enthralled and uplifted by playing quarterback to the best of his ability. He was exhilarated to be in command. He loved running the show, making do – making chicken salad out of chicken manure. Nobody was better at quarterback creativity.

When he showed up in Athens, Georgia had two

quarterbacks who could influence zip on the ball — as much as any coach could want—tight spirals that zeroed like a heat-seeking missile to the target. Nobody thought that Tarkenton could compete with Charley Britt and Tommy Lewis, but he did. That is what set him apart. He didn't *think* he could compete, he didn't *think* he could play. He KNEW.

So what is sport anyway? "Talent and confidence, and I had them both," he says with the candor that has marked his conversations historically. "I knew at Georgia I was going to play although the one platoon rules at the time meant that I would not be a full time starter, but I knew I could compete. I knew I could play quarterback in the Southeastern Conference.

"Same way in the NFL. When I got there, I expected to play. I believed in myself. I knew I would win the starting job at quarterback. Some of that was because of good schooling at Georgia. It was like I had a masters there under Coach Butts, and I was getting my PhD in the passing game with Norm Van Brocklin. I didn't have to jump from kindergarten to a PhD. I had paid my dues and was ready to go to the next level because of the background at Georgia. I recognized that from the first day in training camp."

There has never been a time when he did not pay tribute to the knowledge his college coach imparted and speaks without reluctance to the enhancement of his career based on the Butts' system. He passionately believes in systems. He always felt he knew what would work and what would not.

"Whenever I talk about my career," he says, "I take the stance that I loved the game, I was eager to learn. When Coach Butts drew patterns on the board, I paid close attention. I was fascinated by that. I knew that he knew what he was doing. He was good for my career.

"During the week at pre-practice, we would have 30 minutes of passing. It would be full contact drills. The defense was not allowed to tackle the quarterback, but we would run patterns full speed. The linemen would block full speed and the receivers ran full speed. The defensive backs would tackle for real, and we would go play after play after play with the ball never touching the ground. No team spent that much time with the passing game, but Coach Butts had a love for the passing game. I never have known why. All I know is that he did.

"Here is a guy who didn't evolve from a passing era, but it was obvious he had a love for passing, and I always appreciated that about him. You learn how to excel in the passing game if you spend time on the passing game.

"It actually was not difficult for me in professional football. I had the background and if I hadn't, I wouldn't have been a 21-year-old rookie starting in the National Football League.

"But now we've gotten so scared and so mechanical that we've taken the power of the quarterback away. Tom Moore, however, has given it to Peyton Manning. If you watch him change plays and improvise, you realize Peyton really runs his game. He may be the only quarterback in football who does, and he's the most effective one. However, we don't trust the quarterback to be able to think like we forced our quarterbacks to think back then. That, in my opinion, takes some of the

Wally reviews a play with Tarkenton and Dye (left); Tarkenton gains yardage in Sanford Stadium

power away from the quarterback.

"If I've got to send the play in from the sideline or the quarterback has got to read his list by the signals – oh that's play number 25 – now then call that play; that's so quick, how can I get a vision of that play? I still maintain, a quarterback who calls his plays has an advantage. When I'm playing, as soon as the play is over, a pass that has been completed or is incomplete, I'm already into the next play while I'm going back to the huddle. I'm thinking and know exactly where I want to go and what I want to do. There's no waiting in the huddle, wondering 'What's this going to be?' Then I am surprised by the play coming in. I think it's harder to be a quarterback today because the quarterback has less control because somebody up in a press box is calling the plays. I will suggest that with all of my knowledge and skills, and I had a lot, you put me up in the press box to try to call plays for somebody else I couldn't do it very well. Nobody can do it well."

Growing up, I became a Boston Red Sox fan, and, naturally, a great fan of the legendary Ted Williams. You can imagine the pure, unadulterated joy I had in having dinner with him one evening in Winter Haven, FL. and later spending an afternoon in his home where he lived out his last years in Hernando, FL.

In two conversations with the great hitter, we talked about baseball, but other sports, too. My Georgia pride went over the top when he, unsolicited, brought up the names of Charley Trippi and Fran Tarkenton.

Trippi, he said, was the greatest back he ever saw, and Tarkenton, "got the most out of his ability. He can do more things with the ball than any quarterback in football."

When I passed on this appraisal on to Tarkenton, he immediately laughed and got right to the point. "He probably felt that way because I did not have a cannon arm. Look at my quickness, look at my awareness — that's athletic ability, so I disagree with Ted Williams. I wasn't just an overachiever; I had an ability to play the position. I wasn't a clumsy, plodding mule. I learned the game, and I learned to execute. When I played in pro bowls with Johnny Unitas, I could throw with him. I didn't have John Elway's arm, but I often think about Joe Montana in Bill Walsh's system.

"You don't throw 80 yard bombs in football. True you need to be able to go to deep, but consider Bill Wash's system. Montana threw a lot of eight-yard slants to Jerry Rice, and he took it to the house. I had enough arm, but more importantly, I could get the ball where I wanted it, but I also knew where to throw it and when to throw it.

"When I started out with Van Brocklin, one who had a cannon arm, he wanted to run 15, 18 yard sideline routes. Quarterback drops back seven, eight yards – then I've got to throw a 45-yard pass to get a 15-18 yard completion. That is tough for any quarterback, and the chances of completing it are, more often than not, unlikely. We shortened it. I threw ten yard outs. I can complete ten yard outs and the percentages are much more favorable if you take that approach."

Long after he took his last snap — after 18 years in which he set records for most attempts and completions; yards and touchdown passes—he owns a forthright, candid and unyielding appreciation for the fundamentals of the game. His candor is always there, right or wrong, which makes him one of the most enjoyable conversationalists ever when it comes to sports.

He couldn't imagine playing football without an emphasis on the passing game. Yet he believes that fundamentals dictate how and who wins championships. A quarterback takes great comfort from having a capable and productive running back lined up behind him.

Tarkenton belongs to that fraternity who suggest winning best comes about for those with the capability of running the football and stopping the run.

In 1952, the Rev. Dallas M. Tarkenton Sr., a struggling Pentecostal minister in Washington DC, decided that what was best for him and his family were two degrees he didn't have – a Masters and a Doctorate.

So, without any leads, contacts or friendships, he picked up and moved to Athens where he took a small church assignment to support his family and became a full time student at the University of Georgia, believing the sacrifice important to all concerned.

In time, the late minister's middle son, Francis Asbury, who was named for a Methodist bishop, came to realize that this was, in some respects, a providential move, at least for the younger Tarkenton's athletic future.

Francis, who attended church regularly, would later become appreciated by many Georgia followers as much for his support of the Fellowship of Christian Athletes, which was in its formative years, as he was for his touchdown passes for the Georgia Bulldogs. But there was never any question in his mind. The preacher's kid was born to be an athlete, born to play quarterback.

Francis was 11 years old when the family left a cramped apartment in the nation's capital and settled in Athens, near the Athens Coca-Coca Bottling Company on Prince Avenue. Tarkenton was enrolled at Child's Street School, which was destroyed many years ago. It was there he gained his first significant athletic break.

The school principal was Mae Whatley, wife of Georgia's giant-of-a-man baseball coach, Jim Whatley, who had just agreed to coach one of four Little League baseball teams in Athens. The late Wayne Satterfield, an Athens dentist and some of his friends were successful in securing a local Little League charter and talked Whatley into coaching a fourth team. What Satterfield and the other two coaches had done at that point, was choose their personnel and had snookered Whatley, taking all the pitchers. This left Big Jim with little talent with which to develop a team.

After hearing her husband complain, Mae, advised him to, "Take this little boy from Washington who has just moved to town. He is the best athlete in our school."

Tarkenton was a pitcher, and as Whatley would learn, a leader with rare insight, perceptiveness and talent for his age. He was one precocious athlete. "He really coached the team," Whatley remembered. "If a boy made an error, Francis would go over and pat him on the back and keep him from getting upset."

Whatley got the last laugh in that Little League season. His team played eleven games, Tarkenton pitched all eleven, and the team finished 11-0.

Tarkenton was having fun; he loved growing up in Athens where there were plenty of pickup games and sports emphasis, but financial conditions remained acutely austere at the Tarkenton house. His father's church couldn't pay very much to begin with, and it took every nickel to support the family and pay for the tuition costs at the University.

Whatley remembers that after those baseball games, he would drive his team over for an ice cream at an establishment, which stood at the corner of Lumpkin and Baxter Streets. He had to pay for Tarkenton's ice cream cones. Whatley would also take the players to the movies, and all would go except Tarkenton. Whatley, chucked at the contrast with Tarkenton's adult lifestyle. As a kid, his family felt it was a bad influence to see Hollywood films; but Tarkenton later cavorted with some of filmdom's elete. He became a TV star pushing national products in network commercials, co-hosting ABC-TV's "That's Incredible" and joining the Monday Night Football announcing team for a couple of seasons.

For Tarkenton's next level of athletic competition, Whatley would again provide opportunity. Francis wanted to join the Athens YMCA which had the best sports programs for youngsters in the community, but could not afford to buy his own equipment which all the Y boys were required to do. Whatley took care of the situation by asking the late Pap Eberhardt (father-in-law of track coach Spec Towns) to give him some old shoes, shoulder pads and a used Bulldog helmet. Tarkenton's career was off and running.

Soon he was a freshman quarterback for Weyman Sellers at Athens High, immediately becoming a co-regular. The next football season, as a sophomore, he was the starter outright with stardom waiting at every level. He would lead Athens High to the state football championship, Georgia to the Southeastern Conference title and the Minnesota Vikings to three Super Bowls, a coach-on-the-field, who didn't shy away from controversy nor weaken at the cry of the critics.

Tarkenton ignored the critics when he wasn't challenging them. He was brash, never loathe to spit out his opinion, never hesitant to pop off. It was his style, he had to prove he could get the job done, and it often began with him informing one and all he could and would do what was necessary in every situation, whether it was a series or a drive or a game. One thing he never suffered from was the lack of an opinion, or confidence.

As a quarterback he was recognized universally for his mental ability. He understood the defenses he opposed; he knew the capabilities of his offense. And he wasn't playing the game just for a check or for the hell of it. He loved what he was doing.

Anyone who has ever criticized him for any phase of his quarterbacking ability should analyze the results. Many veteran observers believe that he got more mileage out of his ability and talents than anyone who played the position. What he may have lacked in pure arm strength, he made up for with his intellectual strengths, his poise, his guile and his insights into his own style of play, that of his teammates and those he lined up against. On the field, the cagey Tarkenton knew what and where to exploit.

There is only one thing missing, and regrettably he can't do anything about that. Not winning one of those Super Bowls has so frustrated him that he has consid-

The fabled pass, Tarkenton to Herron for the SEC title

ered writing a book about the only really big prize to escape him in his lifetime. Fame and fortune have come his way, but no Super Bowl ring.

"It's something that lives with me every day," he says. "There is not a day that goes by that I don't think about not winning the Super Bowl – the failure of those three days that I had a chance to play in that game – the ultimate game in pro football – and not winning. I haven't learned how to deal with it, quite frankly."

For a long time, he tried to forget about it, espousing the view that he tried his best and that was it, *que sera*, whatever will be, will be. He does believe in destiny in sports. He is aware that Ted Williams, for example, never won a World Series and that a lot of great athletes, like Ernie Banks never even played in a World Series.

"I've heard people say they accept it as life, but I can't," Tarkenton once said. "I wish that I could. It absolutely bothers me that I've never been able to live it down. And the sad part about it is that I don't have a tomorrow. I can't go back out there at age 65 and play again, but I've had dreams of going back and playing at 48 and age 50 and age 55, and in the back of my mind I always thought I could if someone would give me the chance. And that's sick, but that is how much it bothers me. I wish I could cope with it and deal with it, but I really haven't been able to."

In many cases, a football player has one shot at a Super Bowl, Tarkenton had three as a Viking: versus Miami in 1974, Pittsburgh in 1975, and Oakland in 1977. He knows in his heart he was good enough, but it didn't happen.

"Well, maybe," he slowly counters, "I wasn't good enough. Certainly, on those days I wasn't good enough, and that's a hard thing to admit – that you weren't good enough, or that you didn't make the big plays at the right time. I played in a lot of big games. All the division championship games were big games. It had nothing to do with 'big game,' but it was those three days in the Super Bowl, which is bigger than life, right? The world certainly sees it as bigger than life. I mean what would I do for a Super Bowl ring that I earned? But the worst is that I know that it can never be."

You get your team to the Super Bowl three times, and that's not failure in the eyes of most observers. For Tarkenton who always wanted to be more than a football player, it is. For a man who has never really failed at anything but those events, it is difficult to put aside. There is no tomorrow, there is no Grand Masters, no Senior Tour in his sport. His Super Bowl record will always be 0-3.

Tarkenton's feelings about those failures may in part explained what has motivated him all these years, to be the best and to never finish second best. That spirit, that drive took him to the top.

Regardless of those afternoons in Houston, Pasadena and New Orleans, afternoons he'd like to forget, the fact remains he was an all-pro quarterback who became eminently successful in business with three NFL career records: most attempts – 6,467; most yards gained passing – 47,003; and most touchdown passes – 342.

His records were broken by Dan Marino, who

played in Miami's sunshine. Marino's team annually played two more games than Tarkenton's, all of which does not bother Tarkenton. "I made the most of my career when I played and he did the same. I tip my hat to him."

The record shows that he was a great quarterback even though he played his first six years with an expansion team and his next five with the New York Giants, languishing in mediocrity and suffering from a dearth of capable talent.

It was Tarkenton who brought the mobile quarterback concept to pro football, it was he who led to the development of the ball control passing attack, getting it started with Joe Walton when the latter was an assistant with the Giants. He then adding the finishing touches with Jerry Burns at Tarkenton's second stop in Minnesota.

The critics always said he couldn't win the big one. They always said a scrambler would never make it to the Super Bowl, they always said his arm was not strong enough, but his performance always refuted what the critics said. Nobody ever could convince him he couldn't play quarterback or with the best. And he did for 18 seasons.

"A lot has been said about my arm through the years. Funny thing, I used to have a much stronger arm, but I got a shoulder separation from a scrimmage in high school and after it healed, my arm was never as strong. We taped the arm up after the injury and I tried to throw, but couldn't, and as a result I developed some bad habits and struggled with my arm from that point on.

"All during my 18 years of pro football, my understudies had stronger arms than I did, but I'll tell you what strong arms mean to a quarterback. The year we played Pittsburgh in the Super Bowl, I hurt my arm in about the third game with Dallas. After that I took a shot prior to the game and during practice – every week. I didn't throw a ball in practice the rest of the season. The week of the Super Bowl, I never threw a ball in practice; I couldn't throw the ball over 10-15 yards because my arm just killed me. Even with the momentum of the game, I could throw it a little more, but I had nothing on the ball. My range was 40 yards. We won our division, we won our playoff games and beat Los Angeles in the championship game to get the Super Bowl with a quarterback who couldn't throw the ball over 40 yards.

"This brings us to a point which I've recognized all my career. There are many facets to playing quarterback and if scouts would understand that you just don't take a guy who's got a strong arm. You've got to get the ball to the receiver, and I proved you could do it with a lame arm. When I couldn't throw but 40 yards, we had a good year passing the football. You've got to read a defense, know who to throw it to and when to throw it. You've got to be a complete quarterback, handling the ball, play calling, leading the team – all these things are the intangibles that separate the average quarterback from a better than average quarterback.

"I could throw the ball 57-58 yards, and you never need more than that. If you throw a ball over 60 yards in a football game, you've waited too long. I remember in a long distance throwing contest for NFL quarterbacks in Miami one year: Bob Griese threw 50 yards, Ken Stabler 53, Terry Bradshaw about 70 and Don Pastorini was the winner at something like 71 yards. So if I could throw it 58 and Bradshaw 70, he could throw it 12 yards farther than I, but you don't throw 70-yard touchdown passes. When I was with New York, I threw plenty of long passes to Homer Jones and it was the same way at Minnesota with Amad Rashad and Sammy White. At Minnesota when we got our good teams together the last of my career, we controlled the football by passing which was the way we felt was to run an offense. You don't need a powerful arm to run a pro offense in my opinion.

"Bill Walsh gets credit for the West Coast offense, and I always admired his system. But we started the same approach when I was with the Giants and we perfected the concept at Minnesota.

"The biggest asset I had was that I had a great sense of presence on the field. I could see things better than others, I could see clearly. I could adjust in the middle of a play and make something out of a play that wasn't so good. I think the greatest asset a quarterback can have is a feel for the game.

"One of my assets also was that I believed I could play, that I was the best. I'm sure John Unitas felt he was the greatest quarterback that ever lived. I am sure that Sonny Jurgenson, Y.A. Tittle and Bart Starr felt they could play better than anybody else. I did, too. Any quarterback worth his salt believes the same way.

"A quarterback needs a great deal of confidence to be able to perform, because people are going to dissect his play after the game and say he should have stayed in the pocket, or should have thrown long instead of short, and so on.

"When I did all that scrambling I was doing it because I couldn't just sit there in the pocket and take a sack. I felt that you should improvise, to make something happen. I was buying time, nothing more. I didn't win any games running the football, but I won some games be being able to move around in the pocket and outside the pocket to buy more time in order to complete a pass. I was a freak, and the old establishment guys that came up in the Fifties said, 'This guy will never last.'

"As a runner I was quick. Never was fast, but I was quick and had a great instinct, knowing where people were all the time. I could sense and feel people and escape them, and for five to ten yards I was about as quick as anybody. I could anticipate, knowing when to move and where to move, which goes back to the feel of the game. I knew where I was on the field at all times. I knew where everybody else was and where I was, where I could move and where I couldn't move. You don't teach that. I think that came from playing in the alleys of Washington, D.C."

FRED BROWN

When he was growing up, Fred Brown lived in the West End section of Atlanta and was extremely popular with all the neighborhood kids. The reason was somewhat unique.

His uncle was a famous movie star and often came for visits. When Johnny Mack Brown showed up, all the neighborhood kids gathered to meet the silver screen cowboy and ask for his autograph.

How Brown became a movie star is an interesting story. Johnny Mack was an All-America halfback at Alabama, scoring the winning touchdown in the Rose Bowl of 1926. He stayed on the West Coast and began making movies immediately. According to "Who's Who of the Cinema," MGM signed him to a contract. He played opposite stars like Greta Garbo, Mary Pickford and Norma Shearer. Johnny Mack was not a great actor but had muscular good looks. He developed into a highly regarded leading man and later focused on B Westerns, remaining very popular for decades. Even in the Fifties he was starring in movies while becoming a successful real estate investor in the Los Angeles area.

Interestingly, Brown's three brothers also played halfback at Alabama – Tolbert, Billy and Fred (Bulldog Fred's father). The late J. B. Whitworth, longtime Bulldog line coach, told Fred that his daddy was the best athlete of the Brown boys, but Fred Sr. came down with malaria in Tuscaloosa and never fully recovered to realize his potential.

With this background, you would have thought Alabama would have had the inside track in recruiting the second Fred Brown, whose exceptional speed earned him the moniker "Flyin' Fred" while in Athens.

When Fred was a senior at Northside High in 1955, playing for a loyal Bulldog, the late Wayman Creel, he developed warm feelings for the University of Georgia. Alabama was going through turmoil, and Fred knew that he wanted to live in his homestate. "If I followed through on that," he says, "I knew that I should go to school in the state where I'd be living. On top of that I really liked Coach Butts."

Fred Brown, nephew of movie star, Johnny Mack Brown

Johnny Mack had become a good friend of Coach Butts, and sent his nephew the following handwritten letter when Fred signed with the Bulldogs.

Fred,

I have just heard from Coach Wally Butts of the University of Georgia that you have been signed to play for him – my sincere congratulations!! Be sure, and I know you will, uphold the "Brown Tradition."

Your Uncle,

Johnny Mack

The cowboy movie star attended many of Fred's games, watching his nephew play and visiting with his friend, Wallace Butts. Johnny Mack occasionally showed up at practice, and the players took note of the fact that on the practice field was a real live movie star whom they had often seen on the screen at their hometown theaters.

While Fred enjoyed a very successful career at Georgia with the team winning the 1959 SEC championship and the Orange Bowl, he never realized his full potential with the Bulldogs. He was often injured and still limps today with a knee that was banged up as a Bulldog halfback. It was the same way with the Buffalo Bills with whom he played for three years.

The early Fifties had not been the best of times for Georgia football, but in December of 1956, Georgia signed a number of highly touted freshmen including Francis Tarkenton, Brown and Pat Dye.

Strong emotional feelings from Georgia followers evolved for that particular recruiting class, and while nobody knew for sure, there were reasons to be optimistic. Things were going to be different. Tarkenton and Dye gathered the freshmen together when they reported in August. There was a pep talk and a vow was made, "Men we are never going to lose to Georgia Tech."

In those days the freshmen of Georgia and Georgia Tech played on Thanksgiving Day, the "Scottish Rite Classic". In 1957 the Bullpups won 7-0 on Thursday and Theron Sapp broke the drought on Saturday, both games on Grant Field. The streak had ended. The vow the freshmen had made was headed to fruition. Those players never lost to Georgia Tech. Their record was a sparkling 4-0.

In 1959 Georgia was far from the favorite in the SEC race. After all, LSU was the defending national champion. Both Ole Miss and Auburn had powerhouse teams. That Georgia won the conference championship in that particular year is one of the biggest upsets in league history.

In Baton Rouge, on Halloween night with Ole Miss leading 7-3, Billy Cannon fielded a punt and went all the way for a touchdown to eliminate Ole Miss from the title chase. The next week in Knoxville, Tennessee upset LSU. Then, in Athens on November 14 Georgia took care of Auburn, which left the Bulldogs all alone at the top of the conference heap. Undefeated and Orange Bowl bound.

Georgia had nothing in the way of strength compared to those teams, but the Bulldogs were a band of players which came together as a team and believed in themselves. Fred Brown was one who made many timely contributions in that Cinderella season.

Brown was not a big back (5-9, 160), but like his famous uncle, he was muscular and not only had extraordinary top speed in the open field, he had that quick burst from a three point stance. At the snap, he was into the line of scrimmage in a flash. Give him a crease and only a good angle, as he danced and dodged down the field, would allow him to be cornered.

Interestingly, Brown saved his best performances

Another big yardage gain by Flyin' Fred Brown

for Georgia Tech. The best example of that came in the 1959 game on Grant Field. Georgia had clinched the SEC title against Auburn two weeks earlier and Tech was primed for a big upset. Georgia scored three touchdowns in the first half, and although Tech rallied in the second half, those three touchdowns were enough for the Orange Bowl bound Bulldogs, 21-14.

Against the Yellow Jackets in 1958, he had a 32-yard touchdown run. In 1959 at Grant Field, in the first quarter, he sprinted 38 yards through the Tech defense to the two yard line to set up Georgia's first touchdown.

Fran Tarkenton, late in the half, threw for Georgia's

second score, but Georgia got the ball back with seconds left. Brown remembers well what took place at that point.

"With only seconds left, our quarterback Charley Britt, who platooned with Tarkenton, was going to run out the clock," Brown says "Coach Butts was going crazy on the sideline. He signaled to Britt to throw the ball and the pattern was for me to sprint straight down the sideline and get behind the secondary, which is exactly the way it worked." Britt hit Brown for a forty-yard scoring play and the Bulldogs went ahead 21-0. It was enough for victory.

At Northside High School, Fred was named "All Greater Atlanta", "All State" and was selected to play in the Georgia All-Star Football Game.

Following is a statistical capsule of his productive career: Brown lettered for three years ('57-'60) and was selected All SEC Freshman in 1957 and All SEC Sophomore in 1958. He led the SEC in yards rushing per carry (6.6). He made All SEC in 1960 and led the SEC in pass receiving with 31 receptions. Brown was voted "Best Runner in the Conference" by SEC coaches. He graduated in 1962 with a B.S.Ed.

His three year career all purpose yards total was 2,133; he scored 13 touchdowns and compiled a 5.14 career rushing average.

Brown played with the Buffalo Bills from 1961-63, returning a kickoff 100 yards his first play as a professional. Fred, who could have played in the NFL, chose the rival AFL because he felt that he had a better opportunity to play regularly. When he got to Buffalo, it was the same old injury story. He would regain his health, display remarkable running ability and then become sidelined again. As a consequence, it was an up and down career until a knee injury forced him out of the game completely.

When he is not selling insurance for State Farm, based in Dunwoody, Brown spends every available moment outdoors. "My family was always fishing and hunting," he says. "The Browns really like the outdoors."

Fishing and hunting were important activities for him when he was at Georgia, and he was often in the company of teammates George Whitton and Cicero Lucas.

As time went by, they purchased or leased land near Lucas' hometown of Washington, and the fall is one of the happiest of times for this threesome, who are outdoor partners. They hang out at respective a rustic retreats near Tignall with water where ducks and geese are prevalent. Of course there are dove and quail opportunities. Often they check out pheasant hunting options in Kansas.

"You just can't beat getting out in the fields and doing a little shooting," Brown says. Scoring, whether from his halfback position or with a shotgun, was, and has always been, a natural for Flyin' Fred Brown.

When he was ten years old, Brown successfully fired a shot from a 410 shotgun, bringing down a nondescript bird. The pure exhilaration overwhelmed him. Hunting and fishing became the more important thing in his life except, of course, running the football.

"That was the thing I enjoyed most," he says. "Unfortunately, I can't run the football anymore. The outdoors I can enjoy as long as I live. At least that is the way I've got it figured."

Flying Fred has hunted for game over the country, and beyond, including Canada but says the best duck hunting is where he and his teammates hunt at Tignall. Hunting wild quail remains his most avid activity, but sadly notes wild quail have pretty much disappeared except with the big plantations in South Georgia.

As quick with his eye as he was with his feet from a three point stance, Fred has, on more than one occasion, killed five wild quail on the rise. He explains: "First of all, you need a little luck. To begin with, tou have to have a delayed flush. If they all get up at once, you can't pull that off."

Most hunters consider it something special to kill two birds on the rise and only a few ever claim three, but Brown has not lost his deadly eye over the years. One reason for that is that he constantly shoots skeet, but never in competition. "I have enough of a challenge," he laughs, "competing with myself."

With the passing of time the outdoor experience remains something important in his very existence. "I don't think I could live without having outdoor opportunity," he says. "It is such a wonderful exercise, such a wonderful experience."

He remains a Georgia football fan, seeing many games each fall between the hedges. "There are some very skilled athletes playing college football now," he says. "But something I have noted that amuses me. I see receivers, for example, making unbelievable catches. Then they drop balls right in their hands. Coach Butts would have gone nuts if that happened when he was coaching."

PAT DYE

You would have thought Pat Dye a perfect choice for the head coaching job at the University of Wyoming where he coached in 1980.

In fact, he was, but while he briefly enjoyed the Cowboy state, his heart belonged to the Southeastern Conference. After one season in Laramie, he saw an opportunity to return to the South to his roots and jumped at the possibility.

When his former coach, Bear Bryant, explained why he accepted the job at Alabama in 1958, leaving Texas A & M in College Station for Tuscaloosa, Bryant said, "Mama called."

In Dye's case, he was calling mama, mama being an SEC school. Initially, mama didn't want him as much as he wanted mama. As it turned out, he got what he wanted, but in a sense it became his stepmama.

At season's end in 1980 Georgia was undefeated and ranked No. 1 in the country. Auburn sought a coach to succeed Doug Barfield. The administration concluded that the best thing to do would be to offer Vince Dooley the job along with the athletic directorship. Dooley initially warmed up to what Auburn was offering and weakened until he was promised the athletics director's job outright at Georgia. He also was advised that an arrangement could be established where he would be given title to the house on Milledge Circle. He had moved to that address soon after arriving in Athens.

While all this was going on, Dye communicated with his old teammate, Don Leebern, who was a member of the Georgia athletic board. They felt Dooley would likely return to his alma mater, which meant that Dye would have jumped at returning to Athens as head coach. There was only one problem. If Vince left, the athletic board would likely have rushed a decision to offer the job to Erk Russell.

After all, Erk was very popular across the state and Georgia would be playing in the Sugar Bowl for the national championship. Although Dye would have been the choice of many Bulldogs in the state, he saw it as a cut and dried deal for Erk if Vince had chosen to leave.

Leebern called him late one day and told him that Vince was staying at Georgia, which opened the door for Dye to aggressively seek an opportunity with Auburn, which had assumed that Dooley was going to be their man – to the extent that they had not interviewed other candidates.

Dye immediately called Fob James, Dooley's one time roommate, and governor of Alabama. The governor suggested that Dye call the President of Auburn, Dr. Hanly Funderburk, who was in a meeting with the search committee at that very minute. Funderburk's secretary got the President out of the meeting, and Pat advised the president that he wanted the Auburn job.

All American Pat Dye

He was passionate with his pitch.

Things moved quickly, and Pat Dye, a Bulldog who had coached with Bryant at Alabama, became the coach and subsequently athletic director at Auburn, a school he helped Georgia beat, 14-13, in that memorable game for the Southeastern Conference championship in late November 1959, his junior year.

All of a sudden, you could say that Dye was perfect for coaching at Auburn. If there has ever been a pickup-truck-driving, down home, camouflage-wearing, shotgun-toting football coach, it was Pat Dye, who settled in at Auburn liked he had been born there. He wore well with the Auburn people who had suffered from the dominance of Bryant for years.

Another thing is that when Dye took over the War Eagle program, the school had claimed only one conference championship in its history. Dye eventually won three SEC titles in a row and began to post victory more often than not in the big battle with Alabama. He became a larger-than-life hero to the Auburn people.

Dye coached for 19 years at East Carolina, Auburn and Wyoming. He had an overall record of 153-62-5. At Auburn he exited with a record of 99-39-4.

He won games because he worked at coaching. When he was hired, he said, "We might not be the most talented team in the country, but there is no reason why we can't be the best prepared, the most disciplined and the best conditioned team in college football."

Dye's team's appeared in nine bowl games in his twelve years at Auburn, five of them on New Year's Day. He believes his one year at Wyoming taught him something about himself. "I certainly didn't go there with plans to stay only a year. I liked the place and the people but felt that if I could get the Auburn job, I would be a fool not to go," Dye says.

When the Wyoming opportunity came up, Dye had just completed his sixth year of coaching at East Carolina and felt that it was time to move on. Dye's teams at East Carolina posted a record of 48-18-1, and he never backed away from playing the Atlantic Coast powers. In fact, he had a difficult time getting schools like North Carolina and North Carolina State to schedule the Pirates. There were not all that many coaching options available to him when the Wyoming job opened up. He made a dedicated effort to become the Cowboy's head coach.

At Wyoming, his only year there, he led the team to its first winning record in eight years and only the second in twelve years. "Wyoming," he says, "is a great little school with a fine academic reputation. I liked the place and went back a few summers ago for a visit after being away for so many years. At Wyoming, I knew that I would find out if I were a big time football coach."

He knew the history and the fact that Wyoming coaches often moved up in the profession: Bowden Wyatt to Arkansas; Bob Devaney to Nebraska; Fred Akers to Texas; Dennis Erickson to Miami.

"It is not an easy place to recruit," Dye continues, but they bring in a lot of tough minded kids, a lot of hungry kids and they like to play football."

If Dye had stayed at Wyoming, he figures that he would have eventually enjoyed the outdoor experience in Laramie since he is passionate about hunting and fishing. "It is a great place if you like that," he says, "but since I stayed only a year, I didn't get to do much outdoors. When I got there, I had to recruit, then hire a staff and start up the program. At the end of that first season, I spent all my time trying to get the Auburn job."

It shocked a lot of Alabama partisans who were great fans of his, when Dye took over at Auburn. He remains a popular man in the state today, appreciated by both Alabama and Auburn supporters.

He lives on a farm near Notasulga, Al., hunts and fishes with abiding relish, speaks to a few quarterback clubs and keeps up with college football which has been good to him. He maintains an office on the Auburn campus and is on call for fundraising and public relations assignments. His health is good, and he enjoys the rural lifestyle which is similar to that in which he remembers growing up.

Before retiring at Auburn, Dye underwent elective major surgery in late May of 1991 to improve the flow of blood through his spleen and liver.

The procedure, a distal-splenorenal shunt, took a vein running from the spleen to the liver and connected it to a vein running from the kidney to the heart, thereby reducing the blood supply and pressure on the spleen.

The need to reduce the pressure on Dye's spleen was the result of hemochramatosis, an excess of iron in the blood, a condition diagnosed in December of 1990.

The excess of iron in the blood had caused scar tissue to develop in Dye's liver and caused a backup of blood around the spleen and the liver. Increased pressure at these locations caused enlarged veins around the stomach and esophagus, a condition doctors compare to varicose veins. The surgery was designed to reduce the chance of an internal blood vessel rupturing. He resumed normal activity in early July of 1991 and has never looked back.

The 1958 Bulldogs (Pat's sophomore season) lost six games by a total of 50 points. One of the victories was a 28-0 defeat of Kentucky in Athens, a game significant in that Pat, on a kickoff, stole the ball from a Kentucky back and returned it for a 28 yard touchdown. More than half the stadium did not know what had happened. The Georgia defense stacked up the ball carrier and Pat simply yanked the ball from the Wildcats' grasp and lit out for the end zone. Pat was recognized by both teammates and opponents as one of those players who was always around the ball.

"When I was playing at Georgia," he says, "if you had told me that I would have the kind of life I've had, then I would have told you you would be looking at a happy man, and that is the way I feel about things today. Things have turned out great for me."

Jimmy Vickers

The 1959 Georgia-Alabama game in Athens was one which the Bulldogs dominated from start to finish, winning 17-3.

Yet, with Bear Bryant entering his second year as head coach, the Tide was favored. The year before, Georgia fielded, perhaps, the best losing team in the country and lost to Alabama at Tuscaloosa, 12-0.

In 1958, the Bulldogs lost six games by a total of 50 points. Only Vanderbilt, South Carolina and Auburn could manage more than two touchdowns against the Bulldogs, but even with Theron Sapp at fullback and Fran Tarkenton and Charley Britt at quarterback, the Bulldogs never found a way to win close games.

"It was different the next year," says Jimmy Vickers the all-conference end and alternate captain. "We played together, but the year before, there were too many individuals. We learned how to win in 1959 and it all started, in my opinion, with the Alabama game."

Georgia moved the ball with terrific success against the Alabama defense, which seldom gave up points in the typical Bear Bryant tradition.

One of the reasons for the Bulldogs' rushing success was the blocking of Vickers, one of those players who enjoyed football contact and one who never had any reluctance to stick his head in the thick of the action.

On defense, he gave ground grudgingly. He was a hard-nosed player, the type who would roll up his sleeves and get to work without any fuss, fear or loathing. Coaches love players like Jimmy Vickers for two reasons: they always get the job done and set a good example for the rest of the team.

In Vickers' time, captains were elected before the start of the season. At the annual spring barbecue at old Poss' Restaurant on the Atlanta Highway, Bulldog lettermen chose Don Soberdash as captain and Vickers as alternate.

Early in the 1959 pre-season drills, Soberdash was hurt and played very little until the Auburn game between the hedges. Vickers led the team competently with the captain sidelined with injuries.

"You know," he says "I will never forget the Alabama game because of what it meant to our team to win that first conference game. But to tell you the truth, I don't remember all that many details. I know one thing; we all felt that we would be a much improved football team. We were very frustrated in 1958. We knew that team should have won more games."

When he finished at Georgia, he had prepared himself to coach. He worked with frosh coach Quinton Lumpkin, and then played a year of professional ball in Canada.

Later, he made coaching stops at Presbyterian, South Carolina, North Carolina, Georgia and Ole Miss, getting out of coaching to enter the insurance business.

Today, he lives in Destin, FL, where fishing opportunity abounds. There is considerable time to reminisce about his past. "For a long time," he says, "I thought about getting back into coaching, but I'm not sure I would enjoy it as much the way things have changed. But I had some great experiences and will always appreciate playing and coaching all those years. I was fortunate to be associated with some outstanding teams that won championships. You especially appreciate that when you get older."

Don Soberdash

The captain of Coach Butts last championship team, Don Soberdash, often wonders what his football life would have been like with healthy and unencumbered knees. Additionally, he contemplates how the medical knowledge and treatment for athletes today would have impacted his recovery from the injuries he suffered while playing for the Bulldogs.

His complications began in high school and lingered throughout his career although the period when he was hobbled the most was in the first half of his final season, the SEC championship campaign of 1959.

By the time his career was winding down, Soberdash had lost that step that would have made him a viable threat at halfback at which he demonstrated toughness as a runner, one whose second effort often brought extra yardage. He possessed other skills, too, like catching the ball out of the backfield and clearing a path for other runners with his crisp and deadly blocking.

A native of Connellsville, Pa., Soberdash takes great pride in the fact that he was voted captain in the pre-season of his final year in Athens. There was good reason for that honor. His teammates had great respect for Soberdash. He never groused or complained, even though he hobbled about on his shaky knees restricting his motion and agility. He was tough, he led by example, he put as much effort into being an effective blocker as he did as a runner.

When you earn the respect of your teammates, it

Captain Don Soberdash slowed by injury

shows up when leaders are being officially identified. Additionally, Soberdash had a compatible personality with his Bulldog teammates. They enjoyed being around him. He was a man's man. The main thing was that respect which came from his competitive style.

He worked hard, he had nothing to carp about. If he could spring Fred Brown, Bobby Towns or Bill McKenny with a block, he took great satisfaction in making that contribution even if the headline writers weren't aware. If he could catch a pass out of the backfield and the headline writers took note, that was not as rewarding as his teammates' appreciation for his keeping a drive alive. "An athlete has pride," he says, "and there is nothing quite like having a teammate recognize your value and your contribution."

Soberdash started his football career at Maryland, and then transferred to Georgia in 1956. He shared halfback duties with Jimmy Orr in 1957, was a starter as a junior a year later—all the while, playing with unstable knees.

Then in the second game with Vanderbilt, he was blindsided and went down with a knee injury that would sideline him for three weeks. "I am sure that today, the doctors would recommend surgery since it was a cartilage injury. They didn't have the surgical expertise for bad knees then like they do now, but somehow or other, it healed well enough for me to get back in the lineup."

Because he was such an effective blocker, Coach Butts moved him to fullback, a move that paid off handsomely in the closing minutes of the fourth quarter of the championship clinching game against Auburn.

During the week, prior to the game, Coach Butts designed a play especially for Soberdash. He would fake a handoff into the line, slip past the line of scrimmage and become a pass receiver over the middle.

The Bulldogs had not used that play until that last chance to win the game which came about when Pat Dye recovered a fumble at the Auburn 35 with less than three minutes to play.

Tarkenton hit Soberdash for 16 yards and then 9 yards to set up a 4th down and 13 yard completion for the winning touchdown.

For Soberdash, that drive will be a lasting and proud memory, but he talks more about Tarkenton's poise, confidence and inventiveness in setting up the winning score.

"Fran made up the touchdown pass in the huddle, and he was so calm and under control. He made us believe the play would work. He told us all to go to the right and told Bill Herron to fake inside and go to the left. Tarkenton rolled to the right, pulled up and threw back across the field to Herron for the touchdown. I blocked down on the end for protection, looked up and saw Herron in the end zone with the ball. You never forget an experience like that."

As often as possible, at least once a year, Soberdash returns to Athens. Usually it is for the annual football letterman's golf outing. "I get a good feeling just driving into town. It is not as quiet and small as it was when I played for the Bulldogs, but there is something refreshing about coming back to the campus. The friendships I made while in college are so rewarding, and I appreciate my teammates and the bond that developed when we helped Coach Butts get back on top. He deserved the '59 championship, and I think all of us are proud that we were part of that comeback for him."

When he finished at Georgia, Soberdash played two years with the Hamilton Tiger-Cats of the Canadian Football League, but those unstable knees kept him from continuing his football career. He settled in Somerset, Pa., and became a successful owner of a coal mining company with Georgia always on his mind.

BILL GODFREY

A pretty, young grandmother answered the portable phone which was ferried to the backyard where her husband of 30 years was interrupted from his weekend chores.

You could hear him say impatiently, "Who is it?"

"Don't know," was the reply.

Soon Georgia's starting fullback from the SEC championship year of 1959 was on the line and saying to an old friend, "You caught me cuttin' grass."

"Shall I call back when you're finished?" he was asked.

"Are you kiddin'?" he laughed when he found out the caller wanted to reminisce about the Georgia/Alabama game in Sanford Stadium three decades ago.

"If somebody wants to talk to me about Georgia football, I've always got time and the grass can wait." In a matter of minutes, he was saying, "If it hadn't been for Coach (Quinton) Lumpkin and Coach (Jim) Whatley, you wouldn't be making this call now. Both of them were like second fathers to me. They got me through Georgia."

Whatley recruited Godfrey out of Harding High in Charlotte and had deep respect for the hard-nosed fullback who had literally known nothing but hard times. Godfrey was adopted, the oldest of seven children, and his stepfather, a plumber, seemed always to be out of work. Bill, in today's vernacular, became a street fighter. Literally.

He was always ready to mix it up at the first opportunity, mainly because he actually was never opposed to a little hard-to-hand combat but more often than not because someone had challenged him without knowing what they were in for. Godfrey was a muscled, compact 185-pounder, but he always appeared short, even though he stood 5-11. "I had short legs," he laughs.

"Don't mess with him" would have been the advice of those who knew Godfrey. Somebody was forever unimpressed with the short guy with the mouthful-of-marbles accent. "They'd say something, and here we'd go," Godfrey remembers. "I had it rough in life, growing up, and I just developed an attitude at an early age that I wasn't going to take nothing off nobody, and I never did. It got me in a lot of trouble, and that is where Coach Lumpkin was so wonderful to me. I think he understood. I knew he thought I could play football for Georgia, but I think he knew what made me the way I was. He wanted to help.

"If people had left me alone, there wouldn't have been any problems, but it didn't take much for me to feel like somebody was putting me down, and I just couldn't take it. I'd have to take 'em on."

To remedy the situation, Lumpkin had Godfrey move in with him and his family on Mitchell Bridge Road. The late Bulldog assistant kept Godfrey out of trouble, willing to go the last mile with him.

"I always believed in giving a man a second chance," Godfrey says today, "but thank goodness Coach Lumpkin would give you a third chance. When he died, I cried like a baby. I named my oldest boy for him, and as long as I live, I'll always appreciate what he did for me."

On the football field, Godfrey was the kind of player who always warmed a coach's heart. He played football for keeps. He understood that the game was, by its very nature, tough, and that was right down Godfrey's alley. When he got into the open field, he liked nothing better than to find somebody in his way. He was not opposed to hunting up a defender and run him over.

But by the time Georgia played Alabama in Athens September 19, 1959, Coach Wallace Butts, a lasting proponent of hard-nosed football, had convinced Godfrey that when he got in the open field, it was best to run to daylight.

No Bulldog back has ever had greater opportunity than Godfrey did in the second quarter of that hot afternoon. Quarterback Francis Tarkenton had directed the Bulldogs down to the Alabama 40 – the big plays, 19-yard and 15-yard passes to right end Gorden Kelley.

Tarkenton called for the fullback off tackle, and when Godfrey got to the line of scrimmage, there was as much daylight as he had ever seen in his football life. He bounded through, cut to his right and lumbered the rest of the way on a near perfectly executed play. Godfrey remembers it in simple and basic terms. "All of my guys were knockin' down their guys. Nobody touched me."

In the press box, the late Gen. Robert Neyland, long-time coach at Tennessee, was quoted as saying it was one of the finest-executed plays he had ever seen in his life.

Godfrey did not start that game, but he was a starter for the rest of his career. "I didn't run the ball more than an average of six or seven times a game," he says. "If I could have run it 20 times like they do now, I would have had some real fun playing football. It was fun as it was, but I'd give anything to run it like they do today. I never gained a lot of yards, but one thing I am proud of is that in my whole career – college and high school – I never lost a single yard."

What made Godfrey an ideal fullback for his day was his strength and quickness. "When I took a step, I was at full speed," he says. "But in the open field, I was so slow, anybody could catch me. Coach Butts used to tell me I was so slow he had to sight me on the goal posts to see if I was movin.'"

Nobody could move Godfrey out of the starting lineup, however, and nobody had a greater appreciation for the SEC title than Godfrey. After a few celebrations following the title-clinching game against Auburn and the victory six weeks later in the Orange Bowl Godfrey, in his slow-as-molasses drawl, pronounced to Coach Butts, "Ain't folks nice to you when you win!"

That classic remark is but one of many that players from that era recall with affection. Godfrey was indeed a funny character. Godfrey was not opposed to self-deprecating humor. He brought the house down when speaking to the Athens Touchdown Club following the birth of his first son. He said that a few days after delivery, he asked the doctor, "When are you going to castrate my baby?" The puzzled doctor replied, 'you mean circumcise your baby?'

"That's the word," Godfrey said as the Touchdown Club audience roared for several minutes.

He always cracked up his teammates with his down home humor, but when the whistle blew, nobody was more serious than Godfrey.

His teammates appreciated his courage in competition and his funny lines, but they also had a high regard for his determination to finish college. "I had to study harder than most," he says, "and I don't mind telling you that English was something I could never get the hang of, but I wasn't going to give up."

His persistence at repeating courses and doing extra work through home study enabled him to complete education degree requirements in 1963, two years after his last football season.

He married his college sweetheart, Lola, a pretty majorette, and began farming with her family for a dozen years, before the an opportunity wit the Agricultural Stabilization and Conservation Service came about.

His longtime friend and teammate, Paul Holmes, via Federal appointment, headed up the statewide agency. "My teammates have always been good to me." A few years back, he called me for Tarkenton's phone number. He called his former teammate and asked him

Fullback Bill Godfrey, nobody tougher, flies into the action

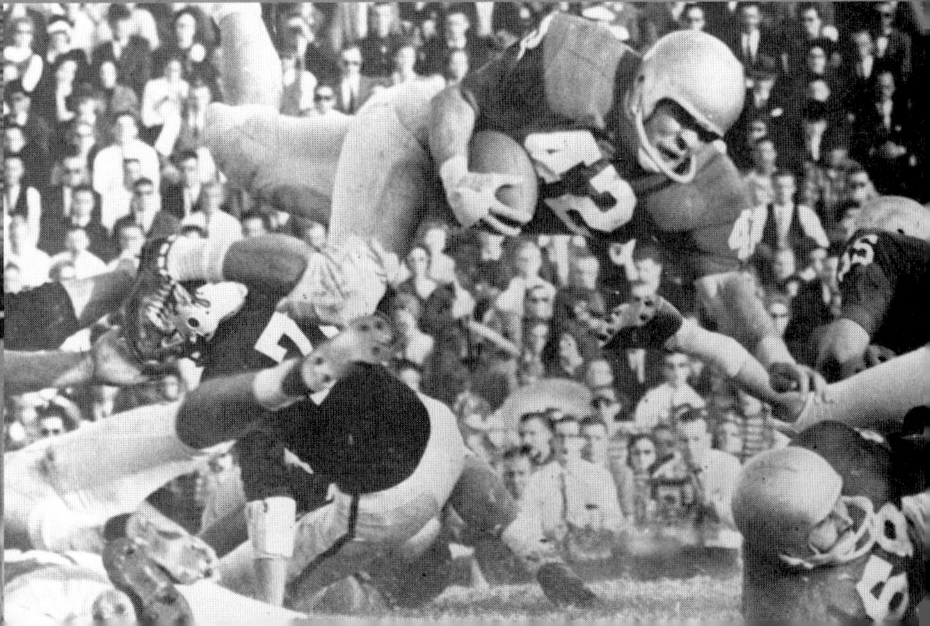

to come speak to the Colquitt Chamber of Commerce.

He began his conversation by saying, "Francis we can't pay a big fee, but we will do the best we can."

Before he could continue Tarkenton stopped him. "Tater Bug (Godfrey's nickname), it won't cost you a penny."

Overwhelmed, Godfrey said later, "You don't know what that meant to me. It brought respect for me in my community. That he would come to our little town and spend time with us is something that will stay with me as long as I live."

"My job took me to Athens a lot" Godfrey says, "and every time I drove into town, I got excited. I think about how lucky I was to play for Coach Butts and Georgia. I can't go anywhere in this state that I don't run into somebody who remembers that 1959 team and my run against Alabama. I think about Coach Whatley and Coach Lumpkin and what could have happened to me if they had ever lost faith in me or given up on me."

There were few times in his life when Godfrey came out second best, whether it was a football scrimmage or game or somebody asked him to step outside.

On the football field, he towered over nobody, he was not fleet of foot, but he would make tacklers pay when he ran the ball. Every inch, every pound of his body was explosive as dynamite. Trouble, very serious trouble lay underneath his down home exterior, if you crossed him.

There will always be room for a competitor, one who asks no quarter and gives none. No player Wallace Butts ever coached would eagerly go tooth and nail with more limitless commitment than Godfrey.

Fran Tarkenton remembers a freshman scrimmage in which there played a big, sleek and tough looking back who stood over six feet and weighed well over 200 pounds. "Looked like Superman in the flesh," Tarkenton says. As it turns out, the big guy was Casper Milktoast inside. Freshman coach, Quinton Lumpkin, wanted to see what the guy was made of and asked one early fall practice, "Who wants some of the big man here?"

A voice spoke up quickly, "I'll take some of the big man." It was Godfrey. In a fierce one-on-one battle, the big man faltered, backed away when Godfrey repeatedly beat him down at close range. He showered after practice and was never heard from again. It was a classic case of a player looking like Tarzan but playing like Jane. Godfrey's appearance, on the other hand, was deceiving. You tangled with a buzz saw when you took him on.

Charley Britt

For many Bulldog fans, the most memorable play of Charley Britt's Georgia career was the return of an interception 100 yards for a touchdown against Florida in the Gator Bowl Nov. 7, 1959. He also chased down Florida's Bobby Joe Green, the fastest man on the field, to save a touchdown in the same game. He tackled Green at the two yard line and the Bulldogs held on four straight downs.

It was, perhaps, his greatest game as a Bulldog. In addition to the aforementioned, Britt directed a nifty 43 yard scoring drive on Georgia's first possession. Britt set up the Dog's second score. Anticipating a quick kick by Green, the SEC's No. 1 punter in 1959, he returned the punt for good yardage. Immediately, he fired a 35 yard scoring pass to Bobby Towns. Georgia was opportunistic in a 21-10 victory in the Gator Bowl.

When the Athens Touchdown club met the next week, Charley was one of the speakers. At TD club gatherings in those years, Coach Butts made remarks but brought along a couple of players who had been picked for back and linemen of the week honors.

Britt regaled the membership with his commentary. He first explained that Coach Butts came up to him after he scored on the interception and provided a critique that included several negative comments. His coach concluded his remarks with, "I didn't like the way you threw the ball up in the air when you crossed the goal line."

After hearing his coach complain about what he did wrong, Britt grinned and said, "But coach how was it for distance?" About overtaking Green on his 70 yard run to the Georgia two, Britt said, "He was running for a touchdown. I was running for my life."

His clever and extemporaneous remarks delighted the Touchdown clubbers who were not surprised in the least when Britt became involved with television work on the West Coast after he was signed to play defensive back with the Los Angeles Rams. Britt, who became a roommate of Ricky Nelson, appeared on the Ozzie and Harriett Show, the family sitcom of Ricky's parents. He also was involved with making several commercials and life after football could have become a show business career.

He never got the big break, but even if he had, he "knew" he would return South at some point. "The West Coast was fun, pro football for six years was fun, but I always felt that I'd come back this way. I enjoyed

California, but I also missed my native South. I knew where I wanted to settle permanently."

Following a tenure with Augusta's WJBF, delivering the six and eleven o'clock news, Britt now publishes a free lance opinion column for several publications in that area.

He often reflects back on his Georgia experience. He was one of the biggest names in high school football in 1955, playing at North Augusta. He had always been emotionally attached to the Georgia tradition and was intrigued by the challenge he saw in Athens. "The Bulldogs had fallen on tough times," he says, "and everybody told me I would be foolish to enroll at Georgia. I liked the challenge, and fortunately, my timing turned out to be rather good. My sophomore year in 1957, fifteen of my freshman class became starters. We improved in 1958 and then won the championship in 1959. When we got to the summit, it was quite rewarding."

Britt and Francis Tarkenton shared quarterback duties in those one platoon days. In game accounts, you frequently read, "Britt's team" or "Tarkenton's team."

Each quarterback made significant contributions to Georgia's success, co-quarterbacks on a conference championship team. The rules required that any player who came out of the game was not allowed to go back until a new quarter had started, which meant that substitutions often were for entire teams.

Tarkenton's touchdown pass to Bill Heron to win the Auburn game and claim the SEC championship is one of the most fabled touchdown passes in Georgia history, but Britt made a significant contribution earlier in the game.

Auburn had taken the lead 6-0 on a second field goal and the Tigers, backed up near their goal line, were punting in the third quarter. Britt returned the kick 39 yards for a touchdown, zig zagging his way through three Auburn All-Americans (Zeke Smith, Jackie Burkette and Ken Rice) for a 7-6 lead.

He had a punt slip out of his hands earlier in the game, the visitors recovered and got a field goal out of it. Later, when Auburn lined up to punt, which turned into six points for the Bulldogs, Britt thought of redeeming himself. "As I looked across the field to the corner of the end zone, I remember spotting a small weed. I had an eerie sensation about that weed. 'I'm gonna take this ball to that weed,' I thought to myself. When I got to the end zone I remember stepping on that weed."

Was this a case of clairvoyance? Perhaps, but while that was to give Georgia a lead that could have been enough for victory, Britt figured into a play that gave the lead back to Auburn. Lining up in the searchlight position on a punt, the seat of his pants is where a hurried Bobby Walden's punt first hit. It was late in the final quarter, and after recovering the fumble, the War Eagles quickly scored to take the lead 13-7.

So many of Coach Butts' teams in the Fifties had trouble winning close games, but 1959 was a year in which it was different. That Auburn lead should have held up in those limited substitution times. But as the clock ticked away, Auburn's Bryant Harvard, on a rollout, fumbled. Pat Dye recovered and set the stage for Tarkenton's heroics.

From the left: A smiling Charley Britt; Britt in action to lead the Dogs over the Gators in Jacksonville; with Fran Tarkenton

"That was a memorable experience, winning the championship," Britt says. "I appreciated the success of my time in Athens, and I was happy to see Coach Butts regain the pinnacle of Southeastern Conference football. He was a colorful character. He was so funny. He was always cracking me up in practice. He had such a graphic way of explaining and teaching. There are a lot of times when I recall something he said on the practice field and just laugh out loud."

CARTER RAMSEY

Carter Ramsey was an all-state player for Ralph Pyburn at Savannah High, and making a decision on where he wanted to play college football was easy. He had always wanted to play for Wallace Butts and the Bulldogs. "There was never any indecision about that," he says.

When he arrived in Athens in the fall of 1956, Georgia was not a power in the Southeastern Conference, and there was a lot of complaining about the Bulldog football program.

It would have been easy for Ramsey and his teammates to develop a poor attitude, but that is not the case. First of all, when he was a sophomore, the Bulldogs defeated Tech in Atlanta to break the drought. The Dogs made it two in a row over Tech in 1958 in Athens.

In 1959, when the Bulldogs won the conference title, Tech fell to the Dogs for the third year in a row. One of the key plays in the game was a blocked punt by Ramsey.

This led to the second touchdown of the game and a 14-0 lead. Ramsey shot the gap and went up and over the blocker, who was positioned to protect the punter. Ramsey came down on the punter in picture-perfect fashion, sailing over the blocker into the punter. It was a classic, one which was prominently featured in all publications relating to the championship year of 1959.

"People still recall that play," he said, "and the older I get, the more I enjoy reminiscing about that game. The entire season as a matter of fact. Makes me proud to be a Bulldog, and I get prouder every year."

Beating your arch rival is always a lot of fun, but the game which has been pretty much forgotten in Ramsey's opinion is the Orange Bowl in Miami when the Bulldogs defeated an excellent Missouri team, 14-0.

"That game," he says, "had to mean a lot to Coach Butts. It was his third trip to the Orange Bowl, and he had gone through so much. To win the conference title and then the Orange Bowl had him on top of the football world again.

"Coach Butts and Coach Lumpkin were so good to me, and I think of them often. I feel that I learned a lot from them and without their influence I'm not sure what would have happened to me in life. They gave me a solid foundation, and I often pay tribute to them when I am alone driving or out on the water fishing by myself."

Ramsey is retired from the Sea Island Company.

HINTON DAVIS

Hinton Davis' father was a logger, and today there remains a strong bond between the former Bulldog tackle and the wood products industry. He'll remind you quickly that he would not be where he is nowadays without his long time association with forestry.

What about today? His companies, the Davis-Garvin Agency and Capital City Insurance Co. of Columbia, S.C., are substantial insurance operations with multi-million dollar sales, licensed to do business in 18 states. "Not bad for an old tackle," he chuckles, but with deep appreciation for the good life he has enjoyed, brought about, in his opinion, by his having matriculated at University of Georgia. More about that later.

And, what about yesterday? That was when he was introduced to football. He grew up 18 miles from Savannah in Richmond Hill. He learned early on to appreciate the fact that his father taught him that to make it in life, he had to take care of himself, and furthermore, he had to look out for himself.

The way of the logging world of his father, was rough and tumble. Up in the morning, out on the job, work like the devil for your pay. Don't stick your nose in anybody's business? If they stuck theirs in yours, put 'em in their place. Hinton became handy with his fists. If somebody pushed him, he pushed back. "If I hadn't, I would have had to deal with my father," he laughs. "He didn't want me going around causing any trouble, but if trouble came my way, he expected me to be able to take care of the situation."

With this background you can appreciate how compatible Hinton became with football. Just one problem, he lived too far from Savannah to associate with a program. He found a way, however, to get around that challenge—by riding the bus. This brings us to an interesting point. In all likelihood, Hinton Davis is the only Wally's boy to ride a Greyhound bus to school to play football.

It all began when he learned about Benedictine School in Savannah. He had gotten exposed to football through an intramural program at Richmond Hill, but, with his class, took a field trip to Benedictine one day.

Immediately, he was fascinated by the military program at Benedictine and learned about the school's competency in football. He wanted to be a part of all that. That daily ride into Savannah and back each day, via Greyhound, made it all possible.

Hinton Davis, success in the line and later in business

While at Benedictine, where he became a starting lineman right away, the team played North Fulton in Atlanta in the fall of 1953. That was another thing about football at Benedictine, he was entitled to travel to several out of town sites, which was interesting and educational. He knew, even back then, that if he played college football, which was a goal, he would enjoy opportunity to visit distant addresses, far from Richmond Hill.

On the way back to Savannah, from that game with North Fulton, the Benedictine team stopped off in Athens to see Georgia play North Carolina. He was overwhelmed with the stadium, the hedges, the color and the pageantry of college football. He was a freshman, and he will never forget his impressions. Not only was he fascinated and enthralled with the game and all the trimmings of college football in Sanford Stadium—from the band to the cheerleaders to the famous hedges—he remembers the pact he made with himself. It would be his goal to prepare for and earn an opportunity to play college football.

"I can remember it like it happened yesterday," Hinton says. "I was so taken by the vivid colors, Georgia's red and North Carolina's blue. It was intoxicating emotionally. I knew right then that I wanted to wear a red jersey and silver britches between the hedges. My ambition to play for Coach Butts and Georgia began on that afternoon.

"Now, I realize that all high school kids have thoughts about things like that, and for a lot of them, it doesn't work out. I certainly had no assurance that it would be the way it was for me, but I can tell you on that afternoon, that experience changed my life. I was willing to work as hard as it took for that dream to come true. Fortunately it worked out for me."

With the military experience at Benedictine, Davis developed discipline which included motivation for efficient grades. When he departed that Greyhound late in the day, he had no reluctance to place high priority on his homework. "I loved the military. Simply loved it and loved it so much that I joined the Marines Reserve, which you could do at that time. This meant that I spent my summers at Parris Island. I was only 17-years-old and I always had lots of energy. The military occupied my time which was good for me at that point in my life."

When he enrolled at Georgia, he easily identified with the practice field work ethic and certainly not an after thought, he paid attention in class. Nobody on the coaching staff had to worry about his eligibility. He was going to apply himself on the field and in class with determination and efficiency. He was not going to allow any bad habit or circumstance to jeopardize that scholarship.

As player, his career was one in which he became consistently reliable. He found a way to block the man in front of him, and on defense, his rugged style, honed in the woods as a kid in Richmond Hill and polished in the trenches of competition at Benedictine, made him effective at getting to the ball carrier.

"With Georgia winning a championship in '59, I appreciated the success. But the thing I appreciate most of all was the fact that we came together as a team which you have to do in football. Of course, all of us appreciated Coach Whitworth's influence. He was like the pied piper. His motivation technique was special. I don't think anybody would deny that his impact made a difference in our team's success. I don't think our championship team was as good physically, as the 1958 team."

Graduation came following the 1960 season. Davis' degree in business was conferred the following summer. Football was over, life in the cruel world had begun, but for Hinton Davis, it would be a good and productive life. He was a successful salesman in insurance from the beginning and still does business today with some of the people he wrote policies for at the outset.

With familiarity with the logging industry, he was the first to develop a program to underwrite insurance for loggers. It was a pioneering program which has resulted in business for life. "One thing that really helped me in business," Hinton says, "is that there are graduates of the University of Georgia Forestry School everywhere, especially in the South. It was easy for me to get in to see people and to establish contacts. People appreciated that SEC championship, and being on that team opened a lot of doors for me."

When Hinton Davis reflects back, it is not lost on him that a field trip to Benedictine High School and a stopover in Athens to see the Bulldogs play between the hedges made a lasting impact on his life and career.

Bobby Green

When Bobby Green finished high school, he joined the Marines, which meant he was immediately undergoing the rigorous training at boot camp in Parris Island, S. C. As a result when he reported to fall football practice at Georgia, he found the regimen to be less taxing that most of his teammates found it.

"Now don't get me wrong," he laughs. "I think Coach Butts was one of the toughest coaches who ever wore a whistle around his neck. To be honest, I liked the way he coached. Football is fundamentals which means you have to scrimmage and try to outfight the guy across the line from you.

"When I finished high school, I went to boot camp with the Marines immediately. It was a reserve program back then which meant that I would spend my summers at Parris Island. This meant I was a step ahead of my teammates when I reported for football in Athens. It was no problem for me to adjust to the discipline that Coach Butts demanded. That boot camp experience gave me an advantage when I got to Georgia."

In the years since he played for the Little Round Man, Green has often thought of his good fortune. "One of the things about Coach Butts that was important to me was that I felt he was loyal to his players. He would fight for us. Throughout my business life, I have appreciated loyalty. If a man is not loyal, there is not much to him. Coach Butts was loyal to us. He was the kind of man I always wanted on my side. He would have been a hell of a Marine."

Green lettered in 1959 as a sophomore and was a regular in 1960 and 1961. His most memorable play came in 1960 in Lexington. Georgia played Kentucky on the road two years in a row, and like it usually was with the Wildcats, it was a hard fought game. The Bulldogs won 17-13 and Green scored one of his team's touchdowns. He tackled the quarterback in the end zone, forcing a fumble and recovering it for the only touchdown of his career.

The highlight of his career? "Well, yes," he says slowly. "In a sense it was. A lineman doesn't get many opportunities to score, and while I appreciate the good fortune that came my way, I think the highlight for me in Athens was the closeness we all felt. We lived in Payne Hall, and we did a lot of things together. We hung out together and we all wanted to help Coach Butts win. We felt he deserved that, and it was wonderful for all of us when he came back to win that championship late in his career. I'm a Wally Butts man."

With a degree in education, Bobby found success in sales. He traveled in the clothing business for 30 years, living in Houston most of that time.

"My business career was rewarding," he says, "but when I had an opportunity to come back to Georgia, I was ready. I feel close to Athens and those hedges, even though I make my home in Carrollton.

In Carrollton, he has embarked on a second career in the restaurant business. He and his son, Billy, own a barbecue restaurant.

The name? "Billy Bob's."

The slogan? "Y'all come!"

Of course.

TOMMY LEWIS

There were many exemplary attitudes in Tommy Lewis' makeup when he arrived at Georgia, a highly touted high school quarterback, in 1957.

To this day, Fran Tarkenton talks about his teammate's golden arm. "He could throw tight spirals, he had pace and zip on the ball. I always admired Tommy's ability to throw the football," Tarkenton says.

Things didn't quite work out for Tommy to achieve in Athens similar success to what he experienced at Decatur. He didn't complain. As a matter of fact the thing that made him different was that he appreciated the opportunity to letter and play in a reserve role on an SEC championship team. It was like he understood there is a role for every player on the team. Everybody couldn't be a star. There is room for those who persevere and accept a reserve assignment. Football is a team game and nobody had more of a team attitude than Tom Lewis.

Nobody ever had a more positive attitude. Even today, he remembers nothing but the good times he experienced in Athens.

An example of what made him exceptional, had to do with the ROTC program. All male students at all land grand colleges at the time were required to take two years of ROTC training. Most guys hated it. Up in early morning twice a week for drills. There were class requirements and shoes to shine.

Tom Lewis was different. He loved the military training. He wanted to be a pilot. He took advanced Air Force ROTC and became cadet colonel. He became a distinguished military pilot, an experience which led to his spending time in cockpits almost all his life.

After seven years in the military, much of the time as an instructor pilot, he flew for Eastern Air Lines for 25 years. When the carrier went under, he joined Knowledgeware, the software firm owned by his teammate, Fran Tarkenton. When Tarkenton sold Knowledgeware, Tommy returned to the cockpit with Air Tran Airways. He is now chief pilot for the airline.

His son, Tom Jr., followed in his footsteps, playing quarterback for the 'Dogs, flew for the Air Force until retirement and now flies for Air Tran. Both former quarterbacks are avid Dog fans.

When he was flying for Eastern we ran the following story for a Georgia football program.

After leaving Georgia, former Bulldog quarterback Tommy Lewis took to the wild, blue yonder. And he's still making touchdowns. At New York's Kennedy Airport, it is cloudy. Visibility is minimum. An 85 ton multimillion dollar jetliner pops through the murky overcast and touches down safely and smoothly on 10,000 feet of concrete. Nothing more than a routine and common occurrence for Eastern Air Lines and Tommy Lewis, Georgia quarterback, 1956-59.

"Although I never had a burning desire to be a pilot and actually got interested in flying while in the Air Force ROTC program at Georgia, I have a tremendous respect for the job done by commercial pilots," he says. "They have to be sharp, alert and dedicated to do their job and, in my case, I fell that I have a big asset by having athletic experience."

Tommy Lewis, fullback on the SEC championship team of 1959

"Coach Butts was a demanding coach; he worked at developing a precision attack in football, and that made my early pilot training much easier."

There is one significant contrast between athletics and piloting a plane, Tommy notes. Mistakes on the football field can often be overcome, but not in the air when you are handling a big jet.

"When I was in the Air Force, I thought that commercial flying was the country club of flying, but it didn't take me long to realize how wrong I was. It is the most exacting and precision work there is. You can never take a chance or risk anything when you are flying.

A pilot has the responsibility of getting his crew and the plane to its destination safe and on time. Beyond that, and more importantly, he has to think of the passengers sitting behind him. It is personally rewarding to us to complete a successful flight that we feel was enjoyable for everyone on the plane. Pilots have a lot of pride in their work, and they are the most dedicated professional people I have ever been around."

A pilot must not only be familiar with the more than 100-plus cockpit controls and switches, the 50 emergency items and a three page checklist for each departure. He must give visible inspection to such things as the wings and tires.

At Georgia, Tommy was an outstanding student and played quarterback with Charley Britt and Francis Tarkenton on the 1959 Southeastern Conference championship team that defeated Missouri in the Orange Bowl.

He was cadet colonel of the Air Force ROTC program and was a member of Sphinx, Gridiron, and KA social fraternity, Blue Key and Arnold Air Society.

BILL MCKENNY

Bill McKenny was one of the few sophomores with playing time as a starter on the 1959 team, but he often played like a seasoned veteran.

With limited substitution rules, Georgia organized two teams, which generally split the playing time. The teams were pretty much known as Britt's team and Tarkenton's team, senior Charley Britt and junior Francis Tarkenton alternating at quarterback. McKenny played on Tarkenton's team, and he didn't get the attention that Britt team halfbacks Fred Brown and Bobby Walden got, but McKenny distinguished himself as a competent back who often made big plays.

One of those big plays came in the first half of the Orange Bowl game New Year's Day 1960. Georgia, the favored team, had its hands full with a solid Missouri team, which played excellent defense all afternoon. It took two big plays to make the difference, two touchdown passes by Tarkenton. The first score of the game came on a Tarkenton pass to McKenny late in the first quarter. On third and 14, Tarkenton fired a 29-yard touchdown pass to McKenny.

"What I remember about the pass is that it was especially designed by coach Butts for the Missouri defense," McKenny said. "Our two ends would go down field and run out routes to the sidelines, taking the two defensive backs to the outside. I was playing right halfback and it was my job to slip through the line and run what we called a banana route to the left side of the field. The ends did their jobs perfectly, and I don't know what happened to the safety because he was nowhere in sight. I ran that curved route to the left end zone and Tarkenton hit me about the five-yard line or so as I recall. It was a 29-yard play."

The score was a particularly big thrill for him since he was a native of Jacksonville and his family and many

Bill McKenny scores in the Orange Bowl

of his friends had driven to Miami for the game. It was a joyful occasion to celebrate a bowl victory after the Bulldogs had paid the price for success.

"Coach Butts kept us in Athens, and we scrimmaged right on up until a couple of days before Christmas. We went to Miami and practiced the afternoon we arrived. We practiced hard, too. It was a fun experience, but I remember working awfully hard for the game. (We really didn't know any difference.) I think Coach Butts appreciated an opportunity to get back into prominence with his team, and he didn't want to take any chances that we might take Missouri for granted. Everybody had us favored and that only made Coach Butts work us harder."

McKenny recalls that the pass play which led to that first touchdown was very important to the Georgia coach. When the team ran it for the first time in practice in Miami, the execution was poor. "Coach Butts was upset the first couple of times we ran the play and he kept after us, running it over and over, until we got it right."

As a sophomore McKenny considered it a big thrill "just to be a member of the team." He was a quiet type, similar to the guy in the white hat in the old Western movies. McKenny belonged to the walk-softly-but-carry-a-big-stick fraternity. He never said much, letting his performance on the field do the talking.

He had played for Landon High in Jacksonville and was a highly regarded high school halfback. Florida put a lot of pressure on him to sign, which bothered McKenny, and when Coach Butts called on him and his family, the Bulldog coach entertained them with stories about Charley Trippi and Frank Sinkwich and told funny jokes. It relaxed McKenny, who appreciated the fact that there were no pressure tactics involved in his recruitment.

"But there was something about the Georgia people that I really liked," he says. "I felt very comfortable in Athens and was sold on the friendly atmosphere."

Lettering three years for the Bulldogs, McKenny played two years for Wally Butts and for Johnny Griffith his senior year. He was elected alternate captain his senior year. Pete Case, another of those sophomores to experience starting time in 1959, was elected captain. McKenny was moved to the left halfback in 1960 and while things didn't go as well on the field for the team, McKenny enjoyed notable success as the key back in the Bulldog offense.

"Hard work is the key to success," he says, "and Coach Butts taught us that you can do anything if you accept the challenge and set your mind to it."

When he left Georgia and entered the insurance business, McKenny often reflected on his days in Athens. "I thought about how it was in college. I enjoyed playing football, and fortunately, for us, we won a lot of games. There were days when practice was a challenge, but we always seemed to get by. Maybe we would rather have had it easier, but life is not easy.

Playing football under Wally Butts enabled me to develop a mental toughness about life and business. You believe when a challenge comes your way that you can handle it. We all have to make a living in this world, and those of us who succeed in life look back on some moment or experience that provided the direction to succeed. With me that confidence that I could succeed came from having played for Coach Butts who taught me that hard work and determination would enable me to handle whatever challenge came my way."

BILLY ROLAND

It was the sage advice of a Georgia alumnus that made Billy Roland aware that if he planned to live and work in the state where he had grown up, it would be to his advantage to enroll at the University of Georgia.

Up until his conversation with a local lawyer, a graduate of the institution, he was headed to Auburn. He never even went to Athens for a campus visit, but Broughton Hayes, a highly respected member of the Colquitt community, had a talk with him that made a lasting impression.

"Son," the gentlemanly lawyer said. "I like you, and I like your family. I want the best for you, and I have not bothered you up to this point. Have you made up your mind about where you are going to school?"

Roland was a little uncomfortable, but he told the truth. "Well, Mr. Hayes, I kinda like Auburn. I have visited over there and they seem to want me."

Without any emotion, Hayes began to point out a few things that Roland had not thought about. "You would be wise to go the University if you plan to live in this state. You'll make friends, you'll meet people who will help you in business. I think you ought to consider that."

Billy did. He saw the logic, and he was ready to ink a grant-in-aid when Spec Towns and Jim Whatley showed up the next day at his principal's office. When the word got out that he had signed with the Bulldogs, a couple of Auburn coaches lit out for Colquitt post haste.

They began to question his decision, but he stood firm. All the time, he was thinking about what Broughton Hayes had told him. It sank in and today he is grateful. "He could not have been more right. I believe things have gone reasonably well for me in life, and I owe it all to the University of Georgia.

"Wherever I go in this state, people talk about Georgia and the Bulldogs. I still meet people who remember our SEC championship team of 1959. Mr. Hayes made me rethink my decision, and I'll always appreciate his advice."

Roland did have second thoughts as a freshman,

however. He was listed on the depth chart at No. 5 at fullback. He foresaw limited playing time, and was not happy. He was sitting on the Payne Hall steps in a disconsolate mood late one day and decided he would transfer to Troy State, where his brother was playing football.

Billy Roland found a home in the line

Assistant Coach Sam Mrvos observed Roland's downcast mood and told him to wait until he had a conversation with Coach Butts. The next day, Roland moved to the line, a decision that was to benefit both team and player.

"We were getting ready to play the Tech freshmen on Thanksgiving Day," he remembers. I didn't know any of the plays. They had to tell me what to do, who to block. I had to feel my way, but on defense, you can hit people and go for the ball carrier. I liked that, and immediately, I realized I had found a home. They had thrown B'rer Rabbit into the Briarpatch."

His sophomore year, things began to change at Georgia. It was not a season to remember when you consider wins and losses (3-7), but that was the year the drought was broken on Grant Field. On Theron Sapp's score for the touchdown, Roland lined up at right guard beside tackle Nat Dye.

"We're going for it, somebody said," Roland recalls. "I was a scared sophomore, but I knew I had to help. I had a good afternoon with the guy in front of me and got down on him pretty good. Nat and Jimmy Orr made their blocks, and when I looked up, I saw Sapp powering through the hole. I knew we had won a game that meant a lot to Georgia and Coach Butts. We all knew he had suffered more than anybody with Tech's good luck against Georgia. All the players wanted to win for him and the Bulldog fans. I felt like I could stop at any town in Georgia after that and get a free lunch. People really appreciated that victory."

After a frustrating season in '58 when the Dogs won but four games, serendipity graced Georgia's season when Roland was a senior. "Winning the championship meant we were back on top where we should be," Roland says.

Following the Orange Bowl, he signed with the Washington Redskins, but a broken ankle in the spring of the year ended his football career. Memory of that off-the-field injury remains regrettable to this day. "It snowed heavily in the spring," Billy painfully recalls. "Most of us had never seen snow like that, and we were sliding down some hills on makeshift sleds. I thought I'd outsmart everybody. I put on my football cleats so I could climb the hills easier, but while on the sled we were using to slide down the hill, my cleats got hung up in some grass underneath the snow. I heard it pop."

The break was really bad, and he was never the same for football. Roland reported to the Redskins, but dejectedly realized he couldn't maneuver like his old self. He went to training camp a year later, and nothing had changed. Football players can't get the job done, hobblingly about on one leg. He joined the national guard, got his degree and became a high school coach. Later, he sold insurance and built houses. After that, he landed a state job with Georgia Correctional Industries following a conversation with former House Speaker Tom Murphy, who remembered him at Georgia.

"When I left the speaker's office, with an attractive job with the state, I thought about that conversation with Mr. Hayes. I sure am glad I chose the University of Georgia."

BILLY SLAUGHTER

Billy Slaughter was one of five players on his Athens High team to earn a scholarship to play for the Bulldogs. After the 1955 Trojans claimed the state championship, the Bulldogs signed him, Carlton James, George Guissler, Sonny Dillard and Bobby Towns.

Slaughter had an inkling that he might be included since Coach Butts told his good friend Fain Slaughter Sr., Billy's father, "we want several of those boys."

The Butts and Slaughters were social friends, and Billy frequently saw the Georgia coach dropping by his house. His dad often traveled with the team.

Nonetheless, Billy knew that when he walked through the practice field gates, friendships and family ties meant nothing to Bulldog head man. "I knew I would be treated like everybody else, which meant I had to buckle my chinstrap and go to work."

He even endured the humorous wrath, on the practice field, that Coach Butts' was famous for. "He had a way of cracking us up in practice. We didn't want to laugh, but it was so hard to hold back," Billy remembers. "One day, he asked me to throw a pass to simulate an opposing team's halfback pass. I was on the B-team, where I spent most of my career, and I had a hurt shoulder. They fitted me with big sized shoulder pads because of the injury, and I thought to myself, 'how can I throw a ball with these pads?' Sure enough I tried, and predictably, the ball missed the receiver by several yards, falling way short."

It turned out to be one of the most memorable moments of Slaughter's days on the practice field. He'll never forget the comment of his colorful coach, who went into a rage at the poorly thrown ball. "That pass of Slaughter's looked like the last shot out of a Roman Candle," Coach Butts screamed.

Slaughter enjoyed a special relationship with line coach J. B. Whitworth. "Even in high school, I was an early riser, and Coach Whit was, too. Our families lived in the Five Points neighborhood, and I often went over to his house for breakfast. We would talk about a lot of things. By just talking, friendly conversation, he gave me a lot of good advice. He wasn't trying to advise me on a particular point, he was just talking. But there were so many things he said about life that made sense, and I will always appreciate having the opportunity to sit and listen to him.

"He and coach Butts were a great combination. Things went downhill after he left, but when he came back in 1959, you saw what happened. I've often wondered what things would have been like in the Fifties if Coach Whit would have still been with Coach Butts."

BOBBY WALDEN

Bobby Walden, Bulldog punter of renown, was pretty much self taught. It was a matter of kicking a football, retrieving it, kicking it again for hours upon hours, creating feel and style by instinct.

His father bought him a regulation Wilson football when he was five years old. Bobby spent a lot of time on his grandfather's farm outside Cairo, and whenever

Bobby Walden was more than a punter

he was there, he was always outside kicking that Wilson ball which became battered and misshapen with the passing of time.

There is something to be said for those times and the lack of organization for kids and sports. If Walden had not grown up with all that time alone on the farm before he got into organized sports in high school, he might not have developed his classic punting style. He could thrust balls in the air that soared up and away. Some of that was leg strength, which certainly enhanced his success.

In his college years in Athens, defense in those one platoon years was, in many respects, more important than offense. A power punter complemented savvy defense. Few punters had the leg power of Bobby Walden, but he developed his style back on his grandfather's farm.

One fall day, he saw his grandfather, with a long fishing pole, trying to knock pecans out of the trees in the back yard. He decided to offer an assist. He began kicking his ball up into the trees, shaking pecans loose. He would also stand a good distance away and kick his ball into the tree. It would rattle around, knocking pecans loose from their clusters.

All the time he was aiming his punts, learning to direct the ball to a specific target—but not with any plan or purpose. He was just a boy having fun, finding something to do.

There was no television, the family didn't subscribe to the newspaper, and the radio was for listening to the weather and the Grand Ole Opry. A country boy had to entertain himself. Bobby Walden did it by kicking that Wilson football.

Little did he know that his early life with that ball would lead to an SEC championship ring with the Dogs and two Super Bowl rings with the Pittsburgh Steelers. His punting artistry, in part, was responsible for his receiving a scholarship to play football at the University of Georgia, but he arrived in Athens with interest beyond punting. "I wanted to play," he says. "I didn't consider myself a punting specialist."

He did play, winding up a starting halfback on the SEC championship team of 1959. Here are the highlights of his Georgia career when he was the regular halfback and punter: Led NCAA and SEC in punting as sophomore in 1958 with 45.3 average; as junior in '59, made All-SEC second team as left halfback, also averaged 40.3 yards per punt; led team kickoff returns with 26.8 yard average; as senior in '60 led SEC in punting with 43.6 yards per punt, set Orange Bowl punting record in '61 game with 46.9 yards per kick average on seven punts, and in '61 Senior Bowl, set all-time bowl punting record of 49.8 yards per kick on five punts.

Walden was a complete player but is probably best remembered for his booming punts which led the creative guru of Bulldog football, Dan Magill, to dub him "The Big Toe from Cairo."

After Georgia, Walden signed with Edmonton of the Canadian League. He played halfback and punted, but following an injury his second season, the club released him.

When he started the long drive home, he perused a map and realized Minneapolis would be a convenient stop. He could visit his old friend and teammate, Fran Tarkenton. Good decision. Tarkenton recommended Walden to Coach Norm Van Brocklin, who signed him to a contract with the taxi squad. He later made the team and became the Viking punter for four years. Walden was subsequently traded to Pittsburgh, where he played for 10 years.

His first season in Pittsburgh left him with a sour taste in his mouth. Too much disorganization, no respect for the coach and no unity. He thought that he was finished with the NFL, but that is when the Steeler organization cleaned house, hired Chuck Noll and began the run to four Super Bowl championships. Walden decided he would give it one more year. When he checked in for training camp, he saw stunning change. Chuck Noll was organized. He knew what he was doing. Discipline was underscored, and if you didn't like his rules, you turned in your playbook and hit the road.

"I liked the way Chuck did things, I felt that we could win with him, and I am happy that I chose to stay longer in Pittsburgh," he says. "When you are with a winning team, it is great fun in a community like Pittsburgh where everybody has great feelings for the Steelers."

His professional career highlights: led Canadian Football League in punting, rushing, and receiving in 1961 and '62 with Edmonton; began NFL career with Minnesota Vikings in '63 and led league in punting with 46.4 yards per kick average; traded to Pittsburgh in '67 where he led NFL in punting several times over the next 10 seasons: Steelers all-time leading punter, played on two Steelers Super Bowl championship teams (IX and X), All-Pro selection in 1974.

At age forty, following the 1977 season, Walden decided it was time to retire. The times had been good, he owned two Super Bowl rings and chose to return home to South Georgia. He and his wife, Charlotte, live in Bainbridge and his football is confined to Sunday television. He refuses to fly, saying, "I wouldn't get on an airplane today if you held a gun on me. The big problem is that if I got on a plane, my concern might be that some damn fool might have a gun," holding little regard for security measures in today's high tech world.

Tennessee recruited him heavily when he was a senior in high school. Walden, as an summary of his career indicates, could do more than punt and the Volunteers told him he could be the player to replace their All-American tailback, Johnny Majors. They saw Walden as a triple threat back.

He broke his leg as a high school senior and all interest ceased, except from Coach Butts. "He told me I had a scholarship whether I played football or not. I have never forgotten that. That told me something about him. Everybody else is backing off, and he says I've got a scholarship even if I don't play football. Of course, I was going to play, but I've always appreciated what he did for me."

Walden played left halfback his freshman year, moved to right half for his varsity years, and punted. He surprised a few defenses with the halfback pass and remembers that his freshman team in 1957 could hold its own with the varsity.

What he remembers most, beyond Coach Butts' commitment and the SEC championship, is making the decision to drive through Minneapolis to visit an old friend. "Francis Tarkenton believed I could make it in the NFL, and he sold Norm Van Brocklin. I had a good pro career because of him going to bat for me."

BILL HERRON

Bill Herron spent little time in Athens. He enrolled after graduating from Fresno Junior College, played two years for the Bulldogs and went back after graduation, to his hometown of Sanger, Ca. He returned to Athens in 1979, his only time in the Classic City following graduation, for a 20 year reunion of the team that defeated Auburn 14-13 for the SEC title.

"The Auburn game is important to me today," says Herron, "because of it being for the championship, but there is more to it than that for me. I always felt that Coach Butts expected more out of me because of the junior college reputation I had. I got hurt the first game I played at Georgia, against Texas in 1958. It was a neck injury and was one that lingered on and on. I wasn't really completely well except for my last three games at Georgia. I played my best against Florida, Auburn and Tech and felt like I had repaid Georgia for my scholarship. I had a good feeling at the end of the year for that reason."

Herron was recruited to Georgia because of playing in a junior college all-star game in Jackson, Miss. Frank Jones, Coach Butts' son-in-law, spotted Herron and recommended him to the Georgia coach. Butts sent Wyatt Posey to sign Herron, who was attracted to the campus because of the people he met while in Athens for a visit.

Bill Herron: Auburn game still important to the Californian

"I live a long way from Athens but I think about my time there quite often."

PAT SMITH

Dating back to the days of Harry Mehre, Georgia always had an intermittent presence in Miami. The Bulldogs played the Miami Hurricanes through the years, and in 1956 the underdog team from Athens played the nationally ranked Hurricanes off their feet. The game ended in a 7-7 tie. It was like a big upset for the visiting team, which won only three games that year.

Given the circumstances, it is somewhat surprising that Pat Smith, the son of a rabid Hurricane fan, would wind up at a school which had been experiencing down times. Miami, his dad's favorite team, never arm twisted Pat, and he developed a favorable impression after a visit to Athens.

It would be a good decision in that he would become a member of a championship team (1959) and would wind up playing in the Orange Bowl in his home town.

"We had good high school football in Miami," Smith says, "and Georgia had recruited two players from my team already. They invited Ray Clark and me

Pat Smith: Georgia was in good hands with this Miami native

to Athens for a visit, and we just felt good about being around those guys who were such down to earth people, so we decided Georgia was the place for us.

"Naturally, we wanted to win, but didn't worry about that. We liked Athens, and we believed in Coach Butts. Turns out that we made good decisions."

College football was still governed by one platoon rules. Substitution restriction was eased somewhat for specialists, but for the most part, you had to play both ways. A center-linebacker in high school, Pat was utilized on primarily defense in 1959 when Georgia won the SEC title. "When Don Soberdash, our captain, returned from an injury, I got in there less and less," he remembers.

This meant that on the drive that won the Auburn game and clinching the title, Soberdash was in the lineup when Georgia scored the winning points. "I wouldn't have been in there on offense anyway," Pat remembers, "but I will never forget that drive. I was down about the 35 yard line, and I saw the play—the pass from Fran Tarkenton to Bill Herron—unfold. I saw Herron break open, and I was shouting, like Francis could hear me, 'Throw it to Bill, throw it to Bill.'"

"In a situation like that, the whole play takes seconds, but when you are close to the action, when you are one of the players, you see things develop and you are overcome with anticipation. You know in an instant what can happen. You know there is an opportunity for a play to succeed. When I saw the ball in the air and realized how open Herron was, I said to myself, 'We are going to win this game.'

"It was the most memorable time of my career, and whenever I am around teammates who played in '59, we still enjoy recalling that high moment in Sanford Stadium."

Smith became a regular in 1960, 61, at center. Injured in the final game of his senior season, he never fully recovered. His bad knee was injured again after signing with the Houston Oilers in 1962. He returned and tried to make the team a year later and hurt the knee again.

"I thought then that it was best to get on with some other interest," he says. He began a sales career with State Farm that has been successful and rewarding.

The cousin of Donna Shalala, President of the University of Miami, he has often attended Hurricane games as her guest, but Georgia is always on his mind. "I always check on the 'Dogs," he says. "I never will lose my attachment to the University of Georgia."

With a second home at The Cliffs, a golf resort at Glassy Mountain, S.C., he expects to spend more of his time there in the future. "It is not far from Athens, and one of the reasons I like it is that it is relatively convenient to the Bulldogs. I want to see more games between the hedges."

Whenever he hears All-State's slogan, "You're in good hands," he often reflects back to Bill Herron's catch against Auburn. "I knew if Francis got the ball to Bill, it was a touchdown," he says.

Bobby Towns

When Bobby Towns grew up, he took for granted his special relationship with Georgia athletics, not considering that it was special. It was simply a situation in which he traveled with the team, walked into the locker room or on the sideline whenever it suited. He even had Bulldog equipment at his disposal.

His dad, Forrest "Spec" Towns was a coach and recruiter and his grandfather, Pap Eberhardt, was the equipment manager. Coaches kids of coaches today enjoy similar treatment but don't have it quite like it was in Towns' youth.

Today's kids might get some of the same benefits, but none of them can slide down the hill on the Northwest side of the stadium. They can't watch the game from the sideline if they choose and they are not likely to ride the team buses to the stadium, especially for road games.

"When you are seven, eight years old, you enjoy the excitement of football, but you are a kid and you do what kids do," Towns said. "There were no stands on the Northwest side of the stadium, so we would get cardboard boxes and create makeshift slides and scoot down the hill while the Bulldogs played between the hedges. That was great fun when you were that age."

The hill gave way to the Athens YMCA games at the stadium, and he first played between the hedges when he was one of the YMCA kids. Then he played his high school games at Sanford Stadium, a prelude to wearing the Red and Black for his collegiate career.

Yet, his decision on where to enroll was left entirely up to him. Auburn and Georgia Tech were high on his list, but deep down his heart was always Red and Black. There were a couple of incidents that figured into his final decisions. When he went to Auburn for his official visit they put him in a room with a bed that had dirty sheets, and when Tech invited him over for a game, the opponent was Georgia. He'll never forget.

"It was the game when Bobby Garrard got loose for a long run and lost a shoe. I was running down the sideline with him as he ran toward the goal line. I saw Coach (Bobby) Dodd looking at me cheering for Bobby and I just sort of slipped around the end zone to the Georgia side of the field.

"Later I apologized to Coach Dodd and told him I just couldn't help it, Georgia was in my blood. He said he understood, but that made me realize I could never go anywhere else to school."

He became a starter in the backfield for the Bulldogs and claimed points in the hurdles and sprints on his dad's track team.

He grew up with all the Bulldog stars of the forties, traveling to bowl games in New Orleans, Miami and Jacksonville. He knew the legend of his father, claiming the Olympic gold at Berlin in the high hurdles in 1936.

Bobby Towns, a versatile halfback

Interestingly, he got interested in running hurdles in high school more by appointment than choice. The football coach at Athens High, Weyman Sellers, announced to the players one day that the school would be fielding a track team and told Towns he would run the hurdles.

"Coach I don't know anything about running the hurdles," Towns protested. "You ought to," Sellers shot back. "Your daddy ran the hurdles."

That is how Bobby Towns became a hurdler. He won his first hurdles race in a short week of practice in the less than stunning time of 18.8, a full five and one tenth seconds slower than his dad ran them in Oslo, Norway after the Olympics to set a standard that stood for almost two decades. Bobby's form was awful, his steps between hurdles were out of sequence, and his dad, who happened to see the race, was hot.

When he walked up to his son, Bobby was expecting congratulations. After all he had won the race, but the old man, who seldom was without an opinion or lack of fire when he was perturbed, tersely announced to Bobby. "I never told you that you had to run track, and I sure as hell never told you that you had to run the hurdles—but damnit, if you are going to run the hurdles, you are going to learn how to do it and not embarrass me like this."

Bobby was shocked, but after regrouping his emotions, he realized that he should not have been. His dad never tried to dictate his career, but was only trying to help. By teaching his son "how" to run the hurdles, in the next race, Bobby shaved 3.6 seconds off his time.

His senior year in football was 1959, the championship year. Other than the Auburn game in Sanford Stadium, the toughest game for the Dogs to win was on a bitterly cold night in Lexington, Ky. Georgia won 14-7, and it took two brilliant defensive plays to provide the victory. The late Larry Lancaster blocked a punt for a TD, but Towns got the Bulldogs on the board with one of the most sensational pass interceptions in the history of Bulldog football.

From his defensive back position, and with cagey timing, he, at the last split second leaped up to snatch a Wildcat pass away from a talented pass receiver, Roger Bird, maintain his balance and sprint 43 yards to the end zone for a touchdown. In photos, you can see Bird's hands poised for the catch, which appeared to be a certainty until the quick and cogent Towns literally stole the ball away.

After Georgia, Towns spent three years in pro football, two with the St. Louis Cardinals and one with the Boston Patriots. Following pro ball it was two years in the Army (he played on a team that won the service championship) and into a career in insurance sales.

The way it has turned out, he has never been away from college football since he got away from sliding down that hill in Sanford Stadium as a kid. In high school, he sold programs for the Georgia games and following college, pro and service football, he got into officiating. He was an SEC official for 29 years, officiating two national championship games.

If you show up at a Georgia practice today, he's still out there in his striped shirt with a yellow flag in his back pocket. At Coach Mark Richt's behest, Towns and a crew of officials call infractions in all contact drills. It was Richt's decision with the objective of trying to help his team learn to cut down on rules infractions.

Don Leebern

After his father's death, Don Leebern left Georgia and took over the business, Georgia Crown Distributing Co., in 1960. At the time, the company had warehouse and distributing operations only in Columbus and Albany. Today, Georgia Crown also has operations in Tennessee and Alabama and there is an annual increase in sales. Growth of the company has been as predictable as sunrise.

To begin with, he did start with a good base. His daddy, Don Leebern Sr., had the company well established in Columbus, but when his son took over, he began an expansion that eventually made him one of the largest liquor, wine and beer distributors in the state. Bottled water has become big with Georgia Crown, too, and if you purchase a bottle of Melwood Springs from your favorite grocery shelf, you are taking home North Georgia water labeled under Leebern's middle name.

Donald Melwood Leebern, a successful businessman and former Chairman of the Board of Regents, enjoys reminiscing about his Bulldog football past, which includes starting status at tackle on the '59 SEC championship team. He is quick to point out that his empire was built on the principles he learned on the practice field in Athens. "It is very simple," he says. "Hard work wins out in business just like it does in football. I was motivated to learn, succeed and improve on the field by men like Coach Whitworth, Coach Whatley, and, of course, Coach Butts."

When he talks about Coach Butts, he pauses and speaks with appreciative reverence. He will never forget what the Bulldog coach did for him on a cold December day in 1957. Leebern had driven to Atlanta on a Friday for a playoff game between Columbus High and Northside. His brother, Fate, was the Columbus quarterback. His father was at the game, too, but Don left early and spent the night with friends in Atlanta. Nobody knew where he was. Consequently, he was unaware his father had suffered a fatal heart attack at the game and had died.

Upon returning to Athens the next morning, he was met by Coach Quinton Lumpkin, who told him he needed to go to Stegeman Hall and to see Coach Butts. Don's first reaction, because of deep and abiding respect for his coach, was to wonder what he had done wrong.

Don Leebern will always remember Coach Butts' kindness

When he walked into the head coach's office, he saw Coach Butts with his head on his desk. The coach was mourning the death of a close friend, Don's daddy. After breaking the news to Don, his coach took him by Payne Hall where his teammates had packed his clothes for him.

Coach Butts then drove Leebern to Columbus, an act of friendship that overwhelmed the young tackle. "You can't imagine how much respect I had for Coach Butts," Leebern says. "And for him to drive me home when I was in such a state of sorrow is something I will never forget."

That respect, in part, motivated Leebern to make the first $500,000 contribution to the Butts-Mehre Building. If you tour the ground floor locker rooms today, you will find Leebern's name above the entrance.

"I feel I owe Coach Butts and Georgia so much," Leebern says. "It was an easy decision for me to contribute to that campaign. I experienced some great times playing football in Athens, and I am one of those former players who wants the best for the young men who play for us today."

Then he laughs and notes, "Because of my dad's friendship with Coach Butts, I saw him around the house from time to time, but that didn't mean anything when I walked on that practice field. There was no way he would let up on me because he was friends with my father. My teammates knew that, too. Friendships stopped when you went out to practice."

He remembers his collegiate days with great affection. "Those friendships, the buddies you make while you play football last a lifetime. I never pass up an opportunity to laugh and recall those times on the practice field when a coach would say something that would stick in your mind forever.

"I remember one day, we were scrimmaging longer than usual. We were tired and someone mumbled something about that under their breath. Coach Whatley overheard the comment and said: 'How can you be tired. Fatigue is a state of mind and not a damn one of you out here has a mind.' There were a lot of times when things were said like that which made us laugh about it later. I always thought our coaches had an innate ability to read the situation so well.

"When I talk to my old teammates today, we remember some of those practice field conversations, we laugh about it, and we'll never tire of recalling those days."

"What I appreciate most about my time as a player are the friendships that I made. I learned about dedication too. I learned that when you got hurt, you kept on playing. Sometimes in business, things might go differently from what you want, but you don't hang your head, you just keep on persevering."

Leebern became a starter at tackle his junior year. He wasn't a heralded lineman, but his dedication and fight warmed his line coach's heart. Whitworth appreciated No. 77's ambition and commitment. The guy who lined up across from Leebern knew he would be in a dog-fight. All afternoon. His daddy raised him to appreciate the tough side of life, which was good experience when he fought for a starting position with the Bulldogs.

How often does he think about his practice field training when he walks into his high tech office and warehouse which covers much of a forty acre plot near McDonough?

"Every day," he smiles with appreciation.

Lee Cummings

Life for Lee Cummings, Georgia halfback in 1959, has been an accumulation of experiences. Lettering on the '59 SEC championship team was one of them. "I got more out of that one year—experiencing Coach Butts at his best with an underdog team and making life long friendships—that some who started every year and made All-America," he says.

While in college, he found summer jobs in Hawaii and Alaska, seeking every opportunity to explore the West, which so fascinated him that he has spent considerable time in the summers reconnoitering landscapes in the Midwest, the Rockies and beyond.

He is a dedicated Lewis and Clark aficionado and has followed their pioneering excursion from St. Louis to their destination to the Pacific and back to the starting point, the city on the Mississippi famous for its Arch, Budweiser and Cardinals. He has made his treks by land, but don't count him out when it comes to following the path of the two 19th century advocates of "Undaunted Courage," by boat. There's time left.

Lee has followed portions of the Oregon Trail in reverse from Portland to its starting point, Independence, Mo. He has retraced Mormon trails across Utah and has explored the Grand Canyon.

His deep and abiding affection for the West began when he hitched hiked across the country and up to Alaska where he found a job in the summer of 1957. Another summer he hitchhiked to New Mexico and worked on a ranch. While he has never been moved to take up permanent residency out West, he retains an enduring passion to revisit the area of the country which captivated him at a time when your poised thumb on the side of the road was often greeted by hospitable motorists, who were obliged to offer a young college age traveler a lift.

After playing football at West Georgia in 1956-57, Cummings transferred to Georgia in 1958 and walked on. The appropriate term in those days was, "try out." Coach Butts took a liking to him, much of it having to do with Cummingss' attitude.

"I grew up with a stern father, who felt that you ought to work hard at anything and everything. Coach Butts reminded me of my daddy. In fact, I was scared to death of both of them. I was used to firm discipline when I got to Athens, so it never bothered me that the scrimmages were long, hard and demanding. I wasn't much player, but I actually enjoyed those physical scrimmages. I think Coach Butts appreciated that. At least he made me feel that way."

The summer of '59 Lee enjoyed an experience which graphically explains how different those times were, compared to today. He explains:

"I knew some girls, who were at Auburn, and who planned to travel to Los Angeles and take a boat over to Honolulu where they had jobs for the summer. I thought I ought to get on that boat, but I had two things to take care of. First, I needed to complete one course to become eligible for football in the fall. My professor told me he would help me out by sending correspondence course materials to Hawaii.

The other matter was a bill that I had at Dick Ferguson's. It wasn't much, about $25.00 or $30.00 as I recall. I went down and explained to the folks there that I would be working all summer and should be able to pay them off when I returned for fall football practice. They were understanding, so I hitchhiked to L.A., and got on the boat to Hawaii with those girls. I found a construction job, completed my correspondence course, saved enough money to pay off Dick Ferguson's and enough to fly home.

"When I got back, I went up to pay off my bill at Ferguson's, and they told me it had been taken care of. They didn't tell me who, but I knew who it was. Coach Butts wasn't just generous to those who could play, he was equally generous to nobodies like me.

"For the Florida game that year, he called me into his office, gave me a hundred dollars in cash. Then he told me to find four or five other players on the team who were not on the traveling squad and to take them with me to the game. He knew I didn't have a car, so he told me to go out to Heyward Allen's and one would be waiting for me. I drove several of my teammates down to the game, using the money he gave me for gas and food for the group. We stayed at the team hotel where he had arranged rooms for us.

"That meant a lot to those of us who were scrubs on the team, but we were proud to be Bulldogs and Wally Butts' players. I've always thought about his gestures in the short time I was on the team."

With a degree in education, Cummings returned to his hometown of Rockmart and eventually settled in with a real estate and property rental company. His main interests today include his birddogs, wildlife conservation and environmental projects. "Anybody who is not concerned about the environment is damn foolish," he says.

Not as foolish as hitchhiking, perhaps. In an earlier day that was okay. "And so was the environment," he says.

DURWARD PENNINGTON

Nicknamed "the automatic toe" for his consistency as a place kicker on Wallace Butts' last SEC championship team, Durward Pennington remains one of the most successful kickers ever to play at Georgia.

He and Leo Costa are the two kickers from the Butts' era who are best remembered. And for good reason. Costa, too, played on a championship team, including the Rose Bowl. After falling on hard times in the Fifties, Georgia came back to claim the conference title with Pennington, a placement specialist who only missed one extra point in his career.

A check of the records reveals how valuable he was in his time as a Bulldog: His extra point won the Georgia-Auburn game, 14-13 for the SEC title in 1959. His extra point was the margin of victory in 1960 to defeat Georgia Tech, 7-6, and extended the streak over the Jackets to four in a row. He kicked two field goals to beat Mississippi State in Athens in 1960, one to tie and one to win, 20-17. The Bulldogs won only three games in 1961, all on field goals by Pennington. Over South Carolina 17-14 in Athens; Mississippi State 10-7 in Atlanta and Kentucky 16-15 between the hedges.

It was against Kentucky that he missed his only PAT, and as it turned out, no ill effect. That was also the game when he kicked his longest field goal, 52 yards—a record for distance, which was later broken by Rex Robinson. He remembers well what happened prior to that kick. "I made a field goal from 47 yards out, but we were off sides and had to kick it over. Fortunately, I made it."

His kicking career began at Albany High School where Pat Field, former Georgia punter, told him in the ninth grade that he should try placement kicking. He became the team kicker, but was a starter at quarterback his junior and senior years. The Bulldog staff recruited him to play quarterback.

In 1959, the late Sterling DuPree, on a summer trip to Southwest Georgia, took Pennington's equipment to Albany and advised the 6-2 junior that he would be doing all the place kicking.

Why was he a successful kicker? "I'm not exactly sure," he says, "but I did work at it." This meant he was compatible with the lonely life of a kicker, who must work by himself. "Beats all that scrimmaging," he laughs. Tall, with a fluid kicking motion, Pennington possessed exceptional leverage for distance. Hard work gave him a repetitive swing like a golfer hitting long iron shots.

In the off season, he kicked all summer, and when he was kicking during daily practice in the fall, he never goofed off, taking the approach of a dedicated golfer hitting shots over and over on the practice tee. Durward took a bag of balls and kicked each one through the uprights, backing up to varying distances and moving from hash mark to hash mark to practice every conceivable angle. He then would retrieve the balls and would go through the routine again.

If he had any interest in lagging through his work, he knew what would happen. Line coach J.B. Whitworth, also in charge of kickers Pennington's junior year, expected kickers to work hard, "to become good at their specialty." Whitworth, who joined the Bulldog staff from the Canadian League for the championship season, was also notorious for meting out harsh punishment for kickers who looked up when they kicked.

In a previous chapter, we learned what he did to Leo Costa for taking a peek. Durward endured a similar fate. Early in the season, he missed a field goal attempt, and when he came off the field, he was confronted by Whitworth.

"Son, where did you miss the kick?"

"To the right," Pennington replied.

Nothing more was said, but when he showed up for practice on Monday, Whitworth sent him running laps, just like he did Costa for the same offense, nearly two decades prior.

As Durward began his laps around the practice field, Whitworth said, "I'm not punishing you for missing a kick, I'm punishing you for looking up."

It was a lesson that the Bulldog kicker never forgot. "I don't ever recall seeing any of my kicks go through after that. It left an impact on me that I'll never forget. It was invaluable in that lifting your head, just a little prematurely, can affect accuracy significantly.

Pennington used a square-toed shoe, which was manufactured by the Ridell Company. In his days at Georgia, nobody was more accurate in the Southeastern Conference, but he received a big scare during his senior season when somebody stole his kicking shoes from the old field house. It was his only pair.

Dan Magill had it amply covered by the newspapers, and a couple of days later, the shoes were back—returned as mysteriously as they had disappeared.

Graduating on time, Pennington made plans to coach, an ambition when he entered college. He took time out for a brief fling with the pros. Drafted by the Buffalo Bills, he wound up with the Dallas Texans, playing the better part of two years with the Texans and, subsequently, the Oakland Raiders. John Rauch, who had marveled at Pennington's accuracy as an assistant in Athens, brought him out to the West Coast.

He didn't like the California life. His wife, Betsy, had returned to Gainesville, where they would settle, and he wasn't inclined to follow the nomadic life of modestly paid kickers in the pro game of those times. Furthermore, he had always wanted to coach and he was able to work that out after a brief tenure with Southeastern Freezer Co.

After a decade of coaching, he went into the motel business with his father-in-law, but assisted Gainesville High Coach, Bobby Gruhn, with the secondary and kickers.

Today, he remains a volunteer coach. He also has a number of business investments, but is always eager when football practice comes around in August. A young kid might need some encouragement, and he would be pleased to pass on his advice. Like Pat Field did to him in Albany in the mid-fifties.

Aaron Box

Aaron Box scored the second touchdown in Georgia's 14-0 victory over Missouri in the Orange Bowl, New Year's Day, 1961.

It was a 33 yard catch and run, and Box remembers vividly what took place. "If you are a receiver, you can pick up on how the defense will play you. They show certain tendencies, and you can read what they are doing and react to get open.

"In the Orange Bowl, I noticed that the defensive halfback was playing to make sure that I would not break to the outside – to run out routes to the sideline. After a few plays on offense, I could tell that he could be beaten to the inside. I went to the huddle and told Fran Tarkenton I could get open to the inside. Those of us who played with Fran were not surprised that he was a great pro quarterback. He demonstrated back then that he was a special player. He was a thinker. He could react to what the defense was doing.

"Interestingly on the play I scored, I was to run a route to the sideline, but the defensive back committed to the sideline. Immediately, I pivoted and went to the inside, what they call a post route today. Fran was alert, saw what happened and hit me over the middle. I had the middle all to myself. I don't think I have ever been more open for a pass in my life."

That remains a treasured memory for him today. Growing up in Live Oak, FL, it was particularly special to be able to play in the Orange Bowl. "And to have an opportunity to score in that game on national television is something I will always appreciate," Box says. "Everybody in Florida took an interest in the Orange Bowl."

A lasting memory, too, is his recruiting experience. He was recruited primarily by Jim Whatley. He was working in construction when Whatley along with his high school coach came to see him. "I was running a front end loader," Box recalls. "It was hot and dusty; I was dirty and sweaty and I didn't want to talk to anybody."

Whatley immediately saw in Box a positive work ethic that would make him compatible with the practice field style of Coach Butts. Box liked Whatley, and he liked Coach Butts, but what sold him on Georgia was that first visit to the campus.

"I had confidence in my ability," Box says. "I had good speed for a receiver, and I didn't mind the tough scrimmaging. I had grown up working outdoors and football wasn't work the way I saw it.

"Coach Towns drove me to Athens in the fall of my senior year in high school. It was October, and the leaves were turning. It was at the peak of leaf season, and growing up in Florida, I didn't see as many hardwoods as there were on the Georgia campus. It was so pretty. I was taken by the scene immediate, but what really sold me on Georgia was the players.

"The first player I met was Billy Roland. I was raised around people like him, people who worked hard and would do anything in the world for a friend. I met other players who were just like him, and realized right away Athens was the place for me. Georgia didn't have to sell me any further. I was ready to sign. I knew I would fit in Athens."

He played a year in Canada after college, having to give up football due to a stomach condition which resulted from an accident as a kid when he accidentally pierced his stomach with a sharp pointed branding iron. The accident left scar tissue, which resulted in a latent infection that permanently sidelined him while he was playing for Edmonton.

Returning to Live Oak, he sold textbooks and later worked for a chemical company. Still active in business, he raises and trains horses. "I can train any kind of horse," he says proudly. There is only one difference between horse training and football.

If you teach a horse to make a move, he never has the option to improvise or change directions like Aaron Box did with the Missouri defender on Aaron's big day in the Orange Bowl in 1961.

Gorden Kelley

If you consider Gorden Kelley's high school reputation—recruiters weren't knocking down his door—and the summary of his career, you can see overachieving, blue collar success that "ain't" bad.

He became a starter at Georgia, played six years in the National Football League and one year in the Canadian League. "I don't think anybody would have thought that I would make it at Georgia when I was coming out of high school," Gorden says. "I know if anybody who saw me play in college was taking bets on me playing pro ball, they would wager that I wouldn't make it through that first training camp."

An overachiever for sure, Kelley is a classic example of how determination, work ethic and commitment enable athletes with lesser natural ability to succeed when greater talent fails.

Kelley worked hard. He gave second effort, and he was mentally attuned to doing whatever it took to play the game he learned to love, while he was growing up in Decatur.

In his time there was plenty of tryout opportunity, but not a lot of colleges sought him out. Furman offered scholarship aid, but Kelley wanted to see if he could make it at Georgia, which never offered him a scholarship. Only an opportunity to see what he could do. "As soon as I got there, they told me I was on scholarship, which was overwhelming," he recalls. "I'm sure it had to do with the recommendation of my high school coach, Clyde Ehrhardt, who played for Coach Butts."

It didn't take long for the Bulldog coaches to realize they had a rugged end who was stout on defense. He wasn't a natural pass catcher with graceful moves and velvet hands, but he was a player who could be relied on whenever a pass came his way. In the Florida game in 1959, he caught a fourteen yard touchdown pass from halfback Bobby Walden. Kelley made a fighting catch fro the touchdown in the end zone.

When he finished Georgia, the San Francisco 49ers signed him to a free agent contract. There were no rave reviews preceding his arrival in training camp. But with a tenacious, unyielding modus operandi and an intense desire to succeed, Kelley played three years with the 49ers and was traded to the Redskins, where he lasted two more years. A leg injury forced him out of the Canadian League, and he made comeback with the Falcons in 1967. He had been out of football a couple of years, but still made the team in Atlanta. Unfortunately, his amazing comeback story ended soon afterwards. The leg would not hold up.

His post football years included furniture sales, work with a pharmaceutical company, and, more recently, a security business. When he reflects back on his football days in Athens, he enjoys recalling the championship season of 1959. "I wasn't on the field, but a highlight of my career as a Bulldog was seeing Bill Herron make that catch to beat Auburn and bring us the conference championship. That made us a champion and is my favorite memory."

After a slight pause, he volunteers one regret. "It meant a lot to me to have an opportunity to play college football and the coaches at Georgia trained me well enough that I got to play in the NFL. I appreciate that, and I regret that I didn't not make it a point to say thank you. Most of us appreciate the influence coaches have on our lives, but we don't always take the time to say thank you. Its not that you don't appreciate their influence and help but you just don't think about those things until you get older.

"I never told Coach Butts how much I appreciated him, and I regret that. He came to my wedding. A lot of his family, including Nancy, came. Some of the assistant coaches were there. I didn't think about how nice that was at the time, but I do now. Those are the people who taught me to succeed, never quit, never give up and believe in yourself. I am indebted to all of them."

1960

This would be Wallace Butts last year as coach although nobody would have forecast such a decision at the beginning of the season.

He would end up with a team that would win six games, but lost three tough outings, falling to Southern Cal 10-3 in Los Angles, 22-14 to Florida in Jacksonville and 9-6 to Auburn at Auburn all of which conceivably, could have gone his way,. Close game failure had again collared him in his last campaign, but there was good news with the fourth straight victory over Tech in Athens, 7-6.

To conclude his career with a conference championship and his third trip to the Orange Bowl in 1959 and to go out with a fourth straight state championship had to make his departure from the coaching ranks something to savor.

The one thing missing in his bittersweet career was induction into the College Football Hall of Fame. He did not live to experience that honor, but for his family and his loyal players and friends, it was a memorable evening at the Waldorf Astoria in New York when his election was confirmed in 1997.

Freddy Farah

Over the years, I've come to appreciate the many Bulldog football lettermen.

The headline makers will never fail to get their due, and I certainly have no quarrel with that. But on every team you find an assortment of contributors from starters to those who never see any game day action. They may have toiled in anonymity as B-teamers, Scout team in today's football world. Never make a headline. They get their hands dirty their noses bloodied, giving the varsity – the mainliners – the opposing team's look during the week and finding their spot on the bench come Saturday.

These players serve an important role for the team. They work as hard as anybody. They give as much as the touchdown producers. When it is all over, more often than not, the players in this category feel for Georgia more than any former player. Their hearts bleed red and black. One of those with deep and abiding emotions for the Bulldogs is a former roommate of mine, Fred Farah of Jacksonville.

Since graduation, Freddy has supported Georgia football with heart, soul and enduring, almost combustible passion. He has answered every request for every project initiated in the last two decades. He graduated in 1960 and immediately purchased season tickets.

When his business became established and successful, he bought an interest in an airplane. You know what that meant. It flew to Athens for all home games and whenever the Dogs traveled out of town.

When he arrived in Jacksonville, an immigrant Arab from Ramallah, which is part of the West Bank, Freddy Farah knew nothing about football. When he learned, he had no idea that it would pay for his education and enable him to realize the American dream. What Esa Farah, his father, had in mind is pretty much what has taken place in the life of his youngest son whose college education and successful pursuit of business is why the senior Farah came and settled in America.

Fred Farah is grateful to an enterprising and adventuring father who came here for a better way of life. He has, in his view, been blessed by the American way.

Once he learned English, Freddy caught on fast with the kids on his block. As a boy, he was athletically proficient. His sense of humor was laced with a constant cynicism that kept him alert, keen and upbeat.

There was a football scholarship to the University of Georgia, and no one has ever left Athens with an abiding affection for the institution that was greater than Farah's. With a prosperous business and a lifestyle that is the envy of his Palestinian cousins back in

Ramallah, you would think that Fred Farah is a man with little to worry about. But that is not the case.

Heart disease has been his family's greatest enemy. The Grim Reaper prematurely claimed his father and two brothers. Fred became the head of the family clan by the time he turned 50 and has undergone bypass surgery, which is why he must stay on his diet. His survival is important to a lot of people. But his heart is heavy for relatives in Ramallah. He knows the pressures they must endure, frightful of that powder keg environment.

Even he asks the questions so many of us ask. Why does that Arab-Israeli hatred run so deep? Many of Fred Farah's customers are Jewish. His annual guest list for a variety of functions includes numerous Jewish friends. Seldom does he attend a wedding or a business party without mixing and mingling with countless Jewish customers and associates.

Fred Farah: From Ramallah to Athens with love

"I just wish some of those fanatics could come over here and see what it is like with all of us," Farah says. "There just ought to be some way for people to get along."

When the Butts-Mehre Building was under construction, he was one of the first former athletes to step forward with a six-figure commitment. "I feel that I owe Georgia so much," he said.

Farah has always been on the giving end, never asking for anything in return. Every athletic program turns out the great player, the one remembered for the unforgettable moment which brought unparalleled glory and honor to the institution. Those players will never be forgotten and they played an important rule in the tradition and heritage which the school builds on – and benefits from – over the years.

But just as important to the success of any athletic program are those players who were limited in ability but who possess unlimited heart and commitment. Like Freddy Farah. His life over the years has centered around his expansive family and The University of Georgia. Nothing is good enough for either.

This is a man who never threw the block that sprung a heralded running back free; rather simply dress out on game day with the team was an honor for him. Strange as it may sound, sitting on the sidelines was a big thrill for this former player. This one man who never got his picture in the paper and never was asked to pose before the camera on the eve of a big game, but Georgia has benefited from his having come our way.

When he was a year old, his father joined brothers who had settled in the United States with plans to bring the family as soon as there was enough cash saved for that purpose. World War II broke out, and he had to wait eight years.

"Although there are many things that I don't remember about those yearly years," Freddy says, "I'll never forget the ride over on that boat.

"It was a converted freighter and I believe it was an American ship, operated by an American crew and everybody on it was emigrating to the U.S." His mother stayed sea sick for 21 days. Freddy learned two words of English on the trip "Coke," and "Hershey." "If I hadn't, " he grins, "I probably wouldn't have made it. They didn't have any Arabic food on the ship, and I spent all of my mother's money on Coca-Cola and Hershey bars."

Fred has visited Ramallah a couple of times, but realizes it is not safe to return. "Ramallah is a resort area, and when King Abdullah used to come there, he would stay at my grandparents house because there were no hotels in the town and my mother would look after his grandson." That grandson was the late King of Jordan, Hussein, whose son is now king.

Fred was named the outstanding lineman in the city of Jacksonville as a high school senior and became an American citizen on the day he signed a football grant-in-aid with Georgia.

That was a memorable day. He was proud to be an

American. He appreciated what it meant, and he was not only proud, but humble, for it was a touching moment, one which he'll never forget.

Additionally, he was appreciative that he would have an opportunity to receive an education and play football. Football had become very important to him, but his family wanted him to get an education and sports would make it possible.

"That was the greatest day of my life," he says. "It meant something special to me to become a U.S. citizen and to sign with Georgia, all on the same day. Although I really was happy about being a Bulldog at the time, I didn't realize what was going to happen to me. My years in Athens were the best. It was such a wonderful experience and I will always appreciate the University of Georgia. I'm lucky that my father decided to come to this country, but I'm even luckier that I became a Georgia Bulldog. The friends I made in Athens are still my close friends. Someday, I hope to move my family to Athens. The place is heaven for me."

Pete Case

In every player's experience, there is an unforgettable moment with his coach. It might be something that was spoken on the practice field or a pre-game admonition. It might be a quip at a banquet or a quote in the paper, a dressing down, a private conference because of which an attitude is adjusted or an incentive is born or rekindled.

With Pete Case, he always chuckled under his breath at the things he heard from Coach Butts on the practice field. After all, his coach was an accomplished raconteur with an alluring conversational style. His salty and caustic commentary became legendary. Coach Butts could apply the needle when an assignment was missed a breakdown of a play set him off. Pete heard the Little Round Man on the field and at banquet halls, but there remains an indelible pre-practice incident that brings forth prolonged chuckles today when he recalls what happened.

"We had some new dummies that were weighted in the bottom," Case laughs in describing the incident. "You could knock those dummies over, and they would spring back to their upright position," Case explains. "One day I was upstairs in the field house with several others and saw Coach Butts out on the field surveying those dummies. All of a sudden he took a boxer's stance and punched one of the dummy, knocking it over. It sprang back, and he punched it again. He began to dance around that dummy, obviously enjoying himself as he kept punching it. He certainly had technique and must have had some boxing training at some point in his life. I can tell you that was one of the funniest things I ever saw in my time at Georgia. We were afraid to bring it up to him afterwards, but we sure had fun watching him punch that dummy that afternoon."

Case learned to respect the serious side of football by playing for Coach Butts, appreciating the intense commitment that he saw in his coach and his ceaseless fighting spirit. "I don't think he ever expected a player to do more than he could physically do, but there was no question that he expected you to get the most out of your ability," Pete says.

Pete Case (at Georgia) was big with the New York Giants

"When I made it to the NFL, the first thing I realized was that practice at Georgia was a lot harder. The pros probably hit harder, but I never worked as hard in my career as a professional as I did in Athens. I always felt that gave me an advantage when I got into the NFL."

Case had a distinguished pro career, playing offensive tackle for the Philadelphia Eagles (three years) and the New York Giants (six years). There was a Bulldog connection at each stop: With the Eagles, there were three former teammates from Athens—Theron Sapp, Dave Lloyd and Riley Gunnels. Another Bulldog letterman, Bobby Walston, was still an offensive star at end with the Eagles. Walston was also the leading place kicker in the NFL. A sixth Bulldog,

Marion Campbell, had retired after the 1960 season, Case's junior year at Georgia. After Case settled in with the Giants, Fran Tarkenton arrived. He teamed with his old pal from Georgia to give the Giants an abundance of creative offense.

"We weren't much on defense in those days," Case says, "but Fran was an exciting player who was very smart and innovative. He really could move the ball."

Case blocked for two Hall of Fame quarterbacks in his pro career: Tarkenton and Sonny Jurgenson when he was with the Eagles. "Sonny," he says, "was smart, too. He had a quick release and was as good of an athlete as you could want at the position. Tarkenton's mobility changed the offense in the NFL. He could really make things happen. When the pocket broke down, he just wasn't going to take a sack. You sometimes felt you needed eyes in the back of your head when that happened because you never knew where he would be or what he would do to turn a bad play into a gain. You had to get a feel for his style, but I always appreciated his ability to make something out of nothing. They talk about the West Coast offense today—I hear it all the time—but we had it with Fran in New York.

"Another thing I admired about Fran was his durability. He had to be durable to play 18 years in the NFL. He knew how to avoid a direct hit, but he was banged around a lot. It didn't matter. He would always bounce up, ready to go back for more.

"He and Coach Allie Sherman could cook up some offensive schemes. Our game plans were exceptional. With a better defense during Fran's time as a Giant, we could have won a lot of championships."

Toward the end of his career, Case was summoned to owner Wellington Mara's office one day. The grand old man of pro football asked if Case would like to be traded to the Falcons. "I was grateful for that," Pete says. "He really appreciated his players and thought that I might be able to play another year in Atlanta. I thanked him for his consideration but told him no. I wanted to finish my career as a Giant. I'll always consider myself a Giant."

Following football retirement, Case held an ownership position with a popular lounge in Atlanta, The Brave-Falcon, and later worked as a food broker until retiring to his place on Lake Lanier.

He was captain of Johnny Griffith's first team in 1961. "I appreciated that honor, but I didn't like it that we had a losing season," Pete says. "We didn't have a lot of players, and we lost a couple of games we should have won. Still, I look back on my Georgia career as a highlight of my football experience. When there is a championship to remember, that is special, and I'll always cherish that Orange Bowl experience in '59. We were all very happy to play in a major bowl, but most of all, we were happy for Coach Butts to return to the top."

FRANK ORGEL

When Frank Orgel finished high school in Albany, an assistant coach Lou McCullough recruited him to Wyoming. Then the coaching staff left – every one of them – and Orgel could have gone to Indiana with Phil Dickens, who moved on to Bloomington as head coach. The transfer rule at that time in the Big Ten was that you not only had to redshirt but you also lost a year of eligibility.

Orgel went home and talked with Bernie Reid, his high school coach, who called Georgia's Wallace Butts, who, subsequently, offered him a scholarship. That led to a memorable championship experience and paved the way for a successful career in football coaching.

Orgel played on the SEC championship team of 1959 and following graduation began a coaching career that included his final stop at Georgia.

On remembering his college days, Orgel speaks passionately about friendships. "I knew a lot of those players would go on to success. I felt Francis Tarkenton, Pat Dye and Don Leebern would excel and succeed. My plans were to coach, and I was fortunate to be friends with Pat. That association turned out good for me. I've always told my players to be nice to your teammates. You never know when one will be successful and will offer you a job. Today, my best friends are my former teammates.

As a football player, Frank was not blessed with great ability, but when it came to fight and heart, nobody had more. His former Bulldog teammate, Pat Dye, puts it this way. "Frank didn't have things like foot speed, but he certainly was not shy on guts. He would fight you tooth and nail."

Orgel had the type qualities that Dye knew would make him an effective college coach. So when Dye signed on to coach at East Carolina in 1974, the first coach he hired was Orgel.

"I was at Alabama and we were playing for the national championship and I couldn't leave Tuscaloosa until after we played the bowl game. I sent Frank up to Greenville (N.C.) and told him to run things until I could get there."

When Dye arrived, he immediately named Orgel defensive coordinator. "Are you sure Pat?" Orgel asked. "I've only been coaching in college for a year." Dye had no concerns about his old roommate's inexperience.

"I knew he would be hard nosed which is the way you have to teach defense," Dye says. "At Georgia he played defense with the greatest heart and fight you could imagine. All I wanted him to do was to approach coaching like he played."

Orgel coached at several college addresses, including Georgia, and retired as athletic director of Dougherty schools in 2001.

Don Tomberlin

Don Tomberlin could have enrolled elsewhere—he had several options—but he chose Georgia because of an incident at Grant Field in 1957.

It was a bitter grudge match between the Bulldogs and Tech that would bring endless celebration across the state with Georgia breaking the drought.

Tomberlin was at the game as the guest of the Bulldogs. He was a highly regarded high school prospect from Waycross and watched the action from the Georgia sideline. When he accompanied the team into the locker room at the half, he noticed that Theron Sapp had taken a hit on the chin, leaving him with a nasty split.

Tomberlin watched as doctors put stitches in Sapp's chin with no deadening agents. "They put some gauze on it, taped it over, and Sapp never winced one time. He was ready for the second half. I watched and thought to myself, 'I want to go where folks are that tough, where they want to play no matter how rough it gets.'"

A freshman in 1958, Tomberlin was redshirted in the championship season of 1959, but began to play more in Coach Butts' final year. He was a starter in 1961 at end although he occasionally saw action at fullback.

A car accident ended his football career, but there was an upside resulting from a bad circumstance in his life. The accident required plastic surgery. He had no insurance, but Coach Butts told him not to worry.

"He took care of me, and I have never forgotten that," Tomberlin, known as Stumpy, said afterwards.

"I have the satisfaction of having been associated with a championship team. I played for one of the outstanding coaches in college football, and I developed lifetime friendships. College football offers a lot of opportunities and memories for those who play the game. My career wasn't one in which there was a lot of recognition, but I learned about the tough side of the game.

"There is a tough side in life, and football helped me manage things when there was a challenge or crisis. When I watch a game on television today, I wonder if those kids appreciate the experience they are having. I enjoyed my time between the hedges, and there are a lot of days when I wish I could do it all over again."

Dale Williams

In 1957, Valdosta played Thomasville in the AAA semi-final game at Thomasville. Dale Williams was the quarterback, but suffered a ruptured kidney and was unable to join his team for the championship game versus Rockmart.

Suddenly, football was not so important. Initially, he was fighting for his life. As he began to recover, he got a surprise visit one day from Georgia assistant Sterling DuPree.

Coach Butts and the staff had offered him a scholarship, and they were not backing away although at one time it appeared that he might not play anymore football.

DuPree showed up at his hospital room with a grant-in-aid and signed Williams to a scholarship. When you ask him to identify his favorite memory as a Bulldog he says, "It was when I became one officially."

Over the years, he has never failed to pay tribute to Coach Butts for his gesture, sending DuPree to his room in a hospital to confirm that he was still wanted in Athens.

A man with a quiet spoken way, Williams doesn't show a lot of emotion, but you can sense the humility in his voice when he recalls that long ago day when Sterling DuPree came to visit him.

Williams played for the '59 SEC champions, moving over to defense by the time he was a senior in 1961, playing his final season for Johnny Griffith.

He entered Georgia with plans to coach, and two years after he got his dipoloma, he was head coach at Dodge County High in Eastman. From there he went to Baker High in Columbus and finally settled in at Waycross where he coached until retirement in 1995.

One of the highlights of his career was coaching his son, Todd, who lettered at quarterback for Georgia, 1982-86.

PAUL HOLMES

Paul Holmes was a tall, lanky, deep-throated tackle with a smile as wide as a xylophone, which he sounded like when he let loose with a spate of booming and uproarious laughter for which he is generally known.

There has never been a Bulldog lineman with a greater propensity for laughing with prolonged gusto. If it were a funny incident or even an incidental comment, he never has been able to contain himself. And like the best of raconteurs, he usually tells the funniest yarns on himself.

He was a good teammate, because he fit in. He tried hard, and he saw the good side of the drudgery of football. He became an effective administrator and executive because he made everybody feel good when the workday began. He was and is a successful salesman because of his magnetic personality. A pleasant man with whom to do business, is the way many of his insurance clients identify the gregarious Holmes.

Anything Paul Holmes wasn't good at? "I'll tell you one," he begins with an increasing volume of laughter. "Pro football. Those boys were too fast and mean for me. Talk about playing ugly! It has a different meaning now, but when I played, 'ugly' meant some snaggle-toothed linebacker knocking you head over heels when you were trying to make a good impression in training camp."

Paul experienced training camp success with the Dallas Cowboys, reaching the final cut in 1963. He didn't make it with the Cowboys, but he reaped considerable fodder for after dinner speeches.

This one is a staple. "One day after I had dressed for practice early in the pre-season, Coach Tom Landry called to me as I went out to the field. He began to talk to me about my college background. He knew that I had played for Coach Butts, whom he knew, but then asked, 'Did you all do things differently at Georgia?'

"I didn't know what he meant and I said, 'Coach I'm not sure I understand.' Landry said, 'Well I don't know how you dressed at Georgia, but in the NFL, we put on our jock strap before we put on our pants.'"

It brought hails of laughter when Holmes told the story of going to practice with his jock strap on the outside of his pants. Apocryphal? Doesn't matter. The point is, Holmes knew how to make those around him enjoy themselves.

His friendship with Charley Trippi, an assistant coach during Holmes' days on campus, remains a highlight of his football experience. Trippi, forever an accomplished needler, took a liking to Holmes, who always enjoyed the banter that took place on the practice field.

Trippi used to say for road trips, "We're taking 50 players and Holmes." Later, after his coaching career had ended, Trippi wisecracked at a letterman's barbecue to Holmes: "It was you, John Paul, who got me out of coaching." He once told Holmes that he was so slow that he should pay for a ticket to get into the games.

Paul Holmes puts away his smile for a serious practice session

Holmes was at practice the day when the wind was whipping about fiercely. Quarterback Larry Rakestraw directed an out pattern toward the concrete fence that encircles the Georgia practice field. A gust of wind lifted the ball up over the wall and out into the street. Trippi cracked, "Touch 'em all, Rakestraw. That one's out of here."

Lettermen barbecues have been fun through the years for Holmes, mainly because he usually meets up with his friend, Trippi. "The one thing all of us appreciate about our college days are the memories," Holmes says. "In my professional life, I have had the good fortune to travel the state for many years. Every town I go into, I bump into an old friend. We enjoy a meal together and most of the time we talk about the University and the Bulldogs. Georgia for all of us was such a great experience."

Looking back, he recalls, with special affection, the 1959 team and season. Although he was a redshirt, he appreciated what Coach Whitworth told him and his teammates on the B-team. "You worked hard," Whit told them. "You pushed the varsity. Much of our success was because of the way you scrimmaged and challenged the varsity. They tried to work you over, but you never gave in."

Holmes reveres Whitworth's memory. "Nobody ever cared about the B-team before, but he made us feel important. He made us feel we were part of the team. I will always remember 1959 as being part of a championship team although I never got into a game. Coach Whit made us all feel that we had made an important contribution."

Today, Paul is an executive with Life of the South, and makes his home in Monticello, the hometown of his wife, Susan, longtime mayor of the city country singer Tricia Yearwood made famous.

TOMMY THOMPSON

Once he had completed degree requirements, Tommy Thompson had two central objectives in his life, beyond family and earning his keep.

He would follow the Dogs wherever and whenever he could, and he would never pass up an outdoor opportunity. He never knew the exhilaration of catching a pass and weaving his way long distance for a touchdown, except vicariously.

Over the years, he has found rapture with the outdoors. He has had countless moments of exhilaration with his fly rod and shotgun, which, to him, is akin to scoring a long TD. With the patience and curiosity that typifies accomplished outdoorsmen, Tommy's outdoor experiences are like that of an avid golfer.

For example, with an accomplished and motivated golfer, there is the idea that you can compete and enjoy the game all your life. You work to improve, and you play as often as possible. You seek out every course and venue, the well known and the local. Same with Tommy. He has experienced wing shooting all over America.

A native of Vidalia, Tommy grew up in Jacksonville but always had Georgia on his mind. When the Bulldogs expressed interest in him, he was overjoyed. "I always thought about how nice it would be for me to have an opportunity to play for Coach Butts and the Bulldogs," he says. "I didn't play much, but I got to know and enjoy some outstanding players and coaches. The friendships from my Payne Hall days are one of the things I appreciate so much today. If I need anything, I know there is a Payne Hall buddy out there somewhere who can deliver. Fortunately, I don't have to call on anybody, but it is comforting to know that I can."

Following an injury to his hand, Tommy was allowed to remain with the team as a manager and lettered for the Bulldogs in 1960. "You can be sure that I am as proud as anybody to be a Wally's boy. I admired him and respected him, but the thing that meant so much to me was that he gave me an opportunity. When I look at my diploma today, I think about how fortunate I was. How many people get to attend college on football scholarship? How many earn a letter? How many are associated with a championship team? All of that happened to me, and I will always be grateful."

He began a career in sales after Georgia and often drew on his football experience. "When you aren't making any sales, you get depressed," he says. "That happened to me a lot of times, but I knew I could not give up. I would always remind myself, 'What would Coach Butts say?' He always reminded me that I had to pay the price. When I recalled that it would make me work harder, and sometimes things just got easier. Sales would come, and I would keep reminding myself to pay the price like I was taught."

Thompson was another one to experience the soft heart of Coach Butts. One year, he wanted to go home but did not have a means of transportation to return to Jacksonville. Coach Butts lent him his car, and Thompson and a couple of teammates from Jacksonville were able to travel home for a weekend to see their families.

At the end of his sophomore year, his football career ended. He went down in a pileup, tackling halfback Bobby Walden. The fingers on his left hand were forced back over his wrist. Permanent tendon damage resulted. He realized after talking to the doctor, it would not be advisable to continue playing football.

"That is when I really appreciated Coach Butts," Thompson says. "He could have run me off by terminating my scholarship, but he told me I still had my scholarship and I could finish out my time on scholarship as a manager. You'll never hear anything but good things from me about that man."

All's Well That Ends Well

Wally Butts Hall of Fame Recognition Long Overdue

When his Georgia career ended, Wallace Butts had become a broken man.

After beating Georgia Tech four years in a row and winning the Southeastern Conference championship in his next to last season, he was pressured to resign as coach. After that came the heavy-handed and unfounded Saturday Evening Post story suggesting that he and Bear Bryant tried to fix a football game. The story was ludicrous and the Post lost so badly in court that it hastened the magazine's business collapse.

The day the Post story was revealed, I went by his house on Highland Avenue and talked with him. I was young and impressionable and very much taken by the Butts' image and mystique. After a couple of phone calls about the magazine's accusation, he hung up the phone and began to cry. I cried with him. He deserved better.

He then resigned as athletic director, flat broke and with no assurance that he could pay the grocery bill. But he fought back, developing a successful insurance agency that not only paid the bills but also developed a few assets to make life pleasant for him and his wife, Winnie.

He did what he always advised his players to do. When adversity hits, fight back, never giving up. He practiced at a critical juncture, what he always had preached.

Like most of us, he made mistakes. That's life, but I have never known anybody who truly knew the man who didn't develop warm affection for him. He was such a lovable person, feisty but gentle, generous and caring. His daughters, Faye, Jean and Nancy, would fight you about their dad.

There were times when Wallace Butts didn't win key games. There were seasons when he came up short. There were times when a different decision here or there might better have served him administratively, but in the final analysis most people who knew him felt that he really did love the University of Georgia.

Coach Butts was elected to the College Hall of Fame in 1997 after a long wait. It was a victory for his former players, many of whom worked tirelessly to see him elected to the Hall.

If you know anything abut his background, you know that Wallace Butts was tough on the football field. You had to be in the times in which he coached. There were critics among some of his former players, but if you check the record, you will find that most of them made a brief stop in Athens and moved on.

Those players who stayed, those who could look beyond a few tough, grueling scrimmages hold him in the highest regard. They knew that they had learned under their old coach the things that would get them through tough situations in life. There are coaches whose players respect them but don't love them. The Georgia players both loved and respected Coach Butts.

I have thought about it often over the years and have concluded that the reason his players loved him so much was the fact that he gave of himself.

He is the coach who brought the first championship to the University of Georgia and got the Bulldog bowl tradition started. He initiated the tradition that came to mean so much to the football program over the years. He laid the foundation, and any tribute to the Little Round Man, however belated, was well deserved.

1939 Lettermen
Allen, B. Heyward
Brown, Woodrow W.
Cate, Vassa "Gus" (Captain)
Eldredge, W. Knox
Fordham, James E. "Jim"
Goodman, Winfred "Goodman"
Greene, Thomas E. "Tommy"
Guest, C.B. Jr.
Halliburton, Julian D. (Manager)
Hughes, Steve G.
Hunnicutt, Oliver "Honey"
Johnson, Howard "Smiley"
(Alternate Captain)
Keltner, J. Green, Jr.
Kimsey, Cliff C.
McCaskill, K. Alex
McKinney, Lee
Malone, Tom "Chief"
Mathews, W. Dooley
Mims, William Freeman "Billy"
Nelson, Curtis "Spike" "Spider"
Nowell, Robin S. Jr. "Bob"
Posey, J. Wyatt
Powers, Henry "Hank"
Salisbury, G. Robert "Bob"
Simonton, Abner A. "Abe"
Skipworth, James "Jim"
Stegeman, John F.
Wilfong, Walter
Williams, Charles, "Charley"
Witt, Tom "Tommy"

1940 Lettermen
Allen, B. Heyward
Blanton, Charles Brooker Jr.
Brown, Woodrow W.
Burt, Will
Costa, Leonard Jr. "Leo"
Davis, R. Lamar, "Racehorse"
Davis, Van A.
Dudish, Andrew C. "Andy"
Ellenson, Eugene "Gene"
Goodman, Winfred "Goodman"
Grate, Carl
Greene, Thomas E. "Tommy"
Guest, C.B. Jr. "C.B."
Horne, Everett
Hughes, Steve G.
Jamison, Joe "Tex"
Keuper, Kenneth E. "Ken"
Kimsey, Cliff C.
Kluk, Paul P.
McKinney, Lee
Malone, Tom "Chief"
Matthews, Jack B.
Newton, Lee T. (Manager)
Nowell, Robin S. Jr. "Bob"
(Alternate Captain)
Passmore, Homer
Pittman, Marvin "Sonny"
Poschner, George
Posey, J. Wyatt
Ruark, J. Walter "Chief"
Sinkwich, Frank B. "Frankie" Flatfoot
Frankie" Frankie the Fireball"
Skipworth, James "Jim" (Captain)
Todd, James Conway, Jr. "Jim:
Witt, Tom "Tomy"

1941 Lettermen
Allen, B. Heyward (Captain)
Bray, Mell F.
Burt, Will
Cocke, E. Erle Jr. (Manager)
Conger, Melvin R. "Duck"
Costa, Leonard Jr. "Leo"
Davis, R. Lamar "Racehorse"
Davis, Van A.
Dudish, Andrew C. "Andy"
Ehrhardt, Clyde
Ellenson, Eugene "Gene"
Goodman, Winfred "Goodman"
Godwin, William D. "Bill"
Greene, Thomas E. "Tommy"
Horne, Everett
Hughes, Steve G.
Keltner, J. Greene Jr.
Keuper, Kenneth E. "Ken"
Kimsey, Cliff C. (Alternate Captain)
Kuniansky, Harry P. "Koon"
Lee, James L. "Jim"
Letchas, Gus
Lewis, Jim
McPhee, Richard H, "Dick"
Marshall, Earl J. "Flathead"
Miller, James Pinkney "J.P." "Preacher"
Nunnally, Jerry
Phelph, Morris O.
Poschner, George
Posey, James Wyatt
Powers, Henry "Hank"
Ruark, J. Walter "Chief"
Sinkwich, Frank B. "Frankie" Frankie the
Fireball" Flatfoot Frankie"
Todd, James Conway Jr. "Jim"
Welch, Clarence W. "Nub"

1942 Lettermen
Ainslie, James William "Bill" (Manager)
Boyd, Carl Willard "Red"
Costa, Leonard Jr. "Leo"
Davis, R. Lamar "Racehorse"
Davis, Van A.
Dudish, Andrew C. "Andy"
Ehrhardt, Clyde
Ellenson, Eugene "Gene"
Godwin, William D. "Bill"
Keuper, Kenneth E. "Ken"
King, Lafayette
Kunianksy, Harry P. "Koon"
Lee, James L. "Jim"
Lee, Ryals
Lloyd, Mayfield "Sonny"
McClure, Ardie E. Jr.
McPhee, Richard H. "Dick"
Maguire, Walter A.
Miller, James Pinkney "J.P." "Preacher"
Nunnally, Jerry
Pierce, H. Brooke
Polak, Joe F.
Poschner, George
Richardson, Dick
Ruark, J. Walter "Chief"
(Altnernate Captain)
Sinkwich, Frank B. "Frankie" (Captain)
Strother, F. Clinton Jr.
Tereshinski, Joe P. "Terry"
Todd, James Conway, Jr. "Jim"
Trippi, Charles L. "Charley"
Vickery, John Farrar "Red"
Williams, Garland "Bulldog"
Williams, James (Manager)

1943 Lettermen
Barrett, Pearce L. Jr.
Belk, Robert Michael "Bobby" "Flap"
Benton, Gene
Bratton, Edgar
Burke, Fred
Buttolph, Lyman, Jr. (Manager)
Byrd, Henry L.
Castronis, Mike J. "Black Mike" (Captain)
Chonko, Bill
Cook, Johnny
Cox, Bryant A.
Eaves, Charles P. "Beefy"
Garasic, George
Hague, Bobby
Harris, Henderson "Buck"
Hollingsworth, Joe D.
Janko, Morris
Jernigan, George T. "Goat"
MacKenna, Bill "Sleepy" (Manager)
Meeks, Calvin S. "Junior"
Moseley, O. Reid Jr.
Perry, Bill F.
Phillips, Benjamin Carlso
Rutland, James William "Billy"
Simons, Walter
Smith, Charles H. "Rabbit"
Smith, Paul

1944 Lettermen
Alexander, Eugene P. "Gene"
Bailey, Sam M.
Barbas, Constino John "Tino"
Bouley, Laurent Henry "Larry"
Bowles, Jesse G.
Bradbury, George "Buck"
Brown, John "The Greek"
Bryan, William P. Jr. "Billy"
Castronis, Mike J. "Black Mike"
(Alternate Captain)
Chonko, Bill
Cooley, Michael Thomas "Mike"
Deavers, V. Clayton "Straw"
Eaves, Charles P. "Beefy"
Edwards, Dan M.
Furchgott, Charles M.
Gibson, Quinton Lamar "Swampy"
(Manager)
Green, Floyd
Haley, Bill
Hiers, William Lee, Jr. "Dub"
Hipps, Claude
Hodges, Billy
Jackura, Joseph "Joe"
Jernigan, George T. "Goat"
McCall, Kenneth Earl "Ken"
Moseley, O. Reid, Jr.
Perhach, Andrew "Andy"
Perl, Al
Phillips, Benjamin Carlso
Reid, Bernie
Rutland, James William "Billy" (Captain)
St. John, Herbert "Herb"
Singletary, Wilson Eugene "Gene"
Skipworth, George
Smith, Charles H. "Rabbit"
Wells, Don Ray

1945 Lettermen
Alexander, Eugene P. "Gene"
Bailey, Sam M.
Bouley, Laruent Henry "Larry"
Castronis, Mike J. "Black Mike"
Chesna, Joe L.
Chonko, Bill
Cooley, Michael Thomas "Mike"
Deleski, Gerald J. "Jerry"
Donaldson, John C.
Eaves, Charles P. "Beefy" (Captain)
Edwards, Dan M.
Furchgott, Charles M.
Gordon, James T. "Jimmy"
Hiers, William Lee, Jr. "Dub"
Hill, Cliff R. (Manager)
Jeffrey, Al N. "Jeff"
Jernigan, George T. "Goat"
Ledsinger, C. Lewis, Jr. (Manager)
Lee, Ryals E.
Miller, James Pinkney "J.P." "Preacher"
(Alternate Captain)
Moseley, O. Reid, Jr.
Perhach, Andrew "Andy"
Phillips, Benjamin Carlso
Plant, Frank M.
Pope, James Thomas "Tommy"
Rauch, John "Johnny"
Reid, Floyd "Breezy"
Sanders Carl
Sanders, Robert T. "Bob"
Sellers, Weyman "Zeke"
Smith, Charles H. "Rabbit"
Steiner, Godfrey B. "Goot"
St. John, Herbert "Herb"
Tereshinski, Joe P. "Terry"
Trippi, Charles Louis "Charley"

1946 Lettermen
Alexander, Eugene P. "Gene"
Bradbury, George "Buck"
Bray, Mell
Bush, Albert Jackson "Jack"
Chandler, Earnest Eugene, Jr. "Gene"
Cook, Johnny
Cooley, Michael Thomas "Mike"
Deavers, V. Clayton "Straw"
Deleski Gerald J. "Jerry"
Donaldson, John C.
Edwards, Dan M.
George, Carl Ogeltree
Geri, Joseph Steven "Jose"
Henderson, William Bradford "Billy"
Hobbs, Homer B.
Hodges, Billy
Jenkins, Donald R. "Chubb"
Jernigan, George T. "Goat"
Johnson, Howard T.
McPhee, Richard H. "Dick"
Maricich, Eli Joseph, Jr.
Moseley, O. Reid, Jr.
Payne, Porter O.
Perhach, Andrew "Andy"
Rauch, John "Johnny"
St. John, Herbert "Herb"
Sellers, Weyman "Zeke"
Smith, Charles H. "Rabbit"
(Alternate Captain)
Strickland, Allan (Manager)
Tereshinski, Joe P. "Terry"
Terry, John N.
Trippi, Charles L. "Charley" (Captain)
Williams, Garland "Bulldog"

1947 Lettermen
Bodine, Alvin A. "Al"
Bradbury, George "Buck"
Bradshaw, William T. "Bill"
Brunson, Stephen Lewis "Lukie"
Bush, Albert Jackson "Jack"
Chandler, Earnest Eugene, Jr. "Gene"
Christian, Robert Vernon "Bob"
(Manager)
Cooley, Michael Thomas "Mike"
Deavers, V. Clayton "Straw"
Donaldson, John C.
Edwards, Dan M. (Captain)
Feher, Nick John
Gatewood, James Hawkins "Chicken"
George, Carl Ogeltree
Geri, Joseph Steven "Jose"
Gulick, John A. "Jack" (Manager)
Henderson, William Bradford "Billy"
Hobbs, Homer B.
Hodges, Billy
Jackura, Joseph "Joe"

Johnson, Howard T.
Lorendo, Eugene "Gene"
McCall, Kenneth Earl "Ken"
Maricich, Eli Joseph, Jr.
Nestorak, Stan G.
Payne, Porter O.
Perhach, Andrew "Andy"
Pope, James Thomas "Tommy"
Rauch, John "Johnny" (Alternate Captain)
Reid, Bernie
Reid, Floyd "Breezy"
Sellers, Weyman "Zeke"
St. John, Herbert "Herb"
Taylor, Spafford "Spaf"
Walston, Robert Harold "Bob"

1948 Lettermen

Bodine, Alvin A. "Al"
Bradbury, George "Buck"
Bradshaw, William T. "Bill"
Brunson, Stephen Lewis "Luckie"
Bush, Albert Jackson "Jack"
Chandler, Earnest Eugene, Jr. "Gene"
Conally, Joe H.
Donaldson, John C.
Duke, John Henderson
Feher, Nick John
Field, Patrick Parfit, "Pat"
George, Carl Ogletree
Geri, Joseph Steven "Jose"
Greer, Robert Sidney "Bob"
Gulick, John Aloysius "Jack" (Manager)
Henderson, William Bradford "Billy"
Hobbs, Homer B.
Hopp, Clifford "Cliff"
Jackura, Joseph "Joe"
Johnson, Howard T.
Lee, Richard
Lorendo, Eugene "Gene"
Love, Henry A. "Monk"
McCall, Kenneth Earl "Ken"
McCarley, Hugh, Jr. "Hemo"
Maricich, Eli Joseph, Jr.
Mixon, Billy Raymond
Payne, Porter O.
Pope, James Thomas "Tommy"
Prosperi, Raymond A. "Ray"
Rauch, John "Johnny"
Reid, Bernie (Co-Captain)
Reid, Floyd "Breezy"
Sellers, Weyman "Zeke"
Tanner, Elijah Hampton "Hamp"
Taylor, Spafford, "Spaf"
Tillitski, John Edgar "Bull"
Walston, Robert Harold "Bob"
Yelvington, Richard J., Jr."Dick"

1949 Lettermen

Bodine, Alvin A. "Al" (Alternate Captain)
Bond, Claude (Trainer)
Bradshaw, William T. "Bill"
Brunson, Stephen Lewis "Lukie"
Campbell, Francis Marion, "Swampfox"
Chandler, Earnest Eugene, Jr. "Gene"
Cook, Malcolm Travis "Mal"
Duke, John Henderson
Durand, Robert Phillip "Bob"
Feher, Nick John
Field, Patrick Parfit "Pat"
Filipovits, Edward R. "Ed" "Flip"
Ford, George Edward "Iggy"
Greenway, Charles Edward "Ed"
Greer, Robert Sidney "Bob"
Henderson, William Bradford "Billy
Hipps, Claude M.
Hlebovy, Gus
Jackura, Joseph "Joe"
Lorendo, Eugene "Gene"
Love, Henry A. "Monk"
McCall, Kenneth Earl "Ken"
McCarley, Hugh, Jr. "Hemo"
McHugh, Jack
McManus, Fred "Mac"
Maricich, Eli Joseph, Jr.
Merola, Michael Eugene "Mike"
Mixon, Billy Raymond
Morocco, Anthony "Zippy"
Payne, Porter O. (Captain)
Pope, James Thomas "Tommy"
Principe, Rocco "Rock"
Prosperi, Raymond A. "Ray"
Raber, Richard Edwin "Dick"
Reid, Floyd "Breezy"
Rocco, Patsy John
Shiver, Ivy M., III "Chick"
Steele, Richard "Dick"
Tanner, Elijah Hampton "Hamp"
Thompson, Albert Matthews "Al"
Tillitski, John Edgar "Bull"
Walston, Robert Harold "Bob"
Yelvington, Richard J., Jr. "Dick"

1950 Lettermen

Anglin, Robert Joseph "Bobby"
Babcock, Harry Louis
Beckwith, Charles A. "Charlie"
Bilyeu, Fred Glenn "Buzzard"
Bradshaw, William T. "Bill"
Brunson, Stephen Lewis "Lukie"
Burgamy, John Jeff, Jr.
Campbell, Francis Marion "Swampfox"
Caprara, Anthony John "Tony"
Carson, Johnny Richard
Cook, Malcolm Travis "Mal"
DeCarlo, Arthur A. "Art"
Dobbs, George Calvin
Duke, John Henderson
Durand, Robert Phillip "Bob"
Feher, Nick John
Field, Patrick Parfit "Pat"
Filipovits, Edward R. "Ed" "Flip"
Ford, George Edward "Iggy"
Grant, William Carl "Billy"
Greenway, Charles Edward "Ed"
Greer, Robert Sidney "Bob"
Hargrove, Lauren "Fitzgerald Flash"
Hill, Jack Donald "Bunker"
Hipps, Claude M.
Hlebovy, Gus
Hyde, Glenn "Wide"
Langley, Derwent, Jr.
McClung, Jerry Ellis "Moe"
McManus, Fred "Mac"
Madray, Clint S., Jr. "Coon"
Magoni, John Charles "Chuck"
Merola, Michael Eugene "Mike" (Captain)
Mixon, Billy Raymond
Morocco, Anthony "Zippy"
Morris, Robert Eugene "Bobby"
Poss, Dexter C. "Cicero"
Principe, Rocco "Rock"
Prosperi, Raymond A. "Ray"
Raber, Richard Edwin "Dick"
Roberts, James Thomas "Jackie"
Rocco, Patsy John
Salerno, Frank V.
Scichilone, Joseph F. "Joe"
Shiver, Ivy M. III "Chick"
Steele, Richard "Dick"
Tanner, Elijah Hampton "Hamp"
Thompson, Albert Matthews "Al"
Tillitski, John Edgar "Bull"
Walsh, William Alfred, Jr. "Bill"
Walston, Robert Harold "Bob"
West, Robert Kenneth "Bob"
Yelvington, Richard J., Jr. "Dick"
(Alternate Captain)

1951 Lettermen

Anglin, Robert Joseph "Bobby"
Babcock, Harry Louis
Beckwith, Charles A. "Charlie"
Bilyeu, Fred Glenn "Buzzard"
Bratkowski, Edmund R. "Zeke"
Burgamy, John Jeff, Jr.
Campbell, Francis Marion "Swampfox"
(Alternate Captain)
Caprara, Anthony John "Tony"
Cook, Malcolm Travis "Mal"
DeCarlo, Arthur A. "Art"
DiPietro, Francis "Ducky"
Dobbs, George Calvin
Earnest, Charles B. "Charlie"
Farish, James "Jim"
Filipkowski, Chris
Filipovits, Edward R. "Ed" "Flip"
Grant, William Carl "Billy"
Greenway, Charles Edward "Ed"
Griffith, Vernon L. "Snap"
Gunn, Earl W.
Hargrove, Lauren "Fitzgerald Flash"
Harrison, Clyde
Hill, Jack Donald "Bunker"
Hipps, Claude M. (Captain)
Jones, Hurley D. Jr.
McClung, Jerry Ellis "Moe"
Madray, Clint S., Jr. "Coon"
Magoni, John Charles "Chuck"
Makowski, Henry "Hank"
Malinowski, Francis William "Frank"
Manisera, Conrad "Connie"
Morocco, Anthony "Zippy"
Morris, Robert Eugene "Bobby"
Mrvos, Samuel Raymond "Sam"
Poss, Dexter C. "Cicero"
Principe, Rocco "Rock"
Raber, Richard Edwin "Dick"
Ragsdale, Randolph
Roberts, James Thomas "Jackie"
Salerno, Frank V.
Scichilone, Joseph F. "Joe"
Steele, Richard "Dick"
Walsh, William Alfred, Jr. "Bill"
West, Robert Kenneth "Bob"
White, Gene Carlton "Crane"
Yelvington, Richard J, Jr. "Dick"

1952 Lettermen

Anglin, Robert Joseph "Bobby
Babcock, Harry Louis
Bilyeu, Fred Glen "Buzzard"
Batkowski, Edmund R. "Zeke"
Campagna, James Henry "Jimmy"
Campbell, John "Johnny"
Caprara, Anthony John "Tony"
Carson, Johnny Richard
Clemens, Robert Norwood "Bob"
Chandler, Charles E. "Chuck"
DeCarlo, Arthur A. "Art"
Dellinger, Robert Edward "Bobby"
Earnest, Charles B. "Charlie"
Farish, James "Jim"
Filipkowski, Chris
Garrard, Robert Inman "Bobby"
Griffin, Gerald D., Jr. "Jerry"
Griffith, Vernon L. "Snap"
Gunn, Earl W.
Hargrove, Lauren "Fitzgerald Flash"
Harper, James Keller, Jr. "Jimmy"
Hill, Jack Donald "Bunker"
Jones, Hurley D, Jr.
Langley, Derwent, Jr.
Locke, James "Baby"
Madison, Charles N. "Charlie"
Makowski, Henry "Hank"
Malinowski, Francis William "Frank"
Mathis, Buddy Thomas
Mrvos, Samuel Raymond "Sam"
O'Malley, Joseph Patrick "Joe"
Orris, Frank Norman "Norm"
Poss, Dexter C. "Cicero"
Ragsdale, Randolph
Richardson, William H. "Bill" (Manager)
Ringwall, Richard
Roberts, James Thomas "Jackie"
Roberts, Joe Wayne
Salerno, Frank V. (Alternate Captain)
Scichilone, Joseph F. "Joe"
Sherrer, Bobby Donald
Snider, Billy Horace
West, Robert Kenneth "Bob" (Captain)
White, Gene Carlton "Crane"
Williams, James Henry, Jr. "Jimmy"
Williams, Edmund Ronald
Wimberly, Bruce William
Young, William David "Bill"

1953 Lettermen

Andeson, Charles "Chuck"
Arthur, Matthew Coan "Shorty"
Bell, John Taylor
Bratkowski, Edmund R. "Zeke" (Captain)
Burt, William Sineath "Billy"
Campagna, James Henry "Jimmy"
Carson, Johnny Richard
Clark, Thad Cleve
Clemens, Robert Norwood "Bob"
Cook, Harold Dean
Earnest, Charles B. "Charlie"
Fruehauf, Ben F.
Garrard, Robert Inman "Bobby"
Graff, Joseph Edmund "Joe"
Griffin, Gerald D., Jr. "Jimmy"
Harper, James Keller, Jr. "Jimmy"
Kelly, Howard Patrick
Langley, Derwent, Jr. (Alternate Captain)
Madison, Charles N. "Charlie"
Malinowski, Francix William "Frank"
Mrvos, Samuel Raymond "Sam"
Mulherin, William Butler "Butch"
Nutt, Fred L., Jr.
O'Malley, Joseph Patrick "Joe"
Reed, Robert Leonard "Bob"
Saye, William Albert "Bill" "Bird"
Shea, Donald Patrick "Don"
Veazy, Charlton (Trainer)
White, John Walter
Wilkins, Roy Lee
Williams, James Henry, Jr. "Jimmy"
Wimberley, Bruce William
Young, William David "Bill"

1954 Lettermen

Arthur, Matthew Coan "Shorty"
Bell, John Taylor
Brown, James Kenneth "Jimmy"
Campagna, James Kenneth "Jimmy"
Carrollton, Ronald William "Billy"
Clark, Thad Cleve
Clemens, Robert Norwood "Bob"
(Alternate Captain)
Culpepper, Walter Knox
Cushenberry, Anthony Sydnor "Tony"
Dye, Wayne, Jr.
Fowler, William Charles "Willie"
Fox, Glenn (Manager)
Fruehauf, Ben F.
Garrard, Robert Inman "Bobby"

Graff, Joseph Edmund "Joe'
Griffin, Gerald D., Jr. "Jerry"
Harper, James Keller, Jr. "Jimmy"
Harris, Charles Edward "Charlie"
Kelly, Howard Patrick
Kotes, John Harry
Luck, John Louis, Jr.
MacDonald, Alexander William "Alex"
Madison, Charles N. "Charlie"
Methvin, Eugene Hilburn "Gene" "Tiger"
Mitchell, George William
Mosteller, James Andrew "Pud"
Nutt, Fred L., Jr.
O'Malley, Joseph Patrick "Joe" (Captain)
Pilgrim, Harold Henderson, Jr.
Roberts, Lovis Laneair, "Red"
Saye, William Albert, "Bill" "Bird"
Shea, Donald Patrick "Don"
Spadifino, Leonard Peter "Len"
Tarleton,, Wendell Earl
Van Buren, Robert C. "Bob"
White, John Walter
Wilkins, Roy Lee
Williams, James Henry, Jr. "Jimmy"
Young, Richard R. "Dick"

1955 Lettermen

Arthur, Matthew Coan "Shorty"
Baccus, Pat (Manager)
Bartenfeld, Charles "Charlie" (Manager)
Bell, John Taylor
Brown, James Kenneth "Jimmy"
Carrollton, Ronald William "Billy"
Clark, Thad Cleveland "Cleve"
Comfort, Joseph Donald "Joe"
Cooper, Elmer Clenton "Ken"
Culpepper, Walter Knox
Cushenberry, Anthony Sydnor, "Tony"
Davis, J.B.
Dukes, Henry Calhoun, Jr.
Dye, Wayne, Jr.
Fowler, William Charles "Willie"
Garrard, Robert Inman "Bobby" (Captain)
Griffin, Gerald Dunn, Jr. "Jerry"
Grubbs, Clayton H.
Harper, James Keller, Jr. "Jimmy"
Harris, Charles Edward "Charlie"
Lofton, Wilbur Mayes, Jr.
Luck, John Louis Jr.
MacDonald, Alexander William "Alex"
Manisera, Conrad L. "Connie"
Meatheringham, Michael Robert "Mike"
Monti, Angelo Joseph Jr. "Angie"
Mosteller, James Andrew "Pud"
Mulherin, William Butler "Butch"
Orr, James Edward Jr. "Jimmy"
Roberts, Lovis Laneair, "Red"
Saye, William Albert "Bill" "Bird"
Schopen, Joseph Leroy "Joe"
Shea, Donald Patrick "Don"
(Alternate Captain)
Spadafino, Leonard Peter "Len"
Tarleton, Wendell Earl
White, John Walter
Wilkins, Roy Lee
Williams, James Henry, Jr. "Jimmy"
Young, Richard R. "Dick"

1956 Lettermen

Anderson, Dudley Michael "Mike"
Bartenfeld, Charles "Charlie" (Manager)
Bishop, Alan Steven "Al"
Brown, James Kenneth "Jimmy"
Burkhalter, Edward Lewis "Ed"
Bush, Marion Jordan
Byars, Charles Ray "Charlie"
Comfort, Joseph Donald "Joe"
Cook, Harold Dean
Cooper, Elmer Clenton "Ken"
Culpepper, Walter Knox (Captain)
Cushenberry, Anthony Sydnor "Tony"
Davis, J.B.
Dukes, Henry Calhoun Jr.
Dye, Nathaniel Slaughter "Nat"
Gunnels, John Riley
Hearn, William Waller Jr. "Billy"
Littleton , Jack Eugene "Gene"
Lofton Wilbur Mayes Jr.
Lucas, Cicero Gordon
Luck, John Louis Jr.
MacDonald, Alexander William "Alex"
Manning, Carl Edward
Meatheringham, Michael Robert "Mike"
Monti, Angelo Joseph Jr. "Angie"
Mosteller, James Andrew "Pud"
Nunley, Glen Murphy
Orr, James Edward Jr. "Jimmy"
Pilgrim, Harold Henderson Jr.
Roberts, Lovis Laneair "Red"
(Alternate Captain)
Sapp, Theron Coleman
Schulte, Kenneth Francis "Ken"
Short, George
Spooner, Johnny Mack
Strumke, William Henry "Bill"
Tarleton, Wendell Earl
Vinesett, Travis Holmes
Watkins, William Parker "Bill"
White, J. Harry
Whitton, George Mortimer
Wilkins, Roy Lee
Wilson, Gene Everett

1957 Lettermen

Adams, Donald Brian "Ace" (Trainer)
Anderson, Dudley Michael "Mike"
Bartenfeld, Richard Turner (Manager)
Box, Aaron
Bracco, Nicholas Terrence "Nick"
Britt, Charles William "Charlie"
Casey, J.V. "Sonny"
Cleveland, Robert James "Bob"
Comfort, Joseph Donald "Joe"
Cooper, Elmer Clenton "Ken"
Davis, J.B. (Captain)
Dukes, Henry Calhoun, Jr.
Dye, Nathaniel Slaughter "Nat"
Francis, Albert John "Al"
Guisler, George Howard
Gunnels, John Riley
Hansen, George Earnest
Hearn, William Waller, Jr. "Billy"
Horton, Dwight, Jr.
Kelley, Gorden Bond
Leebern, Donald Melwood, Jr. "Don"
Lewis, Thomas Howell, Jr. "Tommy"
Littleton Jack Eugene "Gene"
Lloyd, David Allen "Dave"
Lofton, Wilbur Mayes, Jr.
Lucas, Cicero Gorden
Manning, Carl Edward
Meatheringham, Michael Robert "Mike"
Miller, Thomas Welch "Red-Eye" (Trainer)
Orr, James Edward Jr. "Jimmy"
Roland, Billy Gray
Sapp, Theron Coleman
Schulte, Kenneth Francis "Ken"
Sedlock, Robert John "Bob"
Smith, Don Eugene
Smith, Iran Quinton
Soberdash, Donald Andrew "Don"
Thompson, Billy Joe "Dude"
Towns, Robert Forrest "Bobby"
Vickers, Jimmy Franklin
Vinesett, Travis Holmes
(Alternate Captain)
Wilson, Gene

1958 Lettermen

Alexander, Brantley
(Manager)
Anderson, Dudley Michael "Mike"
Ashe, Phillip Neil "Phil"
Box, Aaron
Bracco, Nicholas Terrence "Nick"
Britt, Charles William "Charlie"
Brown, James Fredrick "Fred"
Casey, J.V.
Cooper, William Anthony "Bill" (Trainer)
Cunard, John Vernon
Davis, N. Hal
Dye, Nathaniel Slaughter "Nat"
(Alternate Captain)
Dye, Patrick Fain "Pat"
Galbreath, Robert Joe "Bobby"
Gilbert, William Wayne "Billy"
Guisler, George Howard
Gunnels, John Riley
Hansen, George Ernest
Herron, William Lester "Bill"
Judson, Ronald Douglas
(Manager)
Kelley, Gorden Bond
King, Norman Neilsen
Lancaster, Robert Larry
Lawrence, Amon Fredrick "Bubba"
Leebern, Donald Melwood, Jr. "Don"
Lewis, Thomas Howell, Jr. "Tommy"
Littleton, Jack Eugene "Gene"
Lloyd, David Allen "Dave"
Lucas, Cicero Gorden
Manning, Carl Edward
Nunley, Glen Murphy
Paris, Thomas Hanie "Tommy"
Ramsey, Carter Matthew, Jr.
Roberts, James McMullan, Jr. "Jim"
Roland, Billy Gray
Sapp, Theron Coleman
(Captain)
Sealy, James Felton "Jimmy"
Soberdash, Donald Andrew "Don"
Tarkenton, Francis Asbury
Thompson, Billy Joe "Dude"
Towns, Robert Forrest "Bobby"
Vickers, Jimmy Franklin
Walden, Bobby Earl
Whitton, George Mortimer
Wilson, Gene

1959 Lettermen

Ashe, Phillip Neil "Phil"
Bedingfield, William Walter
Betsill, Roy Johnson
Box, Aaron
Bradley, Richard Young "Bo"
Britt, Charles William "Charlie"
Brown, James Frederick "Fred"
Case, Ronald Lee "Pete"
Christie, Robert Fales (Manager)
Cummings, David Lee
Davis, Hinton Guerry
Dye, Patrick Fain "Pat"
Godfrey, David Aaron "Bill"
Gray, Daniel Warren
Green, William Bobby
Guisler, George Howard
Herron, William Lester "Bill"
Kelley, Gorden Bond
Lancaster, Robert Larry
Lawrence, Amon Frederic "Bubba"
Leebern, Donald Melwood, Jr. "Don"
Lewis, Thomas Howell, Jr. "Tommy"
McKenney, William Dee "Bill"
Orgel, Frank
Paris, Thomas Hanie "Tommy"
Pennington, Thomas Durward, Jr.
Ramsey, Carter Matthew
Roland, Billy Gray
Shamblin, Jackson Benjamin "Jack"
Slaughter, William Nathaniel "Billy"
Smith, Patrick Fred "Pat"
Soberdash, Donald Andrew "Don"
(Captain)
Tarkenton, Francis Asbury
Taylor, Fredrick Wayne "Wayne"
Thompson, Billy Joe "Dude"
Thornhill, Thomas Lee "Tommy"
Towns, Robert Forrest "Bobby"
Vickers, Jimmy Franklin
(Alternate Captain)
Walden, Bobby Earl
Walker, James Panknin "Jimmy" (Trainer)
Williams, Langdale "Dale"

1960 Lettermen

Allen, Robert Bernard "Bobby"
Amtower, Fredrick Lewis "Freddy"
Ashe, Phillip Neil "Phil"
Ashe, Thomas Harold "Tommy"
(Manager)
Bailey, George Robert, Jr. "Bobby"
Bedingfield, William Walter
Betsill, Roy Johnson
Blackburn, Donald Burrell "Don"
Brown, David Irvin "Dave"
Brown, James Frederick "Fred"
Case, Clifford Leslie, Jr. "Bud"
Case, Ronald Lee "Pete"
Childers, Clyde Joseph
Clark, Raymond David "Ray"
Cone, James Daniel "Jim"
Davis, Dan Thomas
Davis, Hinton Guerry
Dye, Patrick Fain "Pat"
(Alternate Captain)
Farah, Freddy Easa
Garrett, Thomas Leroy "Tommy"
(Trainer)
Glover, Gary Augustus
Godfrey, David Aaron "Bill"
Green, William Bobby
Hearin, Gerald Wayne "Jerry"
Holmes, John Paul, Jr.
Ivey, William Frederick "Bill"
Jackson, William Edward "Bill"
Kelly, Richard Edwin
Landry, Hilton John, Jr.
Lawrence, Amon Fredrick "Bubba"
McEachern, Philip John Clarence
McKenny, William Dee "Bill"
Orgel, Frank
Paris, Thomas Hanie "Tommy"
Pennington, Thomas Durward, jr.
Saye, Jake Lee
Shamblin, Jackson Benjamin "Jack"
Shimkus, Dennis John "Denny"
Smith, Patrick Fred "Pat"
Tarkenton, Francis Asbury (Captain)
Taylor, Fredrick Wayne
Thompson, Thomas Jackson, Jr. "Tommy"
(Manager)
Tomberlin, Donald Lester "Don"
Vann, Kenneth Espy
Vella, Leonard Samuel "Lenny"
Walden, Robert Earl "Bobby"
Williams, Langdale "Dale"
Williamson, Robert Wallace "Wally"
Worreil, Billy Joe "Bill"